HODDER
EDUCATION

Hodder Education, an Hachette UK company, 338 Euston Road, London NW1 3BH

Orders
Bookpoint Ltd, 130 Milton Park, Abingdon, Oxfordshire OX14 4SB
tel: 01235 827827
fax: 01235 400401
e-mail: education@bookpoint.co.uk
Lines are open 9.00 a.m.–5.00 p.m., Monday to Saturday, with a 24-hour message answering service. You can also order through the Hodder Education website: www.hoddereducation.co.uk

ISBN 978-1-4441-8145-6

First printed 2013
Impression number 5 4 3 2 1
Year 2018 2017 2016 2015 2014 2013

Cover photo reproduced by permission of agsandrew/Fotolia

Typeset by Datapage (India) Pvt. Ltd.
Printed and bound by CPI Group (UK) Ltd, Croydon, CR0 4YY

This text has not been through the Cambridge endorsement process.

Hachette UK's policy is to use papers that are natural, renewable and recyclable products and made from wood grown in sustainable forests. The logging and manufacturing processes are expected to conform to the environmental regulations of the country of origin.

Get the most from this book

Everyone has to decide his or her own revision strategy, but it is essential to review your work, learn it and test your understanding. This Revision Guide will help you to do that in a planned way, topic by topic. Use this book as the cornerstone of your revision and don't hesitate to write in it — personalise your notes and check your progress by ticking off each section as you revise.

My revision planner

1 The Core Studies	Revised	Tested	Exam ready
1.1 The cognitive psychology studies			
9 Suspects, lies and videotape: an analysis of authentic high-stakes liars	☐	☐	☐
11 The formation of false memories	☐	☐	☐
14 The reading of the mind in the eyes test (revised version)	☐	☐	☐
17 Movement-produced stimulation in the development of visually guided behaviour	☐	☐	☐
1.2 The social psychology studies			
20 Behavioural study of obedience	☐	☐	☐
23 A study of prisoners and guards in a simulated prison	☐	☐	☐
25 Good Samaritanism: an underground phenomenon?	☐	☐	☐

☑ Tick to track your progress

Use the revision planner on pages 4 and 5 to plan your revision, topic by topic. Tick each box when you have:

- revised and understood a topic
- tested yourself
- practised the exam-style questions

You can also keep track of your revision by ticking off each topic heading in the book. You may find it helpful to add your own notes as you work through each topic.

4 Specialist Choices

4.1 Psychology and education

Perspectives on learning — Revised ☐

At AS we defined a perspective (see page 87) as a way of explaining behaviour according to certain principles, concepts and ideas, as opposed to an approach, which refers more to *areas* of research interest (regardless of the perspective adopted). The three perspectives for the Education option are behaviourist, cognitivist and humanistic. Generally behaviourists focus on behaviour, cognitivists on thinking and humanists on the person.

Features to help you succeed

Expert tip

Throughout the book there are tips from the experts on how to maximise your chances.

Typical mistake

Advice is given on how to avoid the typical mistakes students often make.

Now test yourself

These short, knowledge-based questions provide the first step in testing your learning. Answers are at the back of the book.

Tested ☐

Definitions and key words

Clear, concise definitions of essential key terms are provided on the page where they appear.

Key words from the syllabus are highlighted in bold for you throughout the book.

Exam-style questions

Exam-style questions are provided for each topic. Use them to consolidate your revision and practise your exam skills.

Exam ready ☐

Cross check

These quick cross-references to other parts of the book will help your revision.

My revision planner

Countdown to my exams

6–8 weeks to go

- Start by looking at the syllabus — make sure you know exactly what material you need to revise and the style of the examination. Use the revision planner on pages 4 and 5 to familiarise yourself with the topics.
- Organise your notes, making sure you have covered everything on the syllabus. The revision planner will help you to group your notes into topics.
- Work out a realistic revision plan that will allow you time for relaxation. Set aside days and times for all the subjects that you need to study, and stick to your timetable.
- Set yourself sensible targets. Break your revision down into focused sessions of around 40 minutes, divided by breaks. This Revision Guide organises the basic facts into short, memorable sections to make revising easier.

Revised ☐

4–6 weeks to go

- Read through the relevant sections of this book and refer to the expert tips, typical mistakes and key terms. Tick off the topics as you feel confident about them. Highlight those topics you find difficult and look at them again in detail.
- Test your understanding of each topic by working through the 'Now test yourself' questions in the book. Look up the answers at the back of the book.
- Make a note of any problem areas as you revise, and ask your teacher to go over these in class.
- Look at past papers. They are one of the best ways to revise and practise your exam skills. Write or prepare planned answers to the exam-style questions provided in this book. Check your answers with your teacher.
- Try different revision methods. For example, you can make notes using mind maps, spider diagrams or flash cards.
- Track your progress using the revision planner and give yourself a reward when you have achieved your target.

Revised ☐

1 week to go

- Try to fit in at least one more timed practice of an entire past paper and seek feedback from your teacher, comparing your work closely with the mark scheme.
- Check the revision planner to make sure you haven't missed out any topics. Brush up on any areas of difficulty by talking them over with a friend or getting help from your teacher.
- Attend any revision classes put on by your teacher. Remember, he or she is an expert at preparing people for examinations.

Revised ☐

The day before the examination

- Flick through this Revision Guide for useful reminders, for example the expert tips, typical mistakes and key terms.
- Check the time and place of your examination.
- Make sure you have everything you need — extra pens and pencils, tissues, a watch, bottled water, sweets.
- Allow some time to relax and have an early night to ensure you are fresh and alert for the examinations.

Revised ☐

My exams

Paper 1

Date:...

Time: ....

Location:...

Paper 2

Date:...

Time: ....

Location:...

Paper 3

Date:...

Time: ....

Location:...

1 The Core Studies

10 key components of core studies

Revised

(1) Background to the studies (the context)

The **background** or **context** to a study explains the reasons why a particular piece of research was conducted. The research may be a response to an earlier study. It could have been done to support a theory proposed by the author or someone else, or to investigate further or explain a real-life event.

Expert tip

A little knowledge goes a long way. Knowing a little of the background to a study, such as why it was done, is always useful and shows understanding.

(2) The theory or theories on which studies are based

Studies are often based on a particular theory or theories. For example, in 1960, Stanley Schachter proposed the *two-factor theory* of emotion. In 1962, along with Jerome Singer, he conducted a piece of research designed to support the theory. Sometimes, the reverse of this occurs, where research is conducted and a theory is then proposed to explain the findings. The 'Subway Samaritans' study by Piliavin et al. illustrates this point. In this study, the researchers found no diffusion of responsibility, which was contrary to their expectations. To explain bystander behaviour, they proposed 'a model of response to emergency situations', where each witness considers the costs and benefits involved in helping or not helping a person in need.

Expert tip

Suppose you had to summarise a core study in 10 key terms. What terms would you use and then learn? For the Held and Hein (kitten carousel) study, 10 key terms are: sensory–sensory associations; neonatal kittens; Group X and Group Y; active and passive kittens; kitten carousel (gondola); locomotor movements; visually guided paw placement; avoidance of visual cliff; blink to approaching object; developmental process.

It may take a while, but list 10 key terms for the remaining 19 studies.

(3) What are the key words (the jargon)?

Wherever you can, write like a psychologist. Use the jargon!

(4) What methods are used in the studies?

What **method** was used by the researchers conducting the core study? There are experiments, observations, self-report questionnaires and a number of others. See the methodology section starting on page 77. Some of these methods have different types (such as laboratory and field experiments) and sometimes more than one method will be used.

Expert tip

Know the method that was used in each of the core studies.

(5) Who were the participants, and how were they recruited?

Who the participants are (the **sample**) and how they are recruited (the **sampling technique**) can affect the outcome of a study and the conclusions that can be drawn – not least of which is the issue of **generalisation**.

Many studies use participants who are **restricted** in some way. For example, participants may be all students (as in the Schachter and Singer study or the study by Billington et al.), or they may be all male (as in the Maguire et al. study) or all female (as in the Demattè et al. study). They may have been paid for participating (as in the Milgram study). In fact, there are limitations in every study whether the participants are very young infants, children, animals, mentally ill or just telling lies!

Expert tip

Know the difference between the sample and the sampling technique.

How participants are recruited is also important. If participants respond to a newspaper advertisement (as in the Haney et al. study) then they are 'volunteers', and they may behave in ways that are different from those who do not or would never volunteer. In some studies the participants do not even know that they are taking part (as in the Rosenhan study). So, for each study, you should be able to identify the sampling technique, know how the participants were recruited and other relevant details such as how many took part, and be aware of at least one limitation of the sampling technique.

(6) Does the study contravene any ethical guidelines?

The answer is almost certainly 'yes'. Many studies contravene the ethical guidelines laid down by the BPS (British Psychological Society) and the APA (American Psychological Association). A common question asked by students is whether *any* study is actually ethical.

Expert tip

For each study know which ethical guidelines were broken and which ethical guidelines were upheld.

(7) How were the data collected?

The method may be an experiment, but data can be gathered in many different ways. Data can appear as response categories (e.g. a tally chart), such as in the Bandura et al. and Piliavin et al. studies, but they can also be in the form of numbers, or what people say. This introduces two sets of issues that are outlined below.

Data in the form of numbers are known as **quantitative data**. These are data that are based on numbers and frequencies rather than on meaning or experience. **Qualitative data** describe meaning and experience rather than providing numerical values for behaviour. So which is better? Each has its advantages and disadvantages, and you could be asked an examination question about them. You should know whether a study gathers qualitative or quantitative data, or both.

The second issue concerns the time period over which data are gathered. Data may be collected over a short period, perhaps a few minutes. These are known as **snapshot** data because, in the context of an entire lifetime, a few minutes in a study provides merely a snapshot of a person's behaviour and experience. Alternatively, data may be gathered over a longer period, perhaps days, months or years. These are known as **longitudinal** data. You should know whether a study gathers snapshot or longitudinal data.

(8) What are the results of the study? What conclusions can be drawn?

Once the data have been gathered, we need to know what they mean. If we accept the data as valid, how can we summarise what has been found? If we go back to the original aims of the study, what do the results tell us? Sometimes it is possible to explain the same data in more than one way. The crucial aspect of statistics is to know about significance and p (probability). You will see $p < 0.05$ and similar expressions, but what do they mean? You do not need to know all the names of the statistical tests, or calculated values. Knowing a 'p' or two is useful but, crucially, just knowing that a result is **significant** is sufficient.

A result is said to be statistically **significant** if it is unlikely to have occurred by chance.

At what point does the probability of the differences having occurred due to chance factors mean that we can be sufficiently satisfied that the results are due to a genuine difference between the two conditions (i.e. that the IV really has had an effect on the DV)? The standard level for a test showing significance is $p = 0.05$. This means that there is 5% (or less) probability that the differences are due to chance factors and so, conversely, that there is 95% (or more) probability that the differences are due to the IV. At this point, we can generally accept that the results are significant. When $p = 0.05$ it is just significant; when $p < 0.05$ it is slightly better. When $p < 0.01$ it is better still. Generally, the lower the value of p the more significant the difference and the more likely it is that the result is due to the IV.

Expert tip

Don't get stressed about statistics. Knowing what was found is more important than trying to remember all the statistical details.

(9) Methodological issues (reliability and validity)

There are always other methodological issues involved in any study. For example, in experiments, in order to make sure that the manipulation of the independent variable is *causing* the change in the dependent variable, it is important for the researcher to **control** any **confounding variables**. It is also important that a study is **valid** and **reliable**. We will look at these terms and many others in detail in Chapter 2.

Expert tip

Know the difference between reliability and validity. Never write '...this improves the reliability and validity' without saying why. Show you understand the terms and can apply them.

(10) Strengths and limitations of the studies

The CIE syllabus requires you to provide some evaluative comment about the studies. You should remember that evaluation can be positive (a strength) or negative (a weakness, limitation or criticism). For more details on evaluation, see chapter 3.

A good starting point is to consider the method. What are the strengths and limitations of the method used? Was the study ethical? Was it low in ecological validity? Was the sample representative? Were the findings of the study useful? Can the findings be generalised? You can apply these questions to every study, as well as the other evaluative points that apply specifically to each study.

1.1 The cognitive psychology studies

Suspects, lies and videotape: an analysis of authentic high-stakes liars

Revised

Authors: Mann et al. (2002)

Key term: Lying

Approach: Cognitive psychology

Background/context: Do you think you know when someone is telling you a lie? Most people think they can, but are they right? Liars are said to avoid eye contact and show signs of fidgeting such as touching their face, playing with objects and putting a hand over their eyes or mouth. Research shows these things to be wrong because research into lying is usually done artificially in a laboratory, with actors telling lies that are not important and have no consequences; where they have no guilt and they know they are being videotaped. What is needed is a study of 'real' people telling lies that matter, with major consequences if they are found out. In other words, a study of **authentic high-stakes liars** is needed.

Cross check

Approaches: cognitive psychology, page 87

Authentic high-stakes liars are those who tell real lies, when there is much to gain or much to lose.

Aims/hypotheses: To conduct a study examining the behaviour of liars in very high-stakes situations – real people in police custody who are telling genuine lies (along with some truths).

Based on research it is expected that:

- liars will make fewer movements (e.g. hand movements)
- liars will show an increase in speech disturbances, with longer pauses
- liars will blink their eyes less

Now test yourself

1 What **two** things are people said to look for to determine whether a lie is being told?

Answer on p.193

Tested

Method: Natural experiment with 'naturalistic' observation because the participants did not know their behaviour would be analysed for a psychological study.

Cross check

Methods: experiment, page 66; observations, page 75

Variables: The researchers did not manipulate an IV. It was the choice of a suspect whether to tell a lie or the truth, but the IV could be said to be a truth or a lie. The dependent measure was the behaviour shown by the suspects on the videotape, which was observed and categorised.

Design: As the IV was 'truth' or 'lie' and as all participants told both 'truths' and 'lies', the design was repeated measures.

Observation coding/response categories: The two observers were told to 'code the video footage'. They were not told what the study was about or that truths and lies were involved. They had to code (mark on a sheet if a behaviour happened) eight different behaviours: gaze aversion, blinking, head movements, self-manipulations, illustrators (supplements to speech), hand/finger movements, speech disturbances and pauses. At the end of the tape it could be determined which behaviours happened the most and whether these were during the telling of a lie or truth (which the experimenters knew, but not the observers).

Typical mistake

The participants in this study are the suspects, not the observers, because it is their behaviour being analysed.

Participants and sampling technique: 16 police suspects (13 male and three female) aged between 13 and 65. Suspected crimes included murder, attempted rape, theft and arson. Interviews with suspects had been videotaped by Kent police and the tapes were used in the study. The sample was self-selecting because the suspects were known to have made both truth and lie statements. Lies were known because the suspects later confessed to the crimes.

Cross check

Sampling, page 83

Experimenters: Mann et al. set up the study and then analysed the results. The coding of the video clips was done by the two naïve observers.

Apparatus:

- A 1-hour videotape with 65 clips of the 16 suspects. Of the 65 clips 27 were truths and 38 were lies. Each suspect had between two and eight clips; each clip lasted between 41 and 368 seconds.
- Coding scheme/response categories on which the observers could record their observations.

Controls:

- The researchers (Mann et al.) did not code the video clips because they may have been biased and 'seen what they wanted to see'.
- The suspects' truths and lies were confirmed by police and because the suspects later confessed and admitted lies.
- The observers were not told what the study was about. They did not know whether a statement was true or false. They merely recorded the number of times each of the eight target behaviours occurred.

Cross check

Controls, page 71

Procedure:

1. Video tapes of authentic liars from police records were obtained. Clips were broken down so there was at least one truth and one lie per participant. A final tape was created, lasting 1 hour.
2. Observer 1 watched the videotape, coding (recording if a behaviour happened) the eight behaviours in the response categories. The observer was told nothing more than to 'code the video footage'.
3. Observer 2 watched a random sample of 36 clips (at least one of each suspect) rather than all the clips.
4. Checks were done to see if there was good agreement (inter-rater reliability).

Now test yourself

2 One observer coded all 65 clips on the tape but the second observer only watched a random sample of 36 clips. Give two reasons for this.

Answer on p.193

Tested

Inter-rater reliability between the two observers was excellent. Observations were analysed with a correlation test (Pearson product-moment test) with correlations on a scale of 0 (no agreement) to 1 (perfect agreement). Agreement was: gaze aversion 0.86, blinking 0.99, head movements 0.95, self-manipulations 0.99, illustrators 0.99, hand/finger movements 0.99, speech disturbances 0.97 and pauses 0.55.

Cross check

Inter-rater reliability, page 82

Data: Quantitative data were gathered: each time a target behaviour occurred a mark was placed on the tally chart or sheet of response categories. The eight categories were: gaze aversion, blinking, head movements, self-manipulations, illustrators, hand/finger movements, speech disturbances and pauses. Observations were converted to give a truth-telling score and a lie-telling score for each participant. The mean number of instances are shown in Table 1.1.

Typical mistake

The inter-rater reliability data are not the results of the study. They are just a check of the amount of agreement between the observers.

Table 1.1 Behaviours as a function of veracity

	Truthful	Deceptive
Behaviour	*M*	*M*
Gaze aversion	27.82	27.78
Blinks*	23.56	18.50
Head movements	26.57	27.53
Hand/arm movements	15.31	10.80
Pauses*	3.73	5.31
Speech disturbances	5.22	5.34

* Significant difference ($p < 0.05$) between lying and truth telling

Expert tip

In Table 1.1 self-manipulations, illustrators and hand/finger movements are grouped together in the hand/arm movement category.

Cross check

Types of data, page 80

Findings:

- There was no behaviour that all liars exhibited. This means that there were many individual differences, making generalisation problematic.
- No difference was found for head movements and speech disturbances, with 50% of suspects showing an increase and 50% a decrease when lying.
- No difference was found for gaze aversion, with 56% showing more gaze aversion and 44% showing less gaze aversion while lying.
- More participants (69%) showed a decrease than an increase (31%) in hand and arm movements during lying.
- The most reliable indicators of lying were blinking and pauses, where the majority of participants paused longer (81%) and blinked less (81%) while lying. Both these showed significance levels of $p < 0.05$ between lying and truth telling.

Conclusion: These findings contradict the popular belief that liars behave nervously by fidgeting and by avoiding eye contact. They confirm the hypotheses and it can be concluded that the most reliable indicators of telling a lie are pausing for longer and blinking less.

Now test yourself

Tested

3 What two things do Mann et al. suggest people should look for to determine whether a lie is being told?

Answers on p.193

Cross check

Validity, page 86
Designs, page 68
Controls, page 71
Applications/usefulness, page 95
Double blind, page 71

Expert tip

There are three evaluation issues to consider:

- **Validity** – as the videotape consists of genuine police interviews with suspects the study really is measuring what it claims to measure: *authentic* high-stakes liars.
- **Double blind design** – the suspects did not know their behaviour would be analysed and so they were naïve. The two observers did not know what they were looking for – they simply coded the behaviour. The study is double-blind.
- **Usefulness** – in what ways is this study useful?

Expert tip

Also think about ecological validity, ethics, determinism and free-will, and inter-rater reliability.

The formation of false memories

Revised

Authors: Loftus and Pickrell (1995)

Key term: False memories

Approach: Cognitive psychology

Background/context: False memories happen when post-event information changes the original memory so a person believes that the false information really was part of the original event, even though it never existed.

Cross check

Cognitive approach, page 87

False memory is where people remember events that never actually happened.

Aim/hypothesis: To discover whether is it possible to implant an entire false memory for an event that never happened.

Method: Experiment with self-report (semi-structured) interviews.

Variables: IV – the three stages of booklet completion, Interview 1 and Interview 2. (Note that the *time interval* between the three was abandoned because of unavailability of participants.)

DV1 – percentage of participants recalling true and false events at all three stages; DV2 – ratings of clarity of memory 1 (not clear at all) to 10 (extremely clear); DV3 – ratings of confidence in ability to recall more detail, scored from 1 (not confident) to 5 (extremely confident).

Design: Repeated measures, because all participants completed all conditions of the independent variable (booklet, Interview 1 and Interview 2).

Participants and sampling technique: 24 participants (3 males and 21 females) aged 18–53 years. Each participant had a relative (usually parent) knowledgeable about the childhood experiences of the participant.
The sample was an opportunity sample because participants were recruited by University of Washington (USA) students.

Experimenters: Two female students from the University of Washington recruited the participants and the same two conducted and recorded the interviews.

Apparatus: A five-page booklet with a covering letter and instructions. The booklet had four short stories, three true (story given by family relative) and one false (about getting lost in a mall). Each story was a paragraph with space below for recording details of memories about the story.

Controls: All four stories were a paragraph long and each false story appeared in third position in the booklet.

The 'Lost in mall' false story was constructed from an interview with a relative who confirmed that the participant had not actually been lost. *All* false stories included the following *true* features: where the family shopped; family members who usually went shopping; shops that would attract interest.

The 'Lost in mall' false story also included *lies*: lost for an extended period; crying; lost in the mall or large store at about 5 years of age; found by elderly woman; and reunited with family.

Procedure:

1 Interview with relative to obtain three true stories about the participant that happened between ages 4 and 6. Also details to allow construction of false event (see controls).
2 Participants sent booklet, which introduced the study (with some deception) and participants filled in any memories they had about each of four events listed. Booklets posted to researchers.
3 Researchers conducted Interview 1 at university (or by telephone) 1–2 weeks after completion of booklet.
4 Same researchers conducted Interview 2 at university (or by telephone) 1–2 weeks after Interview 1.
5 Interviews asked participants to recall each event, adding as much detail as possible. Participants asked to rate clarity of memory (scale 1–10) and confidence of recalling more in future (scale 1–5).
6 Participants debriefed at end of Interview 2 and apologised to for the deception.

Data: Quantitative data were gathered – percentages of recall, number of word descriptions, clarity and confidence ratings. Qualitative data were also gathered because the study included some word-for-word descriptions of exactly what was said by participants.

Now test yourself

4 How does a false memory happen?

Answer on p.193

Tested

Cross check

Interviews, page 73

Now test yourself

5 Identify the three dependent variables, including rating scales.

Answer on p.193

Tested

Cross check

Designs, page 68

Cross check

Sampling, page 83

Cross check

Controls, page 71

Now test yourself

6 Identify the **three** stages of the procedure, briefly outlining what happened at each stage.

Answers on p.193

Tested

Cross check

Types of data, page 80

Results:

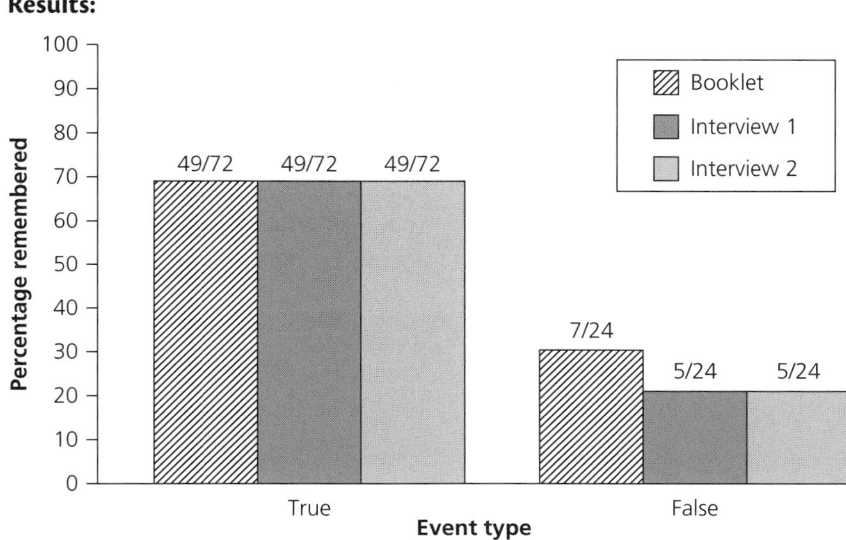

Figure 1 Twenty-four subjects were asked to remember true and false events over three stages – booklet and two interviews. The percentage remembering is shown

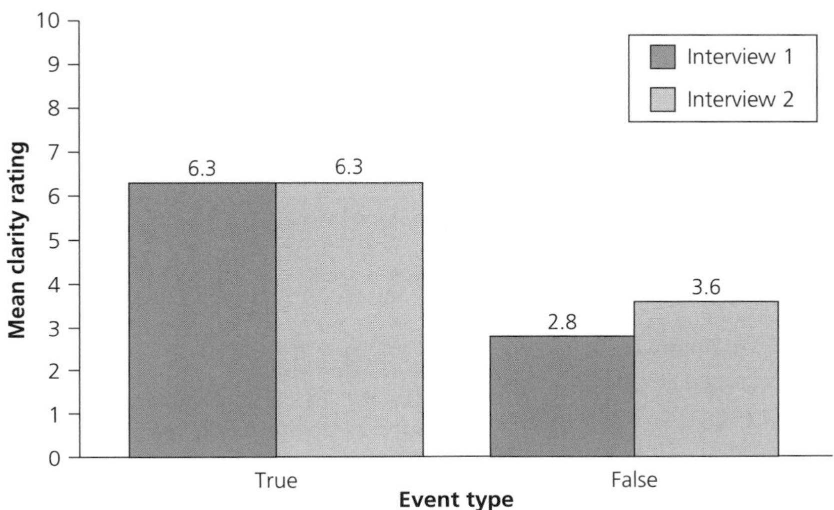

Figure 2 Clarity ratings of subjects who believed the false event during the first interview, compared with the clarity ratings they gave to the true events

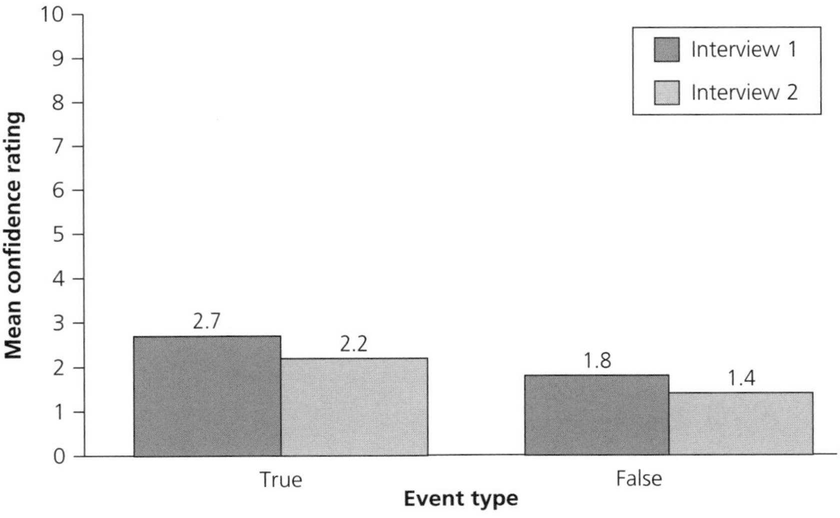

Figure 3 The subjects who believed the false event at first interview were asked to rate their confidence that they would be able to recall additional details of this event at a later time. They also rated their true memories

Findings:

- 49 out of 72 (68%) of the true events were remembered across the booklet, Interview 1 and Interview 2 (Figure 1).
- Seven of the 24 participants (29%) remembered the false event but one participant after recalling the event in the booklet decided that she did not remember (Figure 1).
- Participants used more words to describe true memories (mean of 138) than false memories (mean of 49.9).
- 17 participants (75%) said they had no recollection of the false event at the booklet or interview stage.
- Clarity ratings: mean of 6.3 during Interview 1 and 6.3 during Interview 2 for true events. For the false event, 2.8 during Interview 1 and 3.6 during Interview 2 (Figure 2).
- Confidence ratings (for five participants only): true memories 2.7 (Interview 1) and 2.2 (Interview 2); false memories 1.8 then 1.4 (Figure 3).
- At the end of the study 19 of 24 chose the 'lost in mall' story as the false one while five decided that a true event was false.

Conclusion: People can be led to believe that entire events happened to them after suggestions to that effect. Memory can be altered just by suggestion.

Expert tip

Think about other evaluation issues that apply to this study.

Cross check

Ethics, page 79
Interviews, page 73
Applications/usefulness, page 95

Expert tip

There are three evaluation issues to consider:

- **Ethics** – in what ways is this study unethical? Can we conduct a study on false memory without deception?
- **Interviews** – what are the advantages and disadvantages of interviews in research?
- **Usefulness** – in what ways is this study useful?

The reading of the mind in the eyes test (revised version)

Revised ☐

Authors: Baron-Cohen et al. (2001)

Key term: Eyes test

Approach: Cognitive psychology

Background/context: One feature of autism is a lack of theory of mind. This was first tested by Baron-Cohen et al. in 1985 using a procedure called the Sally-Anne test. In 1997 Baron-Cohen et al. devised a theory of mind test for adults called the 'eyes test'. A number of methodological weaknesses arising from this test were resolved and the revised version was published in 2001.

Problems with the original eyes test:

- There was a choice of only two words for each set of eyes, meaning the answer could be a 50/50 guess. Four words were added in the revised test.
- Parents of children with AS/HFA scored at the same level. The test did not differentiate widely enough as scores covered a very narrow band. The revised test had 40 (reduced to 36) not 25 items.
- Ceiling effects (too many at the top end of the mark range) were observed with too many people scoring too highly. Having 36 items and 4 words aimed to remove the ceiling effect.
- Some test items were too easy, again causing ceiling effects. The revised version had fewer easy items.
- Some items were guessed by checking gaze direction (e.g. 'noticing'). These items did not assess mental states so were excluded from the revised version.
- The original version had more female faces than male. In the revision there were equal numbers.
- In the original the semantic word and foil (the other word) were semantic opposites, such as sympathetic and unsympathetic. Again this could be too easy and contribute to ceiling effects. If three words are not semantic opposites then the level of difficulty increases and ceiling effects should be removed.

Cross check

Cognitive approach, page 87

Typical mistake

The 1997 Baron-Cohen original study appears on some syllabuses. Don't get confused. This syllabus covers the 2001 revised version.

Now test yourself

7 Briefly describe the background to the 2001 core study by Baron-Cohen et al.

Answer on p.193

Tested ☐

Expert tip

You will never be asked for all eight of these problems. A typical question will ask for one or two and possibly ask how the problem was solved.

- The words used might not have been understood by all participants (i.e. comprehension problems). In the revised version a glossary of terms was included, which participants could refer to.

Aim/hypothesis:

1. To test a group of autistic adults to see if the revised version 'works'.
2. To see if there is an inverse correlation between the eyes test and **AQ** for a sample of normal adults.
3. To see if females have superiority on the eyes test.

The study made five predictions:

1. The AS/HFA (autistics) will score lower on the eyes test than other groups.
2. The AS/HFA (autistics) will score higher on the AQ test than other groups.
3. 'Normal' females will score higher than males on the eyes test.
4. 'Normal' males will score higher than females on the AQ.
5. Scores on the AQ and eyes test will be inversely correlated.

Explanation: (Aim 2/Predictions 1, 2 and 5) Those with AS disorders score *high* on the AQ. One feature of AS disorders is a lack of theory of mind, and such people score *low* on the eyes test. This means that there should be an inverse (or negative) correlation with AS people scoring high on one variable and low on the other.

(Aim 3/Predictions 3 and 4) Baron-Cohen suggests that autism may be due to what he calls an 'extreme male brain' and that males in general have more autistic tendencies than females. If this is true then a 'normal' female should score higher on the eyes test than a 'normal' male and inversely a 'normal' male should score higher on the AQ test than a 'normal' female.

Method: Natural experiment; questionnaire

Questionnaire design: The **eyes test** consists of 36 black-and-white photographs of different male and female eye regions taken from a magazine. The images are all the same size (15 × 10 cm). Each photograph has four words that describe the mental state of the person. A participant is presented with a set of eyes and four words and is asked 'Which word best describes what this person is feeling or thinking'. One answer is correct the other three are incorrect. After completing all 36, the total number of correct answers is added to give an overall score.

The words for each set of eyes (the foils) were initially chosen by two of the authors and judged by a four-male and four-female member team. At least five of the judges had to agree that a particular word was the correct one. As a check, at least 50% of participants from groups 2 and 3 had to choose the correct word. Four items did not achieve this level of consistency and so were dropped. Note the original test had 40 items, reduced to 36. This means that there was a check (of validity) to see if the correct word really was describing the mental state.

The **AQ** test consists of 50 statements to which a participant chooses one of four answers, which are always: 'definitely agree', 'slightly agree', 'slightly disagree' and 'definitely disagree'. There is no mid 'opt-out' choice, so this *forces* the participant to either agree or disagree. Actually there is no difference between 'definitely' and 'slightly' in scoring, simply 1 point is given to 'agree' on half the items and 1 point to 'disagree' on the other half. The total score is out of 50. The AQ test is both **reliable** and **valid**. These tests are both **psychometric** tests.

Participants and sampling technique:

- **Group 1**: 15 male adults with **AS/HFA** (asperger syndrome/high-functioning autism) recruited from an autistic society magazine advertisement. Their IQs had a mean score of 115.

Now test yourself

8 Describe **two** problems with the original (1997) version of the eyes test.

Answer on p.193

Tested

AQ (or autism spectrum quotient) is a test devised by Baron-Cohen et al. (2001) to assess autistic spectrum conditions.

Expert tip

AS/HFA means asperger syndrome/high-functioning autistic. You can use abbreviations rather than writing the full terms.

Now test yourself

9 The revised (2001) version of the eyes test made five predictions. Outline **two** of these predictions.

Answer on p.193

Tested

Cross check

Questionnaires, page 72

Expert tip

Go oline, search for The Autism Research Centre, find the AQ and eyes tests, and try them for yourself.

Cross check

Psychometric tests, page 98

- **Group 2**: 122 normal adults (the **control group**) selected from community classes or public libraries in Cambridge and Exeter. There was a mixture of occupations and educational levels.
- **Group 3**: Normal adult **students** (Cambridge undergraduates); 103 (53 male and 50 female) with a much higher than average IQ.
- **Group 4**: IQ-matched controls; 14 normal adults (randomly selected from the population, but with no explanation how) IQ matched with group 1 (mean of 116).

Cross check
Sampling, page 83

Design: Groups 1 and 4 were matched (as above) but each group was independent. For example, it was impossible for a participant to be male with AS/HFA and also be a 'normal' adult female student.

Apparatus: The AQ, the 'eyes test' and a quiet room in Cambridge/Exeter.

Cross check
Designs, page 69

Procedure:

1 All four groups were given the eyes test to complete in a quiet room.
2 Participants in groups 1, 3 and 4 were given the AQ.

Data: Quantitative data were gathered because both the eyes test and AQ test gave numerical scores. Participants were not asked any 'why do you think…' questions or open-ended questions.

Results:

Table 1.2 Performance on the revised eyes test and AQ

		Eyes test		AQ	
	N	Mean	*SD*	Mean	*SD*
Group 1: AS/HFA adults					
All	15	21.9	6.6	34.4[a]	6.0
Group 2: General population controls					
All	122	26.2	3.6	–	–
Males	55	26.0	4.2	–	–
Females	67	26.4	3.2	–	–
Group 3: Students					
All	103	28.0	3.5	18.3[b]	6.6
Males	53	27.3	3.7	19.5[c]	6.7
Females	50	28.6	3.2	16.6[d]	6.1
Group 4: IQ matched controls					
All	14	30.9	3.0	18.9	2.9

[a] N = 14, due to 1 unreturned AQ

[b] N = 79, due to 24 unreturned AQs

[c] N = 47, due to 6 unreturned AQs

[d] N = 32, due to 18 unreturned AQs

Findings:

1 The *distribution* of the eyes test scores showed no score lower than 17 and none higher than 35 (scale of 0 to 36), and most participants were normally distributed with the modal score being 24.
2 The mean eyes test score was lowest for group 1 at 21.9 and this group scored significantly *lower* than all the other groups (e.g. means of 26.2, 28 and 30.9). Prediction 1 is supported.
3 Sex differences on the eyes test were examined in groups 2 and 3 and females did score *higher* than the males but this difference was not significant. Prediction 3 is supported.
4 For the AQ text, group 1 (mean of 34.4) scored significantly *higher* than groups 3 and 4 (means of 18.3 and 18.9). Prediction 2 is supported.

Cross check
Correlations, page 74

5 Sex differences on the AQ test were examined in groups 2 and 3 and males (19.5) did score *higher* than the females (16.6) but this difference was not significant. Prediction 4 is supported.
6 There was a significant ($p = 0.004$) inverse (negative) correlation of −0.53 between the AQ and the eyes test scores. Prediction 5 is supported.

Expert tip

Always know the aims of a study and whether the conclusions match the aims. Do these conclusions match the aims/predictions?

Conclusions:

1 This study replicates the results found in the original eyes test – that AS/HFA participants are significantly impaired compared with non-AS/HFA participants.
2 The modifications made in this test, compared with the original version, improved the test 'in that the same weaknesses were not observed'.
3 This test helps to validate the eyes test as a useful tool for identifying impairments related to AS/HFA.
4 All the initial aims were met and all the predictions were confirmed.

Expert tip

There are three evaluation issues to consider:

- **Questionnaire design** – do the 'eyes' in the test have an equal male/female positive and negative emotional balance?
- **Ecological validity** – the ecological validity is low because the eyes presented are static, whereas in real life a person is animated and the eyes (and face) move continuously. The eyes presented are also in black and white, whereas in real life people see in colour.
- **Nature and nurture** – what causes a lack of theory of mind? In the latest research Baron-Cohen is investigating the role of gene HSD17B2, so clearly the nature side of the debate. This is biological determinism.

Cross check

Questionnaires, page 72
Ecological validity, page 78
Nature and nurture, page 103
Determinism, page 101

Expert tip

Also think about reliability, validity and usefulness.

Movement-produced stimulation in the development of visually guided behaviour

Revised

Authors: Held and Hein (1963)

Key term: Kitten carousel

Approach: Cognitive psychology

Cross check

Cognitive approach, page 87

Background/context: Is visual perception learned or inherited? Studies have been done on both human and animal *neonates* (newborns), and studies have been done that *deprive* the neonate of some sensory experience. If an animal is deprived of a 'normal' sensory experience the question is to what extent it can then adapt when placed (tested) in a normal environment. More specifically, what if there is *deprivation of physical movement* within an artificial environment?

Aim/hypothesis: The aim of the study is to test the theory that concurrent self-produced movement is necessary for visually guided behaviour. In other words a kitten needs to see *and* move for itself in an environment for it to develop normal movement such as paw placement.

Method: Laboratory experiment

Cross check

Laboratory experiments, page 66

Variables: IV1 – kitten pairs 'X' and kitten pairs 'Y'; IV2 – active kitten and passive kitten

Design: Each kitten performs in only one condition of the independent variable and so the design is independent groups.

Cross check

Animals, page 100

Participants and sampling technique: 10 pairs of kittens; each pair was taken from a different litter.

Apparatus: 'Exposure' apparatus consisting of a striped environment and a carousel (Figure 4). One 'active' kitten can walk about freely (or rather round and round) and through the harness movement is transmitted to the other 'passive' kitten, which is placed into a 'gondola' preventing movement by its own legs.

A comfortable cage with no light, where each pair of kittens spends non-experimental time with their mother and litter mates.

Expert tip

Occasionally you may be asked to draw or sketch things. If you are, your drawing doesn't have to be perfect. It just has to show that you understand what is happening.

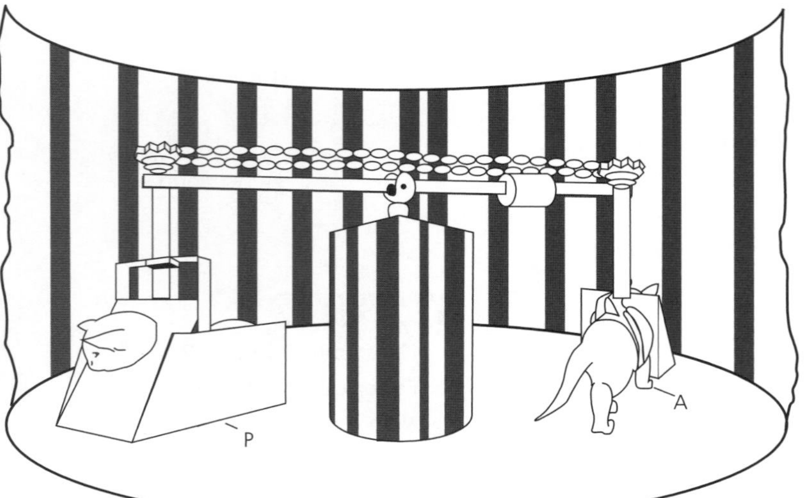

Figure 4 Apparatus for equating motion and consequent visual feedback for an actively moving (A) and passively moved (P) kitten

Controls:

- All participants in each group were exposed to the same environment for the same amount of time and performed exactly the same tests.
- All participants had the same 'living' conditions and spent time with their mother and litter mates.

Procedure:

1 The 10 pairs were divided into two groups, group X of eight pairs and group Y of two pairs.
2 The eight pairs in group X were reared in darkness from birth until one member of the pair was mature enough to coordinate and walk about, which varied between 8 and 12 weeks.
3 The two pairs in group Y were reared in darkness for 2 weeks and then from 2–10 weeks they were exposed to the patterned environment for 3 hours per day. This environment allowed head movement but did not allow then to walk (rather like a 'double gondola').
4 All 10 pairs were then placed in the kitten carousel apparatus for 3 hours per day with one kitten being the 'active kitten' (who could walk around) and one being the 'passive' kitten (whose paws did not touch the floor). When not in the apparatus all the kittens were placed back with mother and litter mates in a dark cage environment.
5 Each kitten was tested with six different tests. There were three main tests and three additional tests:
   Main tests:
   - **Test of visually guided paw-placement**. The kitten was held above a table and slowly moved towards it. A normal kitten would extend its paws to touch the surface.
   - **Avoidance of a visual cliff**. This equipment is like a bridge between two tables with an 'invisible' glass surface between them (so the animal can't fall). One side of the bridge covers a shallow drop and the other side a

Now test yourself

10 Describe **one** difference and **one** similarity in the early visual experience of the kittens in group X compared with the kittens in group Y.

Answer on p.193

Tested

deep drop. A normal kitten walking across from one side to the other will walk onto the shallow surface but avoid the deep drop.
- **Blink to an approaching object**. The experimenter quickly brings his/her hand toward the face of the kitten, stopping before actually touching it. A normal kitten will blink when this is done.

Additional tests:
- **Pupillary reflex to light**. If a light is shone into the eyes of a normal kitten the pupil will shrink in response.
- **Tactual placing response**. This is like the paw-placement test but here a normal kitten when touching a vertical surface will move its paws to touch the horizontal surface.
- **Visual pursuit of a moving object**. If the experimenter's hand is moved about in front of the kitten it will normally move its head and eyes to follow the hand movement.

(i) Group X: the paw placement test was repeated six times after exposure to the carousel and when one of the pair (the active kitten) showed paw placement they were both tested on the visual cliff. Both were re-tested the following day and after the test the passive kitten was exposed to light for 48 hours. The procedure was then repeated.

(ii) Group Y: the paw placement test was repeated six times after exposure to the carousel and when the active kitten showed paw placement it was tested on the visual cliff, but the passive kitten was not. It was only tested after 6 weeks (3 hours per day for 126 hours) of carousel experience.

Expert tip

Know these six tests. A typical question might ask for a description of how the kittens were tested.

Now test yourself

Tested

11 Identify the three tests of visually guided behaviour.

12 What is meant by the term 'visually guided paw placement'?

Answers on p.193

Findings:

1 *All* the kittens responded normally to pupillary reflex, tactual placing and pursuit of a moving object, showing no visual impairment or impaired response to moving objects.

2 When the active kitten in group X showed visually guided paw placement (after around 33 hours of exposures) none of the passive kittens did. The same was found for the blink test.

3 When tested on the visual cliff all the active kittens showed behaviour as if reared normally, whereas none of the passive kittens did.

4 The group Y passive kittens showed the same paw-placement and visual cliff deficit behaviour as the kittens in group X.

5 After 48 hours of freedom in a normally illuminated room all kittens performed normally on all tests, so showing no after-effects of the experimental procedure.

Conclusion: It can be concluded that self-produced movement with concurrent visual feedback is necessary for the development of normal visually guided behaviour.

Expert tip

Also think about ecological validity and use of laboratory experiments.

Cross check

Animals, page 100
Nature and nurture, page 103

Expert tip

There are three evaluation issues to consider:
- **Ethics** – is it ethical to raise kittens in an environment like this? Is the knowledge gained worth it?
- **Generalisation from animals to humans** – can we generalise from studies on animals to humans?
- **Nature and nurture** – do the findings of this study support the nature or the nurture viewpoint?

1.2 The social psychology studies

Behavioural study of obedience

Revised

Author: Milgram (1963)

Key term: Obedience

Approach: Social psychology

Cross check

Social approach, page 90

Background/context: Obedience is productive; and it can be destructive. The slaughter of millions of people from 1933–45 *'could only be carried out on a massive scale if a very large number of persons obeyed orders'*, according to Milgram. He believed that extreme obedience to authority was a one-off, that *'the Germans were different'* from the rest of society. He expected that in 1960s USA no-one would obey if he created an extreme situation.

Obedience is complying with the orders of an authority figure (compliance is obeying an order without agreeing with it).

Aim/hypothesis: To test the hypothesis that the obeying of orders to kill another human was a 'one-off'; that it would not happen again – specifically, that US citizens in the 1960s would not obey the command to give an electric shock to another person.

Method: Laboratory 'experiment' (with minor questionnaire, interview and observation)

Cross check

Laboratory experiments, page 66

Variables: There was no IV in this study and no variables were compared (although the command to obey is sometimes said to have been the single IV). There should be no DV because there was no IV, but 'shock intensity level' is sometimes said to have been the DV.

Expert tip

A stooge (or confederate) is a person pretending to be a participant but is actually working for the experimenter/researcher.

Design: There was no design. Each participant did the 'one condition' of the experiment.

Participants and sampling technique: An advert was placed in a newspaper for a study on 'learning and memory' stating that $4 would be paid (plus $0.50 for travel). 40 males aged 20–50 of various occupations were chosen to participate. As people volunteered, the sample was self-selecting.

Cross check

Sampling, page 83

Experimenters: Also participating as stooges were 'a 31-year-old high school biology teacher wearing a grey lab coat who was the experimenter (not Milgram himself), and Mr Wallace, the 'learner', a 47-year-old accountant trained for the role'.

Now test yourself

13 **(a)** Describe how the participants were recruited.

(b) Outline **one** disadvantage of recruiting participants in this way.

Answers on p.193

Tested

Apparatus: Shock generator labelled from 0–450 volts in 15-volt increments, with labels from 'slight shock' through to 'XXX'. Electrodes attached to the generator and a chair onto which the learner was strapped.

Controls: The procedure was the same for all participants, including drawing lots for teacher/learner, use of equipment, word-pairs and prods.

Procedure:

1 There was a general introduction by the experimenter about punishment and learning to both the participant and Mr Wallace.
2 Choice of who was to be teacher and learner was done by taking a slip of paper from a hat. However, the participant was always the teacher (both slips of paper said 'teacher').
3 Both teacher and learner were taken to the room next door where the learner was strapped into a chair, and electrodes attached to his wrist. A sample shock of 45 volts was given to the teacher and further instructions confirmed the authenticity of the apparatus.
4 The teacher read out word pairs and the learner responded with an answer by pressing a button so it was displayed on a screen in the teaching room.

5 If the learner got the answer right, the next pair was presented, but if the learner got the answer wrong (which the learner did deliberately) the teacher was to give an electric shock to teach the learner to do better.
6 As the 'learning' progressed and the 15-volt shock increments increased, if the teacher showed doubt or did not continue, the experimenter gave a 'prod' – an instruction to continue, whatever the response from the learner.
7 The study progressed with prods either until the teacher pressed the 450-volt switch or until the teacher refused to continue and began to leave the room.
8 The teacher/participant was then given an interview and a debriefing (or 'dehoax' as Milgram called it).

Typical mistake

Don't confuse the teacher (the participant) and the learner (Mr Wallace).

Method: All the participants were given an interview and a debrief after the study. Using a one-way mirror, most of the trials were observed and photographs taken. Often trials were recorded on video-tape.

Data: Quantitative data were gathered – the frequency of participants going to a particular voltage level. Milgram noticed that participants were becoming stressed and although this was noted, it was only reported anecdotally.

Results:

Table 1.3 Distribution of breakoff points

Verbal designation	Voltage indication	Number of subjects for whom this was maximum shock
Slight shock	15	0
	30	0
	45	0
	60	0
Moderate shock	75	0
	90	0
	105	0
	120	0
Strong shock	135	0
	150	0
	165	0
	180	0
Very strong shock	195	0
	210	0
	225	0
	240	0
Intense shock	255	0
	270	0
	285	0
	300	5
Extreme intensity shock	315	4
	330	2
	345	1
	360	1
Danger: severe shock	375	1
	390	0
	405	0
	420	0
XXX	435	0
	450	26

Findings:

1. All participants gave shocks up to and including 285 volts.
2. 5 of the 40 participants withdrew at 300 volts, 4 at 315, 2 at 330, 1 at 345 and 1 at 360 volts.
3. 26 participants went to the full 450 volts.
4. Many participants showed signs of nervousness: sweating, trembling, stuttering, biting lips, digging finger-nails into flesh and nervous laughter. Full-blown uncontrollable seizures were observed in three participants – one was very severe.
5. Most participants were convinced the situation was real. When asked about how painful the shocks at the end were for the learner, on a 14-point scale, the mean rating was 13.42 – 'extremely painful'.

Expert tip

You don't need to remember every voltage level for every participant. Be selective – for example, how many stopped at 300 volts? How many (or what %) went to 450 volts?

Conclusions:

1. Milgram found that the Germans were not different; that US citizens of the 1960s obeyed an authority figure when instructed.
2. Although most of the participants obeyed, they were far from happy in doing so. The signs of tension and stress indicated the mental 'torture' they were experiencing.

Explanations: Why did people obey authority (according to Milgram)? It was conducted at the prestigious Yale University; it was a scientific experiment; the participant felt obliged to continue; the instruction that the shocks were not dangerous; that the experimenter was in charge and so was responsible.

Expert tip

There are three evaluation issues to consider:

- **Newspaper sampling** – what are the advantages and disadvantages of newspaper sampling? Are volunteers different from non-volunteers?
- **Individual and situational** – were those going to 450 volts responding to the situation and were those stopping at 300 volts being individual?
- **Ethics** – a stooge was used in this study (Mr Wallace). This was automatically unethical.

Cross check

Sampling, page 83
Individual and situational, page 102
Ethics, page 79

Now test yourself

Tested

14 (a) Identify **two** features of the experimenter that may have led to obedience.

(b) Identify **two** features of the setting that may have led to obedience.

15 (a) Outline **one** ethical guideline that was broken.

(b) Outline **one** ethical guideline that was not broken.

Answers on p.193

Expert tip

Also think about ecological validity, the ethics of deception and the right to withdraw.

A study of prisoners and guards in a simulated prison

Revised

Authors: Haney, Banks and Zimbardo (1973)

Key term: Prison simulation

Approach: Social psychology

Background/context: What function does prison serve? Because of high recividism (reoffending) rates they do not act as a deterrent and neither do they rehabilitate most inmates. Why are prisons so bad? The simple answer is that it is because they are full of prisoners who by definition are 'bad' people. But is it this simple, and can this **dispositional** assumption be tested? What if 'good' people were to be put into a simulated prison environment. Would this **situational** approach turn them into bad people or would they leave remaining 'good'.

Aim/hypothesis: The main aim was to test the dispositional hypothesis that *'the deplorable conditions of our penal system and its dehumanising effects upon prisoners and guards is due to the 'nature' of the people who administrate it, the 'nature' of the people who populate it, or both'.* To test this, 'good' people were needed (rather than criminals who might already be 'bad') and a prison environment.

Setting/apparatus: For the arrest – police, police car and police station. The main 'prison' was constructed in the basement of the psychology department at Stanford University, Palo Alto, USA. The prison consisted of 'prison cells' with bars, a corridor used as 'the yard', and a 'hole' (a small broom cupboard used for solitary confinement). There were no windows or clocks, and no contact with the outside world was allowed. An intercom was set up to record conversations and a video-tape to record everything that happened. Each cell had mattresses, sheets and pillows.

Participants and sampling technique: The participants were 24 male students, selected from 75 who replied, who had volunteered to take part in a study on 'the psychological effects of prison life'. After responding to the advert (so they were a self-selecting, volunteer sample), they completed a number of tests to ensure they had committed no crime and that they were mentally stable. They were paid $15 per day. 21 participants were actually involved.

The participants were randomly allocated to the role of prisoner or guard. The nine guards (with one on stand-by) worked three 8-hour shifts shared between them. The prisoners were allocated three to each of the three cells (with two on stand-by).

The uniforms: The **guards** were dressed identically in khaki. They carried a big billy club (night-stick), a whistle around their neck, and they all wore reflecting sun-glasses. The **prisoners** wore a muslin smock, with no underclothes. On the smock, front and back, was an identification number. Each prisoner had an ankle chain and wore rubber sandals. On the head they wore a stocking cap.

Now test yourself

Tested

16 **(a)** Identify **two** features of the guard uniform.
(b) Identify **two** features of the prisoner uniform.

Answers on p.193

Expert tip

Rather than Haney et al. this study always appears as Haney, Banks and Zimbardo.

Cross check

Social approach, page 90

Expert tip

This study is often referred to as the SPE (the Stanford Prison Experiment).

A **dispositional** hypothesis is the view that the cause of behaviour is due to some feature or characteristic located within an individual – due to their disposition – rather than being due to the situation a person is in.

A **situational** hypothesis is the view that the cause of behaviour is due to some feature or characteristic of a situation, rather than being located within an individual.

Expert tip

This study appears in several publications and each describes a slightly different version. Zimbardo has a website where the story is again told, along with photographs and video-clips. Don't worry if you have a different account from what is written here. These minor variations will all receive credit in an examination.

Cross check

Sampling, page 83

Typical mistake

Students often get simple details wrong. The muslin smock often becomes a Muslim smock and even neon socks! Try to get facts correct.

Procedure – the arrest and induction: On a quiet Sunday morning a California police car went through the town picking up college students as part of a mass arrest for armed robbery and burglary. Each suspect was arrested at his home, charged, read his legal rights, spread-eagled against the police car, searched and handcuffed as neighbours watched. The suspect was put into the car and taken to the police station. At the station, the suspect was taken to a cell where he was left blindfolded.

Each prisoner was taken from the police cell to the 'prison', where he was searched, stripped naked, deloused with a spray and issued with his uniform.

Effects of arrest, induction and uniform: The arrest in front of neighbours was humiliating and embarrassing. The smock was designed to extend the humiliation (as was the delousing) and to create a sense of emasculation (removal of masculinity). Wearing a number and being known by a number rather than a name, and wearing a cap, created de-individuation (removal of individuality).

Now test yourself

17 Identify **three** features of the arrest procedure for the prisoners.

Answer on p.193

Tested

Procedure – life in the prison: Nine guards and nine prisoners began the study. To assert their authority the guards would bring the prisoners out of their cells and do a roll-call. This could be done at any time, and often during the night. The prisoners were lined up against the wall and called out their numbers. The prisoners tried to assert some independence, but any dissent led to the guards asserting authority and forcing the prisoners to do press-ups as punishment.

On the morning of the second day the prisoners rebelled: they removed their caps, tore off their numbers and barricaded themselves in the cells. The guards on duty called in those who were off-duty to help. They met force with force. Using a fire extinguisher they forced the prisoners away from the doors, broke into each cell, stripped the prisoners naked, took the beds out, and forced some of the prisoners into solitary confinement. The rebellion was over.

To prevent further problems the guards decided to use 'psychological tactics', which meant using solitary confinement as punishment and a privilege cell as a reward. Some prisoners had uniforms and beds returned but others did not. Some were allowed to go to the toilet, but others had to use a bucket in the cell. This created disquiet among the prisoners, who began to trust each other less and less.

At the end of the first day, prisoner #8612 had to be released because he was suffering from acute emotional disturbance, disorganised thinking, uncontrollable crying, screaming and rage.

The second day included visiting hour. The prisoners were well prepared by being fed, shaved and washed and having clean cells but this didn't stop the visitors from noticing the fatigue and distress that was becoming evident in the prisoners. Also, on the second day there was a rumour of an escape plot. Although just a rumour, to prevent anything vaguely challenging the guards increased their levels of harassment and humiliation.

Results – pathology of power: By the fifth day the guards were enjoying their roles. Some were even volunteering to come in on their day/time off. The guards were of three types: (i) those who were tough but fair and who followed the rules; (ii) the 'good guys' who helped the prisoners and never punished them; and (iii) those who were extremely hostile, were aggressive and caused degradation and humiliation whenever possible. One of the worst and most brutal was nick-named 'John Wayne'.

Results – pathological prisoner syndrome: The mental state of the prisoners was going downhill rapidly. They were helpless and powerless to do anything about their predicament. One developed a psychosomatic rash and four others often broke down in tears. They were destroyed, isolated and obedient.

Procedure – the end: The study ended after 6 days, rather than the 2 weeks planned. One reason for this was that the guards were becoming even worse in their treatment of the prisoners, especially at night when it wasn't being recorded. Second, Christina Maslach (who later became Zimbardo's wife) could not believe what was happening and told Zimbardo to stop the study.

Conclusions: The study did not happen according to prediction so the dispositional hypothesis had to be rejected. The idea that 'bad' people make prisons 'bad' places had to be rejected because the student participants were not 'bad' at all. Instead the situation in which they were placed and the roles to which they were allocated caused them to behave in 'bad' ways. Although there were some individual differences, most adopted their given role and behaved according to how they thought that role should have been played out in that situation.

Now test yourself

18 (a) What was the dispositional hypothesis that was proposed?
(b) Did the results of the study support the dispositional hypothesis?

Answers on p.193

Tested

Expert tip

The dispositional hypothesis is crucial to the whole study, so be sure you know what it is.

Expert tip

There are three evaluation issues to consider:

- **Individual and situational** – Haney, Banks and Zimbardo proposed the dispositional hypothesis, but at the end of the study concluded that the behaviour of both the guards and prisoners was due to the roles allocated to them in the situation of a mock prison.
- **Ethics** – quite a number of ethical guidelines are broken in this study. Do you know which ones?
- **Social approach** – this study tells us quite a lot about our relationship with the society in which we exist, the roles we play, and how we respond to the situations in which we are placed.

Cross check

Individual and situational, page 102
Ethics, page 79
Social approach, page 90

Expert tip

Also think about newspaper sampling, and the ecological validity of the study.

Good Samaritanism: an underground phenomenon?

Revised

Authors: Piliavin et al. (1969)

Key term: Subway Samaritans

Approach: Social psychology

Cross check

Social approach, page 90

Background/context: Following the 1964 murder of Kitty Genovese and the apparent apathy of 38 witnesses, where no-one telephoned the police or went to help, many psychologists began to conduct laboratory studies into what became known as bystander behaviour – in particular, Darley and Latané. They conducted studies such as 'a lady in distress' and 'the smoke-filled room experiment'. All these studies showed that as group size increased the amount of helping behaviour decreased and this was termed **diffusion of responsibility**.

Diffusion of responsibility is based on the idea that if one person witnesses an event he or she is 100% responsible for helping. If there are more people then responsibility is diffused among them. If there are 10 people then they are each only 10% responsible. This means that they are less likely to help.

Aims/hypothesis:

1 To test the diffusion of responsibility hypothesis in a real-life setting. Previous laboratory experiments showed diffusion of responsibility in a laboratory but not in the 'real world'. Would the same effect be found?

2 To look at the effect of type of victim and race of victim on the speed of helping, frequency of responding, and the race of the helper. Would helping differ according to the *type* of victim? Would someone who needed help (an ill person) be helped more than a person whose need was their own fault (a drunken person)? Other research suggested that a person is more likely to help someone of his or her own race. Would this be true when a person needed help in an emergency?

Now test yourself

19 What murderous event triggered all the research into bystander behaviour?

20 Describe what is meant by the term 'diffusion of responsibility'.

Answers on pp.193–194

Tested

3 To look at the effects of modelling in emergency situations. Research by Bryan and Test (1967) found that people are more likely to help when they have seen another person helping. If a model was used to help, would other people join-in and help too?
4 To examine the relationship between size of group, and frequency and latency of helping response with a face-to-face victim. This was because previous laboratory studies had shown that group size made a difference to the frequency of helping (because of diffusion of responsibility).

Method: Field experiment and non-participant, naturalistic observation

Cross check

Field experiments, page 67
Observations, page 75

Variables: IV1 – type of victim (ill/cane and drunk); IV2 – race of victim ('black' and 'white'); IV3 – model conditions (see procedure 3, below) DVs – frequency of helping, speed of helping, race of helper, sex of helper.

Design: The design is **independent groups** because a group of people on the subway train only experienced an ill black trial, an ill white trial, a drunk black trial or a drunk white trial.

Setting: New York subway, IND (Independent line) 59th Street station to 125th Street station – a 7½ minute journey.

Experimenter(s): Students from Columbia University (New York): four male victims (three white and one black, aged 26–35); four male models (all white, aged 24–29) and eight female observers. The experimenters were divided into four teams of one victim, one model and two observers.

Participants and sampling technique: 4450 men and women travelling between 11 a.m. and 3 p.m. unaware that they were involved in an experiment (naïve). The racial composition was about 45% black and 55% white. The sample was self-selecting because it consisted of participants who just happened to be on that train at that time of day.

Apparatus: A subway train (an old model in which the observers could sit in the same places each time) and which had 13 seats only. All victims were dressed in Eisenhower jackets and old slacks (no tie). In the ill condition a black cane was carried; in the drunk condition the victim smelled of alcohol and carried a liquor bottle in a brown paper bag. Response categories were used to record the observations (as outlined for the DVs above).

Controls: The same 7½-minute train journey for all trials. Victims wore the same clothes and fell over at the same time (after 70 seconds) in the same place and in the same way on every trial. Each team member started the journey in the same place (e.g. observer 1 in the adjacent carriage near the exit door and observer 2 in the adjacent carriage in the far corner).

Procedure:

1 Four members of the team position themselves in a specific location on the subway train.
2 The subway train leaves the station. 70 seconds later, the victim (black or white, drunk or ill condition) staggers forward, collapses and remains on the floor, looking at the ceiling of the carriage.
3 If no-one helps then a model intervenes. There are four model conditions:
   - Critical-early (model in same carriage as victim) and helps 70 seconds after falling over.
   - Critical-late (model in same carriage as victim) and helps 150 seconds after falling over.
   - Adjacent-early (model in adjacent carriage to victim) and helps 70 seconds after falling over.
   - Adjacent-late (model in adjacent carriage to victim) and helps 150 seconds after falling over.

4. Observer 1 records: sex of passengers, race of passengers ('black' or 'white'), location of passengers (seated or standing) in critical carriage, total number of people, and total number who went to help. Observer 2 records: sex, race and location of people in adjacent area. She also records time taken for first observer to help, and time taken for someone to help the model. Both observers record comments by passengers sitting next to them.
5. If no-one helps, the model helps the victim to his feet. At the next station the team of four gets off the train, crosses over and repeats the procedure on a train going in the opposite direction. 6–8 trials are completed each day.

Typical mistake

There was no inter-rater reliability done in this study. As you will see, the observers recorded different things.

Data: Quantitative data were gathered: demographic characteristics, frequency of helping, etc. Qualitative data were also gathered through the comments that were made to the observers.

Results: The results tables for this study are numerous and complex. They have not been included and are replaced by detailed findings.

Cross check

Quantitative and qualitative data, page 80
Ethnocentrism, page 96

Findings:

1. The victim with the cane received spontaneous (before the model) help on 62 out of 65 trials. This means that the model only helped on 3 occasions. The drunken victim received spontaneous help on 19 of the 38 trials. The median helping time for cane victims was 5 seconds; for the drunken victim, 109 seconds.
2. When people did give spontaneous help, on 60% of the 81 trials there was helping from two, three and even more people. There was no difference on this between black and white, or drunk and ill. A first helper is the crucial thing: if one person helps then others join in.
3. Who helped? 60% of first helpers in the critical area were males; 90% of people helping were male. Racial composition was 55% white, 45% black and 64% of first helpers were white – not a significant difference.
4. Was there same-race helping? When the victim was white 68% of first helpers were white (32% black), significantly above the 55%. When the victim was black, only 50% of first helpers were white (and 50% black). There was a tendency toward 'same-race' helping.
5. In the ill condition there was no difference between black or white helpers. In the drunken condition mainly members of the same race came to help.
6. Other responses:
   - People left the critical area only 20% of the time and totalled only 34 people. More people left when the victim was drunk rather than ill.
   - Most comments happened during the drunken trials, particularly when no-one helped until after 70 seconds. This may be due to the discomfort of not helping and a need to justify inaction, such as saying 'it's for men to help' and 'I'm not strong enough'.
7. Was there diffusion of responsibility? The simple answer is no, and the simple explanation is that in this situation the victim and the witnesses were face-to-face, whereas they were not in the laboratory studies. Further, diffusion of responsibility predicts that the more people there are the less helping there will be. In this study helping was faster when there were more people.

Conclusions:

1. An individual who appears to be ill is more likely to receive help than a person who appears to be drunk.
2. Even when an audience includes both men and women, men are more likely to help than are women.
3. Same-race helping is more likely, particularly when the victim is drunk as compared with ill.

4 There is no strong relationship between the number of bystanders and the speed of helping; the expected diffusion of responsibility was not observed.
5 The longer the emergency continues without help being offered (a) the less impact a model has and (b) the more likely it is that individuals will leave the immediate area.

Model of response to emergency situations:

1 Observation of any *emergency situation creates arousal* in a bystander.
2 *Arousal* is an *unpleasant* feeling, and the bystander has a *need to reduce it.* The arousal will be differently interpreted in different situations (see Schachter and Singer, page 43) as fear, sympathy, etc., and possibly a combination of these. Arousal can be higher (a) the more one can empathise with the victim (e.g. same-race helping), (b) the closer one is to the emergency, and (c) the longer the state of emergency continues.
3 *Arousal is reduced* by the following responses: helping, going to get help, leaving the scene of the emergency, or concluding that the victim doesn't deserve help.

What *determines response* is the **cost–reward matrix**. This means we weigh-up the costs and benefits and then make a decision. What are those costs and benefits? They include: (a) the costs of helping (e.g. possible physical harm); (b) the costs of not helping (e.g. damaged self-esteem); (c) the rewards of helping (e.g. social approval such as a 'thank you'); and (d) the rewards of not helping (e.g. getting to work on time, or not getting harmed).

As Piliavin et al. state, all of the effects observed in this study can be explained by this model.

Expert tip

There are three evaluation issues to consider:

- The **model of response to emergency situations** has much in common with Schachter's two-factor theory of emotion. Both models have a stimulus that creates arousal (physiological component) and then there needs to be a psychological (cognitive) component for a decision or conclusion to be made.
- **Design weaknesses** – it is possible for a person to travel on the same train at the same time every day. The study was only conducted between 11 a.m. and 3 p.m. This limits the sample.
- **Generalisations** – Piliavin et al. suggest that the model of response to emergency situations can be generalised and it explains what all people experience in an emergency situation. Is this true?

Now test yourself

21 Piliavin, Rodin and Piliavin drew five conclusions from their data. Outline **two** conclusions.

Answer on p.194

Tested

Expert tip

It is important to know this model. It brings together physiological arousal and psychological or cognitive interpretation, showing how these two components interact.

Cross check

Physiological approach, page 89
Cognitive approach, page 87
Schachter and Singer, page 43
Determinism and free-will, page 101
Generalisations, page 97

Expert tip

Also think about observations, inter-rater reliability, ethics and ecological validity.

Experiments in intergroup discrimination

Revised

Author: Tajfel (1970)

Key term: Intergroup categorisation

Approach: Social psychology

Background/context: What causes prejudice and discrimination? Tajfel argues that we categorise *everything* (e.g. the foods we like and don't like; tastes and smells we like and don't like) – and this includes people. From a very early age we decide which children we like and which we don't and we do this to put order into a complex world, to make it much simpler to understand and deal with. It means that we categorise people into 'us' and 'them', or 'we' and 'they' or an 'in-group' and an 'out-group'. The implication of this **prejudice** is that we develop a 'generic norm of behaviour' – a 'rule of thumb', and according to this we act toward others, favouring those in the in-group and **discriminating** against those in the out-group.

Cross check

Social approach, page 90

Prejudice is the thought (the cognitive component); **discrimination** is the action (or behaviour).

Aim/hypothesis:
Study 1: To test the theory that in-group favouritism and out-group discrimination will be shown on the basis of categorisation into minimal groups.

Study 2: To validate study 1 using different criteria for categorisation (artistic preference).

Method: Laboratory experiment

Variables:
Study 1: IV – two conditions – randomly allocated 'over-estimators of dots' and 'under-estimators of dots'.

Study 2: IV – two conditions – randomly allocated 'preference for Klee' and 'preference for Kandinsky'.

The DV for both studies was the choice of points allocated on each matrix.

Design: The logical assumption is that the design is independent groups because each boy is either an under- or over-estimator for study 1 and has a Klee or Kandinsky preference in study 2. This is not true. This is what the boys think, but actually each boy is in both the in-group and the out-group and the booklets are completed for boys in the in-group judged against boys in the out-group. The design is therefore repeated measures.

Participants and sampling technique:
Study 1: 64 boys aged 14–15 years from a comprehensive school in Bristol, UK. All the boys knew each other.

Study 2: Three new groups, of 16 boys in each group, from the same school as for study 1.

The sampling technique is not specified but was probably opportunity sampling where the school sent boys who were free one afternoon to the university.

Now test yourself

22 Describe the sample of participants in study 2.

Answer on p.194

Tested

Experimenter(s): It isn't known who conducted the study – most likely Tajfel himself.

Apparatus:
Study 1: Booklet with 18 matrices. Matrices were: (a) **in-group choice** – in-group boy + in-group boy (see Figure 5); (b) **out-group choice** – out-group boy + out-group boy; (c) **intergroup choice** – in-group boy + out-group boy. Cubicle with pencil for completing booklets.

Member 04 of own group	–19	–16	–13	–10	–7	–4	–1	0	1	2	3	4	5	6
Member 03 of own group	6	5	4	3	2	1	0	–1	–4	–7	–10	–13	–16	–19

Figure 5

Study 2: 12 slides – six pictures by the artist Klee and six by the artist Kandinsky. Booklet with matrices. The matrices were the same as study 1: (a) **in-group choice** – in-group boy + in-group boy; (b) **out-group choice** – out-group boy + out-group boy; (c) **intergroup choice** – in-group boy + out-group boy (Figure 6). However, they differed according to whether the top row was in-group or out-group; and also according to whether the largest rewards were to the left or to the right of the matrix.

Points allocated to Kandinsky member 62	7	8	9	10	11	12	13	14	15	16	17	18	19
Points allocated to Klee member 14	1	3	5	7	9	11	13	15	17	19	21	23	25

Figure 6

Controls: All the boys received standardised instructions in both study 1 and study 2. The matrices were all the same. Each boy completed each matrices booklet in an individual cubicle, eliminating any copying or conformity.

Typical mistake

There are two studies here, each looking at the same thing but from a slightly different angle, but students often blend them into one.

Procedure:
Study 1: The boys arrived at the laboratory in groups of 8. They were told that it was 'an experiment on visual judgements'. They estimated the number of dots on a screen. They were divided into over-estimators and under-estimators (but actually allocation was done randomly) creating four groups of eight boys in each condition.

Working alone each boy was required to complete a booklet (of matrices) of rewards and penalties. They simply chose a number they wished to allocate to a boy as indicated in the booklet (see apparatus above).

Study 2: The boys arrived at the laboratory in groups of 16. They were told that it was about aesthetic preference for two 'foreign painters'. They viewed six slides of paintings by Klee and six by Kandinsky. They chose their favourite painting. They were put into two groups: 'Klee' and 'Kandinsky' (but actually allocation was done randomly).

As for study 1 the boys completed a booklet (the matrices) of rewards and penalties but which was different slightly from that in study 1 (see apparatus above).

Now test yourself

23 (a) Why is this study a snapshot study?

(b) Give a disadvantage of a snapshot study.

Answers on p.194

Tested

Data: Quantitative data were gathered: boys chose points from each matrix and they were totalled. They were not asked about why they had allocated points in the way they had.

Results:
Study 1: The boys gave rewards that were fair to both in-group boys, and the boys gave rewards that were fair to both out-group boys. When given an in-group boy and an out-group boy, more points were given to the in-group boy than the out-group boy. This difference was statistically significant.

Explanation: A number of different strategies could be applied. Strategy 1 – when it came to judging in-group with in-group, to be fair to both groups, they chose to give equal points. They also adopted this strategy when comparing out-group with out-group. However, when comparing in-group with the out-group they could have been fair to both or they could have chosen a different strategy, strategy 2 – a 'maximum joint profit' strategy – and allocated as many points as possible for *all* the boys, whatever group they were in. They didn't. They could also have chosen (a third strategy) to give more to the in-group irrespective of what the out-group got. They didn't. Instead they opted for strategy 4 – maximum difference – and allocated more points to the in-group than the out-group, maximising the difference between them.

It was decided to investigate further (in study 2) the relative weightings given to each of these three groups of maximum joint profit, maximum in-group profit and maximum difference.

Study 2: The boys did not choose the maximum joint profit (MJP) option (giving maximum rewards to both in-group and out-group) despite them all being boys from the same school and knowing each other. The boys did not choose the maximum in-group profit (MIP) option (giving maximum to their in-group and a little less to the out-group). The boys chose the maximum difference (MD) option, meaning their in-group got less overall, but much more than the out-group. Maximising the difference between the two groups, even though it meant less profit for them, was more important than taking the maximum profit.

Findings:

Study 1: The boys discriminated, showing in-group favouritism and out-group discrimination on the basis of 'flimsy and unimportant criteria' (i.e. over- and under-estimating dots).

Study 2: The boys discriminated, choosing to maximise the difference between the two groups and showing in-group favouritism and out-group discrimination on the basis of 'flimsy and unimportant criteria' (i.e. artistic preference).

Conclusions: Whenever we are confronted with a situation in which some form of intergroup categorisation appears relevant, we are likely to act in a way that discriminates against the out-group and which favours the in-group. If boys do this on the basis of trivial differences, as shown in two studies, then it will certainly apply to more obvious differences and lead us to believe (and show in-group favouritism) that all our in-groups, such as ethnic group, nation or football team, are automatically superior to all others.

Cross check

Generalisations, page 97
Ecological validity, page 78
Reductionism, page 104

Expert tip

There are three evaluation issues to consider:

- **Generalisations** – for Tajfel the cause of intergroup categorisation (favouritism and discrimination) is simple. It is the mere categorisation of people into any two (or more) groups. He believes this explanation can be generalised to all people all of the time.
- **Ecological validity** – the setting was a psychology laboratory. The task (estimating dots and artistic preference and allocating points) was also low in ecological validity.
- **Reductionism** – can prejudice and discrimination be explained by nothing more than the mere categorisation of people into groups? Is it really so simple? Tajfel argues that it is.

Expert tip

Also think about snapshot studies and ethics.

Now test yourself

24 Give **two** ways in which the boys were deceived.

Answer on p.194

Tested

1.3 The developmental psychology studies

Transmission of aggression through imitation of aggressive models

Revised

Authors: Bandura et al. (1961)

Key term: Aggression

Approach: Developmental psychology; behaviourist perspective

Cross check

Developmental approach, page 88
Behaviourist perspective, page 92

Background/context: Behaviourists believed that all behaviour is learned. This was shown in studies by Pavlov on dogs (classical conditioning) and in studies by Skinner on rats and pigeons (operant conditioning). Watson (1923) classically conditioned 'Little Albert' to be fearful of a white rat. Bandura outlined observational learning, suggesting that if behaviour of a model is observed then it will be copied (imitational learning). The model (a parent or a teacher, for example) is crucial in providing a suitable environment for a child to observe. To test his theory Bandura designed a laboratory experiment. He could choose any behaviour to study because *all behaviour is learned*. Bandura chose to teach aggression.

Aim/hypothesis: To show that observed behaviour is imitated. There were four hypotheses:

1. If a behaviour is observed it will be imitated.
2. If a behaviour is not observed it cannot be imitated.
3. Boys will copy a male model more than a female model and girls will copy a female model more than a male model.
4. Boys will be more predisposed than girls towards imitating aggression.

Method: Laboratory experiment with controlled observation

Variables: IV1 – three conditions – aggressive model group, non-aggressive model group and a control group who were not exposed to any model; IV2 – sex of model; IV3 – sex of children.

Group 1: aggressive group – six boys with male model and six girls with male model, six girls with female model and six boys with female model.

Group 2: non-aggressive group – six boys with male model and six girls with male model, six girls with female model and six boys with female model.

Group 3: control group: 12 boys and 12 girls who saw no model at all.

DV – number of behaviours out of 240 maximum in each of the response categories (see Table 1.4).

Design: Matched pairs, because the children were matched for pre-existing levels of aggression. Also independent groups, as outlined in the three groups above.

Participants and sampling technique: 36 boys and 36 girls aged 37–69 months from Stanford University nursery school. The sampling technique is unspecified, but was likely to be children who were there at the time and so was an opportunity sample. There was quota sampling to achieve 12 participants in each sub-category.

Apparatus:

Room 1: Potato prints and picture stickers, table and chair, Tinker Toy set, mallet and inflatable 5-foot bobo doll (adult-size)

Room 2: Fire engine, locomotive, doll set, spinning top

Room 3: One-way mirror for observations; a 3-foot bobo doll (child-size), mallet and peg board, two dart guns, tetherball with a face, tea set, three bears, cars, farm animals, ball, crayons and colouring paper

Controls:

- Children were matched for pre-existing levels of aggression, meaning that a child rated as 5 (very aggressive) was matched with a child also rated 5 (with one going to the 'aggressive group' and one to the 'non-aggressive group'). This reduced confounding variables.
- The toys in rooms 1, 2 and 3 were always the same and always in the same position when a child entered the room.
- The actions of the aggressive model were always the same, in the same order and for the same length of time.
- Observations were done by two independent observers. The 20-minute session was divided into 5-second intervals, giving 240 response 'units'. Observer data were compared (to assess inter-rater reliability) and showed correlations in the 0.9 range.

Procedure:

1 Pre-existing levels of aggression were determined by the experimenter and nursery teacher, by rating each child on four aspects (e.g. physical aggression and verbal aggression), using a five-point scale.

2 Each child was shown to room 1. He/she played with potato prints and stickers to 'settle-in'. The child was taken to other side of room where the model behaved either in a non-aggressive way or in an aggressive way. Aggressive (and associated verbal) actions were as follows: sits on bobo and punches on nose (saying 'sock it on the nose'); hits bobo on head with mallet ('hit him down'); throws bobo up in air ('throw him in the air'); kicks bobo about the room ('kick him'). After 10 minutes, the child left the room.

Cross check

Laboratory experiment, page 66
Controlled observation, page 75

Cross check

Designs, pages 69–70

Expert tip

There were two different designs in this study: children were matched for aggression and then put into independent groups.

Cross check

Sampling, page 83

Typical mistake

Don't confuse the toys in the original room (1) with the toys in the 'aggression arousal room' (2) and the toys in the test room (3).

Expert tip

To help to clarify a procedure or to help you understand and remember, you can use your own words and descriptions to help you.

Cross check

Controls, page 71

3 The child was taken to room 2 for 'mild aggression arousal'. He/she played with the toys but was then frustrated when told 'these are not for you to play with' and taken to room 3. (The **frustration-aggression hypothesis** means the child was highly likely to behave in an aggressive way given the opportunity.)

4 Room 3 (the test room) contained aggressive toys and non-aggressive toys plus additional toys (e.g. dart guns). The child was left alone and his/her behaviour observed for 20 minutes. The child was then taken back to nursery school.

The **frustration-aggression hypothesis** is the belief that aggression (whatever type) will *always* result when a person is frustrated.

Cross check

Quantitative data, page 80
Observations, page 75

Data: Quantitative data were gathered because the observers used 'response categories' to record the number of times each behaviour occurred. The response categories were: imitative physical aggression; imitative verbal aggression; partial imitation – mallet aggression; sits on bobo doll; non-imitative aggression – punches bobo; aggressive gun play. A record was made every 5 seconds (time sampling) and as the test lasted for 20 minutes. 240 instances of behaviour were recorded.

Now test yourself

Tested

25 (a) Describe the observation sampling strategy used by Bandura et al.

(b) Suggest why this observation strategy was used.

26 Give **two** types of behaviour (the response categories) that the observers looked for when they observed the children

Answers on p.194

Results:

Table 1.4 Mean aggression scores for experimental and control subjects

Response category	Experimental groups				Control groups
	Aggressive		Non-aggressive		
	F model	M model	F model	M model	
Imitative physical aggression					
Female subjects	5.5	7.2	2.5	0.0	1.2
Male subjects	12.4	25.8	0.2	1.5	2.0
Imitative verbal aggression					
Female subjects	13.7	2.0	0.3	0.0	0.7
Male subjects	4.3	12.7	1.1	0.0	1.7
Mallet aggression					
Female subjects	17.2	18.7	0.5	0.5	13.1
Male subjects	15.5	28.8	18.7	6.7	13.5
Punches Bobo doll					
Female subjects	6.3	16.5	5.8	4.3	11.7
Male subjects	18.9	11.9	15.6	14.8	15.7
Non-imitative aggression					
Female subjects	21.3	8.4	7.2	1.4	6.1
Male subjects	16.2	36.7	26.1	22.3	24.6
Aggressive gun play					
Female subjects	1.8	4.5	2.6	2.5	3.7
Male subjects	7.3	15.9	8.9	16.7	14.3

Findings: All four hypotheses were supported. There were many more instances of aggression in the aggression group than in the non-aggression group and the control group. Boys showed more physical aggression when with a male model; girls showed more verbal aggression when with a female model. Children in all groups, both male and female, showed aggressive gun play even though this had not been observed in the room 1 ('exposure') situation.

Conclusion: Behaviour that is observed is likely to be imitated.

Cross check

Nature/nurture, page 103
Determinism and free-will, page 101
Children, page 99

Expert tip

There are three evaluation issues to consider:

- **Nature/nurture** – behaviourists believe that all behaviour is learned (**nurture**) and that nothing is inherited (**nature**). Is this viewpoint true?
- **Environmental determinism** – behaviourists believe that all behaviour is learned and so the learning environment is crucial.
- **Children** – there are always issues when **children** participate in research. They cannot give full, informed consent because they are under age. Do they fully understand the task and what the experiment requires? How does the child respond: does the experimenter interpret behaviour (or what a child says) in the correct way?

Expert tip

Also think about ethics, observations and inter-rater reliability.

Now test yourself

Tested

27 **(a)** Describe how the children were matched for pre-existing levels of aggression.

(b) Explain why the children were matched for pre-existing levels of aggression.

Answers on p.194

Analysis of a phobia of a 5-year-old boy

Revised

Author: Freud (1909)

Key term: Little Hans

Approach: Developmental psychology; psychodynamic perspective

Cross check

Developmental approach, page 88
Psychodynamic perspective, page 93

Background/context: There are many facets to the work of Freud: his theory of personality involving the id, ego and superego; his unique psychodynamic perspective emphasising the role of the unconscious mind and psychoanalysis; and his theory of psychosexual development. Freud proposed that children develop through a number of psychosexual stages: oral, anal, phallic, latency and mature adult. During the **phallic stage** a boy focuses sexual attention towards the mother and Freud calls this the **Oedipus complex**. Freud's evidence for this is the case study of a little boy called Hans.

The **phallic stage** is the third stage of psychosexual development in which the libido is focused on the genitals.

The **Oedipus complex** is part of the phallic stage. It involves a desire for sexual involvement with the parent of the opposite sex and rivalry with the parent of the same sex.

Method: Case study and longitudinal method

Freud's case study of Little Hans

Freud began the case study of Little Hans with the following comment: 'I must deal with two objections which will be raised against my making use of the present analysis for this purpose'. Freud writes: 'The first objection is that Hans was not a normal child; it would be illegitimate, therefore, to apply to other normal children conclusions which might perhaps be true of him'. If Hans was not a normal child then the findings of any study should not be generalised, but it is debatable as to whether Hans was normal or not.

Typical mistake

Don't write too much about the psychosexual stages. It is important to know a little about Freud's theory of psychosexual development, but this core study is about Little Hans, so focus much more on that.

The second objection according to Freud was that: 'an analysis of a child conducted by his father, who went to work instilled by my theoretical views and infected with my prejudices, must be entirely devoid of any objective worth'. Freud went on to write that any child is highly suggestible, but also 'we

Cross check

Case study, page 76
Longitudinal method, page 84

can quite clearly distinguish from one another the occasions on which he was falsifying the facts or keeping them back and the occasions on which he burst into a flood of information about what was really going on inside him and about things which, until then, no one but himself had known'. Freud also wrote that 'during the analysis Hans had to be told many things that he could not say himself', that 'he had to be presented with thoughts which he had so far shown no signs of possessing', and that 'his attention had to be turned in the direction from which his father was expecting something to come'.

Expert tip

This study does not (and cannot) follow the usual format of studies in this guide. It is a very different approach. Don't worry about it being different – just read the story.

Apparently Hans's father had heard Freud speak and, being interested in his views, had begun to study his son and report the findings back to Freud. Freud then analysed the behaviour of Hans on the basis of stories told by the father and on just one meeting with Hans.

Now test yourself

28 Freud writes that his approach does not have any scientific value for **two** reasons. What are those **two** reasons?

Answer on p.194

Tested

Evidence for the phallic stage (and the Oedipus complex)

The first trait in Little Hans that can be considered to be evidence of him being in the phallic stage is his lively interest in his 'widdler'. Hans assumed that all animate objects also had widdlers, including his parents. His mother, he thought, 'must have a widdler like a horse'. Driven by natural (and normal) curiosity Hans asked both his mother and father about their widdlers. Rather than answering a simple question, which would have satisfied his curiosity, they said nothing. Undeterred, Hans tried to observe other people's widdlers. He watched his 7-day-old sister being given a bath and commented, 'But her widdler's still quite small', assuming that it would grow in size as she grew older.

More evidence for the phallic stage was provided when his mother found him touching his widdler when he was 3½ years old. She threatened him with: 'If you do that, I shall send for Dr A to cut off your widdler. And then what'll you widdle with?' Apparently he liked giving himself feelings of pleasure by touching his widdler and masturbating every evening.

Evidence for the early beginnings of the Oedipus complex is provided in a number of claims about Hans's behaviour. When he was 4¼ Hans was being given his usual daily bath by his mother, and afterwards dried and powdered. As his mother was powdering round his penis and taking care not to touch it, Hans said: 'Why don't you put your finger there?' Mother: 'Because that would be priggish.' Hans: 'What's that? Priggish? Why?' Mother: 'Because it's not proper.' Hans (laughing): 'But it's great fun.'

The second piece of evidence is 'the giraffe episode'. Hans told a story about a big giraffe in a room and a crumpled one. Apparently the big one called out and Hans took the crumpled one away. Later Hans said he then sat down on top of the crumpled giraffe. Puzzled, Hans's father asked Hans to clarify. Hans brought a piece of paper, crumpled it and then sat on it. Still puzzled, the father told Freud, who interpreted the story. Freud believed that the big giraffe was the father and the crumpled giraffe was the mother, and Hans wanted the father removed so he could be with his mother. As Freud put it: 'In his attitude towards his father and mother, Hans really was a little Oedipus who wanted to have his father 'out of the way', to get rid of him, so that he might be alone with his beautiful mother and sleep with her.'

Expert tip

Typical questions ask for one or two pieces of evidence that support Hans being in the phallic stage or having an Oedipus complex. Know two pieces of evidence.

The phobia

One day when Hans was out in the street with his mother, he was seized with an attack of anxiety. He was terrified that a black horse would bite him. Apparently Hans had seen a 'bus horse' fall down and he thought the horse was dead. His father suggested to Hans that when he saw the horse fall down Hans must have thought of him (a leading question) and wished that he, his father, might fall down in the same way and be dead. The reason why Hans made this association was that Hans's father looked like a horse! Freud wrote: 'the black on horses' mouths and the things in front of their eyes (the moustaches and

Now test yourself

29 Give **one** piece of evidence from the study that suggests that Hans was a 'little Oedipus'.

Answer on p.194

Tested

eyeglasses) seemed to me to have been directly transposed from his father onto the horses'. But Hans was afraid of both black and white horses. The answer was that Dr A looked like a white horse and Hans had been threatened that Dr A would come and cut off his widdler, so it was not surprising that Hans feared white horses.

Hans was also afraid of carts, furniture vans and buses that were heavily loaded. Hans seemingly was occupied with 'lumf' (faeces) and showed disgust at things that reminded him of evacuating his bowels. His father recognised a similarity between a heavily loaded cart and a body loaded with faeces, such as the way a cart drives out through a gateway and the way in which faeces leave the body. However, Hans was not in the anal stage; according to Freud's theory of psychosexual development this could not be possible. The answer was that the heavily loaded carts represented his mother's pregnancy. The fantasy by Hans about a plumber confirmed this: 'Daddy, I thought something: I was in the bath, and then the plumber came and unscrewed it. Then he took a big borer and stuck it into my stomach.' This could only be a remoulding of a *fantasy of procreation*, distorted by anxiety.

Finally, Hans had a fantasy about imaginary children. Hans was the father, his father the grandfather and his mother the grandmother. This saw Hans moving towards normal sexual development and in the process his castration anxiety and phobias were resolved.

Expert tip

There are three evaluation issues to consider:

- **Longitudinal studies** – there are advantages and disadvantages to longitudinal studies. Do you know what they are?
- **Generalisations** – Hans is described as 'abnormal'. Perhaps the only thing abnormal about Hans is that he was entering the Oedipus complex early.
- **Children** – there are always issues when children participate in research. Little Hans is no exception.

Expert tip

Also think about self-reports, and the case study method.

Now test yourself

Tested

30 **(a)** Give **one** advantage of the case study method as used by Freud.
(b) Give **one** disadvantage of the case study method as used by Freud.

Answers on p.194

Cross check

Longitudinal studies, page 84
Generalisations, page 97
Children, page 99

Facial diversity and infant preferences for attractive faces

Revised

Authors: Langlois et al. (1991)

Key words: Infant facial preference

Approach: Developmental psychology

Background/context: Langlois asks: (a) Is beauty in the eye of the beholder? Her answer is 'no' because there is a universal standard by which facial attractiveness is judged. (b) Do we judge books (and people) by their covers? Her answer is 'yes' because both adults and infants judge attractive adults and infants more favourably (and treat them more positively) than those who are unattractive. It is logical to research very young infants (such as 6 months old) to see if they find faces attractive, taking into account age, sex and race differences.

Aim/hypothesis: To replicate previous results with adult female faces and to determine if infant preferences extended beyond adult female faces to other types of face.

Study 1: (a) to replicate previous results with adult female faces; (b) to extend this to adult male faces; (c) to investigate whether the order of presentation affects preferences.

Study 2: to extend the findings to non-white faces.

Study 3: to extend the findings to the faces of babies.

Method: Laboratory experiment

Cross check

Developmental approach, page 88
Laboratory experiments, page 66

Variables:
Study 1: IV1 – attractive and unattractive white female faces; IV2 – attractive and unattractive white male faces; IV3 – infants who see either all men then all women (or all women then all men) compared with infants who see alternating men and women.

DV – fixation time (in seconds), i.e. the length of time an infant looks at a face. As each face was presented twice (once on the left side and once on the right side of the screen), the mean time for an individual face could be calculated and as there were two observers the agreement between them could be checked.

Cross check

Inter-rater reliability, page 82

Study 2: IV – attractive and unattractive black female faces; DV – fixation time (in seconds), as in study 1.

Study 3: IV – attractive and unattractive male and female infant faces; DV – fixation time (in seconds), as in study 1.

Attractiveness and unattractiveness were determined in all three studies using people acting as judges and rating photographs on 5-point Likert scales. In study 1 attractiveness had been previously determined by 40 undergraduate judges using a Likert 5-point scale. The mean attractiveness was 3.46 for the women and 3.35 for men. The unattractive faces showed means of 1.44 for women and 1.4 for men. Agreement among the judges revealed correlations of 0.97 for women and 0.95 for men, confirming that the vast majority perceived the faces in the same way as attractive or unattractive. In study 2 the mean attractiveness was 3.41 and the unattractive showed a mean of 1.44. The judges were both black and white and their agreement about attractiveness and unattractiveness was extremely similar. In study 3 again the judging process was used, reliability across judges was 0.97 and the mean attractiveness score was 3.02 and unattractiveness 1.69 on the 5-point scale.

Cross check

Correlations, page 74
Rating scales, pages 72–73

Design: Repeated measures in all three studies because all the infants viewed all stimuli, but each infant only performed in one study.

Participants and sampling technique:
Study 1: 110 6-month-old infants from a subject pool (people who are willing to take part in a study when asked) of participants at the University of Texas, USA at Austin. 50 infants were excluded for (a) fussing (×41), (b) equipment failure (×3), (c) experimenter error (×3) and other reasons (×3). Of the remaining 60, 35 were boys and 25 girls. Most infants (53) were white with the others being Hispanic, black and Asian.

Study 2: 43 6-month-old infants from the same subject pool. Three were excluded leaving 15 boys and 25 girls. 36 were white, two black and two Hispanic.

Cross check

Sampling, page 83

Study 3: 52 6-month-old infants from the same subject pool. 11 were excluded for fussing and two were not tested due to being too close to their 6-month age limit, leaving 39 of which 19 were boys and 20 girls. 37 were white and two Hispanic.

Apparatus: Screen and projector. A standard visual preference technique using a stimulus comprising two faces (one attractive and one unattractive) being presented at the same time for 10 seconds. A video camera situated under the stimulus viewing screen connected to a monitor so the experimenter could record the infants' direction of gaze and fixation time.

Now test yourself

31 What is 'fussing'? How many infants were excluded from each of the three studies for fussing?

Answer on p.194

Tested

Study 1: Colour slides of 16 adult white women (eight attractive and eight unattractive) and 16 adult white men (eight attractive and eight unattractive).

Study 2: Colour slides of 16 adult black women (eight attractive and eight unattractive)

Study 3: Colour slides of 16 3-month-old infants (four attractive male and four attractive female, and four unattractive male and four unattractive female).

Controls, all studies:

- The faces in all three studies were controlled for facial expression, hair length and hair colour. All men were clean-shaven.
- Each child sat at the same distance from the screen and the duration of slide presentation was the same.
- Each parent was blindfolded (using occluded glasses) to prevent any signal about the slides being transmitted to the infant.
- Each stimulus pair was presented twice, once with attractive on left and then again with attractive on right to prevent any left- or right-side bias.
- Two experimenters observed each infant and records were compared (inter-rater reliability). The reliabilities ranged from 0.97 to 0.99. Agreement about fussing was also very high.
- The attractiveness of mothers was also controlled because a child might prefer an attractive face if the mother is attractive, for example.

Cross check

Controls, page 71
Inter-rater reliability, page 82

Procedure:

1 An infant was seated on a parent's lap 35 cm from the screen. A light flashed and a buzzer sounded to get the child's attention.
2 The first stimulus was presented and the infant's response was recorded. The same stimulus was then presented again but with the two faces presented on the opposite sides.
3 The same procedure was repeated until all slides in the study were complete (see each study below).
4 The experimenters observed the gaze direction of the child and the length of time (in seconds) the infant looked at a face.

Study 1: 16 sets of stimuli were presented one after another, either all the men first, or all the women first, or alternately for the order of presentation trials. The infant had a 5–10 minute rest. 16 remaining sets were presented to complete all the sets of stimuli.

Study 2: All eight sets of stimuli were presented one after another. There was no break because the number of stimuli had been reduced from 16 to 8 sets.

Study 3: As done for study 2, all eight sets of stimuli were presented, one after another.

Data: All the data collected (for all three studies) were quantitative – the fixation time in seconds that an infant looked at the slide of a face. Given the age of each infant, no qualitative data could be collected.

Cross check

Quantitative data, page 80

Results:

Table 1.5 Mean fixation times (in seconds) for high- and low-attractiveness slides

	High attractiveness		Low attractiveness	
Type of face	***M***	***SD***	***M***	***SD***
Male and female faces (Study 1)	7.82	1.35	7.57	1.27
Black female faces (Study 2)	7.05	1.83	6.52	1.92
Baby faces (Study 3)	7.16	1.97	6.62	1.83

Table 1.6 Mean fixation times (in seconds) for sex of infant × sex of face interaction

	Male face		Female face	
Sex of infant	***M***	***SD***	***M***	***SD***
Male	7.95	1.45	7.36	1.31
Female	7.69	1.35	7.81	1.33

Findings:

Study 1

1 Infants looked at attractive faces for longer (7.82 seconds) than they looked at unattractive faces (7.57 seconds). This difference is significant ($p = 0.03$).
2 Boys looked at male faces for longer (7.95 seconds) than they looked at female faces (7.36 seconds). The difference is significant ($p < 0.01$).
3 Girls looked longer at female faces (7.81 seconds) than male (7.69 seconds), but this difference is not significant.
4 No significant relationships were found between attractiveness of mother and sex of infant, or sex of stimulus face, or attractiveness of stimulus face.
5 Order of presentation made no difference.

Study 2

6-month-old infants looked at attractive black female faces for longer (7.05 seconds) than they did at black female unattractive faces (6.52 seconds). This difference was significant ($p < 0.05$).

Study 3

6-month-old infants looked at attractive infant faces for longer (7.16 seconds) than they did at unattractive infant faces (6.62 seconds). This difference was significant ($p < 0.001$).

Expert tip

Remember that you don't need to know any statistical test, just that the result is significant or not.

Conclusions:

1 The findings of all three studies show that 6-month-old infants can discriminate between attractive and unattractive faces and that they prefer attractive faces.
2 The findings also show that babies are judging attractiveness irrespective of sex, age and race of faces.
3 Exposure to cultural media does not seem to account for these preferences; rather, preferences for attractiveness are either innate or acquired with only minimal experience of faces in the environment.

Now test yourself

32 Describe **three** conclusions from the study by Langlois et al.

Answer on p.194

Tested

Cross check

Reliability, page 82
Correlations, page 74
Determinism, page 101
Nature/nurture, page 103

Explanations: What makes a face attractive? Rather than cultural variation in the perception of beauty, studies have shown that there are common features across cultures. Ethnically diverse faces have distinct, yet similar, structural features. The diversity of the faces (male–female, black–white, adult–infant) presented to these infants suggests they are identifying these 'universal features of attractiveness'.

Expert tip

Also think about validity, ethics and the use of children as participants.

Expert tip

There are three evaluation issues to consider:

- **Reliability** – this study used inter-rater reliability twice, once when judging the attractiveness of faces and again when judging the fixation time of the infant, and the data were analysed using a correlation with high coefficient values.
- **Determinism** – the findings of this study suggest a 'universal attractiveness'. Is the perception of universal attractiveness biologically determined?
- **Nature/nurture** – could a 6-month-old infant have *learned* what the features of attractiveness are? No. Is preference for attractiveness inherited?

Now test yourself

33 What did Langlois et al. conclude about whether facial preference is learned or inherited?

Answer on p.194

Tested

Factors influencing young children's use of motives and outcomes as moral criteria

Revised

Author: Nelson (1980)

Key term: Children's morals

Approach: Developmental psychology

Background/context: Piaget proposed that children go through three stages of moral development: a pre-moral stage (birth to 4 or 6 years); a stage of heteronomous morality (6–10 years); and a stage of autonomous morality (10 years plus). Using stories Piaget found that children under 10 years old based their judgements on the amount of damage (the consequences or **outcome**), and did not take intentions (i.e. **motives**) into account. Other research suggests that Piaget was wrong. Nelson suggests that Piaget's methodology was at fault because when he told a story the younger child may not have *fully* understood it, whereas if a young child fully understands what the story is, by being shown a picture for example, then he/she *can* understand motive as well as outcome.

Cross check

Developmental approach, page 88

Morality is the ability to distinguish right from wrong and to act on that decision.

Aim/hypothesis: To test the hypothesis that young children do take into account both motive and outcome in making moral judgements.

Method: Field experiment conducted in the school of the child, involving an interview.

Now test yourself

34 What is a motive (or intention) and what is an outcome (or consequence) when applied to this study?

Answer on p.194

Tested ☐

Study 1

Variables:

- **IV1** – **age** – children were 3–4 years or 6–8 years
- **IV2** – **motive** good or bad and **outcome** good or bad:
  1 Boy playing with ball. Wants friend to join in (**motive good**). Boy throws ball to friend to start game of catch. Boy throws ball, friend catches ball and game of catch begins (**outcome good**).
  2 Boy playing with ball. Wants friend to join in (**motive good**). Boy throws ball to friend to start game of catch. Boy throws ball, but ball hits friend on head and makes him cry (**outcome bad**).
  3 Boy playing with ball. Mad at friend (**motive bad**). Boy throws ball at friend to hit him on purpose but friend catches ball and game of catch begins (**outcome good**).
  4 Boy playing with ball. Mad at friend (**motive bad**). Boy throws ball at friend to hit him on purpose. Ball hits friend on head and makes him cry (**outcome bad**).
- **IV3** – **mode of presentation** – verbal only (as done by Piaget); picture motive implicit; picture motive explicit:
  1 **Verbal presentation**. Stories (as above) described to each child. Cartoon-like pictures (Figure 7) showing the actor's motive (good or bad), behaviour and outcome (good or bad) are combined:
  2 **Motive implicit**. One set of the cartoon-like pictures has positive and negative motives merely *implied* by the facial expressions of the boy (the actor).
  3 **Motive explicit**. Another set of the cartoon-like pictures has positive and negative motives conveyed *explicitly* by cartoon-like thought bubbles about the actor's head, showing his motive.

Cross check

Field experiment, page 67
Interviews, page 73

Now test yourself

35 Identify the three independent variables.

Answer on p.194

Tested ☐

Expert tip

There is potential for confusion with all the variables in this study. Think them through carefully so you understand exactly what is going on.

Figure 7 Example of drawings used to convey motive, action and outcome in picture–motive explicit presentations of stories

- **DVs** – the judgement (of good or bad) by the child was done on a 7-point scale by using a series of smiley and frowning faces (figure 8). Both sets of faces were 7.5 cm in diameter (very good or bad), 6.5 cm (good or bad) and 5.5 cm (a little bit good or bad). A 4.5 cm face was neutral. Points were allocated to each face and the scale was therefore: 7 very good > 6 good > 5 a little bit good > 4 neutral > 3 a little bit bad > 2 bad > 1 very bad.

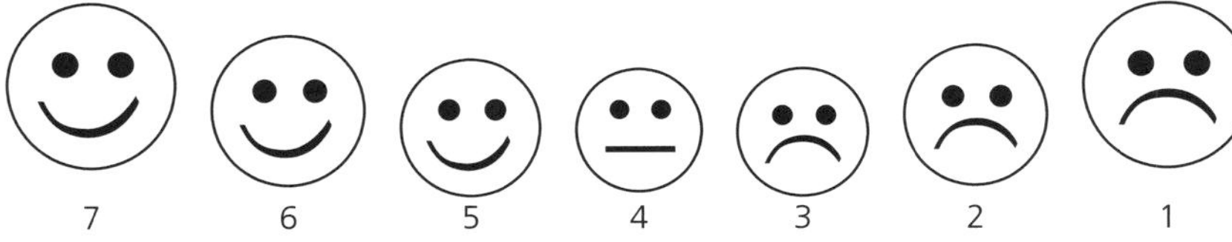

Figure 8

Design: Age was independent groups, as was mode of presentation. Motive and outcome was repeated measures as each child was presented with all four stories.

Cross check

Designs, pages 68–70

Setting: Although not confirmed, schools in and around the University of Illinois, Chicago, USA.

Participants and sampling technique: Study 1 – 60 pre-school children aged 3–4 years and 30 children aged 6–8 years. Half were male and half female in each group. They were mostly white, middle class. A parent gave consent for the child to participate.

Now test yourself

36 Is this study single-blind or double-blind? Explain your answer.

Answer on p.194

Tested

Apparatus: Four stories of cartoon-like pictures showing the actor's motive, behaviour and outcome. Pictures were 25 × 23 cm black-and-white line drawings. One set of four had only facial expressions (implicit) and one set had explicit thoughts bubbles showing the actor's intentions (motives). A third set had no cartoon at all; just the verbal description/words of the story.

Controls: Each child had the four stories, whether they were in the verbal, motive implicit or motive explicit conditions. The same experimenter tested every child irrespective of variable/condition.

The cartoons were all the same, in a standard format. The children were told to listen carefully because they would have to tell the story out loud later on. This was to make sure the child paid careful attention to what was being said.

Procedure:

1 Children in each age group were randomly assigned to mode of presentation groups: verbal only; motive implicit and motive explicit.
2 Children were interviewed by the experimenter and familiarised with rating scales (smiley/frowning faces) and given two practice stories.
3 Children were told to listen to each story and then to point to the face to show how good or bad the boy was.

Data: Quantitative data were gathered – a number was allocated to a smiley face and so the numbers in each condition of the IV could be added and the mean score of each calculated. Statistics for this study were complex because each variable was calculated with and against each other variable. Qualitative data were gathered because the interviewer asked the child to repeat the story. To check interviewer understanding a second rater was used. There was agreement of 97%.

Cross check

Types of data, page 80

Results:

Table 1.7 Mean rating of actor's goodness/badness in Study 1 as a function of participants' age, level of motive, and level of outcome

	3-year-olds ($N = 60$)		7-year-olds ($N = 30$)	
	Good motive	**Bad motive**	**Good motive**	**Bad motive**
Good outcome	6.55	2.27	6.20	3.46
Bad outcome	4.17	1.60	4.47	1.56

Findings:

1 **Motive** – the overall good motive mean was 5.35 ((6.55 + 4.17 + 6.20 + 4.47)/4) while the overall bad motive mean was 2.22 ((2.27 + 1.60 + 3.46 + 1.56)/4), which is statistically significant ($p < 0.0001$). This tells us very little except that the good and bad motives were really 'good' and 'bad', and not similar to each other – i.e. the motives were valid.

2 **Outcome** – the overall good outcome was 4.7 and the figure for bad outcome was 2.92 (calculated as for motive). This is also statistically significant ($p < 0.001$) and it can be concluded that the **outcomes** are very different from each other.

3 What is more important is that when there was a bad motive in the story this appeared to influence judgement much more than a good motive or outcome.

4 **Mode of presentation** – only outcome varied with mode of presentation when it was expected that both motive and outcome would vary. It was also found that when motive information was explicit, good and bad outcomes had a greater effect on judgements than when the presentation was implicit or verbal only.

5 **Age** – 40% of 3-year-olds rated the actor negatively when there was just one mention of 'bad', ignoring any 'good' information. 28% ignored outcome altogether and based judgement entirely on motive. The remaining 32% showed varying patterns of judgement.

Conclusion: Young children place more weight on **valence** (positive and negative, or good and bad) rather than whether the source is motive or outcome. Specifically children are more influenced by something that is bad (see findings 3 and 5 above) than good.

Explanation: An explanation for this might be that they learn the concept of bad before good (and so this carried more weight at age 3–4). It also might be that the first negative information they receive (whether motive or outcome) influences the rest of the story.

However, before there are any further conclusions, there is a design error here. When the stories were presented, the motive information always came first, then action and then outcome. This might have influenced the judgements made. A second study was needed.

Study 2

The participants were 27 pre-school children aged 3–4 (mean age 3.8) randomly assigned to one of the three modes of presentation conditions. Everything was repeated in the same way as study 1 except for a crucial **counterbalancing** difference. This time the outcome was presented *before* the motive.

Findings:

1 As for study 1, anything negative (whether motive or outcome) was more influential on judgement than anything positive.

2 Despite outcome being presented before motive, it did not have more of an effect than motive, suggesting that motive is indeed important and taken into account.

Explanation: Children appear to want a story that is congruent (where all aspects – motive, action and outcome – match each other, being all good or all bad) rather than one that is incongruent (where one aspect is good and another is bad).

Conclusion: Making moral judgements requires understanding of the concepts of both good and bad and a child must understand the relationship between action, motive and goal to make a judgement.

Cross check

Children, page 99
Ethics, page 79
Applications/usefulness, page 95

Expert tip

There are three evaluation issues to consider:

- **Children** – in this study some of the children were as young as 3 years of age. Children of this age might not concentrate or might misinterpret what is required of them.
- **Ethics (informed consent)** – as the children were under 16 years they could not give consent themselves. In this case consent was given by a parent of each child; ethically this is perfectly acceptable.
- **Applications to life/usefulness** – are the findings of this study useful? The answer to this question must be yes because it tells us a little more about what young children are able to understand when it comes to moral decisions and judgements.

Expert tip

Also think about reliability and inter-rater reliability.

1.4 The physiological psychology studies

Cognitive, social and physiological determinants of emotional state

Revised

Authors: Schachter and Singer (1962)

Key term: Emotion

Approach: Physiological psychology

Cross check

Physiological approach, page 89

Background/context: Early theories of emotion were based on physiological factors only and suggested that the physiological response happens at the same time as we experience the emotion. Schachter (1959) proposed the **two-factor theory of emotion**, that emotion is the result of both physiological and psychological (cognitive) components. This is Schachter's *theory* and what is needed is supporting experimental evidence.

Now test yourself

37 What are the two factors in Schachter's two-factor theory of emotion?

Answer on p.194

Tested

Propositions:

1 If a person is physiologically aroused and there is no immediate explanation, the arousal will be labelled as a particular emotion based on the information (or cognitions) available.

2 If a person is physiologically aroused and there is an appropriate explanation, there is no need to seek further information (or cognitions) to label that emotion.

3 If there is no physiological arousal then any cognition we have we dismiss and there is no emotional experience.

Cross check

Laboratory experiment, page 66
Observations, page 75
Self-report questionnaires, page 72

Method: Laboratory experiment with observation and self-report questionnaires

Variables: There are *three* experimental conditions of the IV and *one* control condition:

- EPI INF (epinephrine informed) – injected with epinephrine and told true effects of epinephrine*.
- EPI MIS (epinephrine misinformed) – injected with epinephrine and told false effects of epinephrine.
- EPI IGN (epinephrine ignorant) – injected with epinephrine and told nothing more.
- Placebo (or control condition) – injected with saline solution and told nothing more.

(*Epinephrine/adrenaline causes an increase in breathing and heart rate, possible palpitations, and an empty sensation in the stomach.)

These conditions manipulate the physiological component. The psychological (cognitive) component is manipulated by two further conditions: using a **stooge** in the creation of **euphoria** (happiness/joy) and **anger**.

Thus there are seven sub-groups: placebo anger, placebo euphoria, EPI INF anger, EPI INF euphoria, EPI IGN anger, EPI IGN euphoria, EPI MIS euphoria. There was no EPI MIS anger condition.

There were two DVs: **observation** through a one-way mirror and **self-report** on various measures.

Explanation:

- EPI INF – told effects of epinephrine, so should *not* copy behaviour of stooge.
- Placebo – no epinephrine and told nothing, so should *not* copy behaviour of stooge.
- EPI MIS – misinformed about epinephrine, so seek an explanation, so should copy behaviour of stooge.
- EPI IGN – told nothing about epinephrine, so seek an explanation, so should copy behaviour of stooge.

Design: The design was independent groups because if a participant was to repeat any of the conditions they would immediately understand what was going on and respond falsely.

Expert tip

You can use abbreviations like EPI MIS, but make sure you know which group is which. If you use full words like 'misinformed', then there is no ambiguity as to what they were told.

Participants and sampling technique: The participants were all male college students taking introductory psychology. They were given two extra points on their final examination for participating.

Apparatus: Private room for administering injections, for giving various instructions and for observing through a one-way mirror. Suproxin, i.e. epinephrine (adrenaline), or a placebo (a saline solution). Items for the euphoria condition: paper, wastebasket, manila folders, a hula hoop. 'Ambiguous' questionnaires for the anger condition.

Cross check

Designs, page 69
Sampling, page 83
Controls, page 71

Controls:

- All participants were given an injection.
- All participants in each condition followed the same procedure.
- The stooges repeated the same behaviour, saying and doing the same thing each time.
- Observations were conducted by two observers.

Procedure:

1 Each participant was taken to the private room and told that the study was a test of vision and the vitamin supplement Suproxin.
2 If the participant agreed to do the study, a short while later a doctor arrived and gave an injection of Suproxin.
3 Participants were then given one of three different sets of instructions depending on whether they were in the INF, MIS or IGN/placebo group.

4 Each participant was then placed in a room and introduced to another 'participant' (actually a stooge) and told to wait for 20 minutes. The stooge either behaved euphorically or angrily:
   - **Euphoric** – doodles on paper, crumples it, throws it in wastebasket and plays basketball. Asks participant to join in. Makes paper plane, flies it. Builds a tower with folders then knocks then over. Plays with a hula hoop.
   - **Angry** – begins to answer a questionnaire, which gets increasingly personal and insulting. Makes aggressive comments about it.

5 The experimenter enters the room and hands out questionnaires for 'feedback on effects of Suproxin'.

6 The experimenter debriefs the participants. (11 of the participants were 'suspicious of the procedure' so their data were discarded.)

Data: Observation – **objective** behaviour coded into categories. Four categories for euphoria: joins in, initiates new activity, ignores stooge and watches stooge. Six categories for anger: agrees, disagrees, neutral, initiates agreement/disagreement, watches, ignores.

Self-report – **subjective** data gathered by a structured questionnaire. Mock questions were asked, then two questions about emotional state: 'How irritated, angry or annoyed would you say you feel now?' and 'How good or happy would you say you feel now?' Answers were on a 5-point scale from 0: 'I don't feel…' to 4: 'I feel extremely…'. Then two questions were asked about physiological state: 'Have you ever experienced any palpitations?' and 'Did you feel any tremor?' Answers were on a 4-point scale from 0: 'not at all' to 3: 'an intense amount'.

Results: there are too many results tables to include. See the original study or look at the summarised findings below.

Findings:

1 Participants in the epinephrine condition experienced more physiological responses than those in the placebo conditions (as would be expected) and the difference was significant ($p = 0.001$).

2 For the **euphoria self-reports**.
   (a) EPI INF reported significantly less euphoria than the EPI MIS ($p < 0.01$).
   (b) EPI INF reported significantly less euphoria than the EPI IGN ($p < 0.02$).
   (c) There was no significant difference between the placebo and the other groups.

3 For the **euphoria observations**. EPI MIS had more instances of euphoric activity (22.56) than any other group; EPI INF had the least at 12.72. This difference was significant ($p = 0.05$). No other comparison was significant.

4 For the **anger self-reports**. EPI INF had the highest anger score of 1.91 and EPI IGN had the lowest with 1.39.

5 For the **anger observations**. EPI IGN had the highest anger score of 2.28 and EPI INF had the lowest with –0.18.

Conclusions: All three propositions are supported and so the findings of the study provide experimental evidence for the two-factor theory of emotion.

Expert tip

There are three evaluation issues to consider:

- **Ethics** – stooges were used in this study. This is automatically unethical because the use of a stooge is deceiving a participant.
- **Sample** – the sample was students receiving exam points for participating, and their teachers were conducting the study. This made the sample biased.
- **Generalisations** – the participants were male and they were all students. However, emotion is partly a physiological process and therefore the same for everyone.

Now test yourself

38 (a) How was the physiological component manipulated?

(b) How was the psychological (cognitive) component manipulated?

39 (a) Give **one** advantage of using a stooge in this study.

(b) Give **one** problem with the use of a stooge in psychological research.

Answers on pp.194–195

Tested

Cross check

Types of data, page 80
Stooge, page 20

Expert tip

This theory is important because it brings together physiological and cognitive components. The study by Piliavin et al. also does this.

Cross check

Ethics, page 79
Sampling, page 83
Generalisations, page 97

Expert tip

Also think about the ethics of deception and individual and situational explanations.

The relation of eye movements during sleep to dream activity: an objective method for the study of dreaming

Revised

Authors: Dement and Kleitman (1957)

Key terms: Sleep and dreaming

Approach: Physiological psychology

Cross check

Physiological approach, page 89

Background/context: In 1953 Aserinsky identified REM (rapid eye movement) and NREM (non-rapid eye movement) sleep. Various studies have confirmed that sleep follows a cycle consisting of alternating periods of NREM (with four stages) and REM, and that REM sleep is strongly associated with dreaming. The reason for this study was to investigate further the features of REM sleep.

REM is the sleep period when there is rapid eye movement under closed lids. **NREM** is the rest of the sleep period, when the eyes do not move rapidly.

Aim/hypothesis: There were three main research questions:

1 Does dreaming occur during REM or NREM sleep?
2 Can participants accurately estimate the length of time they have been dreaming?
3 Do eye movement patterns match dream content?

And one sub-question:

4 Does the duration of REM sleep correlate with the number of words (the narrative) in a reported dream?

Method: Natural experiment conducted in a laboratory; use of self-reports

Cross check

Laboratory experiment, page 66
Self-report, page 72

Variables:
Aim 1 – IV was REM and NREM sleep; DV was number of dreams recalled from each.

Aim 2 – IV was 'woken after 5 minutes' and 'woken after 15 minutes'; DV was number of correct dream length estimations.

Aim 3 – IV was direction of eye movement (vertical, horizontal, mixture and little or no movement); DV was the subjective report of dreaming (or not) when woken.

Aim 4 – DV was the total number of words used to describe a dream correlated with the length of a dream.

Cross check

Designs, page 68

Design: All participants slept and were woken at various times, so the design could be said to be repeated measures.

Participants and sampling technique: initially there were nine participants, but two only slept for 1 night and two for 2 nights before exercising their right to withdraw. Five participants completed between 6 and 17 nights. The sample was self-selecting. Participants were volunteers who slept in the laboratory at the University of Chicago (USA). There are no details of how the participants knew about the study or whether they were students. However, because sleep is a physiological process, it is not important that the sample was varied or large in number.

Now test yourself

40 If the participants slept in their own bed rather than in a laboratory, what effect might this have on the results?

Answer on p.195

Tested

Apparatus: Sleep laboratory with equipment: bed, electrodes connected to EEG, bell and tape recorder. Note that no muscle movements were recorded in this study; the EEG recorded eye movements (i.e. EOG).

Typical mistake

Because sleep can be measured using EEG, EOG and EMG it does not mean that every study uses all three. There is also the assumption that EEG, EOG and EMG are three different recording devices. They are not. An EOG simply involves electrodes near the eyes attached to an EEG.

Now test yourself

Tested

41 Suggest **one** advantage of using scientific equipment in psychological experiments such as this.

Answer on p.195

Controls: All participants were asked not to drink alcohol (a depressant) or caffeine (a stimulant). The way in which participants were woken (by a bell) and the way in which dreams were recorded (tape recorder) were standardised.

Cross check

Controls, page 71

Procedure:

1 Participants arrived at the sleep laboratory at their normal bedtime. They went to bed in an individual room with electrodes attached to eye and scalp areas. The electrodes were connected to the EEG in the room next door.
2 As sleep began the experimenter observed the EEG record and noted when a participant entered REM sleep. At the end of REM sleep the experimenter pressed the button to ring the bell situated next to the participant to wake them. If a dream was recalled the details were spoken into the tape recorder.
3 The same procedure was adopted when the experimenter wanted to wake the participant from NREM sleep – after 5 minutes' or 15 minutes' sleep.

Cross check

Types of data, page 80

Expert tip

This study gathered both quantitative data and qualitative data. Make sure you know the difference between these two and can give an example of each.

Data: The data were quantitative (e.g. instances of dream recall, dream length estimations and number of words in each dream narrative) and qualitative (e.g. descriptions of dreams).

Now test yourself

42 (a) How was the self-report method used in this study?

(b) How was observation used in this study?

Answers on p.195

Tested

Results:

Table 1.8 Instances of dream recall after awakenings during periods of rapid eye movements or periods of no rapid eye movements

S	Rapid eye movements		No rapid eye movements	
	Dream recall	No recall	Dream recall	No recall
DN	17	9	3	21
IR	26	8	2	29
KC	36	4	3	31
WD	37	5	1	34
PM	24	6	2	23
KK	4	1	0	5
SM	2	2	0	2
DM	2	1	0	1
MG	4	3	0	3
Totals	**152**	**39**	**11**	**149**

Table 1.9 Results of dream-duration estimates after 5 or 15 minutes of rapid eye movement

S	5 minutes		15 minutes	
	Right	Wrong	Right	Wrong
DN	8	2	5	5
IR	11	1	7	3
KC	7	0	12	1
WD	13	1	15	1
PM	6	2	8	3
Total	**45**	**6**	**47**	**13**

Findings:

1 Aim 1: 152 dreams were recalled during awakening from REM sleep, with only 11 dreams recalled from awakening during NREM sleep. There were 149 instances of no recall when awakened from NREM.
2 Aim 2: When woken after 5 minutes, 45 out of 51 estimations were correct. When woken after 15 minutes, 47 estimations out of 60 estimations were correct.
3 Aim 3: When woken from a specific eye movement pattern, participants reported a dream that corresponded to that pattern.
   (a) Vertical movement: participants reported standing at the bottom of a cliff and hoisting things up and down; climbing a ladder and looking up and down; bouncing and throwing a basketball into the basket.

(b) Horizontal movement: a participant reported a dream of two people throwing tomatoes at each other.

(c) Little or no movement corresponded to dreams about looking into the distance, such as when driving a car.

(d) Mixed movements: dreams were about people talking or watching objects close to them.

4 Aim 4: The number of words used to describe a dream (dream narrative) correlated significantly with the length of the REM period.

Conclusions: Dreams are more likely to occur in REM sleep. Dreams appear to happen in 'real-time'. Dream content appears to correspond to the direction in which the eyes move.

Cross check

Controls, page 71

Generalisations, page 97

Expert tip

There are three evaluation issues to consider:

- **Scientific equipment** – the use of scientific equipment in psychological experiments has many advantages, such as reliability.
- **Controls** – controlling variables in studies is highly desirable, but sometimes it lowers the ecological validity.
- **Generalisations** – can the findings of this study be generalised to everyone? Do we all have REM and NREM?

Expert tip

Also think about the issues of determinism and free will, and ethics.

Recalling routes around London: activation of the right hippocampus in taxi drivers

Revised

Authors: Maguire et al. (1997)

Key term: Taxi drivers

Approach: Physiological psychology

Cross check

Physiological approach, page 89

Background/context: How do we find our way in the real world from point A to point B? We way-find using a **cognitive map**. Much research has been done on cognitive maps and way-finding but a great deal of insight can be gained with the use of new technology. PET and MRI scanners have allowed researchers such as Maguire to investigate the specific brain regions responsible for topographical memory.

A **cognitive map** is an image we have in our head of how places are arranged.

Aim/hypothesis:

1 To confirm findings of other studies that specific brain regions are involved in semantic topographical memory retrieval.

2 To determine the specific region of the brain associated with landmark knowledge when it is not confounded by location information.

3 To examine topographical memory (landmarks and spatial lay-out) and non-topographical semantic memory to determine whether there is a brain region common to both.

Expert tip

This is the only core study to use a pilot study, which is not on the syllabus. You only need to know what the pilot study was.

Method: Laboratory experiment with pre-study questionnaire

1 Participants completed a pre-study questionnaire asking information about:

(a) familiar areas of London

(b) familiar films from a list of 150 made between 1939 and 1997

(c) world-famous landmarks they could visualise from a list of 20 they had never visited

This information was used to design the study. For example, the films chosen for the study had been seen by the drivers five times or more.

2 A **pilot study** was performed with non-participating taxi drivers to check that all the tasks and equipment were fit for purpose.

A **pilot study** is done on a small sample to decide whether it is feasible (worth doing) with a larger sample.

Design: Note that the study stated that there were six tasks, each done twice. However, the study also stated that 'five of the tasks are relevant to this discussion', meaning that the sixth was not reported in this paper and so can be ignored. The five tasks were:

1 topographical/spatial information sequence task – recalling a London route

In task 1 the drivers were given a starting point and an ending point and they had to describe the shortest legal route between the two – points.

2 topographical/spatial information non-sequence task – describing world-famous landmarks

In task 2 the drivers had to describe world-famous landmarks not in London that they had never visited.

3 non-topographical/non-spatial information sequence task – memory for film sequence

In task 3 the drivers had to recall and describe the plot between given points (i.e. in sequence) of familiar famous films.

4 non-topographical/non-spatial information non-sequence task – memory for non-sequential film frames

In task 4 the drivers had to recall and describe individual frames from famous films (i.e. not requiring sequence information).

5 a baseline task in which participants repeated two four-digit numbers out loud to control for speech output

Explanation:

There are two main variables here: tasks with **topographical** (T+) and **non-topographical** (T–) **knowledge** and tasks with **sequencing** (S+) and **non-sequencing** (S–).

This can be shown in a matrix from the study (Figure 9).

Figure 9

Now test yourself

43 What is 'topographical knowledge'?

44 Describe the questionnaires the participants were given before they arrived for scanning.

Answers on p.195

Tested

Expert tip

There is a lot of jargon used in this study. Take your time to understand what everything means.

Topographical knowledge concerns landmarks and spatial relationships between them.

Non-topographical knowledge simply uses semantic memory with no knowledge of landmarks or spatial relationships.

Sequencing requires items to be placed in order (like a route, or the plot of a film).

Non-sequencing requires no order (like a famous landmark, or an individual scene from a film).

Design: All participants completed all tasks, of which there were five. The order of the tasks was counterbalanced both for each participant and across participants.

Cross check

Counterbalancing, page 69

Participants and sampling technique: 11 right-handed males, qualified and licensed taxi drivers from London. All were experienced drivers with a minimum of 3 years' experience, and their average age was 45 years. There was no detail about how the participants were acquired for the study.

Now test yourself

45 Describe the sample of participants.

Answer on p.195

Tested

Apparatus: A London route (from Grosvenor Square to the Elephant and Castle), world-famous landmarks, films with plots, films with still frames, a Siemens PET scanner, intravenous $H_2{}^{15}O$ bolus and a saline flush.

Control:

- The landmarks chosen were places the drivers had never visited in person.
- The films were those all the drivers had seen at least five times, so they were all very familiar with them.
- The scanner procedure was the same for each participant and the injections given were the same.
- A pilot study was done to ensure all tasks were appropriate.

Procedure:

1 The participants completed the pre-study questionnaire.
2 Each participant arrived at the laboratory and a cannula was inserted into his arm. A blindfold covered his eyes and he was placed into the scanner.
3 The participant received an $H_2{}^{15}O$ bolus through the cannula (taking 20 seconds to enter the arm/bloodstream) followed by a saline flush (also taking 20 seconds). There was then a scan frame time of 90 seconds in which to do the task (because $H_2{}^{15}O$ has a half-life of 2 minutes). One of the five tasks was presented and the participant had to give a description of the route, landmark, film plot or frame, which was digitally recorded.
4 Once the task was completed there was an 8-minute wait before the same procedure was repeated.
5 Steps 3 and 4 were repeated 12 times: each of the five tasks was done twice (remember there were other tasks not mentioned in this paper).
6 Scanning and injections over, the participant was debriefed and the study was complete.

Expert tip

A PET scanner 'detects' radioactivity from the $H_2{}^{15}O$ bolus injected into the participants.

Data: The data gathered comprised the rCBF (regional cerebral blood flow) utilised in specific regions of the brain. This was recorded by the scanner, interpreted and analysed. In this procedure the areas activated 'light-up' on a computer screen and three-dimensional images can be seen showing the exact brain region involved in particular processes.

Results:

The results table for this study is too detailed to be included here. See the findings below. (Note that for the route task the crucial component was the sequence of the route rather than specific details of street names.)

Findings:

- **Route task** – activated areas: bilateral activity in extrastriate regions, medial parietal lobe, posterior cingulate cortex, parahippocampal gyrus and right hippocampus.
- **Landmarks task** – activated areas: medial parietal lobe, posterior cingulate cortex, parahippocampal gyrus, left inferior and middle frontal gyri. No activation of right hippocampus.
- **Films (plot and frames) task** – activated areas: left frontal regions, middle temporal gyrus, left angular gyrus. No activation of medial temporal region.

Expert tip

There are three evaluation issues to consider:

- **Reductionism** – to be able to locate a specific brain region responsible for way-finding, for example, is what physiological psychologists argue that modern psychology is all about.
- **Generalisations** – this is a physiological psychology study, so it is assumed that the finding that the right hippocampus is responsible for way-finding for a small sample will generalise to *all* other people.
- **Ethics** – this study could be said to be very ethical.

Conclusions:

1 Aim 1 is confirmed because the brain regions involved in semantic topographical memory retrieval, such as the right hippocampus, are similar to those found in previous studies.
2 The specific brain locations for landmark knowledge are the same for route (sequence) information, except for the right hippocampus, which is only activated during the recall of routes (sequences).
3 The hippocampus is involved in the processing of spatial lay-outs established over long time courses.
4 The right hippocampus is recruited specifically to enable navigation in large-scale spatial environments (processing survey knowledge as it is also known), whereas non-topographical semantic retrieval involves the left inferior frontal gyrus but not the hippocampus.

Expert tip

Also think about the issues of applications to everyday life, the use of scientific equipment and the use of a pilot study.

Cross check

Reductionism, page 104
Generalisations, page 97
Ethics, page 79

Olfactory cues modulate facial attractiveness

Revised

Authors: Demattè et al. (2007)

Key terms: Smells and facial attractiveness

Approach: Physiological psychology

Cross check

Physiological approach, page 89

Background/context: Facial attractiveness is a socially important cue and has been studied extensively, for example Rhodes et al. (1998) studied facial symmetry and its relationship to attractiveness. Is attractiveness determined by other sensory cues such as olfaction? One study has shown that the perfume 'Shalimar' led to significantly higher ratings of softness and sexiness when compared with a no-perfume condition. This core study looks at unpleasant odours in addition to pleasant odours and focuses on just female participants because females are said to be more sensitive to olfactory cues than males, and that they might rely more on olfactory cues in mating behaviour than males.

Aim/hypothesis: To discover whether olfactory cues influence people's judgements of attractiveness. More specifically, whether pleasant odours cause higher ratings of male attractiveness and whether unpleasant odours cause lower ratings of male attractiveness.

Method: Laboratory experiment (minor use of questionnaire)

Variables:
IV1 – three conditions: pleasant odours, unpleasant odours and neutral odour

IV2 – high facial attractiveness, low facial attractiveness

DV – ratings of attractiveness from 1 (least attractive) to 9 (most attractive)

Cross check

Laboratory experiment, page 66
Questionnaires, page 72

Design: Repeated measures because all participants experienced all conditions of the independent variable. The design included **counterbalancing** to allow each of the 40 faces to be presented with each odour.

There were three blocks of experimental sessions with a 5-minute break between each. The second and third experimental sessions replicated the first. For each session the 40 faces were divided into four sets of 10. Each set of 10 had five attractive faces and five unattractive faces, the order of which was randomised. No two odours were presented together. The order of presentation was as follows:

- Set 1: 10 faces with clean air, geranium and body odour (each face was presented three times, once with each odour, and so there were 30 presentations in total for set 1).

- Set 2: 10 faces with clean air, male perfume and rubber odour (each face was presented three times, once with each odour, and so there were 30 presentations in total for set 2).
- Set 3: 10 faces with clean air, geranium and rubber odour (each face was presented three times, once with each odour, and so there were 30 presentations in total for set 3).
- Set 4: 10 faces with clean air, male perfume and body odour (each face was presented three times, once with each odour, and so there were 30 presentations in total for set 4).

This means there were 120 trials in total for experimental session 1. This same procedure was repeated a second time and then a third time. The four sets were also counterbalanced across participants.

Participants and sampling technique: Sixteen female students (aged 20–34 years) from Oxford University, UK. How participants were selected is not specified.

Apparatus:

- A questionnaire to determine health (e.g. respiratory) problems.
- Forty male faces (13 cm × 17 cm) from a standardised face database (previously categorised into 'high' and 'low' attractiveness).
- Four odours: two pleasant (geranium and male fragrance); two unpleasant (body odour and rubber). Control with no odour (clean air).
- Olfactometer to deliver the odours.
- Computer on which to view the male facial images.

Controls:

- Questionnaire before study to determine ability to detect smell (e.g. 'Are you currently suffering from a cold/flu?' and 'Do you suffer from asthma or any air-born allergy?').
- Presentations of each face–odour were counterbalanced.
- Presentations of pleasant–unpleasant odours were counterbalanced.
- Presentation time was standardised at 500 milliseconds.
- Time for tone presentation and odour release was standardised.
- Odour 'strength' was standardised for each participant.

Procedure:

1. Participants completed a confidential questionnaire regarding health. If healthy, then they proceeded.
2. Participants sat at computer and when they heard a **quiet tone** exhaled. They then inhaled when they heard a **louder tone** (to receive the odour).
3. Participants pressed key on keyboard to indicate that they could smell an odour. At same time as the odour was presented a male face appeared on computer screen for 500 milliseconds.
4. Participants pressed a keyboard number to show their rating of the face on a 1–9 rating scale (least attractive – neutral – most attractive).
5. The procedure was repeated for 40 faces in set 1 with three conditions, followed by a 5-minute break.
6. The procedure was repeated a second time and after a 5-minute break repeated a third time.
7. Participants then rated the odours for intensity, pleasantness and familiarity on a scale of 0–100.

Cross check

Designs, pages 68–70
Counterbalancing, page 69

Now test yourself

46 Give **two** reasons why only female participants were used in this study.

Answer on p.195

Tested

Typical mistake

Fresh or clean air is not an odour. The study had four odours and clean air.

Cross check

Controls, page 71

Now test yourself

47 Identify **three** controls applied in this study.

Answer on p.195

Tested

Results:

Table 1.10 Mean facial attractiveness ratings as a function of the attractiveness group and odour (standard deviations are reported in parentheses)

Facial attractiveness	Odour				
	Clean air	Geranium	Male fragrance	Body odour	Rubber
High	5.70 (0.21)	5.40 (0.23)	5.73 (0.24)	5.39 (0.21)	4.96 (0.25)
Low	4.10 (0.16)	4.06 (0.20)	4.15 (0.20)	3.64 (0.21)	3.72 (0.23)

Findings:

1 The highest mean rating of male attractiveness was for male fragrance at 5.73 (scale 1–9), slightly better than clean air – the second highest at 5.70.
2 The lowest mean rating of male attractiveness was for body odour at 3.64.
3 When the two pleasant odours were combined (mean of 4.42) and the two unpleasant odours combined (mean of 4.85) and compared with fresh air (mean of 4.9) participants evaluated male faces as being significantly less attractive with an unpleasant odour than with a pleasant or neutral odour.
4 Both pleasant and unpleasant odours were perceived as smelling more intense than clean air.
5 Unpleasant odours were judged to be significantly less pleasant than the pleasant odours. Unpleasant odours were judged to not differ significantly from clean air.
6 All three odour categories were judged to be of relatively equal familiarity.

Conclusions: Female participants judged male faces as being slightly (but significantly) less attractive when presented with an unpleasant odour than with a pleasant or neutral odour. They perceived no difference in attractiveness when presented with a pleasant odour compared with a neutral odour.

Now test yourself

48 Briefly describe **three** findings in relation to attractiveness.

Answer on p.195

Tested

Expert tip

There are three evaluation issues to consider:

- **Validity** – do the odours chosen actually smell pleasant and unpleasant to the participants?
- **Applications** – is this research useful? Does it have any applications in real life?
- **Nature/nurture** – is the relationship between smell and attractiveness nature or nurture? This study claimed that females rely more on olfactory cues in mating behaviour than males, so perhaps a good-smelling male (or a clean one) has good genes.

Cross check

Validity, page 86
Applications/usefulness, page 95
Nature/nurture, page 103

Expert tip

Also think about the issues of reductionism, and the use of counterbalancing in the design.

1.5 The individual differences studies

On being sane in insane places

Revised

Author: Rosenhan (1973)

Key term: Sane in insane places

Approach: Individual differences

Background/context: How do we know precisely what constitutes 'normality' or mental illness? These are Rosenhan's opening words. Distinguishing the sane from insane is the domain of psychiatrists and a psychiatrist is medically qualified. Two classificatory systems can be used to diagnose mental illness: the **DSM** and **ICD**. Psychiatrists should be able to distinguish between sane and insane, but can they? Rosenhan questions the validity of psychiatric diagnosis. He states: 'There is a view that psychological categorisation of mental illness is, at best, useless and, at worst, harmful, misleading and pejorative'.

Cross check

Individual differences, page 91

The **DSM** (*Diagnostic and Statistical Manual*) began in 1952; the latest edition (*DSM-V*) is about to be published.

The **ICD** (*International Standard Classification of Injuries and Causes of Death*) began in 1958 and is now in its 10th edition, *ICD-10*.

Aim/hypothesis:

1 To show that psychiatrists cannot *reliably* tell the difference between sane and insane people; that psychiatric criteria for diagnosis are not *valid*.
2 To investigate whether 'the salient characteristics that lead to diagnosis reside in the patients themselves (the individual) or in the environments and contexts (the situation) in which observers find them'.

Cross check

Participant observation, page 75
Individual vs situational, page 102
Sampling, page 83

Study 1

Method: Rosenhan describes his study as an experiment, and in a general sense it was. However, there was no IV that he manipulated and there was very little he could control. The main method was participant observation: the researcher (Rosenhan and pseudo-patients) faked illness to 'hide away' among patients who were mentally ill.

Typical mistake

Because they gained access to the mental institutions, it is often thought that the pseudo-patients were the participants. They were not; the pseudo-patients were stooges working for Rosenhan. The participants were the doctors and nurses at the mental institutions.

Variables: There were no variables to manipulate because of the method used.

Design: There was no experimental design.

Setting: Twelve mental institutions across five different states (USA); some old and shabby, and some new. Some had good staff–patient ratios; others were understaffed. This was an attempt to obtain a 'representative sample' – to generalise the findings.

Participants and sampling technique: The 'participants' were the doctors and nurses who happened to work in the 12 hospitals chosen for the study. They did not know they were taking part in a study.

Experimenters: Rosenhan himself was the first pseudo-patient (faking illness) and then he recruited seven sane people to repeat what he had done. In effect they were all stooges, and comprised a psychology graduate, three psychologists, a psychiatrist, a painter, a paediatrician and a housewife. There were three women and five men.

Expert tip

There were 12 institutions but just eight pseudo-patients, so some pseudo-patients visited more than one institution.

Apparatus: No apparatus was needed or used.

Controls:

- The description of symptoms was standardised.
- The entry/access procedure was also standardised.

Now test yourself

49 Who were the pseudo-patients? Who were the participants?

Answer on p.195

Tested ☐

Procedure:

1 The pseudo-patient telephoned a hospital and made an appointment.
2 The pseudo-patient arrived at the admissions office and complained of hearing voices: the voices were often unclear but said: 'empty', 'hollow' and 'thud'. The voices were unrecognisable but the same sex.
3 Other than making up a name, job (where applicable) and the auditory hallucinations, every other detail (e.g. upbringing, relationships etc.) was true.

Cross check

Reliability, page 82
Validity, page 86

Findings (1): All 12 attempts to be admitted were successful – i.e. the pseudo-patients were admitted with a diagnosis of mental illness 100% of the time. 11 were admitted with a diagnosis of schizophrenia and 1 was admitted with a diagnosis of manic depression.

Conclusions (1):

- **Reliability** – psychiatric diagnosis of mental illness is reliable. This means that all psychiatrists made the same decision to admit. This is good and the way it should be.
- **Validity** – psychiatric diagnosis of mental illness is *not* valid. People with fake symptoms were diagnosed as having mental illness and so psychiatrists cannot distinguish between who is sane and who is insane. This is not good at all and *suggests* incompetence.

Now test yourself

50 (a) According to Rosenhan, to what extent is psychiatric diagnosis of abnormality reliable?
(b) According to Rosenhan, to what extent is psychiatric diagnosis of abnormality valid?

Answers on p.195

Tested ☐

Explanation (1): The psychiatrists were not incompetent and did their jobs very well. So why diagnose as insane people who are sane? Symptoms: sane people do not telephone a mental institution and ask for an appointment; sane people do not claim to hear voices; hearing voices is a legitimate symptom of schizophrenia. This creates doubt for a psychiatrist. Is it better to send a sick person away or is it better to test further to be sure and admit? To say a sick person is healthy is a type 1 error and amounts to medical negligence. To admit someone who might be sick but is actually healthy is a type 2 error and, although an error, it is being cautious and, for these psychiatrists, was the correct decision.

Findings (2): Once a pseudo-patient had been admitted to a mental institution, in many respects the 'experiment' was over. However, there was also the issue of getting out of the institution. How could a sane person behave in a sane way? How long did it take for the pseudo-patients to be released?

The earliest release was 7 days. The average release was 19 days and the longest time was 52 days. Notably, on release, they were not 'cured' but had 'schizophrenia in remission'. They had been labelled.

Findings (3) In all the time before release each pseudo-patient was on the ward of a mental institution. This was a perfect opportunity to observe what life on a ward was really like and to see how mental patients were treated by staff. This was participant observation at its best because the staff believed the pseudo-patient was mentally ill, just like all the other patients on the ward.

1 The pseudo-patients talked to other patients, followed orders and accepted medicine (though did not swallow it).
2 Rosenhan (and the others) took notes and hid them. He was spotted and told 'don't worry we'll tell you what you need'. He then took notes openly and no-one ever looked to see what was being written. It was assumed that this behaviour was part of his illness. In his records it was written 'patient engages in writing behaviour'.
3 Any 'normal' behaviour led to a false assumption: a pseudo-patient pacing along a corridor was asked by a nurse: 'Nervous, Mr X?' 'No, bored,' he said. Patients were waiting for 30 minutes for a cafeteria to open. A psychiatrist described it as oral-acquisitive syndrome.

Explanation (3):

1 It is assumed by the nurses, for example, that if a person is on the ward of a mental institution then they must be mentally ill. The **situation** (of being in the institution) determines the assumptions made by the nurses. Only insane people are in insane places.
2 This also means that once a person has been labelled as mentally ill, then it is very hard for that label to be removed (and for the nurses and psychiatrists to view the person as a sane individual). This is the '**stickiness of psycho-diagnostic labels**'.

Findings (4):

1 35 of the 118 real mental patients were suspicious of the pseudo-patients. Some claimed: 'You're not crazy; you're a journalist,' and 'You're checking up on the hospital'. No staff member suspected them. Why not?
2 Staff had very little contact with the patients, staying in their 'cage' – the nurses' station – most of the time.
3 Some staff were verbally and physically abusive in front of other patients but stopped when other staff appeared. If a patient did not go for medication immediately, an attendant sometimes responded with 'Come on you m****r f*****s, out of bed!'.
4 There was no privacy – for example, for safety reasons there was no door on the toilets.

Now test yourself

51 Most of the pseudo-patients were admitted to hospital with the incorrect diagnosis of schizophrenia. Give **two** possible explanations for why the hospitals made these mistakes.

Answer on p.195

Tested

Cross check

Participant observation, page 75

5 To show they were sane, the pseudo-patients asked staff questions such as: 'Hello Doctor X, how are you today?' and 'When am I likely to be discharged?' As can be seen from Table 1.11, staff were uninterested in having even a basic conversation.

Table 1.11 Self-initiated contact by pseudopatients with psychiatrists and nurses and attendants

Contact	Psychiatric hospitals	
	(1) Psychiatrists	(2) Nurses and attendants
Responses		
Moves on, head averted (%)	71	88
Makes eye contact (%)	23	10
Pauses and chats (%)	2	2
Stops and talks (%)	4	0.5
Mean number of questions answered (out of 6)	*	*
Respondents (No.)	13	47
Attempts (No.)	185	1283

* Not applicable

Explanation (4): These findings all show the **powerlessness** experienced by the pseudo-patients, along with **depersonalisation**. They were powerless to do anything: they were seen as mentally ill, so had no rights and had to do what they were told (because they were not of 'sound mind').

At a basic level staff did not want to have a conversation with a 'non-person', and at the other extreme they could have been forced to have treatment (such as ECT – electro-convulsive therapy) as they had no right to refuse it.

Study 2

The staff at one hospital heard these findings but doubted that such an error could ever occur in their institution. Another 'experiment' was set up. The staff were informed that at some time during the next 3 months, one or more pseudo-patients would attempt to gain admittance into the psychiatric hospital. Each staff member was asked to rate each admission on a 10-point scale with 1 and 2 reflecting high confidence that the patient was a pseudo-patient. Over the 3 months data were obtained on 193 patients admitted for treatment. The crucial point about study 2 is that Rosenhan did not send anyone at all. Yet the findings were as follows:

Findings:

1 41 were judged with 'high confidence' as fake by at least one member of staff.
2 23 were judged as 'suspect' by at least one psychiatrist.
3 19 were suspected as fake by one psychiatrist and one other staff member.
4 83 (or 43%) were judged in some way to be pseudo-patients.

Conclusions:

1 Psychiatric diagnosis raises major questions concerning reliability and validity because although study 1 admitted pseudo-patients, study 2 claimed real patients who had been admitted were possible fakes.

Cross check

Observations, page 75
Ecological validity, page 78
Ethics, page 79

Expert tip

There are three evaluation issues to consider:

- **Observations** – the Rosenhan study is a perfect example of participant observation, but what are the advantages and disadvantages of this?
- **Ecological validity** – this is a study about real life; it is a study of psychiatrists and staff in their 'natural environment'.
- **Ethics** – study 1 breaks many ethical guidelines but it could be argued that the ends justified the means.

2 The label of mental illness, once applied, is a difficult one to remove.
3 The experience of life on the ward is depersonalising and creates powerlessness in a patient.
4 The situation of being on a ward affects how behaviour is perceived by staff.

Expert tip

Also think about the issues of individual and situational explanations.

A case of multiple personality

Revised

Authors: Thigpen and Cleckley (1954)

Key term: Multiple personality disorder

Approach: Individual differences

Background/context: Is it possible that a person can have more than one personality in one mind? We all have different personalities, we all play different roles, and we behave differently with different people in different situations. But in everything we do we have a memory of it. A true **multiple personality** would not recall what another personality did or thought. So is multiple personality disorder genuine? Thigpen and Cleckley claim it is, on the basis of their experiences.

Cross check

Individual differences, page 91
Case study, page 76
Longitudinal method, page 84

Expert tip

Multiple personality disorder (MPD) is now known as dissociative identity disorder.

Expert tip

This study does not (and cannot) follow the usual format of studies in this guide. It is a very different approach. Don't worry about it being different – just read the story.

Now test yourself

Tested

52 What is the difference between having different 'sides' to your personality and having multiple personality disorder?

Answer on p.195

Method: Case study and longitudinal method

The story of Eve

It all started when a 25-year-old married lady was referred to the authors suffering with 'severe and blinding headaches'. At the first interview Eve White, as they called her, also mentioned 'black-outs'. Several interviews later, Thigpen reports that 'we were puzzled by a recent trip for which she had no memory'. Apparently Eve White went shopping and bought lots of expensive clothes. She denied doing this when the clothes were delivered (evidence #1).

A few days later Thigpen received a letter (evidence #2; this appears as 'exhibit 1' in the study). It had apparently been written by Eve, but some ambiguous words at the end suggested someone was playing a prank. Not only was the handwriting different, but also the tone changed from serious to light-hearted.

On her next visit Eve remembered the starting the letter but not having sent it. As the interview progressed she '…began to show signs of distress and agitation. Apprehensively and reluctantly she at last formulated a question: Did the occasional impression of hearing an imaginary voice indicate that she was "insane"?' Apparently she had heard a voice talking to her on several occasions (evidence #3).

Then, as Thigpen pondered this latest piece of evidence, 'As if seized by a sudden pain she put both hands to her head. After a tense moment of silence, her hands dropped. There was a quick, reckless smile and, in a bright voice that sparkled, she said, "Hi there, Doc".' When asked by a startled Thigpen who she was, she replied that she was Eve Black. As Thigpen puts it, 'A thousand minute alterations of manner, gesture, expression, posture, of nuances in reflex or instinctive reaction, of glance, of eyebrow tilting and eye movement, all argued that this could only be another woman. It is not possible to say just what all these differences were.'

Typical mistake

Some students who have seen the feature film *The Three Faces of Eve* write about events in that film in their answers. The film is very interesting to watch, but the syllabus is based on the academic core study publication and not the film.

This was a longitudinal study because interviews continued for over 14 months and totalled approximately 100 hours. Apparently Eve Black knew all about Eve White, but Eve White had no knowledge of Miss Black (who said she was *not* married). Miss Black could 'come out' when asked. Miss Black had been part of Mrs White's 'body' since early childhood and a number of events that happened were confirmed by the family. For example, Eve White disappeared into the woods, which were forbidden territory, when she was 6 years old and on her return denied it and was severely punished. According to Eve Black this was a prank to get Eve White into trouble (evidence #4).

This is what was known as multiple personality disorder (MPD) and now known as dissociative identity disorder (DID). The question for Thigpen and Cleckley was how to investigate and treat this rare phenomenon. They decided to conduct a number of different tests (with help from a specialist). The following *psychological* tests were administered to both the predominant personality, Mrs White, and the secondary personality, Miss Black:

- **psychometric tests** – Wechsler-Bellevue intelligence scale, Wechsler memory scale
- **projective tests** – drawings of human figures and Rorschach (ink blot) test

Test results (summary):

- **IQ** – Mrs White obtained an IQ of 110 and Miss Black 104 on the Wechsler-Bellevue intelligence scale. Both scores were lowered by anxiety and tenseness, and superficiality and slight indifference to success, respectively.
- **Memory** – Miss Black's memory function was on the same level as her IQ, while Mrs White's was far above her IQ.
- The **Rorschach** record of Miss Black was by far healthier than that of Mrs White. Miss Black showed a hysterical tendency, while Mrs White's showed anxiety, obsessive-compulsive traits, rigidity and an inability to deal with her hostility.
- The **projective tests** indicated repression in Mrs White and regression in Miss Black.

After approximately 8 months of (unspecified) treatment Eve White seemed to have made encouraging progress with no headaches or 'blackouts', while Eve Black was causing less trouble and she seldom 'came out'. Then things changed: the headaches returned, grew worse and more frequent, and so did the 'blackouts'. Eve Black denied all responsibility. Thigpen describes the next episode: 'One day as Eve White spoke her eyes opened, blankly staring about the room, trying to orient herself. When her eyes finally met those of the therapist, slowly, with an unknown husky voice and immeasurable poise, she said, "Who are you?" It was immediately and vividly apparent that this was neither Eve White nor Eve Black!'

A third personality had emerged. She called herself Jane. Thigpen and Cleckley decided to examine the EEG record (electrical activity of the brain) of all three personalities. Surely this objective physiological test would reveal some interesting results. The results showed Eve Black to have a 'normal to slightly fast' basic alpha rate of 12½ cycles per second, compared with a 'normal' 11 cycles per second for Eve White and Jane. Slightly fast records are sometimes (but not consistently) associated with psychopathic personality.

Jane was now the dominant personality and her thoughts were not available to the other two personalities. The narrative by Thigpen and Cleckley ends at this point without completing the story of the three personalities.

Because of all the evidence gathered, Thigpen and Cleckley were convinced that this was a genuine case of MPD.

Now test yourself

53 **(a)** Outline **two** anecdotes (stories told about the behaviours of Eve) told to the therapists.
(b) What is the problem with this type of evidence?

Answers on p.195

Tested

Typical mistake

Some students confuse test terminology, for example assuming that projective tests are psychometric tests.

Expert tip

It is easy to confuse the terminology here. Make sure you know what are psychometric tests and what are projective tests. Also note that the use of EEG is neither psychometric, projective nor psychological. It is a physiological test – a record of brain function.

Cross check

Psychometrics tests, page 98

Now test yourself

54 Identify (a) **one** psychometric test, (b) **one** projective test and (c) **one** physiological test conducted on Eve.

Answers on p.195

Tested

Expert tip

There are three evaluation issues to consider:

- **Psychometric tests** – the Wechsler-Bellevue intelligence scale, and the Wechsler memory scale were used. There are advantages and disadvantages of psychometric tests.
- **Case study** – this is a case study and there are many advantages of this method. There are disadvantages too, and you should know them.
- **Generalisations** – just like the case study by Freud, case studies cannot be used to generalise to the 'normal' population, and this case study is unique.

Cross check

Psychometric tests, page 98
Case studies, page 76
Generalisations, page 97

Expert tip

Also think about the issues of sampling and ethics.

Cognitive style predicts entry into physical sciences and humanities: questionnaire and performance tests of empathy and systemising

Revised

Authors: Billington et al. (2007)

Key terms: Empathising and systemising

Approach: Individual differences

Cross check

Individual differences, page 91
Cognitive approach, page 87

Background/context: Why do more men have science-related careers? Why do fewer women enter the sciences? Why do more men take science at university (in the UK, possibly worldwide)? Is the answer because of **cognitive style**?

Two cognitive styles are **systemising** and **empathising**. The cognitive component of empathising is also referred to as 'theory of mind' (see the Baron-Cohen et al. core study, page 14). Self-report questionnaires (psychometric tests) have been designed by Baron-Cohen et al. (2003 and 2004) to test systemising (the SQ-R) and empathising (the EQ). The E–S (empathising–systemising) theory (Baron-Cohen, 2002) categorises the result of these two questionnaires into five types: extreme empathising (EE), empathising (E), balanced (B), systemising (S) and extreme systemising (ES). Baron-Cohen et al. predict that females have a stronger drive to empathise and males to systemise. The question asked by Billington et al. is whether this cognitive style determines choice of university subject and career.

Cognitive style is the way in which people perceive, learn, think about and recall information.

Empathising is the drive and ability to identify another's mental states and to respond to these with one of a range of appropriate emotions.

Systemising is the drive and ability to analyse the rules underlying a system in order to predict its behaviour.

Aim/hypothesis: There were four main research questions:

1 Do males take science subjects and females humanities subjects?
2 Are males systemisers and females empathisers?
3 Are science students systemisers and humanities students empathisers?
4 Does cognitive style (systemiser or empathiser) predict choice of degree subject?

Two other research questions were tested:

(a) Are males better at the forced-choice embedded figures task (FC-EFT) test than females? Are females better at the eyes test than males?
(b) Are science students better at the FC-EFT test than humanities students? Are humanities students better at the eyes test than science students?

Cross check

Natural experiment, pages 67–68
Self-report questionnaires, page 72
Psychometric tests, page 98

Method: Natural experiment; self-report questionnaires

Variables: There were a number of different IVs and DVs:

- Aim 1 – IV is male and female; DV is percentage taking science and humanities subjects.
- Aim 2 – IV is male and female; DV is percentage ES/S or EE/E.
- Aim 3 – IV is science and humanities students; DV is percentage ES/S or EE/E.
- Aim 4 – IV is brain type (ES/S and EE/E), FC-EFT and eyes test; DV is degree subject choice.
- Aim (a) – IV is male and female; DV is score on eyes test and FC-EFT test.

Now test yourself

55 Why is this study a natural experiment?

Answer on p.195

Tested

- Aim (b) – IV is science and humanities students; DV is score on eyes test and FC-EFT test.

Design: Independent groups, because participants are either male or female; they take either science or humanities subjects.

Participants and sampling technique: 415 students – 203 male, 212 female – from the University of Cambridge, UK. A self-selecting sample – participants were volunteers who replied to an email or an advertisement within the university. For participating there was a reward of entry into a prize draw (but the prize was not identified).

Apparatus:

- SQ-R (revised version of the systemising questionnaire) – 75 questions scored between 0 and 150.
- EQ (empathy questionnaire) – 40 questions scored between 0 and 80. Both SQ-R and EQ were answered on 4-point scale: 'definitely agree', 'agree', 'disagree' and 'strongly disagree'.
- FC-EFT (forced-choice embedded figures task) – 12 pairs of diagrams each with a small shape embedded either in the left or right side. Participants had to respond as fast as possible. Score (0–24) was based on the number correct out of 12 plus a bonus point if in the fastest 25%.
- The revised eyes test – see, page 15 for full details. (Scoring was 0–72.)

Brain types EE, E, B, S and ES were calculated using a formula with SQ-R and EQ and then percentiles (top and bottom 2.5% as ES and EE, below 35th and above 65th as E and S, and those in between as type B).

Controls: All participants completed the same tests. The order of tests was not fixed (so there were no order effects), but neither was it counterbalanced, so all participants could have done the same test first and perhaps created an order effect.

Procedure: Participants responded to the request for participants and, after registering, they accessed the computer program that took them through each test. All tests were completed on-line.

Data: All the data were quantitative, with most of them being analysed using chi-square and *t*-tests.

Results:

Table 1.12 SQ-R, EQ, FC-EFT and eyes test scores by degree category and sex

			Mean
Female	Physical	SQ-R	61.23
		EQ	43.48
		FC-EFT	15.05
		Eyes test	32.86
	Humanities	SQ-R	51.54
		EQ	46.82
		FC-EFT	14.07
		Eyes test	35.69
Male	Physical	SQ-R	65.46
		EQ	35.59
		FC-EFT	15.03
		Eyes test	31.83
	Humanities	SQ-R	58.65
		EQ	40.56
		FC-EFT	14.14
		Eyes test	33.79

Expert tip

The number of abbreviations (FC-EFT etc.) in this study is high. Although they can be confusing, it is better to know them than use the full names each time.

Cross check

Designs, pages 68–70

Cross check

Sampling, page 83

Typical mistake

This study extends from the eyes test study (page 14) and because the eyes test itself is used here, students often get the two muddled.

Now test yourself

56 How is the reliability of a questionnaire such as the SQ-R (or EQ) usually tested?

Answer on p.195

Tested

Findings:

1 59.1% of males chose science subjects and 70.1% of females chose humanities subjects. The difference is significant ($p = 0.001$). The answer to research question 1 is true.
2 66% of males were ES/S compared with 25.8% of females. 36.8% of females were EE/E compared with 10.3% of males. The answer to research question 2 is true.
3 56.3% of science students were ES/S and 41.5% of humanities students were EE/E. The answer to question 3 is yes.
4 The strongest predictor of degree choice was cognitive style ($p < 0.001$). The answer to question 4 is yes.
(a) Females performed significantly better than males on the eyes test ($p < 0.005$) with no significant difference on the FC-EFT test.
(b) Science students performed significantly better than humanities students on the FC-EFT and humanities students performed significantly better than science students on the eyes test (both $p = 0.001$).

Conclusion: Cognitive style is the best predictor of degree subject entry.

Now test yourself

57 What was aim 1 and to what extent did the findings support the aim?

Answer on p.195

Tested

Cross check

Reliability, page 82
Validity, page 86
Questionnaires, page 72
Sampling, page 83

Expert tip

There are three evaluation issues to consider:

- **Reliability and validity** – both SQ-R and EQ are standardised psychometric tests and have been tested for reliability (such as using test–retest). They are also valid (e.g. they have construct and criterion validity).
- **Questionnaire design** – is it better to have a forced (or fixed) choice, or should there be a 'neutral' option?
- **Sampling technique** – inviting participation via email or an advertisement is very similar to a 'newspaper sample'. Volunteers in this case may win a prize. There may be demand characteristics.

Expert tip

Also think about the issues of psychometric tests, reductionism, biological determinism.

The psychopathology of mirror gazing in body dysmorphic disorder

Revised

Authors: Veale and Riley (2001)

Key words: Body dysmorphic disorder

Approach: Individual differences

Cross check

Individual differences, page 91

Background/context: There are some people who have a preoccupation with an imagined defect in their appearance and this causes them clinically significant distress or impairment in social, occupational or other important areas of functioning. This is BDD, or body dysmorphic disorder. It is where people imagine they have a defect when to other people no defect exists. For those with BDD no amount of cosmetic (or plastic) surgery will remove the problem because the disorder is *psychological* rather than *physical*. Common behaviours of those with BDD are camouflaging (reported in 91% of cases), comparing with others (88%) and checking appearance in mirrors or 'mirror-gazing' (87%). Veale and Riley investigate mirror gazing because a patient of theirs reported spending 6 hours gazing at himself in a mirror.

Body dysmorphic disorder is a preoccupation with some imagined defect in appearance in a normal-appearing person. If a slight physical anomaly is present, the person's concern is markedly excessive.

Aim/hypothesis: To investigate the nature and function of mirror gazing in body dysmorphic disorder patients compared with a control group.

Method: Self-report questionnaire. A mixture of question types was used.

Participants and sampling technique: 52 patients diagnosed with BDD and 55 controls (recruited from personal contacts). The BDD patients were self-selecting and the control group was an opportunity sample.

Now test yourself

58 Name the **three** most common behaviours in BDD patients.

Answer on p.196

Tested

Cross check

Questionnaires, page 72

Design: Matched pairs, because participants were matched on age (30.1 years compared with 33.4 years) and sex (40.4% male and 48% male).

Question sections, types and responses:

1 Length of time mirror gazing
Assessing: duration of 'long' sessions and duration of 'short' sessions
Response: estimation of time in minutes

2 Motivation before looking in a mirror
Assessing: strength of agreement with named statements that motivated them to use a mirror
Response 1: 5-point scales – 1 = strongly disagree, 2 = disagree, 3 = neither disagree nor agree, 4 = agree, 5 = strongly agree
Response 2: an open-ended section enabling them to write anything else that motivated them

3 Focus of attention in mirror
Assessing: whether the focus was internal or external (for both long and short sessions)
Response: a visual analogue scale from +4 (I am entirely focused on an impression or feeling that I get about myself) through to −4 (I am entirely focused on my reflection in the mirror), i.e. a nine-point scale
Assessing: whether whole body or a specific body part is the focus of attention
Response: on a scale of 0–100 (where 100 = specific)

4 Distress before and after looking in front of a mirror
Assessing: degree of distress (a) before looking in mirror, (b) immediately after looking and (c) after resisting the urge to look, applied to both long and short sessions
Response: a visual analogue scale between 1 and 10, where 1 represented 'not at all distressed' and 10 was 'extremely distressed'

5 Behaviour in front of a mirror
Assessing: activities done in front of a mirror in relation to nine named activities (e.g. combing or styling my hair; trying to see something different in the mirror)
Response 1: answers to the questions as a percentage of time spent on each activity (with the instruction that it must total 100).
Response 2: an open-ended section enabling them to write anything else they did in front of a mirror

6 Type of light preferred
Assessing: preference for natural or artificial light
Reponse: a visual analogue scale, but no numerical indicators stated in the study

7 Types of reflective surfaces
Assessing: whether just a mirror is used or whether any reflective surface is used
Response: participants listed any other surface

8 Mirror avoidance
Assessing: avoidance of types of mirrors and the situations in which this happened
Response: an open-ended question asking for a description of types and situations

Cross check

Designs, pages 68–70

Typical mistake

Confusing what was found for short mirror-gazing sessions with what was found for long mirror-gazing sessions.

Expert tip

There are quite a few different types of answer used in this questionnaire. It is worth double checking that you know about questionnaire design (see, page 72).

Results:

Table 1.13 Characteristics of BDD patients and controls

	BDD mean (S.D.)	Controls mean (S.D.)	Significance
Age	30.1 (8.6)	33.4 (8.9)	$p < 0.09$
Sex (% male)	40.4%	48%	$p < 0.43$
Mean duration of long session (minutes)	72.5 (94.8)	21.3 (19.6)	$p < 0.04$
Maximum duration of longest session (minutes)	173.8 (205.3)	35.5 (29.3)	$p < 0.01$
Mean number of short sessions	14.6 (13.6)	3.9 (3.4)	$p < 0.00$
Mean duration of short sessions (minutes)	4.8 (5.4)	5.5 (12.8)	$p < 0.77$
Type of light preferred (natural daylight or artificial) on a visual analogue scale	38.5 (32.4)	41.6 (27.0)	$p < 0.75$
External or internal focus of attention (–4 to +4) for long sessions	–0.49 (2.9)	–2.2 (1.9)	$p < 0.04$
External or internal focus of attention (–4 to +4) for short sessions	–1.12 (2.7)	–1.15 (2.1)	$p < 0.77$
Attention on the whole or specific parts of appearance (0–100 on visual analogue scale) in long session	70.5 (24.3)	44.5 (34.02)	$p < 0.03$
Distress before long session (1–10)	6.44 (2.3)	1.6 (0.83)	$p < 0.00$
Distress after long session (1–10)	7.63 (2.2)	2.40 (2.3)	$p < 0.00$
Distress resisting gaze for long sessions (1–10)	6.82 (2.6)	2.38 (2.5)	$p < 0.00$

Table 1.14 Motivation for mirror gazing as measured by strength of beliefs (on a scale between 1 and 5)

Beliefs	BDD mean (S.D.)	Controls mean (S.D.)	Significance
(1) The hope that I might look different when I first look in the mirror	4.2 (0.9)	1.9 (1.0)	$p < 0.00$
(2) The hope that I can feel comfortable with my appearance	4.6 (0.8)	3.1 (1.3)	$p < 0.00$
(3) I have to know what I look like and I can't until I look in the mirror	4.1 (1.0)	2.3 (1.5)	$p < 0.001$
(4) The belief that I make myself look better or hide myself (e.g. use make-up)	4.0 (1.0)	3.0 (0.9)	$p < 0.012$
(5) I look in the mirror to see how I feel	3.0 (1.2)	2.1 (1.0)	$p < 0.00$
(6) I have to know for certain how I appear in public	4.7 (0.5)	3.1 (1.1)	$p < 0.00$
(7) I have to make myself look my best	4.4 (1.0)	3.3 (0.9)	$p < 0.00$
(8) I believe that if I stare long enough, I might see a different image	3.1 (1.3)	1.2 (0.4)	$p < 0.00$
(9) If I resist looking in the mirror then I will feel worse	3.7 (1.1)	1.4 (0.7)	$p < 0.00$
(10) I need to see what I don't like about myself	3.7 (1.1)	2.0 (0.9)	$p < 0.00$
(11) I need to see what I like about myself	3.2 (1.1)	2.9 (1.1)	$p < 0.30$
(12) I can make myself look presentable (e.g. brush my hair, use make-up)	3.7 (1.0)	4.4 (0.5)	$p < 0.021$

Findings:

1 Length of time mirror gazing (Table 1.13)

BDD participants spent an average of 72.5 minutes mirror gazing compared with 21.3 minutes for controls.

BDD participants had an average of 14.6 short sessions (controls, 3.9) but BDD participants spend less time on these than the controls. All these differences are significant.

Expert tip

The probability values (p) in this table show p as less than 0. No p value can be less than 0.

2 Motivation before looking in a mirror (Table 1.14)

Using a 5-point scale, on 10 out of the 12 belief statements, BDD participants were significantly more likely to strongly agree or agree with the statements than were controls. On statement 11: 'I need to see what I like about myself' there was no significant difference and on statement 12: 'I can make myself look more presentable' controls scored significantly higher than the BDD participants.

3 Focus of attention in mirror (Table 1.13)

BBD participants were more likely to focus on an internal impression for long sessions (−0.49 compared with −2.2) but not for short sessions (−1.12 compared with −1.15). BDD participants were more likely to focus on a specific part (70.5 compared with 44.5 on a scale of 0–100). These differences were significant.

4 Distress before and after looking in front of a mirror (Table 1.13)

Long sessions: BBD participants were significantly more distressed, with a mean of 6.4 compared with 1.6 on a scale of 1–10 ($p = 0.00$).

Short sessions: BBD participants were significantly more distressed, with a mean of 7.3 compared with 2.4 on a scale of 1–10 ($p = 0.00$).

When trying to *resist* checking in a mirror, BDD participants were significantly more distressed (mean 6.82) compared with controls (mean 2.38), which was also very significant ($p = 0.00$).

5 Behaviour in front of a mirror

Long sessions: BDD participants were significantly more likely to use a mirror for (a) comparing what they see with an ideal image and (b) trying to see something different. Controls were significantly more likely to use the mirror for removing hairs or shaving. There was no significant difference between the two in using make-up, combing or styling hair, picking their spots or feeling their skin with their fingers.

Short sessions: BDD participants were significantly more likely to use a mirror for (a) checking their make-up, (b) practising the best position or face to pull or show in public and (c) comparing what they see with an ideal image. Controls were significantly more likely to use the mirror for shaving.

6 Type of light preferred

There was very little difference (not significant) between BDD participants (38.5) and controls (41.6) in terms of preference for natural or artificial light.

7 Types of reflective surface

BDD patients reported using a variety of reflective surfaces such as car mirrors, cutlery, TV screens, table tops and the backs of CDs.

8 Mirror avoidance

67% of BDD participants reported they **selectively avoided** (compared with 14% of controls) certain types of mirror. These types were (depending on the individual): avoidance of looking at a specific defect, using only 'good' mirrors and not 'bad' mirrors (sometimes dependent on light), using private mirrors rather than public mirrors, and using only mirrors that were obscured (e.g. cracked) so that a full reflection could not be seen.

Conclusions:

1 Mirror gazing is complex, being viewed as a series of idiosyncratic and varied safety behaviours designed to prevent a feared outcome.

Now test yourself

59 Identify the **four** types of mirror avoidance.

Answer on p.196

Tested

2 BDD patients always hope that they will look different from their internal body image.
3 BDD patients demand to see exactly how they look.
4 BDD patients believe they will feel worse if they resist mirror gazing.
5 BDD patients have the need to camouflage by excessive grooming – what could be called *mental* cosmetic surgery.
6 Based on the findings of the study, BDD patients can be helped to manage their mirror-gazing strategies, and the following recommendations are made:
   - Use mirrors so they show most of the body, or the whole of the face, rather than a specific part.
   - Focus attention on reflection rather than internal impression of feelings, and do not make an automatic 'ugly' judgement.
   - Use a mirror for a function, such as shaving or to do make-up.
   - Use different mirrors rather than the 'trusted' one and do not use magnifying mirrors or mirrors that give ambiguous reflections.
   - Do not use a mirror when they have the urge but to delay and do other things instead.

Expert tip

There are three evaluation issues to consider:

- **Sampling** – Veale and Riley describe the acquisition of the control group as being recruited through 'personal contacts' without any clarification of what this might be.
- **Matched pairs** – participants were matched on age (30.1 years compared with 33.4 years) and sex (40.4% male and 48% male). It could be argued that this matching process was not rigorous because the percentages were not that close.
- **Applications/usefulness** – this study is very useful. Not only does it give an understanding of the nature of mirror-gazing behaviour, but it also allows the author (David Veale) to recommend ways in which mirror-gazing can be managed when treating BDD patients.

Now test yourself

60 Identify **three** ways in which BDD patients are advised to manage mirror-gazing.

Answer on p.196

Tested

Cross check

Sampling, page 83
Designs, pages 68–70
Applications/usefulness, page 95

Expert tip

What other issues are related to this study?

2 Themes in Psychology

2.1 Research methods in psychology

There are five main research methods: experiment, self-report, correlation, observation and case study. This section will describe each in turn, before summarising their strengths and weaknesses.

Expert tip

All these methods also relate to the A level options. Cross checks appear with each option.

Experiment

Revised

One of the ideas behind the experimental method is that of cause and effect – that changes or differences in one factor bring about changes in another.

An **experiment** is where the independent variable (IV) is the factor that is thought to be the cause, and the dependent variable (DV) is the effect.

Three types of experiment

There are three different types of experiment: laboratory experiment, field experiment and natural (or quasi-) experiment. In both a laboratory and field experiment, the researcher manipulates the IV and controls any variables extraneous (or irrelevant) to the study. In a natural experiment, the IV varies naturally, without the researcher's intervention, for example where people who are left-handed are compared with people who are right-handed.

Typical mistake

Many students get the IV and DV the wrong way round.

The laboratory experiment

A **laboratory experiment** takes place in a laboratory where conditions are controlled and IVs manipulated in order to discover cause and effect. It is probably the method psychologists use most often to conduct research. There is an IV, all extraneous variables are controlled and the DV is measured.

Now test yourself

1 Give **one** similarity and **one** difference between a laboratory experiment and a field experiment.

Answer on p.196

Tested

Examples of laboratory experiments

- The study by Langlois et al. was a laboratory experiment. The attractive and unattractive photographs were shown on a screen for a fixed period of time and the responses of the babies were recorded on a video camera. Many controls were applied.
- The study by Maguire et al. was a laboratory experiment because it involved the use of a PET scan. This large and expensive piece of equipment is fixed in one place, which means participants for any study using it must come to the laboratory. In this experiment Maguire et al. examined the brain patterns of London taxi drivers while they recalled a route.

Cross check

Langlois et al., page 36
Maguire et al., page 48

Alternative examples of studies with laboratory experiments are: Bandura et al., page 31; Dement and Kleitman, page 46; Demattè et al., page 51; Schachter and Singer, page 43; Milgram, page 20; Held and Hein, page 17.

Advantages of laboratory experiments

- The manipulation of one IV while controlling irrelevant variables means that cause and effect are much more likely to be shown.
- They allow for control over many extraneous variables, e.g. temperature and noise levels.
- Standardised procedures mean that replication is possible.
- In a laboratory, participants must have given some degree of consent to take part. This reduces ethical issues.

Disadvantages of laboratory experiments

- The results may be biased by sampling, demand characteristics or experimenter bias.
- Some people regard the process as dehumanising, with participants being treated like laboratory rats by having *something done to them.*
- Controlling variables is reductionist as it is unlikely that any behaviour would exist in isolation from other behaviours.
- Artificial conditions (setting and task) can produce unnatural behaviour, which means that the research lacks ecological validity.
- For the IV to be isolated, participants might be deceived about the true nature of the study. There may be other ethical issues.
- It is more likely that the data will be snapshot.

Now test yourself

2 Give **one** disadvantage of conducting a study in a laboratory.

Answer on p.196

Tested

The field experiment

A field experiment takes place in a natural or normal environment for the behaviour being studied. For example, to conduct a field experiment about how children learn, the logical place to do this is in a classroom.

A **field experiment** is a form of research that takes place outside a laboratory, where conditions are controlled and IVs manipulated in order to discover cause and effect.

Examples of field experiments

- The study by Piliavin et al. was a field experiment. There were IVs, DVs and many controls, but the study was conducted in a New York subway where the natural behaviour of participants could be observed without their knowledge that they were participating in a study.
- The study by Nelson was an experiment because there were hypotheses, IVs and DVs. It was a field experiment because of where the study was conducted. The children were aged 3–4 and 6–8, so taking children of this age to a laboratory would have been inappropriate. The interviews were conducted in pre-schools and schools surrounding the University of Illinois (USA).

Expert tip

An experiment always has an IV and a DV, whether it is conducted in or outside a laboratory.

Cross check

Piliavin et al., page 25

Nelson, page 39

Advantages of field experiments

- There is greater ecological validity because the surroundings are natural.
- There is less likelihood of demand characteristics (if people are unaware of the research taking place).
- The features of an experiment (IV, DV etc.) are retained.
- The behaviour is natural and so tells us how people behave in real life.

Disadvantages of field experiments

- There might be difficulties in controlling the situation, and therefore more possibility of influence from extraneous variables.
- The experiment might be difficult to replicate exactly.
- There might be problems of access to where the study is to be done, such as consent from a company.
- There might be ethical problems of consent, deception, invasion of privacy etc.

The natural experiment

In a natural experiment the conditions of the IV happen by themselves. For example, we might be interested in whether males or females are more likely to choose science or humanities subjects. The IV is sex – male or female. This cannot be 'manipulated' by the experimenter – it just happens.

A **natural experiment** is where conditions of the IV are naturally occurring/happen by themselves and are not manipulated or controlled by an experimenter.

Now test yourself

Tested

3 Give **one** advantage of conducting a field experiment.

Answer on p.196

Examples of natural (quasi-) experiments

- The study by Baron-Cohen et al. (the 'eyes test') is an example of a natural experiment because the participants could not be randomly allocated to be either autistic (AS or HFA) or non-autistic. The AS/HFA condition was naturally pre-existing. The eyes test was exactly the same for all four groups of participants without the experimenters creating an experimental and control group. The method can also be classed as a laboratory experiment.
- The study by Billington et al. (empathising and systemising) is an example of a natural (quasi-) experiment because participants were either male or female and studying either physical sciences or humanities. The experimenters did not manipulate any variables, instead placing the participants in naturally occurring conditions. The tests SQ-R, EQ, eyes test and FC-EFT test were the same for all participants.

Cross check

Baron-Cohen et al., page 14
Billington et al., page 59

Advantages of natural experiments

- There is greater ecological validity because the surroundings are natural.
- There is less likelihood of demand characteristics (if people are unaware of the research taking place).
- The features of an experiment – IV, DV etc. – are retained.
- Behaviour is natural and so tells us how people behave in real life.

Disadvantages of natural experiments

- It may be difficult, even impossible, to infer cause and effect due to lack of control over extraneous variables and no manipulation of the IV.
- The experiment may be difficult to replicate exactly.
- The experiment may be subject to bias if participants know they are being studied.

Experimental designs

Because many of the core studies are experiments (field or laboratory), we need to look in more detail at how an experiment works – its design.

There are three types of design: repeated measures, independent groups and matched pairs.

An **experimental design** is how participants are allocated to the conditions of the IV.

Repeated measures

A **repeated measures** (or related samples) **design** is where each participant takes part in *both* (or more) conditions of the IV. For example:

Condition 1	*Condition 2*
Participant A	Same participant A
Participant B	Same participant B
Participant C	Same participant C

Cross check

Demattè et al., page 51
Langlois et al., page 36

Examples of repeated measures designs

- The study by Demattè et al. was a repeated measures design because all participants smelled all four odours and clean air. This meant that ratings of attractiveness were done by the same person across all five conditions.
- The study by Langlois et al. used a repeated measures design because in study 1 each infant looked at faces of adult women and adult men that were both attractive and unattractive. The same design was used for studies 2 and 3 (but with different stimuli).

Typical mistake

Clean/fresh air is not an odour. There were four odours and clean air was a control.

Another example of a study using a repeated measures design is Loftus and Pickrell, page 12.

Expert tip

An easy way to spot a repeated measures design is so see if the same participants do all the conditions of the IV.

Advantages of repeated measures designs

- This design is best for the control of participant variables, because the same people do both conditions and their level of intelligence, motivation and many other factors remain the same throughout.
- Although much less important, it means that only half the number of participants are needed than for other designs because each participant 'scores' in both conditions.

Disadvantages of repeated measures designs

- Some experiments are impossible to do as a repeated measures design, e.g. a participant cannot be both left-handed and right-handed or both male and female.
- If a participant completes both conditions then it may be necessary to duplicate apparatus, such as word lists. But, how can the lists be balanced so they are of equal difficulty? It may be better to use a different type of design.
- A major flaw is that the design can create **order effects**. If a participant performs an activity twice they may become tired or bored the second time (known as the **fatigue effect**) and the result is different from the first time. It might be that the second result is much better than the first because the participant knew what to expect or treated the first as a practice. This is simply known as the **practice effect**.

One way to eliminate order effects is to counterbalance. This is where participant 1 performs in condition 1 first and then condition 2, participant 2 performs in condition 2 and then condition 1, and so on. As a result, both practice and fatigue effects are controlled.

Examples of studies with counterbalancing include: Demattè et al., page 51; Nelson, page 39; Langlois et al., page 36.

Now test yourself Tested

4 What is meant by the term 'repeated measures design'?

5 Suggest **one** way in which order effects can be overcome.

Answers on p.196

Independent groups

An **independent groups** (or independent measures) **design** is where each participant is in just one condition of the IV. For example:

Condition 1	*Condition 2*
Participant A	Participant B
Participant C	Participant D
Participant E	Participant F

Examples of independent groups design

- The study by Baron-Cohen et al. used AS/HFA participants and 'normal' controls. It would be impossible for any participant to be in both conditions, so the design was independent groups.
- The participants in the Schachter and Singer study could only be in one of four groups: EPI INF, EPI MIS, EPI IGN or control/placebo. Further, they could only be in the euphoric or angry conditions. If a single participant had done all four conditions the experiment would clearly not have worked.

Cross check

Baron-Cohen et al., page 14

Schachter and Singer, page 43

Another example of a study using an independent groups design is Billington et al., page 59.

Advantages of independent groups designs

- Participants only perform in one condition of the IV and so there are no order effects.
- Only one word list (or test) is needed for participants.
- Each participant only experiences one condition so it might stop them guessing what the study is all about and so reduce demand characteristics.

Disadvantages of independent groups designs

- Twice as many participants are needed than for a repeated measures design.
- This design does not always adequately control for participant variables. The researcher may end up with participants in one group who are all somehow 'naturally' better at the DV than the participants in the other group, more intelligent, or more suited to the condition to which they have been allocated.

Expert tip

An easy way to spot an independent groups design is so see if there are different participant numbers in the conditions of the IV. If they are unequal it cannot be a repeated measures design.

One way to try to eliminate participant variables is to **randomly allocate** participants to conditions. Random allocation is done by (for example) tossing a coin for each participant, giving them a 50/50 chance of doing condition 1 or condition 2 first. For this design it does not matter if there are unequal numbers of participants in each condition. Note that random allocation is very different from a random sample.

Matched pairs

A **matched pairs design** is where the experimenter tries to match as many aspects as possible, on which participants may differ, that might extraneously affect the DV. If participants are matched, then the design is equivalent to a repeated measures design. However, this design is only as good as the experimenter's ability to match participants. Can *all* relevant variables be matched?

Now test yourself Tested ☐

6 What is meant by the random allocation of participants to conditions?

Answer on p.196

Examples of matched pairs designs

- The study by Bandura et al. matched groups for pre-existing levels of aggression. If they had not done this – if all the 'naturally aggressive' children were in one group and all the 'non-naturally aggressive' children in another group – the result would be confounded and the effect of learning would not be shown. Matching of pre-existing levels was therefore essential to the study.
- The study by Baron-Cohen et al. matched the participants in group 4. These were randomly selected individuals from the general population who were **IQ matched** with group 1 (the AS or HFA participants).

Expert tip

Matched pairs involves the matching of *participants*, as in the study by Baron-Cohen et al. **Matched groups** involves the matching of *groups* of participants, as in the study by Bandura et al.

Cross check

Bandura et al., page 31
Baron-Cohen et al., page 14

Advantages of matched pairs designs

- Participant variables are controlled because participants are matched across the conditions.
- There are no problems with **order effects**.

Disadvantages of matched pairs designs

- This design is only as good as the matching of participants, and it is questionable whether *all* relevant variables can be matched.
- It can be difficult (and time consuming) to find participants that can be matched.

Expert tip

If you cannot identify the design of a study, don't worry; there are many more things that you can focus on.

Experimental controls

In order to make sure that it is the manipulation of the IV that is *causing* the change in the DV, it is important for the researcher to **control** any **confounding variables**. These are factors apart from the IV that may affect the DV.

A **control** is an action taken by the experimenter to try to ensure that the IV causes the DV rather than some extraneous variable.

A **confounding variable** is when an experimenter does not know whether the DV is due to the IV or some other extraneous variable.

Confounding variables

There are three types of confounding variable that need to be controlled:

1 **Situational variables** concern the environment or situation in which the experimental and control groups are participating in the experiment. If one group is tested in one environment and another group in a different environment, then this might cause the result to be different.

2 **Experimenter variables** are where the presence of the researchers themselves may affect the outcome of the experiment. This can happen in two different ways:

(a) The mere presence of the experimenter may cause **demand characteristics**. The one way to control demand characteristics is by using a **single blind** design, in which the participant is unaware of the behaviour that is expected of them (i.e. they are not told whether they are in the experimental or the control group, or they are not told what behaviour is being measured, or why).

(b) **Experimenter bias** occurs when an experimenter who wants to achieve a particular outcome may consciously or unconsciously give different 'signals' to participants, for example smiling if a participant is doing what is desired or encouraging them if they are not. This can be controlled by using a **double blind** design, in which not only is the participant unaware of the behaviour that is expected of them but also the experimenter does not know whether the participant is in the experimental or the control group. Experimenter bias can also be reduced by giving all participants the same **standardised instructions**.

3 **Participant variables** are relevant individual differences between participants, such as level of motivation, eyesight, intelligence or memory. One solution is to have two very large groups (to minimise the effect of a rogue individual or an 'outlier') and to allocate participants to the two groups randomly. Another solution is to carefully choose how participants will be allocated to the two conditions of the experiment.

Now test yourself

7 Why do psychologists try to control extraneous variables?

Answer on p.196

Tested

Demand characteristics are features of the setting/situation that tell the participant what is expected. These can lead the participant to change behaviour, for example in order to please (or upset) the experimenter.

Cross check

Mann et al., page 11

Expert tip

There is a lot of detail about different types of control here. Although you might find this interesting it isn't essential information to learn.

Examples of studies with and without control

- The study by Bandura et al. had many controls. For example, he matched participants for pre-existing levels of aggression (and so controlled **participant variables**). He used the same three rooms, the same toys and in each room even the toys were replaced in their original position before the next child entered. This was to control any **situational variables**. To control **experimenter bias**, Bandura used more than one observer when testing the responses of the children.
- There were no controls in the study by Rosenhan. It was not an experiment and as Rosenhan was deceiving participants about mental illness he could not control any part of the participants (doctors and nurses) or the situation they were in. If any form of control had been attempted he might have been discovered and the study would have been over.

Cross check

Bandura et al., page 31
Rosenhan, page 53

Alternative examples of studies with controls are: Demattè et al., page 51; Dement and Kleitman, page 46; Mann et al., page 9; Langlois et al., page 36.

Now test yourself

Tested

8 What are the **three** types of extraneous variable to be controlled?

Answer on p.196

Advantages of controlling variables

- More control over irrelevant/extraneous variables means that the DV is more likely to be due to the IV; cause and effect are much more likely to be shown.
- Participants are more likely to behave in predictable ways – particularly ways in which the experimenter wants them to behave.
- Controls act as a benchmark of 'normality' against which things can be compared. This is most likely through using an experimental group and a control group, where nothing is done to the control group and a measure of their 'normal' behaviour is recorded.
- The control of variables makes a study more replicable.

Disadvantages of controlling variables

- Controlling variables is reductionist – it is unlikely that any behaviour would exist in isolation from others.
- The more controls, the more artificial the situation becomes and the more participants are likely to respond to demand characteristics. They are less likely to behave naturally. This lowers the ecological validity of the study.
- Attempting to control variables for many different trials can lead to participants becoming suspicious.

Controlling variables is highly desirable but so is high ecological validity. Low control means high ecological validity and high control means low ecological validity. Which is best? The solution to this dilemma is not a desirable one – to be unethical. The field experiment by Piliavin et al. was done in a real-life setting *and* they had many controls. To achieve this, there was no informed consent, many deceptions, no right to withdraw, no debriefing and possible psychological harm.

Expert tip

Don't just think about one evaluation issue (such as controls); think about how two or more interact with each other.

Now test yourself

9 Name **four** controls used by Piliavin et al. in their subway Samaritan study.

Answer on p.196

Tested

Self-reports

Revised

A **self-report** simply means asking participants about something so they can report on it themselves. There are three main components to take into account:

- the specific **method** (questionnaire or interview) used to ask questions and gather data (the answers)
- the format or structure of the **questions** themselves
- the way in which participants will provide **answers** to the questions

Self-reports involve research that uses the participants' own accounts of their behaviour or experience. Self-report methods include questionnaires, interviews, thinking aloud and diaries.

Questionnaires

How questions are asked in a **questionnaire** depends on what type of response or data the researcher is looking for. Data can be quantitative (in the form of numbers) or they can be qualitative (in the form of words). There are advantages and disadvantages to both these types of data (page 80).

A **questionnaire** is where participants read the questions for themselves and then fill in their answers themselves. This can be done on paper or online.

We can ask **open-ended questions**, which are simply questions that ask the participant to give a response in his or her own words, with no pre-determined way to answer. **Closed questions** on the other hand require the participant to choose from a range of pre-determined answers. There are several forms of pre-determined answer:

- a simple yes/no
- a choice from a range of categories such as 0–6, 7–12, 13–18 etc.
- a choice of number on a scale, with or without descriptor words at either end, such as:

  strongly agree 1 2 3 4 5 strongly disagree

  A rating scale like this is often known as a Likert scale and can be 5-point (as in the example above) or 7-point, or it could be 4-point. If a scale is 5-point it gives the participant a chance to opt-out, to be neutral. In the example above the mid-point of the 5-point scale would be neutral or 'neither agree nor disagree'. This may well be the case depending on what question is asked. But what if every participant responded like this? There would be no useful data. Using a 4-point scale, with a fixed/forced choice, means the participant must commit to either agreeing or disagreeing. Think about the advantages and disadvantages of using each type of scale.

Questionnaires can be sent by post or filled in online, allowing a participant to remain anonymous. Think about the advantages and disadvantages of a postal questionnaire compared with one that can be done online.

Now test yourself

10 Describe what is meant by a forced-choice questionnaire. Give an advantage of this type of questionnaire.

11 Describe the two main types of questionnaire.

Answers on p.196

Tested

Examples of studies using questionnaires

- The study by Billington et al. uses the SQ-R, consisting of 75 questions, and the EQ, consisting of 40 questions. Both questionnaires are closed and force a choice because the answer (on a 4-point scale) is either strongly agree, slightly agree, slightly disagree or strongly disagree. Points are allocated to each and so the final SQ-R total is out of 150 and the EQ out of 80.
- The 'mirror-gazing' questionnaire devised by Veale and Riley uses a 5-point scale (strongly disagree to strongly agree); a 9-point visual analogue scale scoring between +4 and −4 and a 10-point visual analogue scale (1 = not at all distressed to 10 = extremely distressed). Percentages of various items and estimations of time were also required.

Alternative examples of studies using questionnaires are: Demattè et al., page 51; Schachter and Singer, page 43; Baron-Cohen et al., page 14.

Interviews

Interviews can be:

- **structured**, where the questions are pre-prepared and every participant receives the same questions in the same order without variation
- **unstructured**, where there is no pre-preparation of questions and questions are asked depending on the direction in which the discussion goes, or questions are open-ended
- **semi-structured**, where there are some structured questions and some unstructured/open-ended questions.

Cross check

Billington et al., page 59

Veale and Riley, page 61

An **interview** is where questions are asked of a participant and the interviewer notes the responses.

An interview that is **face-to-face** is not anonymous and neither is a **telephone interview**, even if it is not face-to-face.

To check your understanding, suppose I wanted to find out what my students think about my teaching of the AS psychology course. What would be the best method to use, questions to ask and type of data to collect? I could ask:

'My teaching of AS psychology has been superb'

strongly agree 1 2 3 4 strongly disagree

Expert tip

Think about the advantages and disadvantages of answering face-to-face questions compared with answering over the telephone.

This format could be used in a face-to-face **interview**, but answers may be socially desirable to please me. Alternatively it could be part of a **questionnaire** that is completed anonymously. It is a closed question, giving quantitative data, and so I could calculate the percentage of those students who strongly agree, etc. Although this has numerical strength, it has fundamental weakness. It gives no information as to *why* a student thought the teaching was superb or why it was not. Adding an open-ended question such as 'please give a reason for your answer' and leaving a blank space allows the respondents to write their reasons if they so wish.

Now test yourself

Tested

12 Describe the **three** main types of interview.

Answer on p.196

Examples of studies using interviews

- The study by Loftus and Pickrell involves an interview with a relative to obtain three true stories about the participant. The interview has the open-ended question of 'recall each event, adding as much detail as possible' and also closed questions about clarity (1–10 scale) and confidence (1–5 scale).
- The study by Mann et al. involved unstructured interviews conducted by the police in the County of Kent (UK). The suspects being interviewed had been accused of different crimes (theft, arson, attempted rape and murder) and so each interview was different. The police interview procedure is standardised by law (to ensure everyone is treated fairly and lawfully) and, to ensure this, each interview is recorded on videotape.

Cross check

Loftus and Pickrell, page 11
Mann et al., page 9

Other examples of studies using self-reports are: Nelson, page 39; Dement and Kleitman, page 46.

Advantages of self-reports

- Participants are given the opportunity to express a range of feelings and explain their behaviour.
- The data obtained may be 'rich' and detailed, especially with open questions.
- Data are often qualitative, but may also be quantitative depending on the types of question that are asked.
- Closed/forced-choice questions are easier to score/analyse.
- Relatively large numbers of participants can be dealt with relatively quickly, which can increase representativeness and generalisability of the results.
- Questionnaires are relatively easy to replicate.

Disadvantages of self-reports

- Closed questions often do not give the participant the opportunity to say why they behaved or answered a question in a particular way.
- Participants might provide socially desirable responses, not give truthful answers or respond to demand characteristics.
- Closed/forced-choice questions might force people into choosing answers that do not reflect their true opinion, and therefore may lower the validity.
- Researchers have to be careful about the use of leading questions; it could affect the validity of the data collected.
- Open-ended questions can be time-consuming to categorise/analyse.
- If a telephone interview is conducted, a participant can easily withdraw, or might find it difficult to understand how to respond if the questions being asked cannot be seen.

Now test yourself

Tested ☐

13 Describe **three** disadvantages of self-reports.

Answer on p.196

Correlation

Revised ☐

Correlation is a statistical technique rather than a method itself. It looks at whether two variables or factors are related. A **correlation coefficient** is a number between −1 and +1 that expresses how strong a correlation is. If this number is close to 0, there is no real connection between the two at all. If it is approaching +1 there is a positive correlation: in other words, as one variable increases, the other variable also increases (or both decrease). If it is approaching −1, there is a negative correlation: in other words, as one variable increases, the other variable decreases (or one decreases while the other increases).

Correlation is a measure of how strongly two variables are related to each other.

The main strength of a correlation is that it can give precise information about the degree of a relationship between variables. The main weakness it that cause and effect cannot be inferred. This means that however strong a relationship is (i.e. close to +/–1) we can never say that one variable causes another.

Now test yourself

14 What is the difference between a positive correlation and a negative correlation?

Answer on p.196

Tested

Examples of studies using correlations

- The study by Mann et al. found very high inter-rater correlations between the two observers. For example, for *gaze aversion* the correlation was 0.86, for *blinking* 0.99 and for *speech disturbances* 0.97.
- The study by Baron-Cohen et al. found that performance on the revised eyes test was inversely correlated (i.e. negatively correlated) with scores on the AQ (the autistic spectrum quotient). This means that those scoring high on 'autism' scored low on the eyes test. The value found was −0.53.

Cross check

Mann et al., page 9
Baron-Cohen et al., page 14

Alternative examples of studies using correlations are: Bandura et al., page 31; Schachter and Singer, page 43; Dement and Kleitman, page 46.

Now test yourself

15 What can you never conclude from a correlation?

Answer on p.196

Tested

Observation

Revised

In an **observation**, data are collected through observing or watching participants with the aim of recording the behaviour that is witnessed.

Three types of observation

- **Controlled observation** takes place in a controlled environment such as a laboratory. Participants might be given a particular task to do and the observer may record behaviour by either being in the same room or by observing through a one-way mirror. A video camera may be used. Sometimes controlled observation is used to gather data as part of an experiment.
- **Natural observation** takes place in a natural environment (i.e. a situation that is natural for the behaviour the researcher is interested in). The recording of behaviour is much more problematic here because the aim is for the participants to be unaware that they are being observed (i.e. so they behave naturally).
- **Participant observation** is a special kind of natural observation and is where the observer (or researcher) becomes a member of the community (or group of people) he or she is observing. The participants being observed behave naturally and accept the observer as part of their normal routine.

Examples of studies using observation

- An example of a **controlled observation** is the study by Bandura et al. where children were placed in different experimental conditions and their behaviour observed through a one-way mirror.
- An example of **naturalistic observation** is the study by Piliavin et al. They manipulated the situation (the subway carriage) as much as possible, but for the participants this was a natural situation where they did not know they were being observed or taking part in a study. However, because many of the features of the situation were controlled, some argue that this was a controlled observation.
- An example of **participant observation** is the study by Rosenhan, where he gained access to a mental institution. Because the participants believed Rosenhan was mentally ill they behaved naturally (i.e. in the same way they did for actual patients) so allowing Rosenhan to observe openly without arousing suspicion.

Cross check

Bandura et al., page 31
Piliavin et al., page 25
Rosenhan, page 53

Alternative examples of studies using observation are: Mann et al., page 9; Schachter and Singer, page 43.

Recording observational data

Recording behaviour can be done by simply trying to write down everything that is observed. This is known as **unstructured observation** and is where the observer notes down or records all the behaviour, with no predetermined ideas or categories. In his study, Rosenhan did not know exactly what was going to happen so he was not able to pre-prepare.

Now test yourself

16 Name **three** types of observation and give an example of each.

Answer on p.196

Tested

Much more common is **structured observation**, which means that the observer has a predetermined schedule, coding scheme, tally chart or set of categories (often called response categories) that can be ticked when the appropriate behaviour is observed. Structured observation can use:

- **event sampling**, where the observer is looking for certain behaviours and a tally chart or record is kept of every instance of these behaviours (e.g. in the Piliavin et al. study where an observer recorded whether the helpers were male or female, black or white)
- **time sampling**, where the observer notes down or records the behaviour at certain times (e.g. at 5-second intervals, as done in the study by Bandura et al.)

Advantages of observation

- The observed behaviour is natural. As 'real' behaviour is observed, because the person is unaware, it is high in ecological validity.
- The data are often quantitative through using response categories, meaning they can be measured objectively and statistical tests can be applied.
- The data can be extremely rich if unstructured observation or participant observation is used.
- If the participants are unaware of the observation, they are unaffected by demand characteristics.

Disadvantages of observation

- The participants cannot explain why they behaved in particular way.
- Practically, the observer's view might be obstructed and the observations might not be reliable (page 82).
- With natural observation there is a lack of control over variables, making it difficult to conclude cause-and-effect relationships.
- With unstructured observation or participant observation there might be bias, with the observer 'seeing' things he or she desires; with structured observation and no time or event sampling the observer might mis-record instances of a behaviour.
- It might be very difficult to replicate natural observations as some circumstances can be unique (however, a good replication of controlled observation is possible).
- It is unethical if people are observed without their permission in a non-public area; it is also deception if the observer, in order to obtain data, pretends to be something he or she is not.

Now test yourself

17 Using an example, give **one** advantage and **one** disadvantage of an observation.

Answer on p.196

Tested

Case study

Revised

A **case study** is a detailed piece of research involving a single 'unit', for example one participant. It often gives us a detailed insight into unique behaviour and many would argue that this is the fascination of psychology. Others would argue that case studies are often not scientific at all. Some case studies make use of a range of different techniques.

A **case study** involves a detailed description of a particular individual or group under study or treatment.

Examples of case studies

- The case study by Freud of 'Little Hans', who was said to be in the phallic stage and going through the Oedipus complex. Freud admitted that Hans was not a normal child and that his case study had no scientific value.
- The study by Thigpen and Cleckley of 'Eve', a woman said to have multiple personality disorder (now known as dissociative identity disorder or DID). Eve was interviewed, given psychometric and projective tests, and even had an EEG.

Cross check

Freud, page 34
Thigpen and Cleckley, page 57
Little Albert (Bandura et al.), page 31

Advantages of case studies

- There are some circumstances where it is impossible to have a large number of participants, making case studies ideal; rare or unique behaviours can be studied in detail.
- Participants are often studied over a period of time, so developmental changes can be recorded. This is longitudinal, and it often means that the data gathered are detailed.
- The sample may be self-selecting, which means that the participants are not chosen by the researchers.
- Ecological validity is usually very high – the participant is often studied as part of everyday life.
- The data gathered may be rich and detailed.

Expert tip

There are only two examples of case studies at AS. There are more at A level, so this knowledge will not be wasted.

Now test yourself

18 Other than the study on Little Hans, describe a case study of a participant with a phobia.

Answer on p.196

Tested

Disadvantages of case studies

- Case studies rarely produce enough quantitative data for statistical testing; this means that some people regard case studies as little more than anecdotal evidence.
- Because case studies sometimes involve quite an intense relationship between the researcher and the participant, the researcher may lack objectivity. He/she may become too involved and thus alter the natural course of the participant's life events and experiences.
- There might be only one participant (or very few) involved, and so any conclusions cannot be generalised to other people.
- The participant might be unique and possibly not 'normal' in some way. This might mean that the researchers do not know how to proceed, or they might draw false conclusions.

Now test yourself

19 Using an example, give **one** advantage of a case study.

Answer on p.196

Tested

2.2 Methodological issues in psychology

What is a methodological issue? An issue is a topic for discussion and in this case the issues are related to methodology. In many respects some of the issues appearing in this section could easily appear in the issues and debates section, and vice versa. Methodological issues include:

- ecological validity
- ethics
- quantitative and qualitative data
- reliability
- sampling
- snapshot and longitudinal methods
- validity

Expert tip

All these methodological issues apply to the A level options. Cross checks appear with each option.

What follows in this section is a definition and brief explanation of each methodological issue followed by advantages/strengths and then disadvantages/weaknesses. Examples from core studies are given.

You need to know all these methodological issues because questions are asked about them in all three examination papers:

- Learn each issue.
- Know at least two strengths (and examples to illustrate from one study for Papers 1 and 2 or a topic area for Paper 3).
- Know at least two weaknesses (and examples to illustrate from one study for Papers 1 and 2 or a topic area for Paper 3).
- Be able to comment on, or conclude, which side of an issue or debate you support.

Expert tip

Sometimes questions ask for three problems psychologists have when trying to conduct research. Know three problems in relation to all the issues in this section.

Ecological validity

Revised

If a study is close to (or is) real life, we say that it is high in **ecological validity** and we can generalise from it because behaviour is natural and normal. Studies with low ecological validity cannot be used to generalise because they are less true to real life. Experiments low in ecological validity may be of limited value in psychology. Ecological validity can relate to the task that participants are required to do, and it can relate to the location in which the study is conducted. If a study is a laboratory experiment, ecological validity will be low. If an experiment is a field experiment then ecological validity will be higher. However, a field experiment may mean that there are fewer controls. One way of achieving high ecological validity *and* achieve a high level of control is to make the study unethical.

Ecological validity refers to how true a study is to real life.

Expert tip

This is a perfect example of how different issues – controls, ecological validity and ethics – interact with each other.

Examples of studies high and low in ecological validity

- The study by Mann et al. is *high* in ecological validity. The 16 suspects were being interviewed by real police in a real police interview room. The suspects had a genuine reason to lie because if they were convincing they would not be charged with the crime of which they were accused. If their lies were not convincing it could lead to a prison term. The study was therefore of authentic high-stakes liars.
- The study by Demattè et al. could be said to be *low* in ecological validity. The study was conducted in a laboratory and the smells were generated by a machine. There were no actual males present smelling of body odour or perfume, or to be judged on levels of attractiveness. There were just computer images.

Cross check

Mann et al., page 9
Demattè et al., page 51

Alternative examples of studies to consider for ecological validity are: Maguire et al., page 48; Haney et al., page 23; Held and Hein, page 17; Dement and Kleitman, page 46; Rosenhan, page 53; Baron-Cohen et al., page 14; Piliavin et al., page 25

Advantages of high ecological validity

- If a study is located in a real-life setting, participants are more likely to behave 'normally'. There are less likely to be demand characteristics, meaning that, since the participant is not conscious of being studied, there will be no pressure on him/her to perform in a certain way.
- If a study is based on real life, it is more likely that strong generalisations can be made.

Problems when trying to achieve high ecological validity

- It may be impossible, on a practical level, to create a real-life situation or make something happen naturally.

- There may be a lack of control over confounding variables. Experimenters cannot control all variables; they may not be able to isolate one variable from many others.
- If a study is conducted in a natural environment, the experimenter may not have obtained the participants' consent, so the study would be unethical.
- The data may be less reliable, i.e. if the study were repeated entirely different data might be produced.

Now test yourself

Tested

20 Suggest **two** problems when trying to achieve high ecological validity.

21 Suggest a way in which both high ecological validity *and* high levels of control can be achieved in a study.

Answers on p.197

Ethics

Revised

The British Psychological Society (BPS), American Psychological Association (APA) and ethical associations in other countries have guidelines on consent, deception, harm, the right to withdraw, debriefing, confidentiality, the use of children and the use of animals.

Ethics are a set of rules designed to distinguish between right and wrong in the protection of participants in psychological studies.

Informed consent: Participants should (in most cases) be asked if they want to take part in the study and they should be given all the relevant information about what it will involve, what the aims of the research are and so on so they can agree to participate. In the Milgram study, the participants thought they were taking part in a study on learning and memory, not obedience to authority.

Deception: Participants should not be deceived about the aims of the study and should not be deliberately misled about any aspect of the study. For example, the use of a stooge or confederate would be considered to be deception by today's standards. In the Piliavin et al. study, participants were deceived because they thought the victim was genuinely ill or drunk, whereas the male stooge (or confederate) was acting.

Protection of participants (harm): Participants should not be harmed in any way (mentally or physically). This could occur if animals are studied (e.g. the Held and Hein study) or if the participants are exposed to aggression, as in the Bandura et al. study.

Right to withdraw: Participants should be told they can withdraw completely from the study at any time. There should be no pressure to keep them in the study. This cannot be granted if the participants do not know that they are being studied (e.g. the Rosenhan study) or when, as in the Milgram study, the right to withdraw was denied as part of the actual study.

Confidentiality: Participants' data and information about them should not be passed on to other people not directly involved in the research or published in a way that would reveal their identity. No participant is ever named or can be identified in the research, so this guideline is always met. Of course, participants can reveal themselves (e.g. Christine Sizemore, who was studied by Thigpen and Cleckley).

Debrief: At the end of a study participants should be told what has happened, asked if they have any concerns, and given any explanations they require.

Now test yourself

Tested

22 Define (a) deception and (b) debrief.

Answer on p.197

Examples of ethical and unethical studies

All 20 year 1/AS core studies could be examples here. Some break more ethical guidelines than others, but it is also worth considering which ethical guidelines are *not* broken. For example, does any study breach the confidentiality of the participants?

- Milgram's study is seen as unethical. Participants did not give informed consent; they were deceived because they thought it was a study on 'learning and memory'. They were also deceived in many other ways. They were denied the right to withdraw because of the 'prods': 'the experiment requires that you continue' etc. Some participants suffered psychological harm and Milgram states that some participants suffered 'full blown uncontrollable seizures', suggesting they suffered physical harm. To give him credit, Milgram gave a debrief and no participant was identified. Note that participants appearing on the videotape of the study would have given their consent.
- The study by Demattè et al. is seen as ethical. The participants gave informed consent and they were not deceived in any way. They had to smell a smell and give ratings of the attractiveness of a photograph. They could withdraw at any time; they were debriefed and no part of the procedure would harm them in any way.

Cross check

Milgram, page 20
Demattè et al., page 51

Expert tip

Ethics is a student favourite because it is an issue in nearly every study. But other issues are just as likely to appear on a paper.

Alternative examples of studies to consider for ethical issues are: Loftus and Pickrell, page 11; Held and Hein, page 17; Haney et al., page 23; Schachter and Singer et al., page 43; Mann et al., page 9; Bandura et al., page 31; Rosenhan, page 53; Thigpen and Cleckley, page 57; Piliavin et al., page 25.

Advantages of conducting unethical studies

- The knowledge gained may be valuable, so a small amount of harm may be justified.
- Participants behave naively – if they do not know the true nature of the study, they behave more naturally and will not show demand characteristics.
- Being unethical can simulate or help create a more realistic/ecologically valid situation.
- Participants are never really harmed in psychological studies.

Disadvantages of conducting unethical studies

- Being unethical is not ethical! It invades human rights.
- The participant may make a false assumption about the true nature of the study and behave in a way in which the experimenter does not wish.
- Being unethical might discourage future participation in psychological research; it can give psychology a bad name and lower the status of the subject.
- If participants are harmed, something may go seriously wrong; there may be long-term damage.

Expert tip

Which is the most unethical core study? Why is it so? Debate this with your friends. It will allow you to revise the issue with different examples.

Now test yourself

Tested

23 Give **one** reason why studies in psychology should be **ethical** and **one** reason why studies in psychology should be **unethical**.

Answer on p.197

Quantitative and qualitative data

Revised

Quantitative data involve describing human behaviour and experience using numbers and statistical analysis. Examples of quantitative data in research include: a score recorded for each participant; the time taken to complete a task; the number of people in each condition who displayed a particular behaviour.

Quantitative data are data that focus on numbers and frequencies rather than on meaning or experience.

Qualitative data consist of descriptions or words, rather than numbers. These could be descriptions of events, actual quotes from participants, descriptions of participants' responses to a task, etc. Some studies produce a mixture of qualitative and quantitative data.

Qualitative data are data that describe meaning and experience in the form of words rather than providing numerical values for behaviour.

Examples of studies using quantitative data, qualitative data and both

- The study by Veale and Riley gathered quantitative data. Many closed questions were asked, some on a 5-point scale, some on a 9-point and some even on a 10-point scale. Some questions asked for the percentage of time spent on an activity. Results allowed many statistical calculations to be conducted and many activities allowed comparison with a control group.
- The study by Freud of little Hans only gathered qualitative data. The study lacked objectivity and there were no numbers gathered, so no statistical analysis could be done.
- Dement and Kleitman gathered quantitative data largely by the recordings from the EEG machine, which told them whether or not a participant was in REM or NREM and the direction of the eye movements. However, whether the participant was having a dream could only be known if the participant was asked about his or her dream and what they had been dreaming about – qualitative data.

Cross check

Veale and Riley, page 61
Freud, page 34
Dement and Kleitman, page 46

Alternative examples of studies using quantitative data, qualitative data and both are: Loftus and Pickrell, page 11; Mann et al., page 9; Bandura et al., page 31; Schachter and Singer, page 43; Piliavin et al., page 25; Nelson, page 39.

Strengths of quantitative data

- The use of numbers and statistics allows direct comparison of participants in different conditions. It can also allow comparison if the study is replicated.
- The use of numbers and statistics is more objective and scientific, so is more likely to be accepted by the scientific community.
- The collection of data and numbers through 'snapshot' studies can be done relatively quickly; it is the most appropriate way to gather data for some aspects of behaviour.

Weaknesses of quantitative data

- Using quantitative data is reductionist: it often reduces behaviour to a single number or a yes/no, failing to find out why a participant behaved in a particular way.
- It is also reductionist because human behaviour is complex and conclusions drawn from a number or statistic should not be generalised.
- Researchers might misinterpret what is said or observed or put detailed answers into a limited number of categories to enable conclusions to be drawn. There may be bias, with researchers modifying evidence to match the aim of the study.

Expert tip

Make sure in any examination answer that you get quantitative and qualitative the right way round.

Strengths of qualitative data

- The data can be in-depth, rich in detail, insightful and therefore not reductionist.
- The data can help us to understand *why* people behave in a particular way.

Now test yourself Tested

24 Using an example, give a weakness of quantitative data.
25 Give **two** examples of studies obtaining qualitative data.

Answers on p.197

Weaknesses of qualitative data

- There may be problems of interpretation. Words and descriptions are more subjective than numbers, and are more open to bias and misinterpretation by participants.
- Statistical comparisons cannot be made with qualitative data.
- The data might be more prone to researcher bias, as information that best fits the researcher's hypothesis could be selected.
- The participants might give socially desirable answers. Participants might want to look good for the researcher.

Now test yourself

26 What is meant by qualitative data? Give **one** advantage of qualitative data.

Answer on p.197

Tested

Reliability

Revised

If your car *always* starts first time (or indeed *never* starts first time) you can describe it as being reliable. If your car only sometimes starts first time, it is unreliable. In psychology, the **reliability** of a psychological measuring device (e.g. a test or scale) is the extent to which it gives consistent measurements. If an IQ (intelligence) test was given to a person and a few days or weeks later the same test was taken again, the same (or very similar) score should be obtained. If the test gave a very different result the test would be criticised because it would lack reliability.

Reliability refers to how consistent the measure of something is.

The reliability of an **experiment** is the extent to which it can be repeated and produce the same result. Reliability can also be applied to both questionnaires and to observations. The reliability of a **questionnaire**, for example, can be checked in two main ways:

- **Test–re-test method** is this is a system for judging the reliability of a psychometric test or measurement. It involves administering the same test to the same person on two different occasions, such as 3 weeks apart, and comparing the results. The results can then be correlated (page 74).
- **Split-half method** involves splitting the test into two and administering each half of the test to the same person. The scores from the two halves should be the same (but only if certain test items are balanced equally).

Now test yourself

27 What is meant by the term reliability?

28 Using an example, give **one** way in which the reliability of a questionnaire can be checked.

29 Using an example, give **one** way in which the reliability of an observation can be checked.

Answers on p.197

Tested

The reliability of an **observation** is based in part on **inter-rater reliability**, i.e. the extent to which two (or more) independent observers (coders/raters) agree (using a correlation test) on the observations that they have made. Note that inter-rater reliability is merely a *test* of the extent to which the observers agree. It does not improve reliability.

Examples of studies referring to reliability/inter-rater reliability

- The studies by Bandura et al. on aggression and by Mann et al. on lying both used two observers to check the reliability of the observations. Bandura found correlation of 0.89 when judging pre-existing levels of aggression and 'high inter-score reliabilities in the 0.90s' in the test for delayed imitation. Mann et al. also found very high inter-rater correlations between the two observers. For example for gaze aversion the correlation was 0.86, for blinking 0.99 and for speech disturbances 0.97.
- The study by Loftus and Pickrell is all about showing that memory is *not reliable*. Their research showed that people 'saw' broken glass that did not exist following a car crash; that people claimed they shook hands with Bugs Bunny while at Disney World (when Bugs Bunny is a Warner creation and would never be at anything belonging to Disney); that people had a false memory about being lost in a shopping mall when they were never actually lost.

Cross check

Bandura et al., page 31
Mann et al., page 9
Loftus and Pickrell, page 11

Alternative examples of studies to consider for reliability/inter-rater reliability are: Baron-Cohen et al., page 14; Billington et al., page 59; Langlois et al., page 36.

Advantages of reliability

- If a reliable experimental study is replicated exactly, we would expect to achieve very similar results.
- If an observation has high inter-rater reliability, it means that two or more observers are agreed on how behaviour should be categorised.
- If a questionnaire is reliable then it is consistent in its measurement.

Sampling

Revised

The choice of participants for any study is fundamental and is based on two questions:

- What group of people is being studied? (This is the **target population**.)
- How much effort is a researcher prepared to put in to make the sample representative of the target population?

The **target population** is the group to which research is hoping to generalise.

There are different sampling techniques and some are more effective in being representative than others.

Sampling techniques

Opportunity sample

An **opportunity sample** involves the researcher approaching people who are easy to find and available, such as students studying psychology in the same university department. If a researcher is interested in the 'general public', he/she might approach people who walk past in a shopping mall or in a student common room.

An **opportunity sample** is one that is selected by 'opportunity': the researcher simply uses the people who are present at the time that he/she is conducting the research

Advantages of opportunity samples

- It is relatively quick and easy to get participants. A large sample can be obtained quickly and without too much effort.

Disadvantages of opportunity samples

- Participants are unlikely to be representative of the target population. They may be psychology students, have been paid or receive course credits for taking part.
- A researcher might choose people they think look suitable, ignoring others, and so biasing the sample.

Expert tip

Know the difference between describing the sample (details of the participants, such as how many, etc.) and the sampling technique (how the participants were selected, e.g. a newspaper sample).

Self-selecting (volunteer) sample

This usually involves the researcher advertising for participants. An advertisement could appear in a newspaper (as done by Milgram, and Haney, Banks and Zimbardo) or on notice boards. The people who reply are 'self-selecting' – that is, they volunteer themselves for the research. Sometimes volunteers are not paid at all, sometimes they receive a small amount of money, and sometimes students receive course credits.

Now test yourself

Tested

30 Give **two** examples of core studies that used a self-selecting sample (other than those named here).

Answer on p.197

Advantages of self-selecting (volunteer) samples

- They are useful when the research requires participants of quite a specific type or with specific experience.
- It can be easy to place an advert in a newspaper.

Disadvantages of self-selecting (volunteer) samples

- Recruiting a sample in this way can be expensive (advertisements in newspapers cost money, and the researcher may need to pay a participant), and it can take more effort.
- People may not see the advert; they may see it but ignore it; or they may see and read it but will not make the time or effort to reply.
- The type of people who do volunteer to take part may be different in some ways from the type of people who are eligible but do not choose to volunteer.
- We can never really be sure that a self-selecting sample is representative of the target population.
- Participants may only volunteer if they are paid (or receive something in return). This can lead to demand characteristics.

Random samples

This is where each participant is randomly selected from the target population. If the target population is *students* then selecting a sample of students would be representative. But there might be 1000 students and only 20 in the sample. One way to achieve a **random sample** is to put every student's name into a hat and pick out the first 20 names.

A **random sample** is a sample that has been selected in a way that means everyone in the target population has an equal chance of being chosen.

Advantages of random samples

- They are more likely to be representative than opportunity or self-selecting samples.

Now test yourself

31 What is the difference between a random sample and random allocation?

Answer on p.197

Tested

Disadvantages of random samples

- It can be time-consuming to get the right sample.
- Some of the people picked by the random generator may not want to take part and will need replacing; this might end up producing a biased sample.

Examples of sampling techniques

- Volunteer: Milgram advertised in a newspaper in the New Haven district of New York. He asked for volunteers to take part in a study on learning and memory, and from all the replies selected 40 to take part.
- Opportunity: Schachter and Singer used male students who were taking part in introductory psychology classes. They received two extra points on their final examination for every hour they served as participants.

Alternative examples of studies to consider for sampling issues are: Dement and Kleitman, page 46; Freud, page 34; Loftus and Pickrell, page 11; Haney et al., page 23; Piliavin et al., page 25; Demattè et al., page 51; Thigpen and Cleckley, page 57.

Cross check

Milgram, page 20
Schachter and Singer, page 43

Snapshot and longitudinal studies

Revised

Snapshot studies

A **snapshot study** takes place at just one point in time – a one-off picture – perhaps involving a participant in a study for just a few minutes. It may well isolate a behaviour and it might not be known why the participant performed in a particular way.

Examples of snapshot studies

- The study by Tajfel is snapshot because they boys were taken to the laboratory from their school and the entire study probably took no longer than 1 hour. The judgments the boys made were at that moment in time, in that situation.

- The study by Milgram is snapshot because the whole study probably took each participant no longer than 30 minutes of their time. The male participants were introduced to the stooge, drew lots and the study began. The data gathered were about their responses in that situation at that moment in their life.

Alternative examples of studies to consider for snapshot studies are: Mann et al., page 9; Baron-Cohen et al., page 14; Piliavin et al., page 25; Schachter and Singer, page 43; Demattè et al., page 51.

Cross check

Tajfel, page 28
Milgram, page 20

Advantages of snapshot studies

- They are a quick way to collect data, especially if long-term development is not relevant.
- They can be good for obtaining preliminary evidence (testing a small sample in restricted conditions) before committing to expensive and time-consuming longitudinal work.
- They may give an indication of how people are likely to respond/behave.
- The data are likely to be quantitative, so statistical analysis is possible.

Disadvantages of snapshot studies

- It is not possible to study how behaviour might change over time (development), and one cannot see the long-term effectiveness or harm of exposure to certain stimuli.
- The behaviour recorded is limited to that time, in that place and in that culture.
- The data are likely to be quantitative (numbers), and the explanation as to why a participant behaved in a particular way will not be known.
- Snapshot studies are not always 'easier'; they may be more expensive/difficult to set up than longitudinal ones.

Expert tip

Some studies have two, three and even more methods going on at the same time. A study can be a laboratory experiment, it can use observation and it can be snapshot.

Now test yourself

Tested

32 What is a snapshot study?
33 Give **two** weaknesses of snapshot studies.

Answers on p.197

Longitudinal studies

A **longitudinal study** takes place over a period of time, usually following one or more participants throughout the period (or visiting them at regular intervals) to monitor changes. Contrast this with a snapshot study.

Examples of longitudinal studies

- The study by Freud of little Hans is longitudinal because there is a report of Hans's behaviour when he was 3½ years old and also his phobia as a 5 year old. So the study continued for at least this period of time.
- The study by Thigpen and Cleckley of Eve reports that there were over 100 hours of interviews that went on for at least 14 months.

Cross check

Freud, page 34
Thigpen and Cleckley, page 57

Advantages of longitudinal studies

- The development of an individual (or small number of participants) is tracked. A baseline is recorded at the start, and changes that occur over time (e.g. 5 years) in attitudes and behaviour can be measured.
- Studying the same participant means that individual differences such as intelligence are controlled.
- The effects of ageing can be seen, which makes this approach perfect for studying development, both within childhood and beyond.
- The long-term effects of a disorder or treatment, or exposure to a particular situation, can be observed.

Disadvantages of longitudinal studies

- Participant attrition – participants may drop out for a variety of reasons: they may have changed address; they may have died; or they may simply have decided not to continue with the study.
- Once started, the study cannot be changed or new variables introduced.
- The researchers may become attached to the participants. Bias may be introduced, and the study can become less objective.
- Cross-generational effects – those from one generation cannot be compared to another generation due to the social conditions of society changing over time.

Now test yourself

Tested

34 Give **two** examples of studies that are longitudinal.
35 **(a)** What is meant by the term 'longitudinal study'?
(b) Give **one** problem with longitudinal studies.
(c) Give **two** examples where this problem did not apply.

Answers on p.197

Expert tip

There are only two longitudinal core studies. The Rosenhan study is not longitudinal even though it went on for 52 days. The Haney et al. study is sometimes said to be longitudinal because the same people were studied for 6 days.

Validity

Revised

If I devised an intelligence test, how would I know whether it was accurately measuring intelligence? How would I know if my test was valid? If a person scored an IQ of 120 on my test and an IQ of 120 on an existing test, then because the existing test measures intelligence, so must my test. I conclude that my test is valid.

Validity is concerned with whether an experiment or procedure for collecting data actually measures or tests what it claims to measure or test.

There are several ways to assess validity:

- **Construct validity** sees how the measure matches up with theoretical ideas about what it is supposed to be measuring.
- **Criterion validity** compares the measure with some other measure. If the other measure is assessed at roughly the same time as the original one, then the type of criterion validity being applied is **concurrent validity**; if it is taken much later, then it is **predictive validity**.
- **Face validity** is the degree to which a test or measure appears superficially as though it probably measures what it is supposed to.

Expert tip

Know the difference between reliability and validity. Never write 'and this improves the reliability and validity' without saying why. Show you understand both terms and can apply them.

Examples of studies referring to validity

- The study by Mann et al. goes beyond all previous studies where actors tell lies and nothing is at stake. In her study she used real suspects telling real lies to try to avoid punishment and possibly going to prison. In other words she used authentic high-stakes liars.
- The study by Billington et al. states 'The EQ correlates well with the interpersonal reactivity index (IRI) (Davis, 1983), providing evidence of concurrent validity'. This means that it has been compared with another measure and the two confirm each other.

Alternative examples of studies to consider for validity are: Dematte et al., page 51; Rosenhan, page 53; Baron-Cohen et al., page 14; Langlois et al., page 36.

Typical mistake

Don't assume that every psychologist is male. Much research is done by women. For example, Loftus, Maguire, Demattè, Langlois, Nelson and Mann are all female, as well as sub-authors Ross and Ross, Riley and many others.

Cross check

Mann et al., page 9
Billington et al., page 59

Now test yourself Tested

36 What is meant by the term validity?
37 What is the difference between construct validity and predictive validity?

Answers on pp.197–198

2.3 Approaches and perspectives in psychology

An approach is a particular view as to why and how we think, feel and behave as we do. It is an area of research characterised by a particular focus or by a particular set of themes, outlooks or types of explanation. The five approaches for the CIE syllabus are:

- cognitive
- social
- physiological
- developmental
- individual differences

Expert tip
The humanistic perspective only appears in the A level options (e.g. page 118).

What is a perspective, and how does it differ from an approach? Usually, a perspective is more a way of explaining behaviour according to certain principles, concepts and ideas, whereas the approaches refer more to *areas* of research interest (regardless of the perspective adopted). The two perspectives for the CIE syllabus are:

- psychodynamic
- behaviourist

Expert tip
These approaches and perspectives also apply to the A level options. Cross checks appear with each option.

What follows in this section is a definition and brief explanation of each approach and perspective followed by advantages/strengths and then disadvantages/weaknesses. Examples from core studies are given. It is also important for you to think of your own examples.

You need to know all these issues and debates because examination questions are asked about them in all three examination papers. For example, Paper 1 Section B and Paper 2 Section B. For Paper 3 it depends on the options chosen.

- Learn each approach/perspective.
- Know at least two strengths (and examples to illustrate from one study for Papers 1 and 2 or a topic area for Paper 3).
- Know at least two weaknesses (and examples to illustrate from one study for Papers 1 and 2 or a topic area for Paper 3).
- Be able to comment on, or conclude, which side of an issue or debate you support.

Approaches in psychology

Revised

The cognitive approach

Cognitive psychology concerns the mind – thinking (rationally and irrationally), solving problems, perceiving, making sense of and understanding the world, using and making sense of language; and remembering and forgetting. The main assumption of the cognitive approach is that how we think is central in explaining how we behave and how we respond to different people and different situations. In some ways, the cognitive approach sees a human as rather like a complicated computer – information enters the mind (input), it

Cognitive psychology is about mental processes such as remembering, perceiving, understanding and producing language, solving problems, thinking and reasoning.

is processed and stored, and it is sometimes used again later (output) through remembering or responding to a situation.

Examples of the cognitive approach

- The study by Loftus (and Pickrell) showed that one cognitive process, that of memory, is not perfect. In other research, Loftus showed that eyewitness testimony is influenced by many things, such as leading questions, and in the study on false memory she showed that we easily believe things that never happened.
- The study by Baron-Cohen et al. also looked at 'faulty' cognitive processing. Those with an autistic spectrum disorder lack a theory of mind, which means an inability to think what another person might be thinking. The eyes test (as with the Sally-Anne test for children) is just one way in which theory of mind (or lack of it) can be determined.

Alternative examples of the cognitive approach are: Mann et al., page 9; Held and Hein, page 17.

Cross check

Loftus and Pickrell, page 11
Baron-Cohen et al., page 14

Strengths of the cognitive approach

- The cognitive approach uses the experimental method, i.e. manipulation of an IV, and so it is scientific.
- This approach deals with the mind, which many psychologists would say is central to any understanding of human psychology.
- It is the part of psychology that genuinely engages in how we think, and although thinking cannot be measured, decisions about outcomes can be.

Weaknesses of the cognitive approach

- Some psychologists say that this approach is less scientific, as we cannot observe the subject matter directly – we are just inferring or guessing how people think or process information.
- The analogy to information processors is too reductionist. It does not give account of other factors or levels of explanation, e.g. social, emotional or behavioural.
- It assumes all people's cognitive processes are the same. Thus, this approach does not account for individual differences.

Expert tip

Know the strengths and weaknesses of the cognitive approach, because they could appear in Paper 1 or Paper 2 examination questions. Know the four cognitive studies and then you can predict which studies are likely to appear in any question.

Weaknesses of the cognitive approach are also 'problems with investigating cognitive processes'.

Now test yourself

38 Outline what is meant by the cognitive approach in psychology.

39 Give a weakness of the cognitive approach.

Answers on p.198

Tested

The developmental approach

Developmental psychology is sometimes understandably, but misleadingly, thought of as child psychology: understandably, because the major part of the literature in developmental psychology is about children; misleadingly, because it gives the impression that psychological development stops as the child enters adulthood. A truly comprehensive developmental psychology should concern itself with the whole **lifespan** of human development. That said, CIE core studies focus exclusively on child development.

Developmental psychology is concerned with change and development over time.

Examples of the developmental approach

- The work of Freud gives us some insight into the emotional *development* of children. He proposed that each child goes through a number of stages of psychosexual development: beginning with the oral stage, followed by the anal stage, before moving into the third, phallic, stage. In the phallic stage, the Oedipus complex is central for boys, who use their mother to express the desires of the id. The case study chosen is about Little Hans, a boy who was in the phallic stage and going through the Oedipus complex. Freud's interpretations of events, such as the giraffe episode, illustrate the approach he took, and this core study will certainly provoke discussion in

your class. Freud's approach developed into a whole school of thought – the psychodynamic perspective.
- The study by Held and Hein is an example of the developmental approach (in addition to being an example of the cognitive approach). The study looks at how spatial perception and coordination develop in kittens. The active kitten developed visually guided paw placement after 33 hours or so, but not one of the passive kittens had developed this response, showing that active experience is essential for normal paw–eye behaviour to develop.

Alternative examples of the developmental approach are: Bandura et al., page 31; Langlois et al., page 36; Nelson, page 39.

Cross check

Freud, page 34
Held and Hein, page 17

Strengths of the developmental approach

- It emphasises growth and change and how an early life experience can have various consequences at later stages.
- It provides information on what children know and understand and suggests how they may be educated or are likely to behave at different ages. It helps us to understand how to bring them up.
- It could provide useful information on what behaviour is learned and what behaviour is inherited (the nature/nurture debate).
- It provides information on how adults change (in many different ways) through middle-age and into old-age.

Expert tip

The weaknesses of the developmental approach are also 'problems when investigating developmental processes'. The same applies to all five approaches.

Weaknesses of the developmental approach

- Studies on development take time, especially longitudinal studies. Snapshot studies can be used, comparing one child with another, but the children might be different.
- Because of the time needed for such studies, attrition can occur, meaning that participants might drop out of the study.
- Children are children and not adults – we cannot generalise from their behaviour and assume that what they do as children will be what they do as an adult.
- Ethics – children cannot give informed consent and might be studied even though they do not wish to be. They might also not understand that they have the right to withdraw.

Expert tip

Link approaches with methods and issues. For example, the developmental approach often uses the longitudinal method and the issue of the use of children in psychological studies is relevant.

Now test yourself

Tested

40 Name **two** studies that look at actual development and **three** other studies that are part of the developmental approach.

41 Give **one** strength of the developmental approach, using Freud's study as an example.

Answers on p.198

The physiological approach

This approach concerns the physiological (or biological) aspects of humans and how these affect our behaviour, thought patterns and emotional responses. In a way, this approach sees humans as complicated machines, with biological processes such as hormone release and brain activity governing our behaviour. Equally, the body and brain are altered by our experience of the world. Therefore, while much physiological research looks at how the body determines behaviour, there is also research that looks at how our experience shapes our brain development, and so on.

The **physiological approach** explores human behaviour and experience by looking at people as if they were biological machines.

Examples of the physiological approach

- The study by Maguire et al. is an example that uses the latest research tool – that of brain scans. Originally psychologists would study physiological processes using EEG (e.g. Dement and Kleitman) or they would analyse blood or urine samples. MRI scanners use no radioactivity and do not require an injection (unlike PET scans). Using this technique Maguire et al. were able to locate the specific brain region involved in human navigation processes.
- The study by Schachter and Singer shows that although we are often determined by our 'biology', there are many processes that interact with each other, and emotion is a perfect example. The research by Schachter showed that a physiological response needs a cognitive interpretation before it is labelled as a particular emotion.

Cross check

Maguire et al., page 48
Schachter and Singer, page 43

Alternative examples of the physiological approach are: Dement and Kleitman, page 46; Demattè et al., page 51.

Strengths of the physiological approach

- It involves direct observation (such as brain activity), so it is more scientific than a self-report, which is open to bias from the participant.
- It uses the experimental method, with scientific apparatus and controls to try to determine cause and effect.
- The use of recording devices (apparatus) provides consistent (reliable) measurement. For example, an ECG provides a reliable measure of heart rate.
- Human physiological functioning is the same in all cultures.

Expert tip

Link approaches with issues and debates. For example, link the physiological approach with the issue of reductionism and holism, or with determinism. It can also be linked with the cognitive approach, as in the studies by Schachter and Singer, and Piliavin.

Weaknesses of the physiological approach

- It is often reductionist – can we reduce complex intentions and emotions to a part of the brain/physiological processes?
- Findings often show associations (or correlation), but we cannot assume cause and effect.
- Apparatus used may provide false or misleading information – the data may be reliable but are not necessarily valid.
- Subjective (qualitative) data tend not to be used, but can be of equal importance.

Now test yourself

42 Using an example, describe the use of an electroencephalogram.

43 Describe the scientific apparatus used in the study by Maguire et al.

Answers on p.198

Tested

The social approach

Social psychologists look at the numerous complex issues that surround human interactions and human relationships. They look at how the *individual* behaves in relation to other people and also at how that behaviour can be modified by social contexts that both frame and direct the individual's actions and experiences. We like to think that we are true to ourselves in what we do and say, and that we only follow everyone else when we want to. However, we may be more susceptible to social influence than we think. We all play a variety of different roles in our lives: you might be, say, a woman, a student, a friend, and so on. All of these roles are played in relation to other people. The social approach would say we can only understand people in the context of how they operate in their interactions and perceptions of others.

The **social approach** is concerned with how humans interact with each other.

Examples of the social approach

- The study by Haney et al. shows how social roles are determined by others and situations. In the study, Zimbardo took a group of students, allocated them to be either prisoner or guard and, simply because of the role to which they were allocated and the situation they were in, they took on the role and often developed it to an extreme (such as the behaviour of the guard 'John Wayne').

Expert tip

Although the publication is by Haney, Banks and Zimbardo, and so it should be Haney et al., the lead researcher was Philip Zimbardo and so this is often known as the Zimbardo study.

- The study by Milgram is a good example of the extent to which many people have accepted the role of an authority figure in society and so obey on command. Just because they were told to, most of his participants gave electric shocks they thought were real to another person. That said, some of the participants did not continue, showing that the decision an individual makes can be independent of the situation they are in.

Alternative examples of the social approach are: Piliavin et al., page 25; Tajfel, page 28.

Cross check

Haney, Banks and Zimbardo, page 23
Milgram, page 20
Reductionism/holism, page 104

Strengths of the social approach

- We can see how our behaviour is determined by those around us and the society in which we interact (e.g. we can understand what processes are at play in group situations).
- We can discover how we are likely to behave in social situations. We follow a script we have learned from society about society.
- It tends to be a 'holist' approach (i.e. not reductionist), as it usually looks at different levels of explanation.

Expert tip

Link approaches with issues and debates. For example, link the social approach with the issue of individual and situational explanations.

Weaknesses of the social approach

- Social knowledge may become redundant as societies change – i.e. what is true now may not be true in the future.
- Social behaviour is necessarily culture bound. Therefore a study conducted in one culture may say little or nothing about any other culture.
- Because social behaviour is very complex, studying it is difficult in terms of controlling all the variables.
- Problems include distinguishing individual from situational influences, and ensuring that the social behaviour observed is ecologically valid.

Expert tip

Link the social approach with methods. Which method is best to study social behaviour: the laboratory (Milgram), the field (Piliavin et al.) or through a simulation (Haney et al.)?

Now test yourself Tested

44 Give an assumption of the social approach.
45 How does a script help us interact with other people in society?

Answers on p.198

The individual differences approach

This approach is concerned with the differences between people (rather than the things we might have in common), particularly in terms of personality and abnormality. Although we often make *generalisations* (page 97) about people, such as how people behave, think and feel – and sometimes these general statements are quite useful – they often ignore the *differences* between groups of people, and between individuals.

The **individual differences approach** acknowledges that not all people are the same and that there are differences in life experience, intelligence, etc.

One of the assumptions of this approach is that there are differences between the people of any group, in terms of their personal qualities, the ways in which they respond to situations, their behaviour and so on, and it is examining these differences that is most revealing. Research has often focused on trying to measure these differences, for example through the use of psychometric tests such as IQ tests or personality tests. The challenge for psychology is to identify the features that we *share* with other people and still acknowledge the *differences* between individuals.

Generalisations apply to most people for most of the time, but they do not apply to everyone all of the time. For example, some groups of people are much more aggressive than others: men are, on the whole, more aggressive than women, and army commandos are, on the whole, more aggressive than Buddhists. These are groups that have different levels and styles of aggression. Within those groups there will also be some individual differences. You might know some women who are very aggressive and some men who are non-aggressive.

Examples of the individual differences approach

- The study by Veale and Riley compared a sample of people with BDD (body dysmorphic disorder) with a control group who did not have BDD. While there were common behaviours among those with BDD, there were still individual differences in the type and extent of that behaviour.
- According to the Billington et al. study people can be generalised into systemisers or empathisers, but scores on each dimension can vary significantly from one individual to another.

Alternative examples of the individual differences approach are: Rosenhan, page 53; Thigpen and Cleckley, page 57.

Cross check

Veale and Riley, page 61
Billington et al., page 59

Strengths of the individual differences approach

- This approach underlines the differences between us and, arguably, takes a more *idiographic approach* to psychology (i.e. one that focuses on what makes each of us unique) rather than a *nomothetic approach* (i.e. one that focuses on the common features shared by human beings).
- This approach is interested in individual differences, not generalisations. For example, the humanistic perspective sees every person as a unique individual.
- If we look at what is abnormal, we can gain a very good insight into normality.

Weaknesses of the individual differences approach

- Research into individual differences might have limited generalisability and therefore might not be useful for much of the population.
- In looking at individual differences and abnormality, there is an assumption that there is such a thing as normality. However, this is difficult to define or recognise.
- It can be difficult for researchers to conduct research in cultures other than their own – to devise tasks that are not ethnocentric or biased towards their own culture in some way.

Expert tip

Know the strengths and weaknesses of the individual differences approach because they could appear in Paper 1 or Paper 2 examination questions. Know the four individual differences studies and then you can predict which studies are likely to appear in any question.

Expert tip

Link approaches with issues and debates. For example, link the individual differences approach with the issue of generalisation.

Now test yourself

Tested

46 Give an assumption of the individual differences approach.

47 Describe **one** core study from the individual differences approach that shows both generalisations and individual differences.

Answers on p.198

Perspectives in psychology

Revised

The behaviourist perspective

One of the main assumptions of the **behaviourist perspective** is that all behaviour is learned through experience. Another is that the subject matter of psychology should have standardised procedures, with an emphasis on the study

The **behaviourist perspective** focuses on observable behaviour rather than on mental concepts, and explains behaviour in terms of learning.

of observable behaviour that can be measured objectively, rather than focus on the mind or consciousness. There are three sub-strands of behaviourism:

- **Classical conditioning theory** was outlined by Pavlov following his observations of a dog salivating to the sound of a bell. Watson is said to be the first to classically condition a human. This was 'Little Albert', who was conditioned to be afraid of various objects, particularly a white rat.
- **Operant conditioning theory** is based on the principle that if the consequences of a behaviour are good, we are more likely to repeat that behaviour, whereas if the consequences of a behaviour are neutral (or negative), we are much less likely to repeat it.
- **Social learning theory** was outlined by Bandura who believed that humans also learn through observing other people's behaviour (and the consequences they receive for their actions).

According to the behaviourist perspective:

- All behaviour is learned through experience (and so nothing is inherited).
- Learning is through classical conditioning (Pavlov), operant conditioning (Skinner) and social learning theory/observational learning (Bandura).
- The learning environment (e.g. the classroom) is crucial. This is environmental determinism.
- It explains phobias and many mental illnesses. A range of behavioural therapies, such as desensitisation and cognitive-behavioural therapy, have been developed, and are used regularly.

Cross check

Bandura et al., page 31
Determinism, page 101
Nature/nurture, page 103

Example of the behaviourist perspective

- Bandura, like Skinner, is a behaviourist and so believes that all behaviour is learned and nothing is inherited. Watson (of 'Little Albert' fame) believed that a child at birth is a blank slate. Behaviourists believe that the environment is crucial (environmental determinism) and they are therefore on the nurture side of the nature/nurture debate. Bandura believed that all behaviour is learned and he chose to demonstrate in his study that aggression is learned.

Expert tip

Link perspectives with approaches, issues and debates. For example, link the behaviourist perspective with nature/nurture, determinism and reductionism.

Now test yourself Tested

48 Give an assumption of the behaviourist perspective, using examples.
49 Give a weakness of the behaviourist perspective.

Answers on p.198

The psychodynamic perspective

The **psychodynamic perspective** is based on the work of Freud, who distinguished between the conscious and unconscious mind. He proposed a 'tripartite' personality, giving three aspects of self:

- The **id** is what we are born with. It is the 'me, me, me and only me' instinct. It is the 'I want…' part of our personality.
- The **superego** is the part of personality we develop during the phallic stage when we learn to identify with the same-sex parent and internalise their moral code. There is a lot of conflict between the superego and the id – the 'I should' versus 'I want'.
- The **ego** is the part of the personality has the job of mediating between the id and the superego and trying to keep both aspects relatively 'happy' but also in check.

The **psychodynamic perspective** emphasises the role of the unconscious mind – the id, ego and superego – and the influence that childhood experiences have on our future lives.

Freud also outlined **ego-defence mechanisms** (such as repression and displacement) which are strategies that the ego deploys in order to try to minimise the psychological discomfort from the conflict generated between the superego and the id. On top of this, Freud developed a method of psychotherapy that he called psychoanalysis (literally 'analysis of the psyche'). This was based on an understanding of the mind through interpretive methods, introspection and clinical observations.

The psychodynamic perspective can be summarised as follows:

- It emphasises the roles of the unconscious mind: the id, ego and superego.
- Adult behaviour is determined through early childhood experiences and by ego defence mechanisms (repression, displacement, etc.).
- The *unconscious* (the psyche) can be understood through dreams and 'Freudian slips' – psychoanalysis.
- The theory of psycho-sexual development proposes stages (oral, anal, etc.) through childhood. Supporting evidence is the study of Little Hans.
- It explains the cause of many mental illnesses and consequent therapies.

Example of the psychodynamic perspective

- Freud believed in psychosexual stages (oral, anal, phallic, etc.) and that early childhood experiences determine personality. Little Hans was in the phallic stage and Oedipus complex and his phobia of horses was simply an example of how the Oedipus complex dominated his thoughts. The influence of the sub-conscious mind could also be seen in the 'giraffe episode'.

Cross check

Freud, page 34

Now test yourself Tested

50 Give a weakness of the psychodynamic perspective.
51 Summarise Freud's theory of psychosexual development.

Answers on p.198

Expert tip

Link perspectives with approaches, issues and debates. For example, link the psychodynamic perspective with nature/nurture, determinism and reductionism.

2.4 Issues and debates in psychology

What is an issue and what is a debate? An issue is simply a (single) topic for discussion whereas a debate is a topic for discussion with two opposing viewpoints. The use of children in psychological research is an *issue* to be discussed whereas the nature versus nurture *debate* has two opposing viewpoints. There are many issues and debates psychology. For the CIE syllabus these can be divided into the following categories:

Issues	Debates
Application to everyday life (usefulness)	Determinism and free will
Ethnocentric bias	Individual and situational explanations
Generalisations	Nature and nurture
Psychometrics	Reductionism and holism
The use of children in psychological research	
The use of animals in psychological research	

Expert tip

These issues and debates also apply to the A level options. Cross checks appear with each option.

What follows in this section is a definition and brief explanation of each issue and debate followed by an advantage/strength and then a disadvantage/weakness. Examples from core studies are given.

You need to know all these issues and debates because examination questions are asked about them in all three examination papers.

- Learn each issue/debate.
- Know at least two strengths (and examples to illustrate from one study for Papers 1 and 2 or a topic area for Paper 3).
- Know at least two weaknesses (and examples to illustrate from one study for Papers 1 and 2 or a topic area for Paper 3).
- Be able to comment on, or conclude, which side of an issue or debate you support.

Expert tip

Sometimes questions ask for three problems psychologists have when trying to conduct research. Know three problems in relation to all the issues in this sub-section.

Issues in psychology

Revised

Application to everyday life (usefulness)

This refers the contribution that psychology makes to human welfare. Miller (1969) argued that psychology should aim to improve people's quality of life, and that it should be useful to everyone. In psychology, some research is clearly much more useful than other research. Some research naturally lends itself to real-life applications and improvements, for example advice on the best way to raise and educate children, promote health, and diagnose and treat mental illnesses. Other research might appear less useful – though this does not mean that it will never be useful. It could just be that we cannot see the application yet.

Examples of useful and less useful psychological research

- The study by Mann et al. is one of the most useful psychological studies ever conducted. Police are trained to look for lying behaviour when conducting interviews but on what basis? This study suggests that this training is wrong. Instead, police should be trained to look for longer pauses and a decrease in eye blinking.
- The research by Maguire et al. is useful in that it tells us much more about the areas of the brain responsible for way-finding, namely the hippocampus. However, on a practical level a taxi driver knows the route from A to B and can drive that route. For a passenger that is what is important, not what is going on inside the brain of the driver.

Cross check

Mann et al., page 9
Maguire et al., page 48

Alternative examples of useful studies are: Loftus and Pickrell, page 11; Baron-Cohen et al., page 14; Held and Hein, page 17; Demattè et al., page 51; Nelson, page 39; Veale and Riley, page 61; Milgram, page 20.

Strengths of useful psychological research

- If research is useful, it can be of benefit to society. It can improve the world in which we live, e.g. in understanding crime, mental illness and how students can learn more effectively.
- It helps us to understand social behaviour, our interactions with others, obedience, etc.
- If research is useful, it enhances the value and status of psychology as a subject.

Problems when trying to conduct useful psychological research

- A study must be ethical – participants should give informed consent and not be deceived. But a study may need to be unethical to be truly useful, such as the Milgram study.
- A study should be ecologically valid. Studies conducted in a laboratory may not be useful as they are low in ecological validity. Studies involving tasks that are not true to real life may be less useful.

- A study should use a representative sample (not too small or restricted to males or students) and be generalisable. Useful research should apply worldwide so there is no ethnocentrism.
- A study should not be reductionist; it should not only apply in isolation from other behaviours but in various contexts.

Expert tip

Is a study useful or not? This is sometimes difficult to decide and it may be a matter of opinion. Your opinion. Which studies do *you* think are useful and which studies do *you* think are less useful?

Now test yourself

Tested

52 What is good about useful research? Give **three** reasons.

53 Psychologists want their research to be useful. Outline **two** methodological problems psychologists should address if they want their research to be useful.

Answers on p.198

Ethnocentric bias

Specifically, ethnocentrism means being 'nation-centred', but psychologists often take it to refer to much smaller social groupings. Thus, it refers to the belief that our own viewpoint, or the viewpoint of people like us, is superior to that of others, particularly people who are different in some way. The core study by Tajfel (1970) specifically looks at aspects of ethnocentrism such as in-group favouritism and out-group discrimination. We might show in-group favouritism to our own group and show out-group discrimination to those who are not in the same group. This often leads us to believe that our ethnic group, nation, religion, or football team is superior to all others.

Example of ethnocentric psychological research

- The study by Tajfel on boys showed that they favoured members of the in-group and discriminated against members of the out-group by choosing the maximum difference option, and so they behaved in an ethnocentric way.

Cross check

Tajfel, page 28

There is much debate about what ethnocentrism actually is. Some people argue that conducting a study in just one country and not any other is automatically being ethnocentric. But each study has a target population and so the findings apply to that population only. It would be wrong, therefore, to *assume* that what applies in one country also applies to another without actually testing it. It is ethnocentric for a researcher to assume that what is found in one country is more important than what might be found in another.

Reasons for studying ethnocentrism

- It allows us to discover that not all cultures are the same; to discover the diversity of behaviour and experience that people all over the world have.
- It might allow us to discover the causes of prejudice; to realise that our values are not the only ones possible. It educates us not to make value judgments.
- It might allow us to discover which behaviours are inherited and which behaviours are learned through conducting cross-cultural studies.

Problems when studying ethnocentrism

- The sample in a study may be very small or representative of just one culture, and so the findings cannot be generalised to all countries/cultures.
- Many cultures have different philosophies and so cannot be compared. Some cultures are based on cooperation, others on conflict.

- Researchers might speak a different language from participants, so there might be problems in the giving of instructions and the understanding of tasks. There might be misinterpretation of behaviour by the experimenters.

Now test yourself Tested

54 What does the term ethnocentrism mean specifically?
55 According to Tajfel, what are the minimum conditions for creating in-group favouritism and out-group discrimination?

Answers on p.198

Generalisations

One of the aims of psychology is to apply the findings of research to people other than those who participated in the research. This is known as **generalisation**. Generalisations are more likely with physiological studies (because human biology is the same for all), whereas they are less likely with social studies where society has an influence on us. Dement and Kleitman used a very small number of participants in their study on sleep and dreaming, but this is not a weakness of the study because sleeping is something that every human does and findings from the study can be generalised. How do people behave in a restaurant? Shank and Abelson (1973) argued that we all have a very similar mental 'script' of how we behave in a restaurant, so wherever we are in the world we follow the same script of entering, sitting, ordering, eating, paying and leaving. We can generalise this behaviour.

A **generalisation** is when something applies to most people most of the time.

Examples of generalisations in psychological research

- The study by Billington et al. categorises everyone's cognitive style into systemisers or empathisers. Depending on the EQ and SQ-R score people can be placed into five types and there may be individual differences. However, there is the generalisation that every person can be categorised in these ways.
- A generalisation is something that applies to most people most of the time. But some things might apply to everyone all the time. What about the study by Schachter and Singer who claim that emotion results from physiological arousal and cognitive (or psychological) interpretation. Is this something that really does apply to everyone?

Cross check

Billington et al., page 59
Schachter and Singer, page 43

Alternative examples of generalisations in psychological research are: Thigpen and Cleckley, page 57; Freud, page 34; Piliavin et al., page 25; Langlois et al., page 36.

Expert tip

The issue of generalisations should always be considered in relation to the issue of individual differences.

Advantages of making generalisations

- This approach underlines the similarities between us and, arguably, takes a **nomothetic approach** to psychology (i.e. one that focuses on the common features shared by human beings) rather than an **idiographic approach** (i.e. focusing on what makes each of us unique).
- It means we can predict *how* people are likely to behave in a particular situation.
- If research is true of a large number of people in a large number of situations, then research can actually be useful to a large number of people.
- It can simplify complex behaviour.
- It helps most people to interact successfully in society – following 'scripts'.

Disadvantages of making generalisations

- The sample size of the original study might be very small or not very representative (i.e. the sample is restricted in some way).
- The findings of studies performed in one country cannot automatically be generalised to all countries. This would be ethnocentric.
- A study might be laboratory-based and so might not apply to a real-life situation. The study might involve some artificial task and so might not apply to real-life behaviour.
- Generalising assumes a nomothetic approach, i.e. it is concerned with rules and predictability, and so disregards important individual differences.

Now test yourself

56 What is a generalisation?

57 What generalisation can be made from the study by Schachter and Singer?

Answers on pp.198–199

Tested

Psychometrics

Psychometrics literally means measurement of the mind. More formally it is the science of psychological assessment. The emphasis is on questionnaires and tests mainly of intelligence and personality. The first intelligence test was the Stanford-Binet, and the tests devised by Wechsler are very popular. There are many tests used in education (page 129) for measuring and assessing specific abilities such as verbal reasoning.

Psychologists develop tests to assess personality or specifically for use in organisations and employment (page 169). Tests can also be quite specialised and assess things such as cognitive style or mirror-gazing beliefs. The fundamental aim is to ensure that any psychometric test is both valid (page 86) and reliable (page 82). Psychometric tests are standardised, meaning that anyone taking a test can be compared with a sample of results already obtained. For example, if you take an IQ test we know that the score you get can be placed on the same scale as everyone else, with the average score of 100.

Psychometrics is the scientific study of psychological assessment.

Examples of psychometric measures

- Thigpen and Cleckley used an intelligence test, the Wechsler-Bellevue intelligence scale, to test the IQs of Eve White and Eve Black. The average intelligence score is 100, and both were slightly above average.
- A study by Golan et al. (2006) extended the 'eyes test' and looked at 'reading the mind in the voice' (this study is not on the syllabus). The abstract to the study states: 'Results show the revised task has good reliability and validity, is harder, and is more sensitive in distinguishing the AS/HFA group from controls. Verbal IQ was positively correlated.' Not only was there a check on the reliability and validity of this psychometric measure, but verbal IQ was also used, so this is a perfect example.

Cross check

Thigpen and Cleckley, page 57

Alternative examples of psychometric measures are: Veale and Riley, page 61; Billington et al., page 59; Baron-Cohen et al., page 14.

Advantages of using psychometric measures

- The use of standardised measures is objective/scientific.
- They allow comparisons/generalisations to be made with others on a standardised scale.
- Standardised tests are said to be reliable and valid.

Disadvantages of psychometric measures

- The measure might not be valid. What does an intelligence test actually measure?
- Not all people will be familiar with the tests or test items.
- People often generalise and make ethnocentric assumptions based on test results.

Expert tip

Know the strengths and weaknesses of psychometric testing because they could appear in Paper 1 or Paper 2 examination questions.

- Once labelled by a test it can be difficult to remove that label.
- Often tests assume that people do not change. People do.

Now test yourself Tested

58 Give **two** definitions of the term psychometrics.

59 Identify **two** psychometric tests used in the study by Thigpen and Cleckley and describe the findings from both these tests.

Answers on p.199

The use of children in psychological research

Some people treat children as miniature adults, but in reality they are very different. The question is, how much we can generalise from children to adults. Piaget suggested that children think differently from adults, while Freud would place a child in a particular stage of psychosexual development.

If children are used in any study there are advantages and disadvantages in studying them, such as whether they understand the instructions and whether the researcher understands what the child really means by an answer, rather than making an assumption. There are also ethical problems, because a child under 16 years can never give full informed consent. Longitudinal studies with children allow us to see how they grow, develop and change.

Examples of studies using children

- Nelson was interested not in how children develop but in the understanding of morality that young children have. Before her, Piaget suggested there were distinct stages in the levels of reasoning a child has. Nelson questioned the methodology Piaget used, suggesting that young children can understand moral reasoning at a much younger age than Piaget thought.
- Freud was interested in the psychosexual development of children and believed that they progress through a number of fixed stages (oral, anal, etc). However, Freud had limited evidence on which to base his theory and even his study of Little Hans was done through the father.

Cross check

Nelson, page 39
Freud, page 34

Alternative examples of studies using children are: Bandura et al., page 31; Tajfel, page 28; Langlois et al., page 36.

Advantages of studying children

- It is important to study children because they represent the most important and formative period of human development. What happens in early life can determine many things in adult life.
- By understanding children's thoughts and behaviour, it might help us to understand adult thoughts and behaviour.
- In some ways, children are better participants than adults as they are naive and can be more open and truthful.

Expert tip

Know the strengths and weaknesses of the use of children in psychological studies. Studies using children as participants come from many different approaches.

Disadvantages when studying children

- Children might not understand the task or the complex language of an experimenter.
- An experimenter might misinterpret what a child says or how the child behaves.
- Children under 16 years cannot give informed consent and, if debriefed, they might be too young to understand. Children might be more prone to harm or longer-term effects.

Now test yourself

60 Give **three** reasons why we should study children.

61 Why is the study by Freud a study of development?

Answers on p.199

Tested

- Children might be more prone to demand characteristics – i.e. wanting to please the researcher.
- Studies of child *development* need to be longitudinal.

The use of animals in psychological research

Some people argue that animals are no different from humans; they just don't have the influence of society and so we can study much of their behaviour unimpeded. For example, the brain structures involved in eating behaviour are located in the same brain region in many higher-species animals as they are in humans. However, some people argue that animals are different and that what we know about animals cannot be generalised to humans. As always, some things can be generalised and some things cannot. There is also the question of how we can best study animals: in a laboratory (e.g. Pavlov and Skinner) or in a natural environment?

Examples of studies using animals

- The study by Held and Hein raised kittens in deprived environments and then placed them in apparatus (the kitten carousel) to test their paw–eye coordination. This study was useful because we now know that learning experiences and interaction with an environment are essential to normal development.
- The work by Pavlov on dogs showed us that animals can be classically conditioned. Later this was extended to humans (by Watson). Skinner also used animals to demonstrate that if a behaviour is rewarded it is likely to be repeated.

There is no other animal research in the AS core studies but, depending on your chosen option, there might be for A level.

Cross check

Held and Hein, page 17
Behaviourism, page 92
Education, page 118
Health, page 138
Environment, page 146

Advantages of studying animals

- Animal research gives us an understanding of basic learning and motivational systems.
- Some people argue that it is unethical to do certain research on humans but it is acceptable on animals. Ethical guidelines for research on animals do exist and prevent harm.
- It is easier to do longitudinal studies on animals because their life cycle is shorter than in humans.
- In some ways, animals (depending on the study) are better participants, as they are naive and do not respond to demand characteristics.
- Animals are 'simpler' so are easier to study.

Expert tip

Although there can be no Paper 2 questions specifically on animal studies, there can be questions comparing the behaviour of animals with the behaviour of humans.

Disadvantages when studying animals

- We can only observe the way animals behave. We cannot question them.
- The behaviour of animals is more biologically determined; humans are more influenced by culture and society (or so we think).
- As animals cannot give consent or have the right to withdraw we must take special precautions to protect them.
- We can only do relatively simple experiments on animals because their cognitive abilities are restricted.

Can we generalise from animals to humans?

There are some instances and behaviours that we can generalise. For example, we know how motivation centres with regard to hunger and thirst work; we know animals become stressed in crowded conditions just like humans. We learn about human navigation by studying how animals way-find. On the other hand, the behaviour of animals is more biologically determined; humans are more capable of adaptation and adjustment to their environment.

Now test yourself

Tested

62 Should animals be studied in a laboratory or in the natural environment? Answer in relation to controls and ecological validity.

63 Can we generalise from animals to humans?

Answers on p.199

Expert tip

There is only one animal study on the AS syllabus (although the study of animals by Pavlov and Skinner is relevant to behaviourism and the Bandura study). If you take certain A level options then you will come across this issue again.

Debates in psychology

Revised

Determinism and free will

Determinism represents the view that all behaviours and mental acts (thoughts, judgements, decisions) are determined by factors out of our control. **Free will** represents the view that our behaviours and mental acts all come about as a result of our own choices and volition, i.e. we can exercise our own free will.

We have biological determinism – our genetics or our hormones cause us to behave in certain ways – and environmental determinism, which means the environment in which we live, our education and our work cause us to behave in certain ways. There is also climatological determinism – the view that the climate or weather determines our behaviour. Architectural determinism is the view that architecture determines the way that we behave. For example, the design of a gambling casino (high or low ceiling) or shopping mall can have a significant effect on our behaviour inside the building.

Determinism is at the opposite end of the scale from free will, with possibilism and probabilism in between. Things are not so black and white as 'hard determinism' would have us believe. There is 'soft determinism', which says that, although as humans we do have choices to make and can exercise free will, these choices are often constrained (or determined) by factors. Indeed, some choices are more likely than others, and this is determined by, say, previous experiences.

Determinism is the view that we have no (or very little) control over our behaviour or our destiny, but are controlled by factors such as our biology or genetics, or by the environment.

Free will is the view that we have a choice over what we do and the ways in which we behave.

Examples of studies relating to the determinism and free will debate

- Dement and Kleitman studied sleep and dreaming. Sleep is a biological process and so it is biological determinism. We can make the choice to stay awake, but at some point we need to sleep. We cannot choose whether we enter REM or NREM sleep either and if we are deprived of either we suffer. REM rebound exists because we cannot do without it.
- The study by Piliavin et al. might seem to be a strange choice for a determinism and free will debate, but it is appropriate. Piliavin et al. suggest the model of arousal for emergency situations. If we are aroused we are motivated to reduce it. We reduce it by weighing up the costs and the benefits. This might seem like a free choice. We weigh up the pros and cons and we make a decision. But is this truly free or is our choice already determined by what we have learned from society, or from our parents, employers, teachers and other significant people in our lives.

Cross check

Dement and Kleitman, page 46

Piliavin et al., page 25

Alternative examples of studies relating to the determinism and free-will debate are: Mann et al., page 9; Bandura et al., page 31; Freud, page 34; Baron-Cohen et al., page 14; Langlois et al., page 36; and those linked to the physiological approach, page 89, behaviourism, page 92 and the psychodynamic perspective, page 93.

Expert tip

For the debates you only need to know two strengths and two weaknesses.

Strengths of determinism

- If we can establish cause and effect (X causes Y) it makes the world more understandable and predictable. This suggests that it might be worthwhile trying to change certain things (e.g. education systems) because it could benefit everyone.
- Determinism is the purpose and goal of science: to explain the causes of things (of behaviour, in the case of psychology). This makes the subject of psychology more acceptable to society, with its explanations, scientific basis and objectivity.

Weaknesses of determinism

- It does not allow (especially in *hard* determinism) for free will. A hard determinist would say that we *think* we have choice, but free will is just an illusion.
- It is often reductionist. Determinism can never fully explain behaviour because behaviour might be far too complex.

Now test yourself Tested

64 **(a)** Give **one** example of environmental determinism.
(b) Give **one** example of biological determinism.

65 Free will is an illusion. To what extent do you agree with this statement?

Answers on p.199

Individual and situational explanations

Individual and situational explanations refer to the way that we describe the cause of a behaviour as being due to something in that person (**individual** or **dispositional**) or as a response to the situation that they are in (**situational**).

This is another debate that runs through psychology. An individual (dispositional) explanation for an event will look to some feature or characteristic in the person themselves, whereas a situational explanation will look at the wider context – the social group, the environment or even other people influencing our behaviour.

Examples of studies with individual and situational explanations

- The classic example is the Milgram study. Many participants continued to 450 volts because of the *situation* they were in. It was too powerful for them to ignore so they obeyed. However, some participants stopped before 450 volts because their *individuality* allowed them to refuse to obey the demands of the authority figure and the situation they were in.
- In the study by Haney, Banks and Zimbardo the aim was to test the dispositional hypothesis that it is some feature of a prisoner that causes prisons to be 'bad' places. By the end of the study Zimbardo concluded that the dispositional hypothesis was wrong, that 'good' students behaved 'badly' (i.e. those who were guards) because the *situation* in which they found themselves determined how they should behave.

Cross check

Milgram, page 20
Haney, Banks and Zimbardo, page 23

Alternative examples of studies with individual and situational explanations are: Rosenhan, page 53; Schachter and Singer, page 43.

Now test yourself Tested

66 What is meant by a 'dispositional' explanation of behaviour?

67 Name **three** studies where the situation participants were in determined their behaviour.

Answers on p.199

Strengths of studying individual and situational explanations

- If we can discover which behaviours are individually determined and which are situationally determined, such findings may be useful for society.
- Discovering that behaviour may involve a complex interaction between individual and situational factors opens up new directions for further study.
- Reminding ourselves of the power of the situation can help prevent us from blaming people for their behaviour.

Problems when studying individual and situational explanations

- It can be difficult to separate the effects of a situation from the disposition of a participant.
- How can situations be investigated? If investigated in a laboratory there is low ecological validity; if investigated in a natural setting the situation may be difficult to control.
- Rather than individual or situational factors being exclusive alternatives, there may be a complex interaction between the two.
- By investigating the power of the situation, we might expose participants to distressing or harmful situations. There are ethical problems.

Nature and nurture

This debate focuses on whether particular behaviours are innate (inborn or genetically determined – i.e. **nature**) or whether they are acquired through experience and the influence of the environment – **nurture**). In the past psychologists would support one extreme or the other and although there are some who still subscribe to such an extremist view, the 'modern' version considers what percentage is inherited and what is learned.

> **Nature** in this sense refers to the part of us that is inherited and genetic, as distinct from **nurture**, which refers to all influences after our birth (i.e. experience).

Examples of studies relating to the nature/nurture debate

- The core study by Bandura et al. supports the behaviourists' belief that all behaviour is learned (i.e. nurture). Bandura proposed social learning theory to explain how children learn from adults. The learning environment is crucial for the child. If there is aggression in an environment, a child will observe and copy it, whereas if there is no aggression, then a child cannot see it and so cannot imitate it. This is environmental determinism.
- Is perception learned or is it inherited? Do we see the world as it is when we open our eyes or do we have to learn to perceive the world? Held and Hein investigated one small part of this question by allowing kittens different perceptual experiences, with some kittens reared in a 'normal' environment and some in a visually 'restricted' environment. The conclusion was that kittens need to learn from the environment in order to develop normal perceptual abilities.

Cross check

Bandura et al., page 31
Held and Hein, page 17

Alternative examples of studies relating to the nature/nurture debate are: Demattè et al., page 51; Billington et al., page 59; Baron-Cohen et al., page 14; Langlois et al., page 36.

Expert tip

Nurture can be linked to the behaviourist perspective, while both nature and nurture link to reductionism. Both nature and nurture views of humans are determinist, as neither gives scope for free will.

Strengths of studying nature and nurture

- The distinction can help us identify which behaviours are inherited or learned, or allow us to consider the relative contributions of inheritance and learning.

- It can be valuable to discover that some behaviours are due to nature and not to inappropriate upbringing by parents.

Problems when studying nature and nurture

- It is too simplistic to divide explanations into either nature or nurture, as the two often combine in complex ways to influence behaviour.
- Discovering that a particular behaviour or capacity (e.g. intelligence) is inherited might lead to the assumption that much more behaviour is inherited, while failing to consider the effects of the environment. This could encourage eugenics.

Now test yourself

Tested

68 Why are both the nature and nurture arguments deterministic?
69 Why are both the nature and nurture arguments reductionist?

Answers on p.199

Reductionism and holism

Reductionism is the view that complex behaviour can be explained by simple principles; that we can break something down into its component parts and study each more effectively. There is nothing wrong in doing this, but if we break something down into parts, we need to be able to put all the parts back together again. If we do not, we may have an explanation that is too simplistic, exists in isolation and ignores other important aspects or factors that interact to form the whole. A holistic view looks at a person as a whole, or at least looks at a complex of factors that together might explain a particular behaviour. It is often said that the whole is greater than the sum of the parts.

Reductionism is the process of explaining complex psychological phenomena by reducing them to their component parts. This is the opposite of **holism**, where the total is more than the sum of the parts.

Examples of studies relating to the reductionism/holism debate

- The aim of the study by Maguire et al. was to identify which specific part of the brain was responsible for processing information regarding way-finding and cognitive maps. The aim of the study was to be reductionist and the conclusion was that the hippocampus (in the mid-brain) is the brain structure responsible.
- Demattè et al. controlled many extraneous variables and isolated just one (the IV) which was smell, because this is the usual process for an experiment using the scientific method. The result showed the effect of unpleasant smells on the perception of attractiveness and in this respect the experiment was successful. However, the study is reductionist. In the real world how many other variables are present when judging attractiveness? In the real world there is a vast range of different sensory information being processed (in addition to other smells), which might interact with information about smell and result in a different interpretation by a person.

An alternative example of a study relating to the reductionism/holism debate is: Billington et al., page 59.

Cross check

Maguire et al., page 48
Demattè et al., page 51

Expert tip

If you know the strengths and weaknesses of being reductionist, then you also know the weaknesses and strengths of being holist.

Strengths of reductionism

- It helps us to understand the world, because a fundamental way of understanding is to analyse, break things down into component parts, test them and then build them back up again. This is important in studying the world in a scientific way.
- In theory it is easier to study one component rather than several interacting components. If one component is isolated and others are controlled then the study is more objective and scientifically acceptable.

Weaknesses of reductionism

- The components may be difficult to isolate and so manipulate. If a study looks at an isolated behaviour in a laboratory, then it may lack ecological validity.
- If a factor is studied in isolation, this may not give a proper, valid and full account of a behaviour. A behaviour might not be meaningful if it is studied in isolation from the wider social context.

Now test yourself

Tested

70 Outline what is meant by the reductionism/holism debate in psychology.
71 Give **two** arguments supporting reductionism.

Answers on p.199

3 AS Examination Guidance/ Questions and Answers

3.1 AS examination guidance

The AS examination is divided into two papers: Core Studies 1 and Core Studies 2.

Core Studies 1

This paper lasts for 90 minutes and consists of 'short-answer questions' (Section A) and 'structured-response questions' (Section B).

Section A

This section consists of 15 compulsory short-answer questions accounting for 60 marks. Section A examines knowledge and understanding of the details within the core studies themselves. Questions can also be asked about methods, approaches and perspectives, and issues and debates as they apply to each core study.

Exam-style question

Bandura et al. studied aggression.
(a) Describe *one* hypothesis that was proposed. [2]
(b) To what extent did the findings support this hypothesis? [2]

Typical mistake

Bandura proposed four hypotheses. There is no point in writing all four, even though you might know them. You will still only score the two available marks.

Section B

This section consists of two compulsory structured essays accounting for 20 marks, or 10 marks per question. Section B focuses exclusively on your ability to make evaluative points about the studies in relation to methods, approaches and perspectives, and debates and issues. Although both structured essay questions are compulsory there is an element of choice. Each question will have three named core studies from which you choose one study on which to base your answer.

Expert tip

You should know the strengths and weaknesses of every method and methodological issue.

Exam-style question

Evaluate *one* of the studies listed below in terms of the extent to which it supports an individual explanation. [10]

Milgram (obedience)

Haney, Banks and Zimbardo (prison simulation)

Rosenhan (sane in insane places)

Typical mistake

Do not answer the question in relation to all three studies. You will only be marked in relation to one of them and the other two will be ignored. It simply wastes your valuable writing time.

Expert tip

You cannot predict which core studies will be on this examination. You have to cover and revise everything! This is because 15 out of the 20 studies will be examined in Section A and 6 of the 20 studies will appear in Section B.

Core Studies 2

This paper consists of structured essay questions and is assessed by a 90-minute examination. The examination paper consists of three parts:

- Section A – one compulsory **methodology** question (25 marks or 36%) *related to a named core study.*
- Section A – one compulsory **approaches and perspectives, and issues and debates** question (25 marks or 36%) *related to a named core study.*
- Section B – a choice of two questions where one question is chosen and answered (20 marks or 28%). Both questions focus on your ability to make descriptive and evaluative points about **approaches and perspectives, and issues and debates** in *relation to a number of studies.*

Expert tip

You cannot predict which methods, approaches and perspectives, and issues and debates will be in this examination. You have to cover and revise everything!

Expert tip

For each question you should write as much as you can. In 15 minutes you should be able to write one side of A4 examination paper if you have average-size writing. This equates to two sides for each question and six sides in total.

Section A: Methodology question in relation to a named core study

A brief description of a core study will be presented and this will be followed by a suggested alternative way of conducting the same study. This alternative could be a different method altogether or it could be a different type of the same method, such as a field experiment rather than a laboratory experiment, or it could be a different type of observation. The question has three parts.

Part (a) will ask you for a description of the method (or methodological issue) and how it was used in the named core study. This question part usually carries 5 marks.

Part (b) will ask you to design an alternative study based on the suggestion made in the opening sentences of the question. This means that you must know about the different methods and the associated methodological issues. You are usually asked to describe how this study could be conducted, and how your design can be implemented. This is a perfect question for those of you who can think. However, because you are proposing your own ideas there is the temptation to write too much!

Typical mistake

If a question asks you to consider a particular method when designing your own study, then you must not suggest a different method, or describe a study done by someone else.

Part (c) will ask you to evaluate your suggested design from part (b). This could be an evaluation of the **methodology** itself (such as problems with a field experiment or problems with a naturalistic observation); it could be an evaluation of the **practical problems** that may arise when carrying out your suggested study (such as the inability to observe behaviour if other people get in the way); or it could be a consideration of the **ethical problems** that might arise when conducting the study. A question will usually ask for two of these variations.

Expert tip

Ethical and practical problems are *methodological* problems so in an examination you can write about any two (or all three) and not be penalised.

Exam-style question

The study by Bandura et al. was an observation of aggression in a laboratory. An alternative way to conduct this investigation would be to observe the aggression of the children when they went back to the nursery school and went out at break time to play.

(a) Describe controlled observation as used in the Bandura et al. study. [5]

(b) Design an alternative study to observe aggression in a playground and describe how it could be conducted. [10]

(c) Evaluate this alternative way of observing aggression in terms of methodological and practical terms. [10]

Section A: Approaches and perspectives, and issues and debates question in relation to a named core study

This question will introduce a core study, providing sufficient information in the introduction so you know what the question is focusing on.

Part (a) will ask for a definition of the approach, perspective, issue or debate on which the question focuses.

Expert tip

Do not learn a textbook definition for every possible approach, perspective, issue or debate. It is much better to write your own answer, showing that you *understand* the term, rather than writing a definition that you have learned but might not understand.

Part (b) will ask you to relate some part of the named core study to the 'issue' depending on what the 'issue' is. For example, you might be asked to describe a finding from the study.

Expert tip

Write enough to impress the examiner, but do not waste valuable time.

Part (c) is where you have to show your evaluative skills (and in part (d) too). In this question part you have to discuss strengths and weaknesses (or similarities and differences) and you might even have to compare and contrast in relation to the 'issue' in question. The question always asks for strengths and weaknesses in *plural*, so you must include two strengths and two weaknesses in your answer. Check the approaches and perspectives, and issues and debates chapter for details.

Typical mistake

If a question asks for 'strengths and weaknesses', then giving one strength and one weakness, two strengths and no weaknesses or even two weaknesses and no strengths will cost you valuable marks. Writing more than the optimal two strengths and two weaknesses wastes time.

When discussing strengths and weaknesses of a study, give a strength and then say how it relates to the named study. Give another strength and say how this relates to the named study. Then repeat the same for the weaknesses. Crucially, don't make this a *list* of four points. If question asks for a *discussion*, make it a discussion rather than just a list.

A question might ask you to compare and contrast. Generally a comparison is a similarity and a contrast is a difference.

Part (d) asks you to think in a different direction from that of part (c). For example if part (c) concerns the **approach** of the study, part (d) might ask you for the strengths and weaknesses of the **method**. Alternatively, if part (c) asks about one issue, part (d) might ask you about the advantages and disadvantages of a *different* issue. Finally, you might be asked to extend what you wrote in part (c) and be asked to 'discuss the extent to which' in relating how the named study can be applied to an issue.

Typical mistake

Do what the question asks you to do. Do not write about what you want the question to be.

Exam-style question

The study by Maguire et al. investigated the brain activity of taxi drivers using scientific equipment.

(a) What is meant by 'scientific equipment'? [2]

(b) Describe *one* piece of scientific equipment used in the study by Maguire et al. [3]

(c) Discuss the strengths and weaknesses of using scientific equipment in psychological studies such as the one by Maguire et al. [10]

(d) Discuss the extent to which the findings from the scientific equipment of Maguire et al.'s study can be usefully applied in psychology. [10]

Section B: Approaches and perspectives, and issues and debates question in relation a number of named core studies

You have a choice of two questions, so which approach, perspective, issue or debate question do you choose?

Typical mistake

Do not choose the question with your favourite study (or studies) if you cannot answer all parts of the question.

Part (a), just like part (a) for question 2, will be a 'what is meant by' question on the approach, perspective, issue or debate on which the question focuses.

Expert tip

You should know the strengths and weaknesses of every approach and perspective, and issue and debate.

Part (b) asks you to describe how each of the three studies applies to the 'issue' of the question. It is also worth noting that if the question is about an approach (e.g. cognitive or physiological psychology) then of the four studies on the syllabus only three will appear in a part (b) or part (c) question.

Typical mistake

It is very tempting to write all you know about a particular study. Don't be tempted to do this. There is no point in writing a whole page on one study if only 3 marks are available.

Part (c) generally asks for the problems psychologists might have when they investigate the 'issue' of the question, but the question might also ask about the advantages. You need a description of each point that shows you understand what you are writing. A sentence quoted from a book doesn't always show that you understand. Then you need to relate the point to the study. Don't just give a point and then write 'e.g. Milgram'.

Typical mistake

Don't ruin a brilliant answer by naming a study to support the point you are making that is not one of the named three.

Exam-style question

(a) Outline what is meant by the term 'cognitive psychology'. [2]

Using the following studies, answer the questions below:

Mann et al. (lying)
Loftus and Pickrell (false memories)
Baron-Cohen et al. (eyes test)

(b) Describe how data were collected in each of these studies. [9]

(c) What problems might psychologists have when they investigate cognitive psychology? [9]

Expert tip

You should know the strengths and weaknesses of every approach and perspective, and issue and debate.

3.2 AS questions and answers

This section contains exam-style questions followed by example answers. The answers are followed by expert comments (shown by the icon ⓔ) that indicate where credit is due. In the weaker answers, they also point out areas for improvement, specific problems and common errors such as lack of clarity, weak or non-existent development, irrelevance, misinterpretation of the question and mistaken meanings of terms.

Core Studies 1

Section A: short-answer questions

Question 1

The study by Mann et al. (lying) had two observers coding eight behaviours.
(a) Describe *one* behaviour that was coded. [2]
(b) Describe inter-rater reliability and say how it was checked in this study. [2]

ⓔ *(a) There are eight possible answers to part (a), which are gaze aversion, blinking, head movements, self-manipulations, illustrators, hand/finger movements, speech disturbances and pauses. Naming (or* identifying*) one of these eight would score 1 mark. However, the question asks for a* description *(which means providing more detail) so some elaboration of what one of the behaviours actually means is required. Part (b) has two parts and so for 2 marks a relatively brief answer can be given. Crucially, both parts of the question must be answered.*

Answer A

(a) One behaviour was gaze aversion.

ⓔ *This is a correct answer and would score 1 mark out 2 for correctly identifying one of the behaviours. It would not score a second mark because there is no explanation or elaboration to show an understanding of what gaze aversion is.*

(b) Inter-rater reliability is when we can reliably say that the two observers agree about whether a behaviour has happened and, like in this study, the numbers are correlated.

ⓔ *Both parts of this question are answered here, for 2 marks. Inter-rater reliability is having two (or more) people observe the same behaviour and it was checked in this study by correlating the numbers from the two observers. The answer could be more detailed but, importantly, both parts are addressed.*

Answer B

(a) One behaviour was gaze aversion, which was whether the suspect looked directly at the interviewer (when telling the truth) or whether they averted their gaze and could not look them directly in the eye (when telling a lie).

ⓔ *This is a correct answer that would score 2 marks out of 2. It correctly identifies gaze aversion and has earned the second mark by going on to say what gaze aversion is and how it is used by a person telling the truth or a lie.*

(b) Inter-rater reliability is when the accuracy observations by one observer are checked against the observations of a second independent observer to see how much they agree. This is done to avoid bias by one observer and to check that nothing has been missed. In this study it was checked by the first observer coding (or observing) all 65 video clips and then a second observer coding a sample of 36 clips. When the results were correlated on a scale from 0 to 1 and a Pearson statistical test applied the results were found to be excellent for most behaviours. For example, illustrators were 0.99 and speech disturbances were 0.97. Not quite so good was 'pauses' at only 0.55. Overall this means that the first observer 'got it right' and using inter-rater reliability proves it.

ⓔ *Although in many ways this is an impressive answer because it answers both parts of the question in great detail and it would score full marks (2 out of 2), there are some negatives about it. The answer is too long! It can only be awarded 2 marks however much detail there is and to waste time giving too much information is not good examination technique because there may not be enough time to answer all the questions.*

Expert tip

Spend an appropriate amount of time on each question. There is no point in writing too much on one question and scoring full marks if there is no time to answer another question and scoring no marks.

Question 2

Thigpen and Cleckley used a number of tests to assess Eve.
(a) Identify *two* psychometric tests used on Eve. [2]
(b) *Give one* advantage of using psychometric tests in psychological studies. [2]

In part (a) the examiner is looking for the correct identification of two psychometric tests in this question. 'Identify' means to simply say what something is without an outline or description of it, or an explanation of what it means. The psychometric tests used on Eve were an IQ test and a memory test. Giving details of these tests is not required in this particular question. The Rorschach test and 'drawings of human figures' are psychological tests, but they are not psychometric. The EEG recordings taken are physiological measures and are not psychometric.

In part (b) The examiner is looking for one advantage of a psychometric test and this should be quite easy because in your preparation for Paper 2 you should know at least two advantages and disadvantages of psychometric tests.

Answer A

(a) The two psychometric tests used on Eve in the study of multiple personality disorder by Thigpen and Cleckley were the EEG and the IQ tests.

This scores 1 mark only for the correct identification of the IQ test. The EEG test is incorrect. The answer also repeats the question as part of the answer. There is no requirement to do this and it does not add anything to the answer.

Expert tip

Why waste time writing out a question? To do so is poor examination technique.

(b) One advantage of using psychometric tests in psychological studies is that they are standardised. This means that they can be done by anyone anywhere and the score achieved can be placed on a scale and compared with everyone else. For example, in this study Eve White scored an IQ of 110 which places her just above average on a normal distribution curve where 100 is the central and average score. A second advantage of psychometric tests is that they are reliable and valid. Validity means that the test is measuring what it claims and this is known because it will have been compared with an existing IQ test, although I can't remember what this type of validity is called. It is also reliable because the authors of it will have done a test–retest and a split-half test and found that the test was reliable.

This answer also repeats the question. Two advantages are then given when the question only requires one. The whole answer will be marked and credit given to the answer that scores the most marks. In this case both advantages given are correct, are explained, and are related to the study itself (even though relating the answer to this study is not required). Either answer would score 2 marks out of 2. Although answers like this are pleasing for an examiner to read, because they show effort and understanding, they also show poor examination technique.

Expert tip

Just because you know quite a lot about a particular topic, never write more than you need to. You will not get double marks if you give two answers when the question requests one.

Answer B

(a) The two psychological tests given to Eve White and Eve Black were the IQ test and the Rorschach tests.

This answer scores 1 mark only. Everything is correct, because the two tests are indeed psychological, *but this is not what the question asked. The problem is that the Rorschach is a* projective *test and not a* psychometric *test, as the question requests. It is all complex terminology but it is important to know the different types of test.*

(b) The EEG recordings taken of Eve White, Eve Black and Jane are psychometric because they are reliable and valid, and so here are two advantages rather than just one.

This answer would score no marks because EEG recordings are not psychometric. Whilst measures that are both reliable and valid *also* apply to psychometric tests, it does not mean that the answer is worth credit. Making a flippant comment doesn't score any additional marks and it does not impress an examiner.

Core Studies 1

Section B: evaluative essay-style questions

Question 16

Discuss the strengths and weaknesses of the physiological approach, using one of the studies listed below:

Demattè et al. (smells and facial attractiveness)

Dement and Kleitman (sleep and dreaming)

Maguire et al. (taxi drivers) **[10]**

In this question the examiner is looking for two (or more) strengths and two (or more) weaknesses of the physiological approach in relation to one of the named studies. The question does not ask for any description of the study, because the injunction (the order or command) is to discuss strengths and weaknesses.

Expert tip

One way to organise an answer like this is to give a strength and then an example to support that strength. Then give a second strength and another example from the same study. Next, give a weakness, an example, a second weakness and a second example. But, do not make this a list. Answer the question and use this structure to discuss.

Answer A

The physiological approach is about the physiological or biological aspects of the human and how this affects our behaviour, thought patterns and emotions. One advantage is that psychologists use the experimental method, with scientific apparatus and controls. The study by Maguire was conducted in a laboratory and it used a PET scanner. There was a clear independent variable and dependent variable and there were numerous controls, such as the pre-study questionnaires, to eliminate confounding variables. The PET scanner is clearly scientific apparatus that produces data that are reliable (consistent) and valid (it measures what it claims to measure) – in this case, the brain region that is associated with cognitive mapping.

A second advantage of the physiological approach is that the data gathered are objective and not open to bias or opinion by the participant. What this means is that the data are not like a self-report where the participant can answer whatever they wish, perhaps responding to demand characteristics or giving a socially desirable answer. The data cannot be 'fiddled' by the participant. The way in which the brain works is the way in which the brain works. Maguire found that the right hippocampus is associated with the processing of spatial layouts and that is that. Although these are powerful arguments in favour of studying psychology using the physiological approach, there are a number of weaknesses.

I earlier said brain regions were associated with the task. The weakness is that although it is claimed that from physiological data we have cause and effect, an association means that we cannot assume that one thing causes the other. In a study I read on brain scans, mad murderers were said to have different brain structures. But was it the brain structure that caused the murder, or the murder that caused the brain structure. No-one knows!

Another problem with using physiological data is that it is reductionist. Just because this is what happens in a laboratory doesn't mean that it is also true in the real world. When a taxi driver drives, he processes lots of other information too, such as all the road signs, traffic lights and other vehicles too. The study was reductionist in that all the drivers had to do was to recall the route in isolation from other things. If the study could be done in the real world, and so be more holistic, then other brain regions might also 'light up'. All this means is that whereas physiological studies have many advantages, we should be cautious and not accept the data as fact when there could be weaknesses and limitations too.

e *This answer gives two strengths and two weaknesses of the physiological approach with examples from the Maguire et al. study in support. There is also some discussion to show understanding of physiological psychology, rather than just a list of points. It is an excellent answer, which would score the full 10 marks. On the negative side, this answer is too long and this may lead to insufficient time to complete all answers on the paper.*

Question 17

Discuss the advantages and disadvantages of the laboratory experiment using one of the studies listed below.

Held and Hein (kitten carousel)

Schachter and Singer (emotion)

Langlois et al. (infant facial attraction) **[10]**

Answer A

An advantage of using a laboratory in the Held and Hein study was that all the variables could be controlled. For example the kittens could be raised from birth in a restricted environment and put into the carousel. The active kitten was one condition of the independent variable and the passive kitten was the other condition of the independent variable. There was also an experimental design because a kitten could not do both conditions. A disadvantage is that the laboratory environment is low in ecological validity and not like the normal environment of a kitten. Also, because participants know they are in a laboratory they are more likely to respond to demand characteristics. Another possibility is that controlling variables is reductionist and this is likely to affect the validity and reliability of the study.

e *This answer chose the Held and Hein study, but the later points could only be applied to human rather than animal participants. It is always worth thinking about the whole of the answer before starting to write. The answer does have both strengths and weaknesses, as the question requests, but at the start there is an emphasis on the experimental method rather than laboratory experiments. For example, the comment about the design applies to experiments wherever they are conducted and not specifically laboratory experiments. A final weakness is the use of jargon without showing how it applies or what it means. The comment that controlling variables is reductionist is correct, but with no elaboration or explanation there is no evidence of understanding. This answer would achieve no more than half the available marks.*

Core Studies 2

Section A: type 1 – methodology question in relation to a named core study

Question 1

The study by Tajfel used a laboratory experiment to test the boys to see if they would discriminate on the basis of being categorised into minimal groups. An alternative way to test intergroup categorisation is to use a questionnaire.

(a) Describe the main features of a laboratory experiment and how this method was used in the study by Tajfel. **[5]**

(b) Design an alternative study using a questionnaire and suggest how it could be conducted. [10]

(c) Evaluate this alternative way of studying intergroup categorisation in ethical and methodological terms. [10]

Answer A

(a) The main features of a laboratory experiment are that the study is done in a laboratory. This was used in the study by Tajfel so he could control all the variables. Boys came to the laboratory and judged dots on a screen. They then gave money to boys in the other group but not as much as they gave to themselves. This shows they discriminated against the out-group and their own group was the favourite group.

e *This is a poor answer because it does not address the question. Other than stating that 'it is done in a laboratory', there is no evidence of knowledge of the experimental method. With regard to the second part of the question yet again the only reference to the laboratory experiment as a method is that 'the boys came to the laboratory'. There is a little understanding of the study with the reference to 'dots' and the term 'out-group', but this is nothing to do with the method. This answer would score no more than bottom-band marks.*

(b) I would use a questionnaire to find out about intergroup discrimination. My questionnaire would have the following questions: What is your name? How old are you? Are you male/female? If you were asked to give points to someone in the classroom next door would you give them (a) more than someone in your class, (b) the same as someone in your class or (c) less than someone in your class. I would conduct this questionnaire by giving it to all the people in both classes and then I could compare the differences between the two groups to see if there was any discrimination.

e *This answer is very brief for a question carrying 10 marks – there should be much more detail. It shows little understanding about the design of questionnaires (even though those by Billington et al. and Veale and Riley are on the syllabus). There is very little about how the questionnaire could be conducted other than to say 'giving it to people in both classes'.*

Typical mistake

Very few questionnaires done by psychologists ask for personal details, but many students think that every questionnaire asks for name, age, etc. when such details are often irrelevant to what is being studied (and asking for them is unethical).

(c) I think that my questionnaire is entirely ethical. There would be no harm at all to any of the participants, so ethically it would be fine as all questionnaires are. Methodologically my method is good because it would give me the answer to the question as to whether people would discriminate or not. My method would be a questionnaire and I would give it to all the people in both classes and they would answer it truthfully. This method, because it is a questionnaire, would be methodologically good.

e *This answer shows a lack of understanding and there are many things missing. Ethical issues apply to all methods. There is no mention of confidentiality (even though name and other personal details were asked for), consent, right to withdraw or debriefing. It is wrong to assume that automatically there will be no harm when there is always the possibility that some questions may upset a participant – psychological harm. Evaluation of the methodological aspects shows a lack of awareness. For example, there is the assumption that in a questionnaire a direct question can be asked and that participants will answer this truthfully. There is no awareness of the types of data different kinds of questionnaire will produce. Overall this answer would score no more than a bottom-band mark.*

Expert tip

If you you don't know what more to write, then don't simply re-write some or all of what you have already written.

Answer B

(a) The main features of an experiment are the isolation of one variable (the IV), the control of all irrelevant variables that might confound the result, and the measuring of the dependent variable, which will be the result. If the experimental method is conducted in a laboratory then it allows many more variables to be controlled and so the experimenter can be more confident in cause and effect. Tajfel used a laboratory experiment so he could control variables. The boys could not be distracted by anything else going on (situational variables) and just focused on the dots or artistic preference. The boys could also only be in one group so the design was repeated measures. The task of awarding points was also standardised.

e *This is an excellent answer, showing knowledge of the experimental method and the advantage that conducting a study in a laboratory provides. The answer also considers how Tajfel used the laboratory to apply the method and control variables, and uses appropriate jargon. There is ample detail, knowledge and understanding to score full marks.*

Expert tip

Note how this answer uses jargon effectively in answering answer the question. Think about the essential features of all methods and the jargon associated with each one.

(b) I would use a questionnaire to find out about intergroup discrimination. Rather than using an open-ended questionnaire, because that would mean asking a direct question about discrimination and may lead to difficulty analysing and scoring the answers, I would use a closed questionnaire where I would provide a number of different answers from which the participant has to choose. I would not begin by asking for a name because it would break the ethical guideline of confidentiality. I would not ask for any other personal details either. I would state that 'this is a questionnaire about attitudes towards others' and then write 'if any question upsets you in any way, you have the right to withdraw'. I would then have 10 questions asking about attitudes towards others and one of the questions would be: Suppose you found some money that no-one claimed after 7 days. You decided to share it between the two classes. Would you (a) give more to your class than the other class, (b) give the same to your class as the other class, or (c) give less to your class than the other class. This would be a forced-choice question which is better than using a Likert type scale for my purposes. I could then ignore all the other questions and simply add the number of students answering (a), (b) or (c). Hopefully, because this question was hidden among others, participants would not realise what I was investigating and so answer truthfully rather than in a socially desirable way.

I would conduct this study on students in my class and the class next door and I would do an opportunity sample by simply asking people when they were walking past if they would participate. I would get their consent and tell them they could withdraw. I would also tell them to do it at home that evening rather than at school and then they would not copy an answer from a friend. It might mean that some forget to bring back their questionnaire, but I think that fewer returns is better than copying and producing the same answer as a friend. I would score the answers and hopefully this would give me some data that I could analyse statistically.

This is an excellent answer, which addresses both parts of the question in very good detail. It shows very good understanding of questionnaire design, ethics and methodology, and addresses the essential 'what, who, where, when and how' of a study.

Expert tip

Always address the 'what, who, where, when and how' of a study. This is *what* you are doing (a questionnaire), *who* you will do the study on (the sample), *where* the setting is (such as 'at home' in this example), *when* (if applicable) the study will be conducted and *how* it will be conducted (the procedure).

(c) There are always ethical issues to be addressed. My questionnaire asked for no personal information and so maintained confidentiality. I asked each participant for consent but they didn't give full informed consent because I deceived my participants a little. Like Milgram, I didn't give entirely truthful information about the aim of the study. I stated that 'this is a questionnaire about attitudes towards others' and although this is deception, it is necessary to keep the participants naïve about the true aim of the study. This means I can get genuine information and it is said by some that the ends justify the means. All other guidelines I met because I gave the right to withdraw, so no psychological harm was caused.

Methodologically my questionnaire was right for the purpose. I chose a closed questionnaire to get some quantitative data so statistics could be done. However, the weakness with this is that it gives no information or explanation for why a participant made a particular choice. If I had asked an open-ended question, such as 'please state why you chose answer (a), (b) or (c)', then the person may have given a reason for their answer, which would have given me insight into their decision. I should have done that. But, a strength of my method was to do the questionnaire at home. If I had watched while it was completed they may have responded to demand characteristics and if they had done it at school with a friend they may have given a socially desirable answer. My method may have avoided both of these.

As with parts (a) and (b), this answer scores a top mark for the range of different points included and the understanding of both methodology and ethics. Yes, it could be better, but an answer does not need to be perfect to score full marks.

Section A: type 2 – approaches and perspectives, and issues and debates question in relation to a named core study

Question 2

Dement and Kleitman carried out a laboratory experiment to investigate the nature of sleep and dreaming.

(a) What is meant by the physiological approach? [2]

(b) Describe two controls used by Dement and Kleitman in their study. [3]

(c) Discuss the strengths and weaknesses of the physiological approach in psychology using the study of sleep as an example. [10]

(d) Discuss the extent to which the findings of the study by Dement and Kleitman can be generalised. [10]

Answer A

(a) The physiological approach looks at things like the physiology of sleep and dreaming.

This answer would score no marks. The physiological approach does look at physiology, but this is just re-stating the question and can be written with no understanding of the term whatsoever. Given the wording of the question it is obvious that sleep and dreaming are physiological processes.

Expert tip

Don't just re-word the question. You must add detail or an explanation, or use an example.

(b) One control was that no alcohol was allowed and another control was that no caffeine was allowed.

There are two problems with this answer. Firstly, no alcohol or caffeine are both aspects of the same control, so there is only one control here rather than two. Secondly, even if alcohol and caffeine were two controls there is no expansion or elaboration that would take the answer to 3 marks rather than 2 marks.

Expert tip

Why go for the briefest answer possible? Add a little extra detail and try to achieve full marks. Just one mark could be the difference between one grade and another.

(c) The study of sleep and dreaming is a perfect example of the physiological approach. What is good about this approach is that it is direct and obvious. What I mean by this is that what the experimenter observes is a physiological response that is not influenced by anything. It is a direct recording from the brain of the participant, which they cannot do anything about because they are asleep. All the experimenter has to do is to see what the data are and draw a conclusion about them.

This means that all the data that are gathered are scientific and objective. In some ways this is just like biology, and biology is a science. If physiological studies are done in a laboratory then they can be controlled and this makes them more scientific. Further, if the experimental method is used then this also strengthens the scientific approach. All this means that the physiological approach is very scientific, as shown in the study by Dement and Kleitman on sleep and dreaming.

Although this is a good answer in places, it has many weaknesses. The question wants strengths (plural), so does this answer include two strengths? If so, where are they? Try to work out where the first ends and the second begins. If you find this difficult to do then so will an examiner!

A second problem is that there are no weaknesses at all and so any mark scheme would be quite right to award no more than half marks for half an answer. Yet another problem is that there are no examples. It is not enough to write 'as shown in the study by Dement and Kleitman on sleep and dreaming'. If the question requires examples, and this type of question always will, then include them! This answer will score no higher than bottom-band marks.

Expert tip

Make sure that strengths and weaknesses are distinct from each other, and include appropriate examples from the study.

(d) The findings of this study cannot be generalised because the study was conducted in a laboratory and not many people sleep in a laboratory. The findings also cannot be generalised because of the limited sample size. There were so few participants – only five – and as this is a very low sample size nothing can be generalised. What happened in the study is also a problem because the participants were woken up at regular intervals during the night and so they didn't get a normal night's sleep as most people do. According to Freud, if the sample is not normal then generalisations cannot be made from it. Another problem is that the participants were not tested to see if they had any sleep disorders and if they did, this also may be a problem. Also the study was done in just one country and so we cannot generalise to people in other countries. To answer the question, the findings cannot be generalised.

This answer makes quite a wide range of points about generalisations. It covers a wide range of different methodological aspects and should be given some credit for this. However, most of the points made (if not all) do not apply because of the physiological nature of the Dement and Kleitman study, which shows a lack of understanding.

Answer B

(a) The physiological approach concerns the biological aspects of humans and how they affect things such as sleep. In a way, this approach sees humans as complicated machines, with biological processes, such as hormone release and brain activity, governing our behaviour.

The answer, except for a few words deleted and the word 'sleep' added is almost a direct copy of the explanation of the physiological approach given in this guide. While adopting this strategy will score top marks, this example has been included to show what not *to do. Psychology is not about learning definitions; it is about knowing and understanding. There are more important things to life than learning definitions.*

Expert tip

Do not waste time learning definition after definition. It is much better to use your own words and show that you understand.

(b) One control was than no alcohol or caffeine was allowed. This is so a baseline could be established for all participants without a stimulant or depressant affecting sleep patterns. A second control was that the experimenters did not enter the room of any participant but used a bell to wake them. This standardised the procedure and ensured that the presence of the experimenter did not cause demand characteristics.

This is a perfect answer. There are two different controls identified and there is that little extra detail and inclusion of terminology to show understanding *of why these two variables were controlled.*

(c) One strength of the physiological approach is that the use of scientific recording devices results in data that are reliable. For example, an EEG machine can be used to record when a person is in REM or NREM, and this is reliable.

Another strength is that all people have physiological processes such as sleep, and this means that we can generalise more easily across cultures. For example, all people sleep and unless there is some sleep disorder, all people have REM and NREM sleep.

One weakness of the physiological approach is that it does not tell us any 'psychology'. It tells us that a person is in REM sleep but it doesn't tell us whether the person is having a dream. We have to wake the person and ask them to find that out.

Another weakness of the physiological approach is that it is reductionist. Controlling too many variables such as no alcohol or caffeine means that the Dement study does not relate to real life where many variables cannot be controlled.

This is a very good answer in many ways because it conforms to all the components of the mark scheme. It has two strengths and it has two weaknesses and it makes these explicit. It has examples from the Dement and Kleitman study to illustrate each point. In many respects this answer is worth full marks. However, there could be more. The answer doesn't explain what reliability is, or what reductionism is. This would show more understanding and make the answer less formulaic.

(d) The findings of this study can be generalised, which is whether something applies to most people most of the time. Most (if not all) people sleep and go through stages of both REM and NREM sleep. Most people recall dreams when woken from REM but not all the time and most people do not recall a dream when woken from NREM. Both these aspects can be generalised.

It doesn't matter that the study was done in a laboratory because a person goes through REM and NREM wherever they sleep. Because sleep is a physiological process it also means that it doesn't matter whether the participants are male or female, or that Dement and Kleitman only studied a few people. They can generalise the findings to any person wherever they are in the world.

There are some individual differences in the findings as can be seen from the results, but this is the point. A generalisation applies to most people and allows for a few individual differences. For example, most of the time the participants could correctly estimate whether they had been sleeping for 5 minutes or 15 minutes and although there were a few incorrect estimations we can generalise that people estimate the time they have been dreaming. A final point is that the measures taken by the EEG can be taken from any person. This form of data collection can be used anywhere and on anyone, as it is a reliable measure.

This very good answer shows much more understanding of generalisations, the physiological approach and the study itself.

Section B: approaches and perspectives, and issues and debates question in relation a number of named core studies

Question 3

(a) What is meant by the term 'ethical guideline'? **[2]**

Using the studies from the list below, answer the questions:

Piliavin, Rodin and Piliavin (subway Samaritans)
Milgram (obedience)
Rosenhan (sane in insane places)

(b) Describe how one ethical guideline was addressed in each of these studies. **[9]**

(c) What are the advantages of being unethical in psychological research? **[9]**

Answer A

Ethical guidelines are what psychologists must follow to make sure that participants will not be harmed in any study in which they participate and that they leave a study as happy as when they arrive.

This question is only worth 2 marks so you just need to show an understanding of the essential reasons for ethical guidelines, which is the protection of participants. This answer just about does this and so would score full marks.

(b) The participants in the study by Piliavin were deceived in a number of ways. The participants thought that the students doing the study were ordinary people just like them and so to pretend to be normal people rather than experimenters is deception. When the student or victim pretended to be drunk by smelling of alcohol and carrying a brown paper bag, again the public were deceived. The same is true when the victim pretended to be ill. Finally, when the victim fell over and lay there looking at the ceiling and pretending to be ill when nothing was wrong with them was also deception.

The participants in the study by Milgram were deceived in a number of ways. When they arrived at the laboratory they were introduced to a man who was pretending to be Milgram when it wasn't. They were introduced to Mr Wallace pretending to be another participant but he was a stooge and this was deception. The participant then drew lots to decide who was to be learner and who the teacher. But this was faked so the participant was always the teacher. They were given small shocks so they thought the pretend shocks were actually real ones. When asking the word pairs the learner Mr Wallace gave deliberately incorrect answers, deceiving the participant. As a shock was given Mr Wallace screamed and shouted in pain and this was also deception as he was given no shock at all. Finally there was deception because Mr Wallace was not actually screaming, it was all done by playing a tape recorder so that responses were standardised.

There was deception in the study by Rosenhan because the pseudo-patients were pretending they were ill when they were not.

The answer relating to the Piliavin et al. study would score full marks. There are three examples of deception, showing clear understanding of the study. The length of the answer is about right for 3 marks. The answer for the Milgram study is very good because it covers every deception there was – at least six examples. However, in writing all the examples, too much time was wasted for an answer worth only a maximum of 3 marks, which is perhaps reflected in the one sentence on the Rosenhan study, which would only score 1 mark. Interestingly the same issue was discussed for all three studies. Given the wording of the question this is a legitimate thing to do.

Expert tip

Always be mindful to write appropriately balanced amounts for the marks allocated and if the marks are three studies for 3 marks each, then write three similar amounts.

(c) In my view there are no advantages to being unethical and so this is an inappropriate question. One advantage of being ethical is that participants are not harmed at all in research. Another is that if they are harmed then the research is illegitimate because in real life participants are not harmed. If a psychologist kept doing unethical research then they should be struck-off and not allowed to do any research any more. It is bad enough if a person has a small amount of harm for a few days after doing a study, but it is even worse if there is long-term damage. The people doing Milgram's study said after a week that they were glad they had done the study. But, if Milgram had paid them to do the first study he might have paid them to do the second and so we don't know whether they were just saying that or whether they were honest. What he didn't do was to look at the long-term damage that the participants might have suffered. All in all, all studies should be ethical or they shouldn't be done.

This answer may be expressing an opinion but is worth no marks at all. Although it makes some good points, they do not address the question, which is about the advantages of being unethical.

Typical mistake

A common error for a question like this is to mis-read it – in this case a question on 'the advantages of being unethical' has produced an answer on the disadvantages of being unethical.

Answer B

(a) Ethical guidelines were laid down by the APA and BPS after unethical studies were done in the past, such as that by Milgram in the 1960s. They focus on things like consent, deception, harm, right to withdraw and debriefing, all of which are designed to protect participants from anything inappropriate.

This shows understanding of why ethical guidelines exist, has identified the relevant guidelines for humans and has acknowledged the role of the American Psychological Association (APA), for example. This answer would score full marks.

(b) The study by Piliavin et al. may have caused psychological harm to participants and this is unethical. When the ill victim collapses and lies on the floor a passenger doesn't know what is wrong with them. It might be a genuine emergency and some people become upset or panic if they don't know what to do. It is unethical for people to be upset or distressed when it is faked. A passenger may also begin to worry if a drunken person falls over in front of them. A drunken person may be unpredictable and may harm them.

The study by Milgram prevented the right to withdraw. Any participant should be allowed to leave any psychology experiment at any time, and preventing this is a little like kidnapping a person – detaining them against their will. Milgram did this with a prod such as 'you must go on' and then if a participant again wanted to leave Milgram would give another, stronger prod. In fact there were four prods in total, which shows that Milgram clearly wanted to prevent participants from withdrawing.

The study by Rosenhan failed to get consent from the participants. The participants such as the doctors did not know they were in a study and such a lack of consent means that it was unethical. However, it could be argued that consent was not needed because the doctors were doing their normal job in their normal place of work. It isn't unethical to observe a person walking along because they are doing what they wish and normally do. It only becomes unethical when deception is involved, as it was in this case.

This answer well balanced, for full marks – the word count for each paragraph differs by no more than 10 words. This answer uses a different issue for each study, which is fine. For the first two studies the answer has simply described, whereas for the Rosenhan study there is the addition of evaluation, where the answer raises the issue of whether consent is actually needed. Although there are no specific marks for evaluation in this question part, the answer is clearly related to ethics.

(c) There are a number of advantages to being unethical in psychological studies. For example, some people argue that the ends justify the means. What this means is that the knowledge we gain is well worth harming a few people. This is really a philosophical point to be debated. It could be said that we should never harm anyone, but on the other hand if we are to progress in the world, sometimes it may be for the greater good if we did unethical things. This is rather like conducting medical experiments on animals. It isn't desirable, but the knowledge gained may help save human life. Some people say that Milgram's study should never have been done, while others say that it was well worth it. Milgram defends the ethics of the study and many people agree.

Another point in support of doing unethical research is that participants behave as they normally would. If there is a study going on and they are not told, it is unethical. But if they are told their behaviour might change and they might respond to demand characteristics. An example of this is the Rosenhan study where the doctors assessing the mental illness could not be told they were taking part in a study or they would simple say 'you are faking it' and there would be no point in doing the study. Again the ends justified the means.

Another point in support of doing unethical research is that we might want to do a study about normal behaviour and we make something happen without telling them. We do it to create a realistic situation. The study by Piliavin et al. had to have high ecological validity. It also needed to have many variables controlled. The only way to achieve both of these was to deceive participants and not tell them they were in a study. Again, the ends justified the means.

Another point in support of doing unethical research is that the participants in any study are not really harmed at all. Some people just like to complain all the time and so ethics is just another thing they moan about. In the Piliavin study some participants might have been psychologically harmed, as I mentioned above. However, they could be on a real train with no study going on and someone might pass out. So there are lots of points to say that unethical research is okay to do.

e *There are four really good (and different) points here and each point is supported with an appropriate example, to gain full marks. There is even some discussion, which shows understanding. On the negative side each point begins with the same words 'another point in support' and this is unnecessary. There are four points, but only three points are needed to score full marks.*

4 Specialist Choices

4.1 Psychology and education

Perspectives on learning

Revised

At AS we defined a perspective (see page 87) as a way of explaining behaviour according to certain principles, concepts and ideas, as opposed to an approach, which refers more to *areas* of research interest (regardless of the perspective adopted). The three perspectives for the Education option are behaviourist, cognitivist and humanistic. Generally behaviourists focus on behaviour, cognitivists on thinking and humanists on the person.

Behaviourist applications to learning

One of the main assumptions of the **behaviourist perspective** is that all behaviour is learned. This done through classical conditioning (Pavlov), operant conditioning (Skinner) and through observational learning (outlined by Bandura). The learning environment is crucial and determines what is learned and what is not. This has major implications for education.

The **behaviourist perspective** focuses on observable behaviour and the way in which children and animals learn.

Programmed learning is an approach to teaching and learning. Bloom's mastery learning (1971) can be done by a teacher or by an individual student, but crucially there are well-defined objectives organised into small units where the learner is rewarded for learning each unit.

Expert tip

Mention briefly the theory underlying the behaviourist perspective, but emphasise the actual applications.

Keller's **personalised system of instruction** (1968) is composed of small, self-paced modularised units of instructions where study guides direct learners through the modules. Learners must score at least 90% before moving on to the next unit.

Examples from other sub-topics of this option can be used here. See page 127 for examples of corrective strategies for disruptive behaviour and page 125 for applications to motivation.

Cross check

Behaviourist perspective, page 92

Humanistic applications to learning

For the **humanistic perspective** (e.g. Rogers, 1951) every individual is the centre of a continually changing world of experience. Four features are at the heart of this:

- affect (emphasis on thinking and feeling, not just information acquisition)
- self-concept (children to be positive about themselves)
- communication (attention to positive human relationships)
- personal values (recognition and development of positive values)

The **humanistic perspective** recognises the uniqueness of each person's experiences, emphasising the importance of feelings and emotions and a holistic approach to learning.

Maslow (1970) advocates **student-centred learning**, where teachers are learning facilitators rather than didactic instructors. Dunn and Griggs (1988) propose that each child has a personal and unique learning style and so traditional education should change radically, providing a 'staggering range of options'.

Expert tip

Mention briefly the theory underlying the humanistic perspective, but emphasise the actual applications.

Dennison (1969) advocates **open classrooms**:

- They are student-centred and students are free to choose what to study. Grades and tests are unimportant.
- They can use a variety of learning materials and students can work alone or within groups (cooperative learning).

Cooperative learning involves pupils working in teams to solve a task:

- Each child must be specifically responsible and accountable for his or her role.
- A task can only be solved when all pupils make a contribution.
- A task can only be completed when each child has contributed equally and all can share the same success. Five essential elements are: positive interdependence, face-to-face promotive action, individual and group accountability, social skills and group processing.
- Cooperative learning techniques include: the jigsaw technique, jigsaw II and reverse jigsaw; the reciprocal teaching technique; the Williams; and think pair share.

Summerhill School in the UK was founded in 1921. It believes that children learn best with freedom and when they can choose what to do with their time. All pupils have an equal voice and can vote democratically on what happens. Children progress at their own pace and anyone can go to any class.

Cognitive applications to learning

Cognitive applications to education concern how children understand information and concepts using mental processes. The role of the teacher is to structure lessons to facilitate cognitive processing.

The contribution of Piaget and his theory of cognitive development to education is significant. The concern here is with applications that go beyond the work of Piaget.

Vygotsky outlines the **zone of proximal development**. This is the distance between what children can do by themselves and the next learning that they can be helped to achieve with competent assistance. The role of the teacher therefore is to provide support that is just beyond the level of what the child can do alone. **Scaffolding** is a 'framework' by a parent, teacher or other to help the child learn. Vertical scaffolding extends the child's language by asking questions, and instructional scaffolding is to use a more advanced language to help a child explain.

Bruner (1967) has looked at **discovery learning**; the view that children are best educated then they discover information about the world for themselves. A teacher will set a problem to be solved and the child will use what they already know and their experiences to solve the problem and learn from it. This actively engages children, encourages them to research for themselves, motivates them and promotes responsibility.

Ausubel (1977) argues that discovery learning takes time and isn't more effective than **expository teaching** and **reception learning** (the teacher gives information and pupils learn it). However, understanding can only occur when it is related to what is already in mind. **Subsumption** is the linking of new material to existing concepts done either through derivative or correlative subsumption. The role of the teacher is to ensure that what is taught extends from what is already known.

Expert tip

There are three evaluation issues to consider:

- **Comparing and contrasting** – there are competing explanations here – cognitive, behaviourist and humanist. Be able to compare and contrast them.
- **Usefulness/applications** – how useful are the suggestions made by each approach for a teacher in a classroom?
- **Reductionism and holism** – can education be reduced to one viewpoint? Is it not more appropriate to consider education in more holistic terms?

Now test yourself

1 Describe the features of humanistic cooperative learning.

Answer on p.199

Tested

Cognitive psychology is about mental processes such as remembering, perceiving, understanding and producing language, solving problems, thinking and reasoning.

Now test yourself

2 Describe what Vygotsky means by 'zone of proximal development' and 'scaffolding'.

Answer on p.199

Tested

Cross check

Cognitive approach, page 87
Reductionism, page 104
Usefulness/applications, page 95

Expert tip

Mention briefly the theory underlying the cognitive approach, but emphasise the actual applications.

Special educational needs

Revised

Definitions, types and assessment of children with special educational needs

There are many different definitions of special educational need. One approach is to take the statistical definition, placing the minority at either end of the normal distribution curve into the category of needing some form of 'special' or different education from the norm. This means that those who find it difficult to learn are included as well as those who are gifted. It also includes those children whose learning abilities are 'normal' but who have some physical disability such as being partially sighted and so have 'special' needs.

A **special educational need** is where a child who is not educationally 'average', either because of giftedness or disability, may need different educational strategies and/or facilities from the norm.

Special educational needs can be assessed in a variety of ways:

- **Intelligence tests** – performance can be assessed by IQ (intelligence) testing to determine very high or very low IQ.
- **Screening tests** – aim to narrow down children who *might* need a more thorough test for dyslexia for example. There are now on-line tests such as 'Lucid Rapid', 'Dyslexia Screener' and the 'Lucid Programmes' (tests for children of different ages).
- **Comprehensive tests** – are very specific and include assessment of reading, spelling, drawing, mathematics as well as visual tests, laterality tests, visual scanning tests and sequencing.

Types of giftedness

Exceptional performance on an intelligence test is one indicator of giftedness. According to Marland (1972) 'gifted and talented children are those identified by professionally qualified persons who by virtue of outstanding abilities are capable of high performance'.

Gifted children have been found to have specific information processing strategies: they learn quickly, transfer knowledge and skills to new situations with ease, are very aware of their own cognitive ability (meta-cognitive awareness), and process information flexibly.

According to Sternberg and Wagner (1982) giftedness is characterised by insight skills that allow a person to separate relevant from irrelevant material, combine isolated pieces of information into a coherent whole and relate newly acquired information to that already in their possession.

Exceptional ability in mathematics can be determined by Straker's (1983) Mathematics Checklist for Gifted Pupils.

Expert tip

Each type of giftedness is associated with a particular way of assessing it. Link the two together.

Musical intelligence can be measured by the Bentley Test for Music (1966) involving assessment in: pitch discrimination, tonal memory, rhythmic memory and chord analysis.

Giftedness can be identified early. Bridges (1969) lists seven features, such as reading at 3 years of age and having enormous energy. Tempest (1974) lists nine early signs of giftedness, for example such children are likely to be highly competitive or able to deal with abstract problems.

Cross check

Psychometric tests, page 98

Causes and effects of a specific learning difficulty or disability

Dyslexia accounts for 80% of all learning difficulties and it is more common in boys than girls. It can be auditory (dysphonetic dyslexia), visual (dyseidetic dyslexia) or mixed/classic. Typically there is:

- letter reversal or rotation – the letter 'd' may be shown as 'b' or 'p'
- misspelling – 'discutian' for 'discussion'
- transposition of letters – 'brid' for 'bird'
- problems keeping the correct place when reading, and problems when pronouncing unfamiliar words

Many theories explain the *causes* of dyslexia:

- Research with twins and families shows a greater likelihood of dyslexia if one or both parents have the disorder. Owen (1978) reported a concordance rate for monozygotic (identical) twins of 100%.
- Geschwind and Galaburda (1985) believe that 'several behavioural and medical conditions, including dyslexia, are more prevalent in males due to increased levels of testosterone, which inhibits development of the left side of the brain'.
- Modern scanning techniques show that the planum temporale on the left side of the brain is much smaller in people with dyslexia than in non-dyslexics.

The *effects* of dyslexia include the following:

- **Dyscalculia** affects mathematical performance, including processes such as addition, subtraction and dealing with money. It also affects map reading and sense of direction.
- **Dyspraxia** involves problems with fine and/or gross motor coordination, leading to problems with physical activities in subjects like science and sport. It can also affect ability in mathematics.
- **Dysgraphia** is a disorder of writing, which can involve the physical aspects such as pencil grip and angle. It might also involve poor spelling and difficulties when transferring thoughts to paper.

Cross check

Physiological approach, page 89

Now test yourself

3 Briefly describe **three** learning difficulties.

Answer on p.199

Tested

A child with **attention deficit hyperactive disorder** (ADHD) is likely to show:

- hyperactivity – fidgets; leaves seat; runs about – always 'on the go'; talks excessively
- impulsivity – blurts out answers; cannot wait for his or her turn; interrupts others
- inattention – poor attention to detail; makes careless mistakes; has difficulty in sustaining attention; does not follow instructions; is easily distracted

Many theories explain the *causes* of ADHD:

- Research (family, adoption and twin studies) shows a **genetic** link. In identical twins, there is a 72–83% probability that both will have ADHD, but in non-identical same-sex twins the probability is 21–45%
- ADHD might be caused by a **chemical imbalance**, for example involving dopamine and noradrenaline. Both these neurotransmitters are involved in 'executive' functions, which allow self-control. Hyperactivity, impulsiveness and inattention can all arise due to problems with executive functions.
- **Toxic substance exposure** has also been linked to ADHD, for example involving mothers who smoke and drink alcohol in pregnancy, or who have been exposed to the metal lead.
- **Diet**, such as ingesting food additives, sugar and caffeine, is also claimed to affect ADHD.

Cross check

Nature/nurture, page 103

Strategies for educating children with special needs

Children with learning difficulties or disabilities or those who are gifted can be educated in different ways:

- **Segregation** – children are selected for particular schools and so they could be taught on a one-to-one basis or be part of a small group. This is academically effective, but may be unfair, divisive and hard to implement.
- **Acceleration** – gifted children are promoted to a higher class than normal. This is intellectually beneficial, but can be socially and emotionally problematic.
- **Enrichment** – carried out in a normal classroom with extra-curricular activity and individualised independent learning programmes. There is pressure on the teacher to show clear differentiation.

In the USA Renzulli (1977) advocates an **enrichment triad model** (also known as the **revolving door model**), where children in the top 25% on academic ability, creative potential or high motivation can be enriched – but only if they wish. Stanley's (1976) **radical acceleration** is for gifted mathematicians.

Strategies for overcoming dyslexia

- Children having difficulties with reading and writing can be helped through careful choice of font, size, spacing and use of lower case. Paper should be light coloured and text dark; presentation should be in boxes with diagrams, bullets and numbers.
- **Selikowitz** (1998) lists strategies for overcoming dyslexia that focus on errors in reading, spelling and writing.
- Hornsby and Shear's (1976) **alpha-to-omega scheme** is a highly structured multi-sensory approach (using sight and hearing) to writing and reading. The pupil is taught step-by-step, beginning with single letter sounds linked to letter names and letter shapes. Progress leads to learning single-syllable words followed by complex multi-syllable words.

Dyscalculia is addressed by making maths relevant, use of large-squared paper to keep numbers properly aligned and encouraging the pupils to write down the rules for a new theory or process. Pupils with dyspraxia are encouraged to write on alternate lines and benefit from a multi-sensory approach to teaching. Use of computers and audio technology can help with dysgraphia.

Expert tip

There are three evaluation issues to consider:

- **Psychometric tests** – the strengths and weaknesses of psychometric tests are always a big issue for debate in relation to psychology and education.
- **Nature vs nurture** – the causes of many disabilities and difficulties are unknown. The nature and nurture debate is worth having, but there are other possible causes to consider.
- **Competing explanations** – anything can be an evaluation issue and here there are differing ways in which children can be educated. Debate the advantages and disadvantages of each.

Now test yourself

4 Describe **one** way in which children with dyslexia can be educated.

Answer on p.199

Tested

Cross check

Usefulness, page 95

Expert tip

Psychometric measures and associated issues such as reliability and validity feature prominently in the education option. Make sure you know these issues very well.

Learning and teaching styles

Revised

Learning styles and teaching styles

Learning styles are concerned with how learners learn and teaching styles are concerned with how teachers teach.

A **learning style** is the way in which a child learns best.

Curry's (1983) **onion model** describes learning as having four (a fourth has been added) layers, analogous to an onion:

- The outer layer (most observable yet most susceptible) Curry calls **instructional preference** and is the 'learning environment'; a student's preferred way of learning and being taught.
- The second layer, **social interaction**, is the preference (or not) for social interaction during learning.
- The middle layer Curry calls **informational processing style** and is the student's intellectual approach to processing information.
- The inner layer is **cognitive personality style** – the student's relatively permanent approach to thinking itself.

Grasha (1996) outlines six styles of learning:

- **Independent** – works and researches independently, seeking minimal guidance.
- **Dependent** – relies on others. Prefers to be told information and given work. Often learns rather than thinks.

- **Competitive** – a learner motivated to do better than others. Aims high – for top grades – and likes praise.
- **Collaborative** – likes small group discussions and project work.
- **Avoidant** – avoids working, lacks enthusiasm and does not enjoy study. May have learned helplessness.
- **Participant** – enjoys class activities and is eager to please a teacher.

Grasha believes that all students use one or two styles most of the time because this becomes a familiar and comfortable way of learning. However, using more than one or two styles shows flexibility, offering the learner a much wider range of skills.

Learning styles have direct implications for teaching styles.

Bennett (1976) distinguishes between a **formal** and an **informal** style of teaching. In the formal style the teacher is in charge and decides the classroom layout, what is to be taught and how it will be taught. The teaching gives knowledge to students who are passive listeners. This is a **teacher-centred approach**. The opposite from this is the **student-centred approach** or **informal style**. Here the teacher puts much more emphasis on the students, expecting them to take a much more active part in the learning process. In many ways learning becomes a negotiation and even the classroom layout can be decided by both students and teacher.

Fontana (1995) distinguishes between a high-initiative style and a low-initiative style. A **high-initiative teacher** will typically be aware of the needs of individual students, will allow and develop the skills and abilities of students and encourage self-confidence, independence and responsibility for self-learning. The implication of this style is that students will be more active in learning, make more informed decisions and be more confident about what they do. A **low-initiative teacher** will in many ways be the opposite of a high-initiative teacher. However, no teacher will be extreme high or low; most teachers will have some features of each.

Now test yourself

5 Briefly describe Grasha's six styles of learning.

Answer on p.200

Tested

A **teaching style** is the strategy and method adopted by a teacher.

Cross check

Usefulness, page 95

Reductionism, page 104

Expert tip

An exam question might ask you to think about what strategy you would use if you were teacher in a classroom.

Measuring learning styles and teaching styles

How can we find out which learning style a student uses? How can we find out which teaching style is the most effective? To do this we need to find some way of measuring different teaching and learning styles.

Kolb's (1976) **Learning Styles Inventory**, LSI-1 (the latest is LSI-3.1, 2005) is a 'learning cycle' made up of four elements: concrete experience – 'feeling' (CE), reflective observation – 'watching' (RO), abstract concept formation – 'thinking' (AC) and active experimentation – 'doing' (AE). The LSI asks for a choice of four sentence endings that reflect the four types above. When scores are plotted on a graph a 'kite shape' appears, showing which of the following four learning styles a person prefers:

- **diverging** (CE/RO) – feeling and watching
- **assimilating** (AC/RO) – watching and thinking
- **converging** (AC/AE) – doing and thinking
- **accommodating** (CE/AE) – doing and feeling

Ramsden and Entwistle's (1981) **Approaches to Study Inventory** (ASI) has 64 items in 16 subscales under the four headings of 'meaning orientation', 'reproducing orientation', 'achieving orientation' and 'styles and pathologies' (or non-academic orientation). The ASI uses a seven-point Likert scale ranging from 'very difficult' to 'very easy' to assess each of the 64 items. From the score achieved on each of the sub-sections the preferred learning orientation (one of the four above) can be determined. A version specifically for students is the Approaches and Study Skills Inventory for Students (ASSIST), which is a modified version of the original. The latest Revised ASI has six approaches with 44 items.

Kyriacou and Wilkins (1993) assessed teaching styles such as use of a teacher-centred or student-centred approach. They used a semantic differential – a scale with opposite meanings at each end – in this case opposite teaching styles: 'the teacher's role as provider is fixed' to 'the teacher's role is enabler and facilitator', with five points between the two extremes. In the UK (1993) many teachers had moved from a teacher-centred to a more student-centred approach. In many countries the approach is still very teacher-centred simply because it is believed that such an approach is the best way for students to learn.

Expert tip

Try to find and complete one of these questionnaires for yourself to determine your learning style. It is a good experience and will give you a better understanding of the measure itself.

Improving learning effectiveness (study skills)

How can teachers make learning more effective? What can they do to work *smarter* rather than *harder*? This can be approached through the way teaching is organised and/or through the way in which students learn.

Cross check

Self-report questionnaires, page 72
Usefulness, page 95
Reliability, page 82
Validity, page 86

McCarthy's (1990) **4-MAT** is a teacher-based approach that matches teaching styles with learning styles through effective lesson planning. There are four stages:

- Motivation – creating a learning experience.
- Concept development – where the student plans for learning and the learning experience is discussed.
- Practice – where students implement the motivation and concept development stages; they do some work.
- Application – now the students have learned and know what to do, they can apply this to new concepts and situations.

Mulcahy (1986) proposed the **SPELT** method: Strategies Program for Effective Learning and Thinking. This approach makes the assumption that if a student knows *how* to learn then they can go about it more effectively. Mulcahy suggests the following stages in the process:

- raising students' awareness of the learning process
- a teacher developing strategies to allow students to discover learning processes for themselves
- developing independent learners who can think for themselves and work independently

The **PQRST** method is intended to improve the ability to study and remember material in a textbook:

- **Preview** – the student skim-reads or glances over the major headings or sections in the text.
- **Question** – the student formulates questions to be answered after the preview.
- **Read** – the student reads through the text, focusing on the information that best answers the questions formulated earlier.
- **Self-recitation** – the student recites the information either out loud or sub-vocally (to him/herself) to practise accurate recall of the information.
- **Test** – the student answers the questions drafted earlier, testing for accuracy, detail and ease of recall.

Now test yourself

6 Describe **two** ways in which learning effectiveness can be improved.

Answer on p.200

Tested

Cross check

Usefulness, page 95

Expert tip

There are three evaluation issues to consider:

- **Methodology** – self-report questionnaires have many advantages and disadvantages, which are worth debating. Any measure also brings in the issue of reliability and validity.
- **Usefulness** – how useful are SPELT, PQRST, etc? Can you use them? How useful is it to know that there are different teaching styles?
- **Reductionism** – whatever the theory of teaching styles, there seem to be just two types. Is this too reductionist? Maybe teaching is more complex, more holist than this.

Expert tip

When planning an essay don't just re-write what appears in this topic area. This is just information. Show that you understand what it means; explain and impress the examiner.

Motivation and educational performance

Revised

Definitions, types and theories of motivation

Intrinsic motivation is the desire to perform a particular task because it gives pleasure or develops a particular skill. Motivation comes from the actual performance of the job or task and gives a sense of achievement and satisfaction. **Extrinsic motivation** is the desire to do something because of an external reward (e.g. praise from a teacher) or to avoid a punishment.

Motivation is the force that energises, directs and sustains behaviour.

Behaviourists such as Skinner showed that behaviour is affected by its consequences, that positive reinforcement increases the probability of a behaviour happening again. Motivation stems from the way behaviour is reinforced – good behaviour is rewarded, and bad behaviour reprimanded. A powerful reinforcer is praise; Brophy (1981) lists guidelines for the use of effective and ineffective praise.

The **humanistic** view of motivation is focused on the individual as a whole person and looks at his or her physical, emotional, intellectual and aesthetic needs. A positive classroom climate and caring student–teacher relationship is essential to the development of student motivation. Maslow's hierarchy (1970) reflects the individual needs of the 'whole person'. In education the concern is for the need to learn, to have knowledge and to understand the world. This is assuming that more basic needs (physiological, safety, etc.) have been met. Humanists emphasise intrinsic motivation.

Expert tip

In this education option physiological and safety needs are irrelevant. Maslow's 5th need (cognitive: having knowledge and understanding) and his 7th (self-actualisation and realising potential) are relevant.

The **cognitivist** approach to motivation is concerned with what and how we think about our behaviour. McClelland (1961) believes that achievement motivation is determined by how likely we *think* the chances of success or failure in performing a particular task are and how important we *think* the chances of success or failure are to us. Bandura (1977) believes that the extent to which we think that we are competent will determine whether we can succeed at a particular task.

Cross check

Perspectives and approaches, page 87
Generalisations, page 97

Improving motivation

According to Brophy (1981) effective praise should:

- be in response to a specifically defined behaviour
- be sincere, credible and spontaneous
- reward the attainment of clearly defined and understood performance criteria
- provide information about the individual student's competencies in recognition of noteworthy effort or success at a difficult task
- attribute success to effort and ability

To **praise** is to commend the worth of, or to express approval or admiration (Brophy, 1981).

However, praise can be ineffective if it:

- is delivered randomly or unsystematically, or rewards participation unrelated to performance
- is restricted to global positive reactions delivered in a bland fashion with minimal attention to the student or behaviour
- compares the student's performance with that of other students
- is given without regard to the effort needed to complete the task, or attributes success to ability alone or to external factors such as luck or the ease of the task

Now test yourself

7 Give **one** advantage and **one** disadvantage of the use of praise in a classroom.

Answer on p.200

Tested

McClelland (1953, 1961) outlines **achievement motivation**, which he believes is a basic human need. This is made up of **need for achievement** and **need to avoid failure**. Achievement motivation is a result of the desire to achieve success (intrinsic motivation) minus the fear and anxiety a person has about failing. Atkinson (1966) developed a model of motivation from achieving success and avoiding failure.

Need for achievement is the desire to achieve success and to accomplish and master skills by taking on challenges. **Need to avoid failure** is the desire to avoid challenges because of a risk of failure.

- The need for success is determined by: the need for achievement (nAch); the chances of success in performing a particular task; and the incentive for success.
- The motive to avoid failure is determined by: the need to avoid failure (nAf); the chances of failure at a particular task; and the incentive value of failure, i.e. how unpleasant it would be to fail.

If a child's self-confidence is stronger than their fear of failing, then they will be motivated to do a task. The challenge for a teacher is to increase motivation through increasing self-confidence.

Bandura (1977) believes that **self-efficacy** is affected by the following:

- **Performance (experience) accomplishments** – past achievements in the activity encourage a feeling of self-efficacy. Success raises it; failure lowers it.
- **Vicarious experiences** – seeing someone else, whom you believe to be of the same standard or of a lower standard than yourself, complete a task provides confidence to do the same.
- **Verbal (social) persuasion** – encouragement and positive words from those close to you (e.g. a teacher) can instill confidence.
- **Emotional arousal** – control over arousal and anxiety levels provides greater self-efficacy.

Self-efficacy is the extent to which an individual believes that he or she is competent and can succeed at a particular task.

Now test yourself

8 Briefly describe self-efficacy as proposed by Bandura.

Answer on p.200

Tested

Motivation issues: attribution theory and learned helplessness

Attribution theory in education is the way that people attribute their success or failure either to internal (ability, effort) or external (difficulty, luck) factors. According to Weiner (1984) the *explanations* people give to account for success or failure depend on three dimensions: locus (causality), stability and controllability:

- The **causality** is whether the cause is perceived to be **internal** or **external** to the attributor.
- **Stability** is whether the cause is does not change (**stable**) or whether it is changeable over time (**unstable**).
- The **controllability** dimension reflects whether the cause is **controllable** or **uncontrollable**.

Cross check

Perspectives and approaches (behaviourist and cognitive), pages 92 and 87

Usefulness, page 95

Generalisations, page 97

People explain success or failure to maintain a positive self-image. They attribute successes at an academic task to their own efforts or abilities; but when they fail, they will attribute their failure to factors over which they have no control, such as bad teaching or bad luck.

Changing attributions involves changing a person's perception. A student will apply more effort if they attribute success to internal and unstable factors that they control (I have ability; I couldn't concentrate), or stable internal factors that were disrupted by other things that they could not control (I have ability; it was too cold) but which might be different next time. However, it is much more difficult to change perceptions if they are external, stable and uncontrollable.

Expert tip

Think about how you would change the negative attributions of students in your class if you were a teacher.

Dweck (1978) distinguishes between **learning goals** and **performance goals**:

- **Learning goals** are set by those who seek to increase their competence. They believe challenges will lead to greater competence; and they respond to failure by increasing their effort.
- **Performance goals** are set by those who seek to gain favorable judgments or to avoid unfavorable judgments in the eyes of others. These people are likely to avoid challenges unless they can succeed, and respond to failure with feelings of **learned helplessness**.

Learned helplessness is the expectation, based on previous experience, that our actions cannot possibly lead to success (Dweck, 1975).

To counter learned helplessness a teacher can focus on learning goals – what the individual child can achieve rather than performance in comparison with others.

DeCharms (1972, 1977) believes that when children are treated like 'pawns' (who cannot take responsibility and whose outcome is controlled by others) they do not learn and they misbehave. To change this, children should feel internally motivated – their actions are theirs, chosen by them and originated from them. Children must be given a choice that gives them some feeling of personal influence and security. Learning to make choices leads to commitment and to responsibility for the results of those choices. This chain (choice, commitment, responsibility) is the key to motivation.

Expert tip

There are three evaluation issues to consider:

- **Comparing and contrasting** – there are competing explanations here: behaviourist, humanistic and cognitivist. Be able to compare and contrast them.
- **Usefulness** – to what extent can these theories be used in schools? What motivates you and the others in your classroom? Are you motivated by intrinsic or extrinsic factors?
- **Generalisations/individual differences** – to what extent can we apply many of the theories in this topic area to all people? There are always individual differences to take into account.

Disruptive behaviour in school

Revised

Types, explanations and effects of disruptive behaviours

Disruptive behaviour is 'behaviour that proves unacceptable to the teacher' (Fontana, 1995).

Disruptive behaviour might be unacceptable to the teacher, but it also disrupts other children and the child him/herself. Types of disruptive behaviour include:

- **conduct** – distracting other pupils, attention-seeking, calling out, out-of-seat, breaking rules, playing with mobile/cell phone
- **aggression** – verbal abuse of pupils and teacher, impertinence, physical aggression towards classroom itself, teacher and other pupils (e.g. hitting, pushing)
- **bullying**: name-calling, teasing (verbal assault), possible physical aggression

Various authors list the frequencies of disruptive behaviours. For example the *Elton Report* (UK, 1989) found 'talking out of turn' to be the most frequent, accounting for 53% of disruptions each day.

Some children are disruptive not because they are 'bad' children, but because they have some special educational need and cannot prevent themselves from disrupting. Children who have attention deficit disorder with or without the hyperactive element (ADD or ADHD) come into this category (page 121).

One reason why children disrupt is because they are **attention seeking**. Their aim in a classroom is to be the centre of attention so everyone looks at and pays attention to them. The *effects* can involve: shouting out and making inappropriate noises; dominating conversations; turning something small into a major crisis; making a false confession; and manipulating and bullying others. The *cause* may be because of low self-esteem. They may be lonely, need to feel valued or feel jealous. They may even have a narcissistic personality disorder, which includes feelings of self-importance and feelings of superiority.

Attention seeking is where a child uses excessive or inappropriate behaviour in order to gain attention.

A number of teaching issues might cause disruptive behaviour problems:

- poor planning and preparation
- poor management of attention and time
- boring instruction
- confusing presentation

Causes and effects of one disruptive behaviour

Bullying includes three types of abuse: **verbal**, **emotional** and **physical**. **Cyberbullying** is done through the use of technology, for example inappropriate messages being sent by mobile/cell phone while in a classroom.

The concern here is not with the effects of bullying on victims or how bullying can be prevented. It is with the causes and effects of bullying as an example of disruptive behavior. Bullying is learned; it is not innate.

Bullies have the following in common:

- a need to dominate others
- excessive impulsivity
- problems managing anger, anxiety, jealousy and other negative emotions
- difficulty tolerating other children who are perceived as somehow 'different'

There are a number of causes of bullying:

- Bullies often come from (**dysfunctional**) **families** where parents or other relatives:
  - set poor examples of behaviour
  - demonstrate little warmth and interest
  - use force, threats, humiliation or intimidation to get their way, thinking this is normal
  - are overly permissive ('look the other way' when the child shows aggression or violence)
- Because of their difficulty controlling feelings and impulses, children with conditions such as ADHD and oppositional defiant disorder or other **personality disorder** are more likely to bully others.
- Peer influences and possible gang membership. 85% of bullying incidents happen within peer groups.
- Desire for attention and control; envy and resentment.

Cross check

Generalisations, page 97

Bullying is a distinctive pattern of deliberately harming and humiliating others.

Corrective and preventive strategies

Preventive strategies involve anticipating disruptive behaviour and proactively working to stop a disruptive behaviour from starting. This can be done in different ways. General principles for schools include:

- high behavioural expectations by all staff, with commitment to enforcing rules promptly and consistently
- clear rules, sanctions and procedures (all pupils know what is and what is not acceptable)
- a warm school climate; friendly staff with a visible and supportive head teacher

Cotton (1990) brings together the work of many authors, concluding that an **effective classroom manager**:

- has high expectations for learning and behaviour
- establishes and clearly teaches classroom rules and procedures
- specifies consequences and their relation to student behaviour
- enforces classroom rules promptly, consistently and equitably
- shares with students the responsibility for classroom management
- maintains a brisk pace for instruction and makes smooth transitions between activities
- monitors classroom activities and provides feedback and reinforcement

Expert tip

There are seven features of an effective classroom manager. Select three that you might choose to discuss in an essay. Don't automatically choose the first three.

Kounin (1970) believes that effective classroom management includes:

- **with-it-ness** – the teacher communicating to the children that he/she knows what the students are doing and what is going on in the classroom
- **overlapping** – attending to different events at the same time

An **effective classroom manager** is a teacher whose classes are orderly, have high levels of on-task time and have minimal disruption.

- **smoothness** and **momentum** in lessons
- **group alerting** – involving all children in what is going on in the class
- **stimulating seatwork** – work done by pupils should have variety and offer a challenge

In addition to many behaviourist strategies for reinforcing behaviour, Presland (1989) outlines the main stages of any **corrective** behaviour modification programme:

- **Define the problem** – what behaviour(s) need modifying?
- **Measure the problem** – determine how serious the disruption is.
- **Determine the antecedents and consequences** – what causes the behaviour and what reinforces it?
- **Decide what to modify** – if certain consequences reinforce the behaviour new consequences should be identified.
- **Planning and implementation** – devise the programme and put it into action.
- **Evaluation** – evaluate the effectiveness of the programme.

Meichenbaum and Goodman (1971) used **self-instructional training** to modify the behaviour of impulsive and hyperactive children so they would realise that going slower and thinking about what was being done would be successful. They repeated a task (done originally with errors) first by talking out loud about it and then by moving the lips while thinking about it. Finally they did the task in 'silent speech' by sub-vocalising the words without moving the lips. Disruption was reduced and the task was completed successfully.

Expert tip

There are three evaluation issues to consider:

- **Comparing and contrasting** – there are competing explanations here, particularly the behaviourist and cognitive viewpoints. Is the behaviourist viewpoint too reductionist, with everything being reduced to reward and punishment?
- **Usefulness** – strategies for modifying disruptive behaviour are suggested, but how useful are they? To what extent can they actually be used by a teacher?
- **Generalisations** – is disruptive behaviour a 'cultural universal', meaning that it happens in all cultures? Is there disruptive behaviour in your school? Is there bullying?

Now test yourself

9 Suggest **three** things a school can do to prevent disruptive behaviour.

Answer on p.200

Tested

Cross check

Cognitive approach, page 87
Behaviourist perspective, page 92
Generalisations, page 97
Reductionism, page 104

Now test yourself

10 Using examples, explain the difference between preventive and corrective strategies for controlling disruptive behaviour.

Answer on p.200

Tested

Intelligence

Revised

Definitions, types and tests of intelligence

Wechsler (1958) defined intelligence as the global capacity of a person to act purposefully, to think rationally, and to deal effectively with the environment.

Binet (1904) devised the first intelligence test for school children in Paris. Terman (1916) adapted this test and called it the Stanford-Binet test. The latest version was published in 1986.

The concept of intelligence quotient (IQ) devised by Stern is:

$$\text{IQ} = \frac{\text{mental age}}{\text{chronological age}} \times 100$$

Wechsler (1939) devised the Wechsler-Bellevue test, updated to the **Wechsler Adult Intelligence Scale** (WAIS) in 1955. There is also the Wechsler Intelligence Scale for children (WISC). Both have been revised and are now known as WAIS-IV and WISC-IV (2003, 2008). The tests give an overall IQ score resulting from a verbal IQ score and a performance IQ score.

Conceptually, **intelligence** is the ability to learn from experience, solve problems and use knowledge to adapt to new situations. Operationally, intelligence is what an intelligence test measures.

Verbal IQ includes:

- verbal comprehension – similarities, vocabulary
- working memory – digit span, arithmetic, letter–number sequencing

Performance IQ includes:

- perceptual organisation/reasoning – block design, matrix reasoning, picture completion
- processing speed – symbol search; digit symbol coding

The **British Ability Scales** (BAS) are 23 tests covering a wide range of abilities. The six main categories are: speed of information processing, reasoning, spatial imagery, perceptual matching, short-term memory, and retrieval and application of knowledge. BAS-3 was published in 2011.

The characteristics of a good test include:

- **reliability**, which concerns the consistency of a test. A good test should give the same (or very similar) score when applied on different occasions. Reliability is usually determined using test–retest and split-half. (See page 82.)
- **validity**, which is whether the test measures what it claims. There are different types of validity. For example, predictive validity assesses validity by seeing how well the test correlates with some other measure, which is assessed after the test has been taken. (See page 86.)
- **standardisation** – tests themselves should be standardised and all students answer the same questions, in the same conditions, and are scored in the same way
- **norm referencing**, which involves comparing an individual's score with others in the same age group who are taking the same, standardised test
- **culturally unbiased** – tests should be culturally fair, but it may be impossible to create a culturally unbiased test

Now test yourself

11 Describe the main features of the Wechsler Adult Intelligence Scale test.

Answer on p.200

Tested

Cross check

Reliability, page 82
Validity, page 86
Psychometric tests, page 98
Individual differences, page 91

Theories of intelligence

The technique of **factor analysis** revolutionised thinking on intelligence. The aim of factor analysis is to simplify a large number of correlations, to find out whether there is any determining general factor or whether there are clusters of different abilities. Spearman (1904) found that scores on all mental tests came down to one factor that he called **general intelligence** (g). Thurstone disagreed, suggesting seven clusters or primary mental abilities. Cattell (1941) proposed fluid intelligence (the ability to solve problems through reasoning) and crystallised intelligence (knowledge-based and dependent on education). The latest version is the **Cattell-Horn-Carroll theory** (1999) with 'g' divided into 10 broad clusters, each sub-divided into 70 specific abilities.

Gardner (1983) rejects the traditional concept of intelligence, instead preferring aptitudes and abilities. He originally proposed seven 'intelligences':

- **Linguistic intelligence** is sensitivity to spoken and written language, the ability to learn languages and the capacity to use language to accomplish certain goals.
- **Logical-mathematical intelligence** is the capacity to analyse problems logically, carry out mathematical operations and investigate issues scientifically.
- **Musical intelligence** is skill in the performance, composition and appreciation of musical patterns.
- **Bodily-kinesthetic intelligence** involves controlling one's whole body or body parts to handle objects skillfully.
- **Spatial intelligence** involves the ability to recognise and use the patterns of wide space and more confined areas.
- **Interpersonal intelligence** is the capacity to understand the intentions, motivations and desires of other people.

- **Intrapersonal intelligence** is the capacity to understand oneself, and to appreciate one's feelings, fears and motivations.

Gardner (1999) has, in addition, suggested the following:

- **Naturalist intelligence** enables human beings to recognise, categorise and draw upon certain features of the environment.
- **Spiritual/existential intelligence** involves a concern with 'ultimate issues'.
- **Moral intelligence** involves a concern with rules, behaviours and attitudes that govern the sanctity of life.

Sternberg (1988) defines intelligence as mental activity central to one's life in real-world environments. People 'succeed' in life when they use mental skills to adapt to, select and shape external environments. Sternberg's **triarchic theory** (or theory of successful intelligence) comprises three types of intelligence:

- **Analytical (componential) intelligence** is evoked while planning, analysing, evaluating, criticising, reasoning, reflecting and judging.
- **Practical (contextual) intelligence** is used while implying, implementing and using.
- **Creative (experiential) intelligence** focuses on discovering, inventing, applying new ideas and creating.

The theory predicts that 'intelligent' people will identify their strengths and weaknesses, making the most of their strengths and compensating for their weaknesses. Individuals are not limited to strength in only one of the three areas; both integrated and uneven profiles of intelligence are possible. This led Sternberg to identify seven types: the analyser, the creator, the practitioner, the analytical creator, the analytical practitioner, the creative practitioner and the consummate balancer.

Alternatives to intelligence

According to Goleman (1995), **emotional intelligence** is how we handle ourselves (our goals, intentions, responses and behaviour) and how we handle our relationships (understanding others and their feelings). There are five components:

- knowing your emotions (self-awareness, recognising a feeling as it happens)
- managing your own emotions (handling feelings so they are appropriate)
- motivating oneself (marshalling emotions to service a goal)
- recognising and understanding other people's emotions (empathy and social awareness)
- managing relationships (managing the emotions of others)

Emotional intelligence is the understanding of one's own feelings, empathy for the feelings of others and the regulation of emotion in a way that enhances living (Goleman, 1995).

Cross check

Nature/nurture, page 103: Goleman believes emotional intelligence is learned rather than being innate.

Guilford (1950, 1967) distinguishes between **convergent thinking** (focusing on a single, correct solution) and **divergent thinking** (i.e. **creativity**), involving the generation of many different answers to a problem. Guilford devised several tests to measure creativity including: **quick responses** – a word association test; **remote consequences** – the suggestion of radical answers to unexpected events such as loss of gravity; and the more common **unusual uses** test, which asks people to suggest unusual uses for everyday objects, such as a brick. Some people have functional fixity where objects are viewed as being used only for their intended purpose such as a brick being used only for building.

Creativity is the process of thinking something unusual.

Expert tip

You might be asked to devise an 'unusual uses' test of your own.

Problem solving can involve a number of steps or **planning strategies**: identify the problem; define the problem; form a strategy; organise the information; allocate resources; monitor progress; and evaluate the results.

Forming a strategy means that problems can be solved in different ways depending on the individual and the problem to be solved. One strategy is **trial and error** – trying different solutions and eliminating those that are wrong. Another is to use **lateral thinking** (or insight), where solving is

Problem solving is the strategy used to generate solutions from observed or given data.

approached creatively; thinking 'outside the box'. **Means-ends analysis** is a technique used in artificial intelligence computer programs, where a decision is made at each step to move closer to the solution. **Backward searching** is the strategy of working backwards, starting with the end results and reversing the steps needed to get those results, in order to figure out the answer to the problem.

Expert tip

There are three evaluation issues to consider:

- **Psychometric tests** – the strengths and weaknesses of psychometric tests is always a big issue for debate.
- **Reliability and validity** – both are evident in this topic area; you could even deal with them as different issues.
- **Competing explanations** – there are different explanations of what intelligence actually is.

Now test yourself

12 Describe **three** ways in which Guilford tested for creativity/divergent thinking.

Answer on p.200

Tested

4.2 Psychology and health

The patient–practitioner relationship

Revised

Practitioner and patient interpersonal skills

In any medical consultation **interpersonal skills** such as verbal and non-verbal skills are displayed by both the patient and the practitioner. Argyle (1975) suggests that non-verbal communication is four times more powerful and effective as verbal communication, but it should match verbal communication.

Non-verbal communication (NVC) is a process of communication involving the sending and receiving of mainly visual messages between the practitioner and a patient during a consultation. The study by McKinstry and Wang (1991) looked at how acceptable patients found different styles of doctors' clothing and whether patients felt that this influenced their respect for his or her opinion. They dressed a male doctor and a female doctor in various outfits ranging from a white coat to a casual shirt and jumper. Result: most patients preferred the formal, white coat style as this was the most professional looking.

Non-verbal communication is the process of communication through sending and receiving wordless (mostly visual) messages.

Ley (1988) investigated **verbal communication** – specifically what people remember about a consultation after consulting a practitioner. They were asked what the practitioner had told them to do and this was compared with what had actually been said. Ley found that:

- patients remembered about 55% of what was said
- they remembered the first thing they were told (the primacy effect)
- they remembered information that had been categorised
- they remembered more if they had some medical knowledge

Expert tip

Think about what method (questionnaire or experiment) you would choose to use to investigate the preferred dress style worn by doctors in a local hospital. What would be your reasons for choosing this method?

Most people have little medical knowledge. The use of terminology by women on a hospital maternity ward was investigated by McKinlay (1975). On average, terms (e.g. mucus, protein, umbilicus) were understood by fewer than 40% of the women. The practitioners expected even fewer women to understand these terms, but despite this they still used them.

Expert tip

Don't just describe what verbal and/or non-verbal communication mean. Give an example to illustrate.

Patient and practitioner diagnosis and style

A medical practitioner can show a 'personality style' when a patient consults them. After analysing 2500 tape-recorded surgery interviews Byrne and Long (1976) distinguish firstly between a 'diagnostic phase' and a 'prescribing phase' and then go on to distinguish between a **doctor-centred style** (dominated by his or her professional expertise) and a **patient-centred style** (chatting and discussing with the patient and allowing a contribution) for managing the consultation.

Cross check

Field experiments, page 67
Ecological validity, page 78
Self-reports, page 72

In 1990 Savage and Armstrong conducted a field experiment on 359 patients in a London medical practice. When the patient entered the doctor turned over a card that determined the style – either a sharing consulting style (patient-centred) or a directive consulting style (doctor-centred). After the consultation, and at home a week later, the patient completed a questionnaire. Higher levels of satisfaction were recorded for the directive style, particularly so for patients with physical problems.

In order to correctly **diagnose**, a medical practitioner needs information from a patient (**self-disclosure**). Some studies have looked at whether males or females will disclose more to a male or female doctor. Robinson and West (1992) studied people attending a sexually transmitted disease centre and found that more information about symptoms and undesirable behaviours was given to a computer (e.g. the number of sexual partners) than in a face-to-face consultation with a doctor.

Cross check

Field experiments, page 67
Ecological validity, page 78
Generalisations, page 97
Validity, page 86

A medical practitioner hopes to correctly diagnose an ill person as ill and a well (not-ill) person as well. However, sometimes errors do occur. If a practitioner makes a **type 2 error** they diagnose the person as ill when they are not. This means that the person might, for example, take some medicine for no reason. But, it is better to be safe than sorry and, if in doubt, it is better to diagnose illness. This is what the psychiatrists did in the study by Rosenhan (page 53). The worst decision a practitioner can make (a **type 1 error**) is to diagnose an ill patient as being well. This is medical negligence and the consequences for the person can be very serious indeed.

Self-disclosure is revealing personal information to others.

Expert tip

Using the Rosenhan study briefly in this case is good; writing about it in detail is not. Remember, this is the health psychology option.

Misusing health services

Misuse of health services is the extent to which people do not use health services in the usual way. Pitts (1991) suggests that people under-use services for the following reasons:

- Persistence of symptoms – people take a 'wait-and-see' approach and only seek advice if symptoms persist.
- Expectation of treatment – people seek medical advice only if it is thought it will do some good.
- People do not want to waste valuable practitioner time, seeking advice only for serious symptoms.

Now test yourself

13 Give **three** reasons why people might delay seeking help from a medical practitioner.

Answer on p.200

Tested

Safer (1979) found three types of delay in seeking treatment (and treatment only begins when each of these questions is answered with a 'yes'):

- Appraisal delay – Have I got any symptoms? Do I feel ill?
- Illness delay – Do I need medical help?
- Utilisation delay – Will the treatment work? Can I afford it?

Hypochondriacs interpret real but benign bodily sensations as symptoms of illness. They worry excessively about their own health, monitor their bodily sensations closely, make frequent and unfounded medical complaints, and believe they are ill despite reassurances by physicians that they are not.

Hypochondriasis is a preoccupation with health involving exaggerated concerns about having a serious illness.

Barlow and Durand (1995) present the case study of Gail. Minor symptoms (e.g. a headache) would result in extreme anxiety that she had a serious illness because of newspaper and television reports. She avoided exercise and even laughing, and noted anything that could be a symptom. Hearing about a *real* illness in her family would incapacitate her for days at a time. Doctors would always say 'There's nothing wrong with you; you're perfectly healthy'.

Munchausen syndrome includes pathologic lying, peregrination (travelling or wandering), and recurrent, feigned or simulated illness.

Munchausen syndrome is where people seek out excessive medical attention, often going from city to city to get a new diagnosis and new surgical intervention. In very exceptional circumstances, known as Munchausen syndrome by proxy, people seek excessive and inappropriate medical contact through the 'illness' of a relative such as a child.

Cross check

Case studies, page 76
Generalisations, page 97
Individual differences, page 91
Ecological validity, page 78
Usefulness, page 95

Aleem and Ajarim (1995) present the case study of a 22-year-old female who had a painful swelling above her right breast. After many tests an infection was diagnosed and treatment began. Despite treatment the infection got worse and spread to the left breast area. A nurse found needles and a syringe full of faecal material, which the girl had been injecting into herself. Munchausen syndrome was diagnosed.

Expert tip

There are three evaluation issues to consider:

- **Methodology** – this topic area has experiments and it also has case studies. Both can be evaluated and both can be contrasted.
- **Generalisations/individual differences** – what has been found in one study might not be found in another, or might not apply in different cultures.
- **Usefulness** – how useful are the findings from these studies? Do they help our understanding of patient–practitioner interactions?

Expert tip

There are two case studies here. Case studies are a perfectly legitimate method with a range of advantages and disadvantages.

Now test yourself

14 Describe a case study of Munchausen syndrome and give **one** weakness of a case study.

Answer on p.200

Tested

Adherence to medical advice

Revised

Types of non-adherence and reasons why patients don't adhere

Adherence to medical advice includes:

- adhering to requests for short-term treatment regimens (e.g. 'take these tablets twice a day for 3 weeks')
- attending a follow-up appointment
- making a lifestyle change (e.g. quitting smoking or improving diet)
- engaging in more preventative measures (e.g. using condoms)

Taylor (1990) suggests that 93% of patients fail to adhere to some aspect of their treatment regimes, while Sarafino (1994) suggests that people adhere 'reasonably closely' to treatment regimes about 78% of the time for short-term treatments, and about 54% for chronic conditions. The main consequences of non-adherence will be that most people will have a longer recovery period, needing more time off work, a stay in hospital, a second prescription or a second visit to the doctor.

One reason why patients do not adhere to health requests is that they do not believe it is in their interests to do so. The patient is making a *rational decision* not to adhere (they are exercising their **free will**). They might believe that the treatment will help them get better, or they might believe that the treatment will cause more problems than it solves.

Bulpitt (1998) studied male participants taking a new drug for hypertension (high blood pressure). The drug reduced the symptoms such as headaches and depression compared with pre-drug states, but, negatively, the men experienced more sexual problems. These side effects meant many men made the rational decision to stop taking the medicine.

People do not adhere precisely to a treatment regimen and tailor their usage to suit their own particular requirements. They *customise their treatment*. Johnson and Bytheway (2000) found that participants' use of prescribed medicines varied according to their perceptions of: effectiveness, likely dependence, side-effects, and whether they might interact adversely with other medicines being taken.

Expert tip

Rational non-adherence is summarised here. However, there are many other reasons for non-adherence that you can discuss in an exam alongside rational ones.

Measuring adherence/non-adherence

Pitts et al. (1991) suggest that asking a medical practitioner to estimate the level of non-adherence (a subjective self-report) is 'particularly pointless'. Asking a patient is also of little use because of over-reporting, self-administration or the person may simply not know. People also give **socially desirable answers**: they will not always tell the truth, in order to present a good impression to the health practitioner.

Riekert and Drotar (1999) suggest that people who do not adhere are unlikely to participate in non-adherence research. From a sample size of 94, results showed there were three types of participant:

- those completing all parts of the study (n = 52)
- non-returners who completed initial questionnaires but did not return postal questionnaires (n = 28)
- non-consenters refusing to participate at the first contact (n = 14)

Quantity accounting, or a **pill count**, is where the number of pills remaining in a medication dispenser is counted by the practitioner. However:

- the fact that the pill has left the bottle does not mean it has been taken
- patients may simply throw away unconsumed medication
- supplies are divided up; pills may be transferred to other containers

Medication dispensers record and count the number of times they are used. Chung and Naya (2000) developed TracCap, where a microprocessor in the pill bottle cap records the date and time of each use. Over 12 weeks the rate of adherence recorded by TracCap was 71%. This measure is reliable (produces consistent results) but it is not valid (does not measure whether the medicine is actually taken).

Blood or **urine tests** can be used to measure adherence. Roth (1987) reviewed different adherence measures and concluded that blood and urine levels are the best available measures of medicine intake. However, while such measures 'do not lie', they do not measure the degree of adherence; merely that the patient ingested some of the drug at some time; not that they took the proper amount at the proper time. Biomedical checks are much more expensive than any other method, so this approach is unlikely.

Better than the above is recording number of **repeat prescriptions** from a pharmacy. Sherman et al. (2000) checked adherence by telephoning the patient's pharmacy to assess the refill rate. They found that the pharmacy information was 91% accurate. They concluded that telephoning a patient's pharmacy is an accurate method and can be used as basis for estimating medicine use.

Perhaps the best measure of adherence is recording the **number of appointments kept**. This is 100% accurate. It is reliable and valid. It is not time-consuming and does not involve the patient in any direct assessment.

Improving adherence to medical requests

Studies have shown that adherence can be improved through:

- changing practitioner behaviour (DiMatteo and DiNicola, 1982)
- changing practitioner communication style (Inui et al., 1976)
- changing information presentation techniques (Ley et al., 1988)

Ley (1988) recommends that practitioners:

- emphasise key information by stating why it is important and stating it early in the interaction
- simplify instructions and use clear and straightforward language (no medical jargon)
- use specific statements such as 'you should...' and have the patient repeat the instructions in their own words
- use written instructions, breaking down complex instructions into simpler ones
- use a combination of oral and visual information (such as diagrams)

Lewin et al. (1992) looked at how effective providing information in an instruction manual would be when the patients were discharged from hospital

Expert tip

Don't just describe these studies of different measures of adherence. Think about the different methods; think about the advantages and disadvantages of asking a person compared with obtaining data from a biochemical test or recording whether they turn up to an appointment.

Now test yourself

15 Suggest why pill counting may not be a valid measure of non-adherence.

Answer on p.200

Tested

Cross check

Field experiments, page 67
Observations, page 75
Self-reports, page 72
Quantitative and qualitative data, page 80
Physiological approach/measures, page 89

after a heart attack. Patients who received *The Heart Health Manual* adhered more to medical advice. They were judged to have better psychological adjustment, visited the doctors less, and were less likely to be readmitted to hospital than the control group (less than 10% readmission compared with 25%).

Behavioural methods (e.g. Burke et al., 1997) are also effective in enhancing patients' motivation to adhere, and include:

- tailoring the treatment, where the treatment programme is designed to be compatible with the patient's habits and daily routine, for example taking a pill at breakfast
- providing prompts and reminders by telephone, text or email to take medicine or attend appointments
- behavioural contracting, whereby the practitioner and patient negotiate treatment activities and goals in writing and specify the rewards the patient will receive for adhering, such as being healthy again

On the other hand punishments can be used. Wesch et al. (1987) introduced a service charge for missed appointments, which significantly increased adherence.

Expert tip

There are three evaluation issues to consider:

- **Methodology** – as always there are different methods used which can be evaluated. In this topic there are, for example, self-reports, pill counts and field experiments; in other words, lots of choice of method to evaluate.
- **Behavioural methods** – does providing rewards and punishments for adhering/not adhering work? What about using a cognitive approach and addressing the reasons why people do not adhere?
- **Physiological approach** – some studies here gather physiological data. This is objective and more scientific because it cannot lie. But is it valid? Do the data measure what they claim to measure?

Expert tip

There are lots of lists here. Remember that this is a revision guide. You should have more detail to add if you are explaining something in an examination.

Now test yourself

16 Suggest **three** ways in which medical practitioners can improve their communications with patients in order to improve adherence.

Answer on p.200

Tested

Cross check

Usefulness, page 95
Generalisations, page 97
Field experiments, page 67
Cognitive approach, page 92
Behaviourist perspective, page 92

Pain

Revised

Types and theories of pain

There are different types of **pain**:

- **Acute pain** is when, after a relatively brief time period, the pain subsides, the damage heals and the individual returns to a pre-damage state.
- **Chronic pain** is when the pain does not subside even though the damage is apparently healed, and may continue for many months or years.
- **Psychogenic pain** describes episodes of pain that occur as the result of some underlying psychological disorder, rather than in response to some immediate physical injury.
- **Phantom limb pain** is the feeling that a missing (amputated) body part is still there. Many amputees describe it as a burning, tingling or itching feeling that may or may not be painful. Most amputees have at least some phantom limb pain after limb loss.

The **specificity theory of pain** was proposed by Descartes (1644) and his analogy of bell ringing is a good one: 'pull the rope at the bottom and the bell will ring in the belfry'. The theory proposes that there are four sensory receptors (warmth, cold, pressure and pain) in bodily tissue that connect to a pain centre in the brain. Evidence from many sources – clinical evidence (e.g. phantom limb pain), physiological evidence and psychological evidence – show that this theory is wrong.

In 1965 Melzack and Wall proposed the **gate control theory** – the idea that physical pain is not a direct result of activation of pain receptors, but rather that

A nursing definition of **pain** is: 'whatever the experiencing person says it is, existing whenever he says it does'.

Now test yourself

17 Give **one** similarity and **one** difference between acute and chronic pain.

Answer on p.200

Tested

A **theory of pain** is an analytic structure designed to explain an unpleasant sensory and emotional experience associated with actual or potential tissue damage.

the spinal cord contains a neurological 'gate' that either blocks pain signals or allows them to continue on to the brain. Crucially, pain is seen as a combination of both physiological and psychological factors. This explains how the sensation of pain can be dampened or manipulated by thoughts, and explains all the clinical, physiological and psychological evidence that specificity theory could not.

Measuring pain

It is logical to ask a person in pain (in a **clinical interview**) to describe their pain. However, this **self-report** method is notoriously unreliable particularly when many people do not know where the liver, kidneys or stomach, for example, are located in their body.

An alternative is a **visual rating scale**. The visual analogue scale, for example, has a 10 cm line with the descriptors 'no pain' at one end to 'pain as bad as it could be' at the other. An alternative is the **box scale**, which is the same as the visual analogue but with numbers, while the **category (verbal) scale** uses a line with descriptors.

For people with chronic pain, Melzack (1975) developed the **McGill Pain Questionnaire** (MPQ). This is a psychometric measure including words and drawings and consisting of four parts:

1 'Where is your pain?' Patients mark on a drawing where their pain is.
2 'What does your pain feel like?' Patients use descriptor words in 20 categories.
3 'How does your pain change with time?' Is the pain continuous, rhythmic or brief.
4 'How strong is your pain?' Includes a visual analogue type scale using six questions with five descriptors, for example 'Which word describes your pain right now?'

When in pain we display characteristic pain behaviour. According to Turk et al. (1985), these are:

- facial/audible expression of distress – e.g. grimace, groan
- distorted ambulation or posture – limping, rubbing and holding
- negative affect – being irritable, in a bad mood
- avoidance of activity – staying at home, resting, opting out

The **UAB pain behaviour scale** outlined by Richards et al. (1982) is for use by nurses (for example) who observe people in hospital for a week or more. Nurses observe each patient daily and rate each of 10 behaviours, such as mobility and down-time, on a three-point scale, scoring 0/0.5/1 for each. Ratings are totalled so that pain behaviour over a period can be recorded.

The **Children's Comprehensive Pain Questionnaire** (McGrath, 1987) uses pictures of smiley and sad faces and a child's body on which the site of the pain can be drawn/pointed to. The **Wong-Baker scale** is similar. The **Paediatric Pain Questionnaire** (Varni and Thompson, 1976) gets children to pick colours and then colour a box – 'no hurt', 'a little hurt', 'more hurt' and 'a lot of hurt' – with a coloured pencil or crayon. The child then chooses the colour from the 'hurt boxes' to colour the part of the body that is hurting.

Managing and controlling pain

Pain can be managed by medical techniques. **Surgery** such as amputation is possible but can lead to phantom limb pain. Pain can be managed with **chemicals** (medicines or drugs):

- **Peripherally acting analgesics** act on the peripheral nervous system (e.g. aspirin, ibuprofen, paracetamol).
- **Centrally acting analgesics** work directly on the central nervous system (e.g. morphine).

Now test yourself

18 Suggest **three** behaviours people may display when they are in pain.

Answer on p.200

Tested

Cross check

Use of children in psychology, page 99
Observations, page 75
Self-report questionnaires, page 72
Psychometric measures, page 98

- **Local anaesthetics** can work when 'rubbed in' but are more effective when injected into a site (e.g. tooth extraction, epidural).

Psychological techniques can be used to help manage pain, all based on 'controlling the gate'. These include:

- attention diversion – focusing on a non-related stimulus in order to be distracted from the discomfort. It can be passive (e.g. looking at a picture) or active (e.g. singing a song). Even watching television can distract the patient.
- non-pain imagery, whereby the person tries to alleviate discomfort by creating or imagining a mental scene that is unrelated to, or incompatible with, the pain
- cognitive redefinition, where a person replaces negative thoughts about pain with constructive (positive) thoughts. For example, a person can think 'it's not the worst thing that could happen to me'.

One **alternative technique** to manage pain is a **stimulation therapy** based on the principle 'fight pain with pain', or using counter-irritation that directs attention away from the stronger pain to the milder pain. One example is **transcutaneous electrical nerve stimulation** (TENS). Electrodes are placed on the skin near where the patient feels pain and mild electric shocks are given, causing distraction. With **acupuncture** very fine stainless steel needles are used to stimulate the body's 14 major meridians to increase the release of neurotransmitters called endorphins, which block pain.

The term **alternative technique** is used to describe any intervention that is not medical or psychological.

Cross check

Cognitive approach, page 87
Physiological/biochemical approach, page 89

Expert tip

There are three evaluation issues to consider:

- **Approaches/perspectives** – reference can be made here to the cognitive approach, the physiological or biochemical approach, and the behaviourist perspective. This gives a wide range to choose from or to compare and contrast.
- **Methodology** – there are many methods here that can be evaluated. For example, self-reports (clinical interviews), the MPQ and the UAB.
- **Children** – whereas the use of children in a number of core studies is different from examples here, there are issues surrounding children that can be evaluated.

Stress

Revised

Causes and sources of stress

Stress involves an interaction of **cognitive** and **physiological** factors. Stress hormones such as adrenaline and cortisol play a major role. Selye (1956), following laboratory studies on rats, proposed the **general adaptation syndrome** (GAS) model, with three stages:

1. An **alarm reaction**, such as the flight or fight response, mobilises the body's resources and increases physiological arousal.
2. **Resistance**: an attempt is made to counteract the earlier effects and reduce the higher state of arousal.
3. **Exhaustion**: if the high levels of arousal are prolonged, eventually some part of the physiological system will break down.

Stress is the condition that results when a person's environment/transactions lead them to perceive a discrepancy (whether real or not) between the demands of a situation and the resources of the person's biological, psychological or social systems (Sarafino, 1990).

There are many causes of stress:

- Johansson et al. (1978) found **work stress** in a Swedish sawmill where 'finishers' were compared with a group of cleaners. The finishers' work was machine-paced and repetitive, and they were isolated from other workers. Compared with the cleaners, the finishers' levels of absenteeism were much higher and they secreted far more stress hormones.
- Holmes and Rahe (1967) devised the **social readjustment rating scale** (SRRS) to examine the **life events** and experiences (both positive and

negative) that cause stress, such as 'death of spouse'. They found that people scoring 300 life change units (over 12 months) more were more susceptible to illnesses ranging from sudden cardiac death to sports injuries.

- Friedman and Rosenman (1974) outline a **Type A personality** and a **Type B personality**. Type As are said to be aggressive, assertive, competitive and time conscious, and so are more likely to suffer physical and mental illnesses.
- Lazarus et al. (1981) believe that stress is caused by small, everyday frustrations, which they call **daily hassles**. The modified hassles scale now has 117 items. They also have an **uplifts scale**, with 135 events that bring peace, satisfaction or joy.
- Geer and Maisel (1972) found in their laboratory experiment using GSR (see below) that a group of participants without control found viewing photographs of dead bodies more stressful than the group with control.

Cross check

Physiological approach, page 89
Generalisations, page 97

Expert tip

Causes of stress match with measures of stress. For example, if life events cause stress then a measure of life events is needed (see SRRS and Holmes and Rahe, 1967).

Measures of stress

The **physiological component** of stress can be measured using:

- **blood pressure tests**. Goldstein et al. (1992) found that paramedics' blood pressure (using a sphygmomanometer) was higher during ambulance runs or when at the hospital, compared with other work situations or when at home.
- **galvanic skin response** (GSR). This calculates the electrical resistance of the skin, an indicator of arousal in the autonomic nervous system (Geer and Maisel, 1972 – see above).
- **sample tests of blood or urine**. Lundberg (1976 – page 146) collected urine samples to measure the levels of stress caused by commuting to work. Johansson et al. (1978) found that the 'finishers' in a Swedish sawmill produced more stress hormones than cleaners.

The **cognitive** or **psychological component** of stress can be measured using self-report questionnaires:

- Holmes and Rahe (1967) devised the **SRRS** to measure life events and compiled a list of major and minor events, giving each a **rank** and a **mean value**. At the top of the list (rank 1, with a mean value of 100) is 'death of spouse'; at the bottom of the list (rank 43 and a mean value of 11) is 'minor violations of the law'. Points are added to give a total score.
- Lazarus et al. (1981) devised the **hassles and uplifts scale** to record daily hassles. Their original list had 117 hassles with 'concerns about weight' and 'too many things to do' at the top of the hassles list.
- Friedman and Rosenman (1974) devised the **Type A Personality Questionnaire**. There are short and long versions, some requiring yes/no answers and others scoring on a 1–4 scale.

Cross check

Physiological approach, page 89
Self-report questionnaires, page 72
Quantitative data, page 80
Generalisations and individual differences, pages 97 and 91

Management of stress

There are a number of different ways in which stress can be managed. Those adhering to the **medical approach** would opt for **drug treatment**. Two common drugs are benzodiazepines (e.g. Valium, Librium) and beta-blockers (e.g. Inderal), which both reduce physiological arousal and feelings of anxiety by blocking neurones stimulated by adrenaline.

Stress can be managed using the cognitive-behavioural technique of **biofeedback**. For example, we can slow down our heartbeat just by thinking about it. Budzynski et al. (1970) studied patients suffering from chronic muscle contraction headaches. They combined biofeedback with training in deep muscle relaxation in the experimental group, who reported having fewer headaches than the control group. The benefits were still effective after 3 months.

Now test yourself

19 Describe **two** studies in which stress has been measured psychologically.

20 Using examples, give **two** ways in which stress can be measured physiologically.

Answers on p.201

Tested ☐

Bridge et al. (1988) used **relaxation** and **imagery** to reduce stress in 154 women with breast cancer in three different ways: control, relaxation only, and relaxation and imagery. After 6 weeks measures of mood states were significantly less in the experimental group than in the control group, with relaxation and imagery being particularly effective.

Biofeedback is the control of physiological functions through cognitive processing.

Meichenbaum (1985) prevented stress with **self-instructional training** and **stress inoculation training**. Self-instructional training focuses on replacing maladaptive statements with positive, coping statements and relaxation, which leads the person to respond to stress in more positive ways.

Stress inoculation training has three stages:

- **Conceptualisation:** the trainer talks to the person about their stress experiences such as how they would normally cope with stress. Negative thought patterns are identified.
- **Skill acquisition:** the person is educated about the physiological and cognitive aspects of stress, and techniques used to manage stress, such as replacement of negative thought patterns with positive ones.
- **Application and follow-through:** the application of the new skills through a series of progressively more threatening situations to prepare the person for real-life situations.

Cross check

Biochemical treatments, page 157

Cognitive-behavioural treatments, page 157

Field experiments, page 67

Expert tip

There are three evaluation issues to consider:

- **Methodology** – this can be considered for physiological measures and particularly in relation to the many self-report questionnaires in this topic area. Some studies conducted field experiments.
- **Generalisations/individual differences** – what might apply to one person (e.g. daily hassles) may well not apply to another.
- **Approaches** – different approaches/perspectives suggest ways in which stress can be reduced. These can be compared and contrasted.

Expert tip

Any evaluation should include at least three issues and one of these must always be the named issue presented in the question.

Health promotion

Revised

Methods for promoting health

The idea behind **fear arousal** is that if an appeal is very upsetting it scares people into changing their behaviour.

Janis and Feshbach (1953) conducted a study on oral/dental hygiene. Participants listened to either strong (very scary), moderate or minimal fear presentations. Later participants were interviewed about whether they would conform to the advice given in the presentations The minimal fear presentation group showed 36% agreement with the advice but agreement was just 8% with the strong (scary) presentation, suggesting that low levels of fear are best.

Leventhal et al. (1967) showed smokers a 'high-fear' film, which presented a diseased lung caused by smoking. A 'low-fear' film was shown to another group. On leaving, participants in the high-fear condition reported being more vulnerable to lung cancer and more claimed they would give up smoking compared with those in the lower-fear condition. Conclusion: the more fear can be aroused the better, but this was a laboratory study with no longitudinal follow-up.

Hovland et al.'s (1953) **Yale model of communication** looked at persuasive communications:

- **The source of the message** – is the presenter of the message credible, an expert, trustworthy?
- **The message itself** – is it clear and direct; is it one-sided or two-sided?

Health promotion aims to enhance good health and prevent illness.

Fear arousal involves a message being presented to a target audience with the aim of scaring or creating fear in them in order to change their perceptions and motivate them to act.

Now test yourself

21 What is meant by the term 'fear arousal'?

Answer on p.201

Tested

Expert tip

Questions might ask for techniques or methods to promote health. Can you identify the **two** main techniques in this sub-section? Can you describe the techniques and give examples of studies that use them?

- **The medium** – is the message personal; done via television, radio or printed?
- **The target audience** – who is the target audience? School children; communities?
- **The situation** – where will the message be presented? In the home; a medical surgery?

All of these features contribute to the success (or failure) of persuasive communication.

If people want to live healthier lives they need to know what to do; they need to be *provided with information*. Posters placed in medical settings can be a major source of information. Better still is when a practitioner provides information to a patient, but studies have shown (e.g. Ley, 1988) that patients do not remember most of what they are told. Written information is better.

The **Heart Health Manual** devised by Lewin et al. (1992) was tested. In the field experiment, using a double-blind, 176 patients were randomly allocated either to the Heart Health Manual group or to a control group. Patients were assessed at 6 months and 1 year. Key findings: patients with the manual were judged to have better psychological adjustment, visited the doctors less, and were less likely to be readmitted to hospital in the first 6 months compared with the control group (less than 10% readmission compared with 25%).

Health promotion in schools, worksites and communities

Children in schools can be targeted before bad health habits begin. Walter (1985) conducted a 5-year programme (focusing on nutrition, physical fitness, and cigarette smoking prevention) in 2283 children in 22 elementary schools in the Bronx, New York. After 1 year the programme group (compared with the control group) showed improved cholesterol levels, lower blood pressure and improved post-exercise pulse recovery rate.

In the UK Tapper et al. (2000) used role models called the 'Food Dudes' and devised a programme aimed at promoting the eating of fruit and vegetables in schools. It included: a Food Dude adventure video; a set of Food Dude rewards; a set of letters from the Food Dudes (for praise and encouragement); a Food Dude home-pack; and a teacher handbook and support materials. Levels of fruit and vegetable consumption were measured at baseline, intervention and at a 4-month follow-up. Results: lunchtime and home consumption in the experimental school was substantially higher than the control group, so the programme was effective.

Gomel et al.'s (1983) **worksite intervention** research was conducted in 28 Australian ambulance stations with a view to reducing cardiovascular disease. Four intervention programmes were used. Overall results showed that 12-month cessation rates (e.g. of smoking) were far higher for both behavioural counselling groups (7%) compared with 0% for the risk assessment/risk education only conditions.

The **Stanford three-community study** involved three Californian (USA) communities each with between 13 000 and 15 000 people. The programme was delivered in two communities (the third was a control) through various media, including television, radio, newspapers and billboards. Pamphlets, cookbooks and direct mail were also used. Dietary questionnaires were given along with cholesterol tests. Results: after 3 years mass media health education achieved lasting changes in diet, obesity and cholesterol levels.

A follow-up – the **Stanford five-city project** (Farquhar et al., 1985) – went on for longer (6 years rather than 3), involved a wider age-range and monitored change in cardiovascular disease rates. Like the three-community study, results showed that community-wide education is effective.

Cross check

Laboratory experiments, page 66
Field experiments, page 67
Snapshot and longitudinal studies, page 84
Ethics, page 79
Generalisations, page 97
Use of children, page 99

Expert tip

There are five different studies summarised here. You do not need to include all five in your essay. Choose those you can remember or those that relate to the issues being discussed.

Promoting the health of a specific problem

Dannenberg et al. (1993) looked at the wearing of cycle helmets in three counties in Maryland (USA). Howard County introduced a law in 1990 where children under 16 years had to wear a cycle helmet. A nearby county provided a large-scale educational campaign and a third county had no law or educational information. Results: helmet use rates in children increased from 4% in 1990 to 47% in 1991 in Howard County but did not change significantly in the other two counties.

McVey and Stapleton (2000) evaluated television anti-smoking advertising. The adverts used John Cleese (UK actor/comedian) and went to four different regions over 18 months. The results showed that after 18 months, 9.8% of successfully re-interviewed smokers had stopped smoking. Conclusion: the campaign was effective in reducing smoking prevalence through encouraging smokers to stop and helping prevent relapse in those who had already stopped.

Breast cancer is one of the leading causes of cancer deaths and of all deaths in the USA. Testicular cancer is the leading cause of cancer deaths among American men between the ages of 15 and 35. Both forms of cancer can be effectively treated if they are identified at an early stage and this is best achieved through self-examination. The problem is getting people to self-examine.

Also see the Cowpe (1989) report on the reduction of chip pan fires (page 144).

Expert tip

There are three evaluation issues to consider:

- **Children** – a number of studies here use children (e.g. Walter, Tapper, Dannenberg).
- **Snapshot vs longitudinal studies** – some snapshot studies are done here when the findings suggest longitudinal studies would have been better. There are some longitudinal studies done in their own right.
- **Methodology** – a contrast can be made between laboratory, field and natural experiments.

Now test yourself

22 Briefly describe **two** health promotion campaigns that have been conducted in schools.

Answer on p.201

Tested

Expert tip

The syllabus is designed to allow you to choose to promote the health of anything. You can choose from those examples covered here or your own. If you choose your own, choose something with published evidence (a name and date) to support it. Don't give an anecdotal answer.

Expert tip

When you evaluate don't just use the issues listed here. There are many more. All evaluation issues receive credit.

Health and safety

Revised

Definitions, causes and examples of accidents

Reason (2000) argues that **human error** can be placed into two categories:

- **Theory A**: the person (or individual) approach. Accidents are caused by the unsafe behaviour of people; prevention is by changing the ways in which people behave (fitting the person to the job).
- **Theory B**: the systems approach. Accidents are caused by unsafe systems at work; prevention is by redesigning the work system (fitting the job to the person).

However, accidents characteristically have multiple causes, and it is the way these causes come together that makes the event unexpected and an accident.

Familiar theory A (individual) errors include the following:

- The sinking of the *Titanic* (1912) can be blamed on the captain of the ship because of his **illusion of invulnerability**.
- The 1976 airplane crash at Zagreb occurred because an air traffic controller, due to **cognitive overload**, could not cope with the number of aircraft in his sector.

Theory B (system) errors include the following:

- The Three Mile Island (1979) and Chernobyl (1986) nuclear energy technological accidents occurred where workers were working a *rapidly*

An **accident** is an unplanned, unforeseen or uncontrolled event that has negative consequences (Pheasant, 1991).

Expert tip

There is cross-over here with the 'disasters' section from the Environment option. For wider reading, look at how the same information applies more widely.

rotating shift system, and the poor design and layout of the technology meant that it was impossible for the workers to cope.
- The *Herald of Free Enterprise* sinking in 1987 was initially blamed on the workers, but the systems/procedures were really at fault.

Accident proneness and personality

Greenwood and Woods (1919) found that a small number of people have a disproportionately large number of accidents. Robertson et al. (2000) devised a questionnaire to assess accident-prone personality and believe there are three important determinants:

- dependability – the tendency to be conscientious and socially responsible
- agreeableness – the tendency not be aggressive or self-centred
- openness – the tendency to learn from experience and to be open to suggestion from others

People have accidents because of personality factors:

- **Age**: young people have most accidents. There is a decline between 25 and 45 before there is a slow increase towards old age.
- Some people claim **extraverts** are more accident prone (e.g. Furnham, 1999) but other studies contradict this. For example, Liao (2001) found more accidents among **introverted** fire-fighters.
- **Type A personalities** (see page 139) are said to have more accidents (e.g. Magnavita, 1997).

People also have accidents due to **non-personality** factors:

- **Illusion of invulnerability**: accidents are caused by errors of judgement – we take a risk with the belief that we can 'get away with it'. Successful risk taking leads to the illusion of invulnerability, i.e. the belief that 'it will not happen to me'. The *Titanic* sank in 1912 because the captain had the illusion of invulnerability: sailing an 'unsinkable' ship too fast at night when it was known icebergs were in the area.
- **Cognitive overload** is the term given to a situation when a person cannot cope with all the competing mental demands placed on them. Barber (1988) describes the case where an aeroplane crashed over Zagreb in 1976 and 177 people died. An air traffic controller was blamed because it was said he couldn't cope and he was jailed for 7 years. However, he was released after 2 years because it was agreed that the unmanageable *system* was to blame.

Other reasons people have accidents include the following:

- A 'transient state' is where a person is mentally impaired due to drugs, medication or alcohol.
- Some people have accidents because they are tired and fall asleep.
- Shiftwork – there are more errors during an 8 p.m. to 6 a.m. shift than at any other time.
- People make substitution errors – where one instrument is confused with another.
- People have motion stereotypes in which behaviours are done 'automatically' and logically rather than adapting to the needs of a rapidly changing situation.

Reducing accidents and promoting safety behaviour

Safety behaviour can be promoted in the same way as health, using fear appeals (page 140) and by providing information (page 141).

To reduce accidents at work, Fox et al. (1987) studied use of a **token economy** system at an open-cast mine. Employees could earn stamps/tokens (to gain rewards) for working without time lost for injury; not being involved in accidental damage to equipment; and behaviour that prevented accidents

Now test yourself

23 What is the difference between Theory A and Theory B categories of accidents?

Answer on p.201

Tested

Cross check

Real-life examples, page 95
Generalisations, page 97

Accident proneness is a personal idiosyncrasy predisposing the individual who possesses it to a relatively high accident rate.

Now test yourself

24 Using examples, give **two** 'non-personality' explanations for accidents.

Answer on p.201

Tested

Expert tip

Look at question 24 carefully. If you choose a 'transient state' can you give an appropriate example of it, which means a published study? If you cannot, choose one where you can, such as the illusion of invulnerability.

Cross check

Reductionism, page 104
Cognitive approach, page 87
Individual differences, page 91
Questionnaires, page 72
Nature/nurture, page 103

Safety behaviour is maintaining a healthy existence through safe practices at work and in the home.

or injuries. Stamps were lost for unsafe behaviour that could cause accidents. Result: there was a dramatic decrease in days lost through injury and the number of accidents was reduced.

Reorganising shift work can also reduce accidents at work. Using slow rotation rather than a rapid rotation might be effective (page 179).

A common accident in the home (in the UK) is a chip (or French-fry) pan fire (hot oil overheating and bursting into flames). Cowpe (1989) reports on a television advertising campaign that showed viewers how to deal safely with a chip pan fire (providing information) and featuring a chip pan fire victim (fear arousal) who told her tragic story. The campaign was successful but recommended an annual follow-up.

Expert tip

If you are referred to another page/section then follow it up. Information that applies in more than one section is worth knowing about!

Expert tip

There are three evaluation issues to consider:

- **Methodology** – there can be an evaluation of questionnaires at the very least.
- **Reductionism** – can all the causes of accidents be reduced to just two explanations?
- **Nature nurture** – is accident proneness learned? Is it inherited?

Think too about generalisations, the behaviourist technique of a token economy and the longitudinal study reported by Cowpe.

4.3 Psychology and environment

Noise

Revised

Definitions and sources of noise

When sound is unwanted it can be defined as **noise**. Some types of noise are more annoying than others. Kryter (1970) suggests that noise is annoying if it is: loud; uncontrollable; unpredictable. Borsky (1969) adds: if it is perceived as unnecessary; if those making the noise are unconcerned; if the noise is yet another environmental stressor.

Noise is unwanted sound.

Sources of noise include transportation (e.g. air, rail or road). Such noise is predictable and people may be able to choose whether or not they live near an airport or busy road. Noise can be due to construction of buildings or repairs, in which case the noise is temporary. Perhaps the worst type of noise is that from 'noisy neighbours' because the it might be unnecessary and those making it might be unconcerned (Borsky).

Now test yourself

25 Describe psychological features that make noise annoying.

Answer on p.201

Tested

Negative effects on social behaviour in adults and performance in children

Geen and O'Neal (1969) showed participants either a boxing or non-violent film. Participants later could give electric shocks (which were fake) and were exposed to 60 dB of white noise. Those with aggressive film plus noise gave most shocks; those with non-aggressive film minus noise gave the fewest shocks. Conclusion: noise has a negative effect on anti-social behaviour.

Donnerstein and Wilson (1976) conducted a laboratory experiment where participants worked on maths tasks with 95 dB of white noise. Some were made angry and some were not. When giving (fake) electric shocks those made angry (and with no control) gave the most intense shocks. Those giving weakest shocks were the 'non-angry group', particularly those with 'high noise with control' rather than those with no noise at all. Conclusions: unpredictable and uncontrollable noise is more aversive than predictable or controllable noise.

Studies have also been done on the negative effects of noise on pro-social behaviour. In the Mathews and Canon (1975) laboratory experiment, participants were exposed to 48 dB of normal noise, and 65 dB or 85 dB of white noise. As participants waited, another individual (a confederate) dropped papers onto the floor. The DV of helping was whether or not the subject helped to pick up the papers. With no noise helping was 72%, with 65 dB 67% and with 85 dB it was significantly reduced to 37%. Noise had a negative effect on helping behaviour.

In the Mathews and Canon (1975) field experiment a confederate dropped a box of books while getting out of a car. In some trials a plaster cast was worn on the arm. Noise of 87 dB was created by a lawnmower. The DV of helping was how many passing subjects stopped to assist the confederate pick up the dropped books. When a cast was worn helping dropped from 80% with no noise to just 15% with noise. Again, noise had a negative effect on helping behaviour.

Cross check

Laboratory experiments, page 66
Field experiments, page 67
Ethics, page 79
Ecological validity, page 78

Studies have been done on the negative effects of noise on the performance of children. Bronzaft (1981) found that children in 'Public school 98' in New York had low reading ages on one side of the school due to the 89 dB caused by passing 'elevated subway' trains. When soundproofing was installed in the school and rubber tracks laid for the trains, reading ages eventually returned to normal.

Research from Haines et al. (2002) and from other studies at airports all found that transportation noise affects children. Negative effects include: impaired speech perception affecting language acquisition; significantly reduced reading ability; less motivation; learned helplessness; distractibility; less tolerance for frustration/easily annoyed; and, perhaps worst of all, they have higher blood pressure and high levels of adrenaline (evidence of stress).

Positive uses of sound (music)

Research on **consumer behaviour** has shown that the environment (lighting, smell, decoration and music) can influence the behaviour of customers. Fast music speeds up eating; slow music slows it down. 'Muzak' is often used in retail environments to encourage people to buy products. North et al. (1997) played French music and German music, finding more French wine was purchased (compared with other wines) when French music was played. North and Hargreaves (1998) found that the playing of classical music created an 'upmarket atmosphere' and led to increased spending. North et al. (2003) found that classical music resulted in more profit for a restaurant compared with when no music or 'pop music' was played.

Cross check

Naturalistic experiments, page 67
Usefulness, page 95

Now test yourself

26 Describe **one** study to show that music can be beneficial to health.

Answer on p.201

Tested ☐

Sound (music) can improve **health**. Playing music to patients waiting for (and even while undergoing) a medical treatment means patients are distracted and worry less. Chafin (2004) found that listening to classical music could reduce blood pressure. Chafin recorded blood pressure baselines (sitting in silence) and then gave a stressful (mental arithmetic) task to participants to increase blood pressure. Classical, jazz, pop and no music were then played. Chafin found that those played classical music recovered (blood pressure back to normal) more quickly than the others.

Sound (music) can affect **performance**. Fox (1983) found that playing music in factories and to those working on production lines helps to distract from boredom and reduce the tedium of the task.

In 1993 Rauscher et al. showed that listening to a Mozart piano sonata produced significant short-term enhancement of spatial-temporal reasoning in college students. This finding led to the claim that listening to Mozart's music would make people more intelligent! Some research has supported this finding, but many other studies have not, such as that by Steele et al. (1999).

Expert tip

There are three evaluation issues to consider:

- **Methodology** – many studies here are experiments and the three types of naturalistic, laboratory and field are evident.
- **Methodological issues** – the methods have issues related to them. It is worth contrasting the ecological validity of the different studies and debating the high number of controls, or lack of them, in various studies.
- **Ethics** – as some of these studies deceive, this is a valid issue for debate.

Density and crowding

Revised

Definitions, measurements and animal studies

Density refers to *physical* conditions (social or spatial) whereas crowding is a *psychological* state. Some high-density situations are pleasurable with no experience of **crowding**, whereas others are not.

In 1965 Dubos wrote that lemmings jumped of the edge of cliffs because of biological pre-programming in order to regulate numbers due to high **social density**. The Disney film *White Wilderness* 'confirmed' this. However, the Disney film was fiction and studies show that lemmings do not jump off cliffs.

In 1960 Christian et al. reported a real-life event. In 1916 deer were put onto James Island (USA). They bred successfully, but in 1955 half of the population died suddenly. Autopsies revealed significantly enlarged adrenal glands so it was concluded that the deer died from stress due to crowding. The spatial density (size of the island) did not change but the social density (number of deer) did.

In 1962 Calhoun's laboratory experiment investigated social density in rats. His 'rat universe' (or 'behavioural sink'), basically a very large box, was divided into four pens with 36 rats in each. Breeding caused very high social density and problems began. There were high levels of aggression in some, submissiveness in others, significant amounts of sexual deviance (hyper-sexuality and homosexuality) and reproductive abnormalities. Calhoun concluded that the **anti-social behaviour** exhibited was due to the high population/socially dense environment.

Crowding is a psychological state determined by perceptions of restrictiveness when exposed to spatial limitations (Stokols, 1972).

Spatial density is where the number of people remains the same; the size of space varies.

Social density is where the size of space remains the same; the number of people varies.

Now test yourself

27 Describe the differences between spatial density, social density and crowding.

Answer on p.201

Tested

Cross check

Natural observations, page 75
Laboratory experiments, page 66
Ecological validity, page 78
Generalising from animals to humans, page 100

Effects on human health, pro-social behaviour and performance

Lundberg (1976) studied the **health** of passengers on a commuter train travelling from Nynäshamn via Västerhaninge to Stockholm. Male commuters provided a urine sample analysed for stress hormones. Those with a 72-minute commute (from Nynäshamn) showed less stress than those with a 38-minute journey from Västerhaninge. Reason: those from Nynäshamn could *control* where they sat unlike the others who had no control, having to sit next to another passenger or stand for the journey. In all passengers, high social density caused stress (which affects health).

In a cafeteria Jorgenson and Dukes (1976) observed the effect of social density on compliance with the **pro-social** request to 'please return your soiled dishes'. Fewer users complied during high-density periods, showing that high social density decreases helping behaviour. In low-density conditions more people returned dirty dishes.

Bickman et al. (1973) compared pro-social acts in high-, medium-, and low-density student dormitories. Envelopes, which were stamped and addressed, were dropped and helpfulness (the pro-social behaviour) was measured by the

Expert tip

Section B essays on density and crowding always lead to students writing too much about animal studies. They are just one part, so summarise them and include other examples too.

Now test yourself

28 Describe **two** non-laboratory studies of the effects of density and crowding on animals.

Answer on p.201

Tested

number picked up and placed in the mail. Results: 58% were posted when the dormitory was full, compared with 79% with medium density and 88% with low density. Conclusion: high social density decreases helping behaviour.

In the field experiment by Mackintosh et al. (1975) study 1 asked participants to find and describe 12 pairs of shoes and describe three people (in a department store) in high and low social density conditions. Result: there was no difference in focal memory (descriptions of the shoes and people) but there was in incidental memory (recollections of the store itself and the environment they were in), with performance better for those in the low-density conditions. Study 2, conducted in a railway station, also found that high social density impaired performance and led to negative affect in participants.

Cross check

Field experiments, page 67

Validity, page 86

Physiological measures, page 89

Quantitative data, page 80

Preventing and coping with effects of crowding

Architecture can be modified to increase the perception of more space:

- increase ceiling height (Savinar, 1975)
- have rectangular rooms rather than square rooms (Desor, 1972)
- ensure well-defined corners to rooms (Rotton, 1987)
- ensure rooms have a visual escape or distraction such as a window, mirror or picture (Baum et al., 1976).

Similar issues apply to public transport. Evans and Wener (2007) suggest that train seats should be in pairs rather than in threes because sitting in the middle is far more stressful through personal space invasion from people on either side. People sit in window seats as a visual escape from the high social density within the bus or train. Escapes can also be made with books, magazines or by listening to music.

Langer and Saegert (1975) suggest coping with crowding by increasing **cognitive control**. They found that by simply telling people what to expect (in a busy or quiet store and a busy or quiet railway station) this led to a more positive emotional experience being reported than in participants who were provided with no information about social density.

Karlin et al. (1979) trained people in muscle relaxation, cognitive reappraisal (focus on positive aspects of the situation) and imagery (think about a pleasant image), or they were told 'to relax'. Those in the **cognitive reappraisal** group reported less stressful experiences than those in the other groups. Both these studies show that the negative experience of crowding is psychological and so can best be reduced using psychological techniques.

Expert tip

There are lots of studies to describe here, so be selective and don't think you have to include every single study.

Expert tip

There are three evaluation issues to consider:

- **Methodology** – various methods are used here, including observations, laboratory experiments and field experiments.
- **Generalisations** – the extent to which we can generalise from animals to humans can be considered.
- **Physiological measures** – some measures are more objective and scientific than others.

Expert tip

The issue of generalising from animals to humans appears in different topic areas. You can prepare the same arguments for each and just change the examples that you use.

Natural disaster and technological catastrophe

Revised

Definitions, characteristics and examples of disaster and catastrophe

Psychologists make a distinction between *natural* disaster and *technological* catastrophe, although often news reports refer to all negative events as disasters. Some of these events can be easily categorised but some are more problematic:

- Natural disasters are largely unpredictable, uncontrollable, abrupt and acute. No-one is to blame. They include earthquakes, tsunamis, hurricanes, avalanches, floods and fires.
- Technological catastrophes are unpredictable. They can be controllable (and preventable?), abrupt and acute. Someone is to blame (they should not happen). They include nuclear power accidents, mine collapses, most air crashes and space shuttle explosions (e.g. *Challenger*).
- Ambiguous events are those involving interaction between natural and technological factors, such as the Aberfan (1966) mine 'disaster' (mining waste subsided due to very heavy rain).

A **natural disaster** is a naturally occurring event that has extreme negative consequences for those affected by it.

A **technological catastrophe** is when man-made technology fails and has extreme negative consequences for those affected by it.

Expert tip

Add a number of your own examples for 'natural', 'technological' and 'both'. Try to use events that have published research, or which are known world-wide.

Behaviours during events, and methodology

LeBon (1895) outlined the **contagion** explanation of behaviour during emergency events where normally civilised people panic, behave like wild animals and stampede. The aim is to survive at any cost to other people because the goal is to be first to reach the exit and safety. The 1903 Chicago Iroquois theatre fire, where 603 people died because of stampede, is a perfect example.

Contagion is when individuals brought together in an emergency situation, such as a fire, panic and irrational behaviour quickly spreads among all those present.

Schank and Abelson (1977) outline script schemata – mental programmes (logical sequences of events) of how we and others are likely to behave in a particular situation, such as in a restaurant or when leaving aircraft. In an emergency, some people follow the script of usual behaviour without variation.

Drury et al. (2009) argue that people very rarely 'panic' (people misuse the term) and suggest that they develop a **social identity**, a sense of belonging and unity, 'we-ness', because they are in the extreme situation together and to survive 'there is strength in numbers', with people helping each other to escape and survive.

Mintz (1951) conducted a **laboratory experiment** to investigate emergency behaviour. Participants pulled on a string attached to a cone in a bottle. Only one cone could be removed at a time and cones had to be removed before water filled the bottle. The problem was solved if participants took turns, but they did not and instead they all rushed to get their cone out first. Mintz believes this study replicated, safely, the behaviour of people in a real emergency situation.

Following the Manchester (UK) aeroplane fire where 55 people died, a **simulation** was conducted by the Civil Aviation Authority where students were seated on a real plane and on the word 'go' they all tried to escape, the first out being given a reward of money. To be passed as safe any aeroplane world-wide must be able to evacuate all passengers within 90 seconds.

Kugihara (2007) used a computer-generated 'game' to investigate how people behave. Cocking et al. (2005) used **virtual reality** to investigate how people behave when told to evacuate the London underground.

Another method that can be used is to **interview** survivors (e.g. Drury et al., 2009). What can *never* be done (far too unethical) is to deceive participants into thinking that there is a real emergency happening, because people may panic and injure themselves, or worse, and the ethics of this could never be defended.

Cross check

Laboratory experiments, page 66
Ecological validity, page 78
Self-report interviews, page 73
Ethics, page 79

Psychological intervention before and after events

Psychologists study disasters for three reasons:

- To plan escape strategies, so events do not happen or are not repeated (i.e. before the event).
- To determine how people behave during an event.
- To understand how survivors feel and respond (e.g. post-traumatic stress disorder) so that appropriate therapies can be applied (i.e. after the event).

Sattler et al. (2000, 2002) looked at how people in the USA prepare for disasters. Questionnaires were given and people reported that they prepared by having: petrol for the car, bottled water, a flashlight, candles and matches, batteries and tinned food. People more likely to prepare were older, had a larger income and had previous experience of disastrous events. In Japan, for example, there is a regular earthquake drill where all people evacuate buildings. In other countries, people are told to stay inside buildings.

Now test yourself

29 Outline **three** reasons why psychologists study disasters and catastrophes.

30 Describe a laboratory study that investigated how people behave in emergency situations.

Answers on p.201

Tested

Loftus (1972) researched the Bay Area Rapid Transport (BART) subway system following a fire and outlined the features of a good evacuation message. It must:

- get attention but *not* cause panic (*never* use the word 'fire!')
- be short

- have the most important instructions repeated
- give people confidence that someone in authority is in charge
- use simple words, spoken in an accent that everyone can understand

Following a major event people can suffer from post-traumatic stress disorder. The symptoms of PTSD include:

- re-experiencing phenomena, for example flashbacks, and recurrent and distressing memories
- avoidance or numbing reactions – efforts to avoid anything vaguely associated with the event
- symptoms of increased arousal, such as difficulty concentrating or sleeping

Post-traumatic stress disorder (PTSD) is a natural emotional reaction to a deeply shocking and disturbing experience.

Hodgkinson and Stewart (1991) studied the survivors of *The Herald of Free Enterprise* sinking in Belgium in 1987 where 197 people died. 90% of survivors suffered from PTSD, with symptoms being worse on anniversaries. A *Coping with a Crisis* leaflet was issued to survivors explaining the feelings and emotions (of PTSD) they were experiencing. PTSD is often said to be a normal reaction to an abnormal situation.

PTSD can be treated in a number of different ways. **Systematic desensitisation** (page 165), first outlined by Wolpe (1958), trains the person to relax and then exposes them gradually to the feared stimulus. A more recent alternative is EMDR (**eye movement desensitisation and reprocessing**) outlined by Shapiro (2001), where moving the eyes from side to side appears to reduce the disturbance of negative thoughts and memories.

Cross check

Usefulness, page 95
Questionnaires, page 72

Expert tip

There are three evaluation issues to consider:

- **Methodology** – there is a wide range of methods here: experiments, self-report questionnaires, interviews and simulations/virtual reality.
- **Methodological issues** – the methods have issues related to them such as controls and ecological validity. The methods also have implications for types of data (quantitative and qualitative).
- **Ethics** – ethics is a big issue for this topic area because no study could ever be carried out that creates an emergency situation, due to the harm that this might cause.

Expert tip

If different methods are evident they can all be dealt with as different issues rather than just as one 'methodology issue'.

Personal space and territory

Revised

Definitions, types and measures

Hall (1966) outlines four zones of personal space:

- **intimate** – for people in a relationship, close friends and family
- **personal** – for friends and family
- **social** – for interacting work colleagues
- **public** – for speaking in public, e.g. a lecture

Personal space is an invisible boundary surrounding us.

Alpha personal space is an objective, externally measurable distance and **beta personal space** is the subjective, individual experience.

Altman (1975) outlines three types of territory:

- **primary** – a private area owned by an individual, such as a house
- **secondary** (semi-public) – an area used regularly but shared with others, such as a desk/seat in a classroom
- **public** – an area that can only be occupied temporarily on a first come first served basis, such as a seat on a bus or train

There are five main measures of personal space:

- The **simulation method** uses figures of people on a board or dolls. Little (1968) investigated cultural differences. He created 19 social situations and participants had to place dolls at distances at which they would stand in real social situations. Little measured the distances and found that Scottish females were placed furthest apart while Greek females were the closest.

- In the **stop–distance method** a participant stands a distance away and walks toward the experimenter, stopping at a 'comfortable' point. The distance between the participant and the experimenter is measured. Kennedy et al. (2009) report on 'SM', whose bilateral lesion of the amygdala meant she stood at a distance of 0.34 m rather than the 'normal' average of 0.64 m when her stop–distance was measured.
- **Naturalistic observation** is possible, for example observing two people in a conversation, but precise measurements cannot be taken.
- Duke and Nowicki (1972) outline the **comfortable interpersonal distance scale** (CIDS) which involves a person sitting (or standing) and people approaching from different angles until the subject asks them to stop when they feel space is about to be invaded. A pattern of responses can then be drawn for each person.
- Personal space invasion (see below). As will be seen, if our personal space is invaded we experience negative cognitions and affect, and our behaviour seeks escape from the invasion.

Expert tip

Five different methods are too many to evaluate in one answer. Be selective.

Now test yourself

31 Using an example, describe one non-invasive way in which personal space has been measured.

Answer on p.201

Tested

Cross check

Field experiments, page 67
Simulations, page 148
Observation, page 75
Ecological validity, page 78
Ethics, page 79
Reliability and validity of measures, pages 82 and 86

Invading space and territory

Felipe and Sommer (1966) had an experimental confederate approach and sit next to lone patients (in a psychiatric institution). Results: when not invaded (the control) only 3% left within 5 minutes and 7% within 10 minutes. When invaded, 40% had left within 5 minutes and 50% within 10 minutes, showing that space invasion is uncomfortable and that flight or escape is common.

Middlemist et al. (1976) looked at the effects of space invasion on physiological arousal, performing a study in a three-urinal men's lavatory! The three conditions of this field experiment were: no invasion, a stooge at a far distance and one at a near distance (invading space). Results: little difference was found between the non-invasion and far, but the near invasion affected both onset and duration of urination, showing that invasion of space has physiological effects. Urination was being observed through a periscope in a nearby cubicle!

Fisher and Byrne (1975) studied gender differences in the invasion of personal space in a library and how such invasions were defended. There were three conditions to this field experiment: sitting next to a participant, sitting one seat away and sitting opposite. Results showed gender differences, with females preferring an invader to sit opposite and not next to them, whereas the opposite was true for the males in the study. Females defended their space by placing belongings next to them.

Cross check

Controls, page 71
Quantitative data, page 80

Brodsky et al. (1999) conducted naturalistic observation of 12 attorneys in a courtroom covering six different cases. They found attorneys invaded the personal space of witnesses more during cross-examination compared with when they were questioning the person they were defending. Although the invasion of personal space does affect a person in many different ways (as in the studies described above) Brodsky et al. claimed that the invasion did not affect witnesses in these trials.

Defending territory and space

For the defence of primary territory (e.g. a home), Newman (1976) suggests the following:

- A **zone of territorial influence** – an area that appears to belong to someone (such as having a fence around a garden).
- Increasing **opportunities for surveillance** – if an area can be seen by the occupants, then there is much less vandalism.

Expert tip

Invading space is unethical. This is a major issue here, with many examples. But, although you can give many advantages and disadvantages of being both ethical and unethical, don't drift into examples from the AS course.

Newman based his suggestions on the unsuccessful Pruitt-Igoe project and his own housing design projects such as Clason Point (page 152).

Ruback conducted studies on the defence of public territory. Ruback et al. (1989) found that people talking on a public phone spent longer when someone else was waiting to use it than when no-one was waiting. Ruback (1997) conducted three studies in a car park, finding that when no-one else was waiting to use the car parking space drivers departed faster than when someone was waiting to occupy the space. Ruback attributed these behaviours to the occupying of public territory and making others wait for longer to occupy the public territory they had claimed as 'belonging to them'.

Public territory is often defended with bags, books, clothing, etc. In a field experiment in a university library (Hoppe et al., 1972) a stooge occupied a seat and then left, asking another student to 'save his place'. Sometimes the confederate left no marker and sometimes three books (a personal marker). When an invader (another stooge) tried to occupy the space 71% of students told the invader the seat was occupied. When no marker was left, 57% of the students placed an item of their own to mark and defend the territory. It was also found that personal markers, e.g. an item of clothing such as a coat, were more effective than impersonal markers.

Expert tip

There are three evaluation issues to consider:

- **Methodology** – a wide range of methods appears here, including experiment, observations; and simulations.
- **Methodological issues** – the methods have issues related to them, such as controls and ecological validity. The methods also have implications for reliability and validity.
- **Ethics** – the Middlemist study is argued to be one of the most unethical studies ever conducted. It could be contrasted with the stop–distance study, which is ethical.

Now test yourself

32 Give **two** reasons why invading personal space is unethical.

Answer on p.201

Tested

Expert tip

A question could ask you to investigate something like the parking of cars in a car park. You should think about the method you could use and the strengths of choosing this particular method.

Expert tip

Be careful if you try some of these methods for yourself. Some people get upset when you study them without consent, particularly if they want to sit down!

Architecture and behaviour

Revised

Theories and effects of urban living on health and social behaviour

Theories of **urban living** include the following:

- **Adaptation level** – each person has an optimal level of stimulation, sometimes tolerating large crowds that over-stimulate, but sometimes having too little stimulation (getting bored). We therefore regulate the amount of stimulation and *adapt* ourselves to the environment we are in.
- **Behaviour constraint** – people living in cities feel their lives are constrained and they have to modify their behaviour accordingly. There may be more crime, travelling may take longer and going shopping could mean high social density. These factors constrain behaviour and may cause negative feelings and learned helplessness.
- **Environmental stress theory** – Glass and Singer (1972) argue that transportation noise present in a city, or the high social density of a shopping mall, can negatively affect behaviour and cause stress. An individual can respond *constructively* by applying coping strategies to try to reassert control, or *destructively* by behaving aggressively.
- **Overload** – humans have a limited processing capacity and at times, when the amount of information needing to be processed exceeds capacity, overload occurs. Milgram (1970) uses the term **social overload**. When overloaded, some form of adaptation is required to allow the individual

to cope. Coping strategies include attending only to important stimuli or erecting interpersonal barriers.

- **Health behaviour** – Soderberg (1977) measured rates of HIV infection, comparing urban, semi-urban and rural blood donors in Tanzania. Male and female donors from urban and semi-urban villages, non-farmers from urban villages and unmarried donors were identified as high-risk groups and Soderberg concluded that this pattern was consistent with extensive risk shown more in urban communities.

Social behaviour includes the pro-social behaviour of helping. Altman (1969) had participants ask residents if they could use their telephone to call a friend. Altman found that a woman was allowed to use the telephone in 94% of rural homes (40% allowed men) but in city homes this was just 40% (14% for men), showing more helping behaviour in rural communities.

Amato (1983) had a stooge limp down a street then scream, fall over and clutch his leg, which began bleeding profusely (this was fake). In rural communities 50% stopped to help. In a small city this dropped to 25% and in major cities to 15%. Conclusion: city residents help less.

Urban living is having a place of residence in a relatively densely populated area.

Cross check

Field experiments, page 67
Ecological validity, page 78
Controls, page 71
Ethics, page 79
Reliability and validity of measures, pages 82 and 86

Urban renewal and housing design

In the USA the **Pruitt-Igoe Project** was a public housing project in which 12 000 people were relocated into 43 buildings, 11 stories high, containing 2 762 apartments and covering 57 acres. After 3 years there was a very high crime rate. Gangs formed and rape, vandalism and robbery became common.

Because crime frequently took place in elevators and stairwells, the upper floors were abandoned. By 1970, 27 of the 43 buildings were empty. The whole estate was demolished in 1972.

Urban renewal is a program of land redevelopment in an area of moderate-to-high-density urban land use.

Housing design refers to systematic plans for building places for people to live.

Newman (1976) believed that certain buildings (e.g. the Pruitt-Igoe Project) are more likely to be vandalised/burgled because of their design. Crime would be reduced if a design were to include:

- a zone of territorial influence – an area that appears to belong to someone. If there is no apparent owner (i.e. it is semi-public) more vandalism is likely.
- opportunities for surveillance. Vandalism is more likely if the vandals cannot be seen and they know they cannot be seen.

Newman designed a low-cost housing project – Clason Point in New York City – 'cluster housing', with 12–40 families per cluster. He increased defensible space by:

- assigning public space controlled by specific families by using fencing
- reducing the number of pedestrian routes through the project and improving lighting along the paths
- improving the image by encouraging a sense of personal ownership through giving different colours to houses

Cross check

Generalisations, page 97

He found that residents took pride in their homes, planted grass, added personal modifications and even swept public pathways. Serious crimes dropped by 62%. The number of residents who said they felt they had the right to question a stranger in the project doubled.

Another successful project by Newman (1994) was the Five Oaks development in Ohio, USA. Streets were closed, lighting was improved and he introduced speed bumps and divided the estate into 'mini-neighbourhoods'. He also encouraged a sense of personal ownership.

Now test yourself

33 Describe **one** urban housing design project that was unsuccessful.

Answer on p.202

Tested ☐

Community environmental design

The **retail environment** has an impact on a variety of consumer emotions and attitudes. It can include: music styles and tempos; effective exterior store windows; different types and levels of lighting; store layout; and ambient odour. Machleit et al. (2000) studied the perceived crowding in a retail store, while

Michon et al. (2005) investigated the effects of ambient odours on shoppers' emotions, and perceptions of the retail environment and product quality under various levels of retail density. Their field experiment had three IVs: no ambient odour, lavender scent and citrus scent. Using a questionnaire, the results showed that an odour only positively influenced shoppers' perceptions under the medium retail density conditions; not in low or high socially dense conditions.

Finlay et al. (2006) identify two main types of casino design. The Kranes casino 'playground' model includes environmental elements designed to induce pleasure, legibility and restoration (relief from environmental stress), with open space, high ceilings, vegetation and an entertaining, 'fantasy' environment that is comfortable and pleasant. In contrast, the Friedman design proposes a focus on the slot or fruit machines as the dominant feature of the décor. Ceilings are low and bland so the eye isn't drawn above the machines and there is a maze-like design with hard-to-find exits encouraging continuous play. The 48 participants in Finlay et al.'s study found the Krane's design led to more pleasure and restoration.

For community environmental design Whyte et al. (1980) observed and filmed 18 plazas in New York City, counting usage on pleasant days and relating usage to various features of the plaza. Whyte (1980) suggested that urban plazas should promote positive social interaction and include places to sit, trees, amentities such as food outlets, and things to see and to do. Brower (1980) extended this work, adding that a successful design should take into account the reduction of cars, give residents things to do and places to be, keep the street front alive and make places like parks more attractive to adults.

Community environmental design is the design of public places for public use.

Expert tip

An exam question could ask you to design a field experiment (or any other method) to investigate some aspect of a retail environment. Think about designing a study now rather than making one up in the examination.

Expert tip

There are three evaluation issues to consider:

- **Methodology** – a wide range of methods appear here, including field experiments and many real-life examples. Contrasting between the two is always good evaluation.
- **Methodological issues** – the methods have issues related to them – ecological validity contrasts field experiments with real-life examples, and reliability and validity are relevant here too.
- **Generalisations** – can we generalise types of housing design from one culture to another? Pruitt-Igoe may have failed because it was in the USA. Different countries do have different designs and different relationships between people.

Now test yourself

34 Describe **two** types of gambling casino design.

Answer on p.202

Tested

Environmental cognition

Revised

Definitions, measures, errors and individual differences in cognitive maps

Environmental cognition is how we process information about the world so we know where we are. We know the route from home to school and we can recall what other houses, buildings, shops, etc. look like. We do all this because we have **cognitive maps**.

Lynch (1960) identified five common elements of **sketch maps**:

- paths – roads, walkways, rivers (i.e. routes for travel)
- edges – non-travelled lines (e.g. fences, walls)
- districts – larger spaces (e.g. a town square or small village)
- nodes – places, junctions, crossroads, intersections (i.e. where people and transport systems meet)
- landmarks – distinctive places people use for reference points (e.g. the tallest building, a statue)

Moar (1976) used **multidimensional scaling**. Moar asked female participants ('housewives') from Scotland and Cambridge (England) to draw a map of the British Isles. When putting their maps together he found extreme distortions:

Environmental cognition is the way we acquire, store, organise and recall information about locations, distances and arrangements of the great outdoors (Gifford, 1997).

A **cognitive map** is a pictorial and semantic image in our head of how places are arranged (Kitchin, 1994).

Expert tip

We cannot reproduce a cognitive map (of what is in our 'mind's eye'). The best we can do is to draw a sketch map. This gives neither quantitative nor qualitative data.

both sets of participants significantly over-estimated the size of the area with which they were familiar and significantly under-estimated the size of the area with which they were unfamiliar.

People make a range of errors when drawing sketch maps:

- Euclidean bias – people assume roads are grid-like, with right-angles, when they are not (different angles and bends).
- Superordinate-scale bias – we group areas (e.g. counties) together and make a judgement on an area rather than a specific place.
- Segmentation bias – we estimate distances incorrectly when we break a journey into segments compared with estimating a journey as a whole.
- Maps are often incomplete – we leave out minor details and we distort by having things too close together, too far apart or misaligning. We over-estimate the size of familiar areas (e.g. Moar, 1976).

There are individual differences in this area. Bryant et al. (1991) suggest that men are much better than women in the acquisition, accuracy and organisation of spatial information. Appleyard (1976), for example, found overall accuracy was equal, but women emphasised districts and landmarks whereas men emphasised path structure. Holding (1992) found that men began with paths and nodes followed by landmarks; women began with landmarks.

Now test yourself

35 Describe **two** errors made when drawing sketch maps.

Answer on p.202

Tested

Cognitive maps in animals

Tolman (1932) was the first to use the term 'cognitive map' in reference to a mental ability possessed by rats when finding food at the far end of an experimental maze he had built. Since then many researchers have investigated cognitive maps in many species.

Jacobs and Linman (1991) investigated how squirrels relocated buried nuts. Eight squirrels buried 10 nuts, which were then removed by the experimenter to remove the smell of the original nut. Alternative nuts were buried in the area. When looking for their buried nuts 2, 4 or 12 days later, the squirrels easily found the locations of their original nuts, but not the alternative ones. Conclusion: squirrels must use a cognitive map to find the specific locations of their nuts.

Capaldi et al. (2000) tracked the flight patterns of bees, using harmonic radar (with a small aerial attached to each bee). They found young bees take a number of 'orientation' flights to allow them to become increasingly familiar with their environment. Each flight is restricted to a narrow sector around the hive but with experience the bee flies faster and travels further, suggesting that the bee learns the cognitive map of the local landscape in a progressive fashion.

Walcott et al. (1973, 1979) has researched ways in which homing pigeons find their way home. In one study he drugged pigeons while they were being taken away from home, so they could not follow the landmarks of the route, but the pigeons flew home. It is generally now accepted that pigeons (and maybe even humans) have the substance magnetite in their brain, which responds to the magnetic fields of the Earth. This was supported by fitting pigeons with a Helmholtz coil to disrupt magnetic signals; they struggled to find their way home.

Designing better maps; wayfinding

A 'you-are-here' map is a **map design** that has an arrow or marker showing your current location on the map. This type of map is not usually helpful for tourists because it does not translate to reality. Levine (1982) suggests two ways to improve to 'you-are-here' maps:

- Structure mapping. The map should reflect the layout and appearance of the setting it represents. It should be placed near an asymmetrical feature so that more than one building is visible. The map should include a landmark that is visible in reality.

Cross check

Laboratory experiments, page 66
Field experiments, page 67
Ecological validity, page 78
Generalisations from animals to humans, page 100

- Orientation. The map should be aligned to match the setting and it should have forward equivalence (the top of the map should be straight ahead).

To **way-find**, Segal and White (1975) suggest that children learn a sequence, while McDonald and Pellegrino (1993) suggest the same process for adults in a new environment:

- **Landmarks** are noticed and remembered.
- Paths or **routes** between landmarks are constructed.
- Landmarks and paths are organised into **clusters**.
- Clusters and features are coordinated into area or **survey** knowledge.

Aginsky et al. (1997) suggest that this 'stage theory' is incorrect. They propose, after research using a driving simulator to learn a route, that participants either choose a visually dominated strategy (landmarks and routes) or go straight to a spatially dominated strategy (survey maps).

Aginsky et al. (1997) and Maguire et al. (1997, 2000) used real-life knowledge for **virtual way-finding**. Maguire et al. used London taxi drivers (see page 48). Jansen et al. (2001) used a virtual maze to look at factors that determine a detour strategy – what people do if they cannot follow the usual and familiar route. If a person has survey knowledge then a detour is not a problem, but if a person has landmark and route knowledge then a detour causes problems.

Expert tip

There are three evaluation issues to consider:

- **Methodology** – the use of simulations and virtual reality can be contrasted with laboratory and field experiments.
- **Methodological issues** – arising from the methods is the extent to which we can generalise from laboratory studies of virtual reality. We can also consider the extent to which such studies are useful.
- **Generalisations** – studies on animals raise the debate about the extent to which we can generalise from animals to humans.

Now test yourself

36 Describe **two** ways in which 'you-are-here' maps can be improved.

Answer on p.202

Tested

To **way-find** is to successfully follow a route from point A to point B.

Expert tip

Refer to the AS core study by Maguire et al. However, don't just describe that study in this section. Only use information from it that applies to virtual way-finding.

Cross check

Generalisations, page 97

4.4 Psychology and abnormality

Models of abnormality

Revised

Definitions of abnormality

Abnormality has been defined in a number of ways:

- **Deviation from statistical norms**. This is simply deviating from the norm or average, as in a normal distribution curve. Anyone at either end of the curve is abnormal or atypical.
- **Deviation from social norms**. This refers to the commonly held norms of a society, which has expectations of how people should think and how they should behave. Such norms vary from one culture to another and they also change over time.
- **Deviation from ideal mental health**. If the characteristics of ideal mental health could be determined, then anyone not possessing those characteristics, or deviating from them, by definition would be abnormal.
- **Failure to function adequately**. This suggests that people who experience personal distress or discomfort will seek the help of a health-care professional. They would take on what is known as 'the sick role'.

Mental health **diagnosis** differs according to where in the world the assessment takes place. In most places its diagnosis is based on the person's report of symptoms, his or her ability (or inability) to function in society appropriately and

Abnormality is a subjectively defined behavioural characteristic, assigned to people with 'non-normal', rare or dysfunctional conditions.

Expert tip

Note that two definitions of abnormality have nothing to do with mental illness or even health. For example, people who are very tall or very short could be classed as 'abnormal'.

an observation of the person's attitudes and behaviour. Reference will then be made to one of two classificatory guides that list all recognised mental illnesses:

- **DSM** (*Diagnostic and Statistical Manual*) began in 1952. The latest version is *DSM-IV* (1994). *DSM-V* will be published in 2013.
- **ICD** (*International Standard Classification of Injuries and Causes of Death*). This began in 1958 and is now in its 10th edition, *ICD-10*.

DSM lists 16 major categories of mental illness and *ICD* lists 11.

A medical practitioner (whether assessing a mental or physical illness) will always want to make a correct diagnosis. If the practitioner is in doubt they should always assume that an illness is present and refer or admit a person for further testing. The worst thing a practitioner can do is to assume there is nothing wrong and send away an ill person. To do this would be medical negligence and the consequences for the person can be very severe and sometimes result in death.

The study by Rosenhan (1973, page 53) showed that the psychiatric diagnosis was reliable. Although it was claimed that the psychiatrists could not distinguish between the sane and the insane, given the presentation of symptoms, all the psychiatrists made the correct decision to admit because they were in doubt and they were 'being safe rather than being sorry'.

Now test yourself

37 Using an example, explain what is meant by the 'deviation from statistical norms' explanation of abnormality.

Answer on p.202

Tested

Expert tip

Question 37 asks about the 'deviation from statistical norms' explanation of abnormality. There are three others that could also be asked about in an examination. Be active – why not prepare answers for all four.

Diagnosis is the process of identifying a medical condition or disease by its signs or symptoms and from the results of various diagnostic procedures.

Models of abnormality

The **medical/biomedical model of abnormality** focuses only on biological factors to understand a person's illness and excludes psychological and social factors. The model includes all possible biological bases for behaviour — chemical, genetic, physiological, neurological and anatomical. The approach is summarised in a classic quotation from Maher (1966):

Deviant behaviour is referred to as psychopathology, *is classified on the basis of* symptoms, *the classification being called* diagnosis, *the methods used to try to change the behaviours are called* therapies, *and these are often carried out in* mental *or* psychiatric hospitals. *If the deviant behaviour ceases, the patient is described as* cured.

A **model of abnormality** is a collection of assumptions concerning the way abnormality is caused and treated.

Expert tip

Consider these models in relation to what you know from AS and how they relate to treatments in the next sub-section. Then relate them to different types of abnormality in all the other topics in this option.

The medical model of abnormality assumes the following:

- Dysfunctional behaviour has a biological cause.
- Mental disorders are the same as physical illnesses, but are just located in a different part of the body.
- Mental illnesses can be diagnosed and treated in the same ways as physical illnesses – mainly with drugs, but with the options of surgery or electro-convulsive therapy.

The behavioural model of abnormality assumes the following:

- All behaviour (adaptive and maladaptive) is learned through the principles of classical conditioning (association) and operant conditioning (reinforcement).
- Dysfunctional (maladaptive) behaviour is learned in exactly the same way.
- Dysfunctional behaviour can be treated with behaviour therapies, or with behaviour modification, in which maladaptive behaviour is replaced with adaptive behaviour.

The psychodynamic model of abnormality assumes the following:

- Psychological illness comes about from repressed emotions and thoughts from experiences in the past (usually childhood).
- As a result of this repression, alternative behaviour replaces what is being repressed.

Assumptions of the cognitive model of abnormality:

- Cognitive psychologists believe that thinking determines all behaviour and that dysfunctional behaviour is caused by inappropriate or faulty thought processes.

- Cognitive therapy involves helping people to restructure their thoughts and to think more positively about themselves, their life and their future.

Treatments of abnormality

The use of **biochemicals** (drugs) is very common in the treatment of **schizophrenia**. Anti-psychotics were the first to be developed in the 1950s. The next generation were the atypical anti-psychotics, which act by blocking dopamine receptors. A third generation of drugs also block dopamine receptors, but have reduced side-effects.

Drugs are also used to relieve the symptoms of **depression** and include MAOIs, SSRIs and SRNIs. MAOIs inhibit neurotransmitters such as adrenaline and melatonin in addition to serotonin and noradrenaline. SSRIs are sometimes used to treat pyromania, kleptomania and occasionally gambling. If obsessive-compulsive disorder is caused by low serotonin levels, then drugs can be used to increase the activity of serotonin in the brain. This is exactly what clomipramine does.

Electro-convulsive therapy (ECT) is used to treat severe depression. It is sometimes used to treat catatonic schizophrenia.

Behaviour therapies include:

- **token economy** systems. For example, Paul and Lentz (1977) found this to be successful in reducing bizarre motor behaviour in schizophrenics. It has also been used to treat alcoholics.
- **systematic desensitisation** (Wolpe, 1958). This is used specifically for the counter-conditioning of fears, **phobias** and anxieties.
- **flooding** (Stampfl, 1967). This treats phobias using 'in vivo' exposure – actual exposure to the feared stimulus.
- **aversion therapy** (or overt sensitisation). This can be used in the treatment of alcoholics. The drug antabuse is given, and when any alcohol is drunk, the person becomes violently sick.

Sensky et al. (2000) used **cognitive-behavioural therapy** (CBT) to treat schizophrenia, finding it to be effective in treating negative as well as positive symptoms. Cognitive-behavioural treatments are also used for impulse control disorders:

- **Covert sensitisation** involves the person *imagining* associating an aversive stimulus with the impulsive behaviour. For example, Kohn and Antonuccio (2002) used kleptomania-specific covert sensitisation successfully.
- **Imaginal desensitisation** involves teaching progressive muscle relaxation and then the person visualises themselves being exposed to the situation that triggers the drive to carry out the impulsive behaviour. Blaszcznski and Nower (2003) found this technique was particularly effective with gamblers.

Ost and Westling (1995) found that CBT led to a significant reduction in the number of panic attacks. **Exposure and response prevention** is used to treat **obsessive-compulsive disorder**.

Beck et al. (1979) believed in **cognitive restructuring**, finding that 98% of those in their study were better than those following anti-depressant drug treatments. Ellis (1962) outlined the use of **rational emotive behaviour therapy** (REBT) to dispute and disrupt irrational beliefs.

Psychoanalytic psychotherapy uses a 'talking treatment' – encouraging the verbalisation of all the patient's thoughts, including free association, fantasies, and dreams, from which the analyst formulates the nature of the unconscious conflicts that are causing the patient's symptoms and character problems. This addresses the underlying problems generating negative emotions that cause **mania**, and is successful for children who exhibit signs of **pyromania**. It has also been used to treat phobias.

Expert tip

Further details on all these treatments can be found in the topics following this sub-topic.

Expert tip

You might be asked how you find out about the long-term effectiveness of a particular treatment. Logically you would conduct a longitudinal study. Think about it now rather than in an examination.

Now test yourself

38 Briefly describe **three** different cognitive-behavioural therapies.

Answer on p.202

Tested

Cross check

Reductionism, page 104
Behaviourist perspective, page 92
Psychodynamic perspective, page 93
Cognitive approach, page 87
Physiological/biological approach, page 89

Expert tip

There are three evaluation issues to consider:

- **Approaches and perspectives** – there are at least four different ones here. You can evaluate any one of them, or make comparisons and contrasts.
- **Reductionism** – can illnesses be reduced to biochemistry, genes, maladaptive learning or unconscious processes?
- **Generalisations/individual differences** – can any one model explain all abnormalities and/or mental illnesses? Can any one model explain the behaviour of all people with a particular illness?

Schizophrenia

Revised

Types, symptoms and characteristics of schizophrenia

There are five main types of **schizophrenia**:

- **disorganised (hebephrenic)**, involving incoherence, disorganised behaviour, disorganised delusions and vivid hallucinations
- **simple**, involving a gradual withdrawal from reality
- **catatonic**, involving impairment of motor activity, where the person often holds the same position for hours or days
- **paranoid**, where the person has well-organised, delusional thoughts (and hallucinations), but a high level of awareness
- **undifferentiated/untypical**, referring to sufferers who do not fit into any of the above categories

Schizophrenia can be defined as the disintegration of the process of thinking and of emotional responsiveness.

Now test yourself

39 Outline **three** types of schizophrenia.

Answer on p.202

Tested

Depending on the *type* of schizophrenia, symptoms can be 'positive' or 'negative'. 'Positive' (common) symptoms include:

- hallucinations – hearing, smelling, feeling or seeing something that is not there
- delusions – believing something completely even though others do not believe it
- difficulty thinking – finding it hard to concentrate and drifting from one idea to another
- feeling controlled – that thoughts are vanishing, or that they are not your own, or being taken over by someone else

'Negative' (not very common) symptoms include:

- loss of interest, energy and emotions
- feeling uncomfortable with other people

Explanations of schizophrenia

There are many explanations of schizophrenia, three of which are the genetic, the biochemical and the cognitive.

Studies show that 1 in 10 people with schizophrenia have a parent with the illness. While this does not provide proof of a **genetic link** for schizophrenia, such figures add support. Twin studies are also important. Gottesman and Shields (1972) examined the records of 57 schizophrenics (40% monozygotic and 60% dizygotic) between 1948 and 1964. In this sample they found concordance rates (the probability of a twin having schizophrenia if the other twin has it) of 42% for monozygotic twins and 9% for dizygotic twins. This again provides evidence for a genetic link for schizophrenia.

The **biochemical explanation** of schizophrenia is that it is caused by changes in dopamine function in the brain. An excess of dopamine causes the neurones that use dopamine to fire too often and therefore transmit too many messages, overloading the system and causing the symptoms of schizophrenia.

Cross check

Reductionism, page 104
Nature/nurture, page 103
Cognitive approach, page 87

The **cognitive explanation** suggests that schizophrenia is a result of 'faulty information processing' due to specific 'cognitive deficits'. It claims that schizophrenia sufferers have problems with metarepresentation, which is involved with giving us the ability to reflect upon our thoughts, behaviours and feelings, as well as giving us the sense of self-awareness. Frith (1992) took this further and argued that several symptoms of schizophrenia could be explained by mentalising impairment (the ability to attribute mental states such as thoughts, beliefs and intentions to people, allowing an individual to explain, manipulate and predict behaviour) and that theory of mind is impaired in schizophrenics.

Now test yourself

40 Outline the cognitive explanation of schizophrenia proposed by Frith (1992).

Answer on p.202

Tested

Treatments for schizophrenia

The use of biochemicals (drugs) is very common in the treatment of schizophrenia and has gone through a number of phases. The first **antipsychotics** (or neuroleptics) were produced in the 1950s. The first such drug was chlorpromazine, which has a powerful calming effect and was known as the 'chemical lobotomy'. Other phenothiazines act as tranquillisers, sedating the patient and relieving the symptoms of psychosis such as delusions and hallucinations. The second generation of drug treatments were the **atypical anti-psychotics**, which act mainly by blocking dopamine receptors. They also reduce many of the side-effects of the first-generation drugs. The third generation of drugs, such as Aripiprazole, are thought to reduce susceptibility to metabolic side-effects associated with the second-generation atypical antipsychotics.

Electro-convulsive therapy (ECT) was originally developed as a treatment for schizophrenia in 1938 by Cerletti. In its early days it was given bilaterally, where electrodes were placed on each side of the patient's head. However, it was found to be ineffective in reducing psychotic symptoms. It is now used mainly as a treatment for severe depression and is usually only administered when drug treatment has failed. It is sometimes used to treat catatonic schizophrenia.

Psychosurgery has been used as a last resort when drugs and ECT have apparently failed. This involves either cutting out brain nerve fibres or ablating parts of the brain that are thought to be involved in the disorder. The most common form of psychosurgery is a pre-frontal lobotomy, usually used for schizophrenia.

Paul and Lentz (1977) found that the use of a **token economy** was successful in reducing bizarre motor behaviour and in improving social interactions with staff and other patients. Originally devised by Ayllon and Azrin (1968), the token economy system is based on the behaviourist principle of positive reinforcement, which involves giving tokens for good or desirable behaviour; these can be later exchanged for rewards. However, the token economy system does not have any impact on hallucinations and delusions, and any improvements tend not to last once the patients are released.

Sensky et al. (2000) used **cognitive behaviour therapy** (CBT) to treat schizophrenia. The participants had schizophrenia for at least 6 months, despite drug treatment with chlorpromazine. After CBT sessions for at least 2 months, patients showed significant improvements. At the 9-month follow-up evaluation, patients who had received CBT continued to improve and this was not due to changes in prescribed medication. It was concluded that CBT is effective in treating negative as well as positive symptoms in schizophrenia.

Cross check

Determinism, page 101
Perspectives, page 92
Ethics of drug treatments and ECT, page 79
Usefulness, page 95

Expert tip

There are three evaluation issues to consider:

- **Usefulness** – how useful are treatments of schizophrenia? To what extent can the use of a token economy system be generalised. For example, it is good to help social relationships with other schizophrenics, but it is not a *treatment*.
- **Nature vs nurture** – here there is biological determinism (nature/genes) and environmental determinism (learning environment). Is schizophrenia learned or inherited?
- **Approaches and perspectives** – there are different models here, representing different viewpoints, all of which have different assumptions. Comparing and contrasting is a high-level skill and is worth doing.

Expert tip

Don't just choose issues to go into an essay randomly. Think about an issue and the examples you will use as evidence to support your arguments.

Abnormal affect

Revised

Types, characteristics, examples and sex differences in abnormal affect

The term 'affect' relates to mood or feelings. A person with depression will have intense feelings of negativity or despair, while a person who is manic will have intense feelings of happiness and 'over-activity'. A person can have depression (unipolar) or they can be bipolar, which is the alternative name for manic depression, where a person has swings of mood from one extreme to the other.

Abnormal affect concerns disorders of mood and emotion, most typically depression and mania or manic depression (bipolar disorder).

Features of depressive episodes include:

- physically lethargic; a loss of energy
- loss of interest; feelings of unhappiness, inadequacy, worthlessness; possibly thoughts of suicide
- continual urges to cry
- difficulty in concentrating and an inability to think positively, often with hopeless feelings of guilt
- difficulty in sleeping; possible loss of appetite and weight; avoiding other people

Expert tip

Many students think 'abnormal affect' is a generalised term that concerns all 'abnormal' disorders. It does not. It concerns disorders of mood or feelings.

Features of manic episodes include:

- feeling very excited; having lots of energy and enthusiasm
- quickly moving from one thing to another; spontaneous and full of good ideas
- outbursts of exuberance, heightened good humour; often entertaining those present
- talking quickly; feeling less inhibited; making spur-of-the-moment decisions

There are **sex differences** in depression. Studies have estimated that women are 2–3 times more likely than men to suffer from clinical depression. A number of reasons have been proposed to explain this:

- Women have many different hormones (e.g. those associated with menstruation, childbirth and menopause) and these exist in differing amounts.
- Women are more likely to seek medical help than men and so are more likely to be diagnosed.
- Many men (even medical practitioners) see women as inferior and may be more likely to diagnose a women as depressed than they would a man with the same symptoms.

Explanations of depression

Depression may be **genetic**. The closer the genetic relationship, the more likely people are to be diagnosed with depression. First-degree relatives (close family members) share 50% of their genes and according to Oruc et al. (1998) first-degree relatives of people diagnosed with depression are significantly more likely to be diagnosed with depression than non first-degree relatives.

Depression may be caused by **neurochemicals**. Schildkraut (1965) suggested that too much noradrenaline causes mania and too little causes depression. However, serotonin was found to exist in low levels for both depression and mania. What is known is that both serotonin and noradrenaline imbalances are involved in affective disorders.

Beck (1979) proposes a **cognitive theory**, believing that people react differently to aversive stimuli because of the thought patterns that they have built up throughout their lives. **Schemas** (core beliefs) are formed in early life, for example a **self-blame schema** makes the person feel responsible for everything that goes wrong, while an **ineptness schema** causes them to expect failure every time. These predispose the person to have negative automatic thoughts (NATs), but they will only surface if an event triggers them. When that happens,

cognitive errors maintain the negative beliefs. Depression results from the **negative cognitive triad**, comprising unrealistically negative views about the **self**, the **world** and the **future**.

Seligman et al. (1988) extended the original theory of **learned helplessness**, suggesting that a person's **attributional style** determined why people responded differently to adverse events. If a person makes an internal attribution (they are the cause) and if they believe that this is stable and global (the cause is consistent and this applies everywhere) then they may feel helpless and may experience depression. However, if they make other attributions (e.g. that the cause is external or situational; or unstable and specific), then helplessness and depression are unlikely. Attributional style is assessed using the **Attributional Style Questionnaire** (ASQ). Seligman and others have found depression to be associated with an internal/global/stable pattern. After therapy, depression is again assessed and the attributional style is indeed less internal/global/stable.

Treatments for depression

There are three main types of drug that relieve the symptoms of depression:

- MAOIs (monoamine oxidase inhibitors, e.g. Marplan, Nardil, Parnate, Emsam)
- SSRIs (selective serotonin reuptake inhibitors, e.g. Citalopram, Escitalopram)
- SNRIs (serotonin and noradrenaline reuptake inhibitors, e.g. Venlafaxine, Duloxetine)

Anti-depressants affect neurotransmitters. Those relevant to depression are serotonin and noradrenaline. SRRIs inhibit serotonin and SNRIs inhibit both serotonin and noradrenaline. MAOIs inhibit a wider range of neurotransmitters such as adrenaline and melatonin in addition to serotonin and noradrenaline. Anti-depressants do not remove the *cause* of depression but instead relieve the symptoms.

ECT is now used to treat severe depression when other treatments are ineffective. A patient is given a general anaesthetic (unlike in the early days) and an electrical pulse is given to the head. How it works is not known. Some patients are confused afterwards and some suffer memory problems.

Beck et al. (1979) believe in **cognitive restructuring**. This done in a six-stage process, starting with an explanation of the therapy. Next the person is taught to identify unpleasant emotions, the situations in which these occur and associated negative automatic thoughts. Then the person is taught to challenge the negative thoughts and replace them with positive thoughts. Finally the person can begin to challenge the underlying dysfunctional beliefs before the therapy ends. Dobson (1989) compared restructuring scores on the **Beck Depression Inventory** (BDI) with other treatments. 98% were better than controls; 70% better than those in anti-depressant drug treatments and 70% better than those in some other form of psychotherapy.

Ellis (1962) outlined **rational emotive therapy**, which developed into **rational emotive behaviour therapy** (REBT). Ellis focuses on how illogical beliefs are maintained through:

- A: an **a**ctivating event, perhaps the behaviour or attitude of another person
- B: the **b**elief held about A
- C: the **c**onsequences – thoughts, feelings or behaviours – resulting from A

Ellis describes the illogical or irrational beliefs using the terms **musterbating** (I *must* be perfect at all times) and **I-can't-stand-it-itis** (the belief that when something goes wrong it is a major disaster). In order to change to rational beliefs, Ellis expands the ABC model to include:

- D for **d**isputing the irrational beliefs
- E for the **e**ffects of successful disruption of the irrational beliefs

Expert tip

Many students refer to 'anti-depressants' to cover to a wide-range of drug treatments (including those for schizophrenia). It is far more accurate to refer to the drug type (e.g. SSRIs) and then apply it to treating depression, obsessive-compulsive disorder, etc.

Now test yourself

41 Outline drug treatments used for depression.

Answer on p.202

Tested

Cross check

Biological, cognitive and behavioural perspectives/models, page 92
Nature/nurture, page 103
Determinism, page 101
Reductionism, page 104
Usefulness, page 95

Now test yourself

42 Outline the rational emotive behaviour therapy proposed by Ellis.

Answer on p.202

Tested

Expert tip

Rational emotive therapy is the early version and rational emotive behaviour therapy is the later version. A question could ask about one or the other.

Expert tip

There are three evaluation issues to consider:

- **Nature vs nurture** – some theories suggest that abnormal affect is inherited and some theories suggest that it is learned. Which is it?
- **Usefulness** – how useful is REBT or cognitive restructuring? Is it not *easier* just to take a drug? It might depend on what *causes* the depression.
- **Ethics** – is the use of ECT ethical? Is it ethical to give drugs to treat abnormal affect, which are often addictive? People can be addicted to drugs that are prescribed by a medical practitioner.

Addiction and impulse control disorders

Revised

Definitions, types and characteristics of addictions

People can be addicted to many things, not just drugs. People can be addicted to alcohol (alcoholics) and to nicotine (most smokers). However, we may believe that an alcoholic is mentally ill, but perhaps not say that a smoker is mentally ill. Both, however, have the characteristic symptoms of an addiction.

An **addiction** is a condition produced by repeated consumption of a natural or synthetic substance, in which the person has become physically and psychologically dependent on the substance.

Physical dependence (unlike **psychological dependence**) involves **tolerance**, which is when the body increasingly adapts to a substance and requires larger and larger doses of it to achieve the same effect, and **withdrawal**, which is the unpleasant physical and psychological symptoms people experience when they stop using a substance.

Physical dependence is a state in which the body has adjusted to the presence of a substance and incorporated it into the 'normal' functioning of the body's tissues.

Psychological dependence is a state in which people feel a *compulsion* to use a substance for the pleasant effect it produces (this can happen without being physically dependent).

Now test yourself

Tested

43 What is the difference between physical dependence and psychological dependence?

Answer on p.202

Griffiths (2005) believes there are six components that help define *any* addiction (even to coffee, chocolate and the internet):

- **Salience** – when when an activity becomes the single most important activity in the person's life and dominates their thinking, feelings and behaviour.
- **Euphoria** – the experience people report when carrying out their addictive behaviour, such as a 'rush', a 'buzz' or a 'high'.
- **Tolerance** – where an increasing amount of activity is required to achieve the same effect.
- **Withdrawal** – the unpleasant feelings and physical effects that occur when the addictive behaviour is suddenly discontinued or reduced.
- **Conflict** – with those around them (interpersonal conflict), with other activities (job, schoolwork, social life, hobbies and interests) or from within the individual themselves (intrapsychic conflict).
- **Relapse** – chances of relapse are very high, even after a long time.

Expert tip

When you write your essay, don't spend too much time going through each of these features that characterise addiction. Ensure that your essay is balanced, covering something from all three sub-topics.

Impulse control disorders have three typical features:

- Before committing the act there is a growing tension.
- During the act the person feels pleasure from acting, and often feels relief from the urge.
- Afterward the person may or may not feel guilt, regret or blame.

An **impulse control disorder** is a failure to resist a temptation, urge or impulse.

Pyromania is where a person has the urge to deliberately start a fire (and often to watch the fire or emergency services). Specifically, before setting the fire, the person must have felt some feelings of tension or arousal, must show attraction to fire, must feel a sense of relief or satisfaction from setting the fire and witnessing it, and must not have other motives for setting the fire.

Kleptomania is not being able to resist the urge to collect or hoard things. Kleptomaniacs may steal things (even though they have money to pay), even things of little or no value. Sometimes the harder the challenge of stealing the more the thrill, relief and guilt.

Compulsive gambling is where a person has to gamble to gain euphoria or relieve tension. This typically includes feelings of gratification or relief afterward. Here the term compulsive is used because compulsions are recurring actions that the individual is forced to carry out.

Expert tip

In your essay, don't spend too much time describing what pyromania, kleptomania and gambling are. Look at explanations and treatments too.

Causes of addiction and impulse control disorders

Peters and Preedy (2002) suggest that half the people who abuse alcohol have a close relative who also abuses alcohol. Is this because a child inherits genes for it, or is it because a child learns to become an alcoholic? One way to investigate the influence of genes is to do research on twins and adoptions. Generally studies show a vulnerability to alcoholism rather than a specific gene.

Now test yourself

44 What are the typical characteristics of impulse control disorders?

Answer on p.202

Tested

The question is how environmental events might relate to how the biological predisposition toward alcohol dependence is mediated. Schuckit (1985) compared individuals who were genetically at *high risk* (close relatives who abuse alcohol) with those who were at *low risk*. Schuckit suggests that people who are genetically prone to becoming alcoholics may have an impaired ability to perceive alcohol's effects. As a result, they fail to notice the symptoms of drunkenness early enough to stop.

People often become addicted to reduce **negative affect** – to relieve anxiety and tension – or for **positive affect** – stimulation, relaxation and pleasure. The **feeling-state theory** (Miller, 2010) argues that disorders are created when intense positive feelings become linked with specific behaviours. To generate the same feeling, the person compulsively repeats the behaviour, even if detrimental. This re-enactment creates the impulse control disorder.

When **dopamine** is released it gives feelings of pleasure and satisfaction. These feelings of satisfaction become desired, and to satisfy that desire the person will repeat behaviours that cause the release of dopamine. This means that there is a complex relationship between physiological and psychological factors. Now add in **behaviourism**: if a person gambles and wins, the reward (and the thrill experienced) means the person is likely to repeat the behavior. The thrill of stealing or setting fires and the release of dopamine explains why some people repeat these behaviours. The thrill (or high) is so intense the person cannot resist and will do all they can to repeat the experience.

Expert tip

A question could ask you investigate the amount of dopamine that is produced when gambling. What method would you choose and what would be the advantages of this method?

Coping with and reducing addiction and impulse control disorders

Biological treatments such as selective serotonin uptake inhibitors (SSRIs) are used to treat pyromania, kleptomania and sometimes gambling. Other treatments include seeing the patient's actions as an unconscious process and analysing them to help the patient remove the behaviour. This **psychodynamic approach** addresses the underlying problems that generate the negative emotions causing the mania. Treatment appears to work in 95% of children who exhibit signs of pyromania, for example.

Behaviour modification can be used in the form of a **token economy**, where the individual receives rewards for good behaviour (or for non-impulsive behaviour). Tokens can later be exchanged for items or privileges. **Aversion therapy** (or overt sensitisation) can be used in the treatment of alcoholics. The drug antabuse is given and, when any alcohol is drunk, the person becomes violently sick.

Much more effective are **cognitive-behavioural treatments** for impulse control disorders.

Covert sensitisation involves the person *imagining* associating an aversive stimulus with the impulsive behaviour. Glover (2011) used images of nausea and vomiting to treat a 14 year old with a history of kleptomania. At a 19-month follow-up the girl was free of stealing behaviour.

Kohn and Antonuccio (2002) used kleptomania-specific covert sensitisation (images of getting arrested, going to court and spending time in jail) successfully. Crucially this must be accompanied by a programme of reinforcement of appropriate behaviour.

Imaginal desensitisation involves teaching progressive muscle relaxation and then the person *visualises* themselves being exposed to the situation that triggers the drive to carry out the impulsive behaviour. The aim is to relax and leave the situation without having acted on the urge. Blaszcznski and Nower (2003) found this technique was particularly effective with gamblers.

Alternative sources of satisfaction involves finding alternative socially and individually acceptable sources of pleasure and excitement to replace the problem behaviour.

Expert tip

There are three evaluation issues to consider:

- **Ethics** – is flooding ethical? Many cognitive-behavioural treatments are. What about aversion therapy? Certainly a debate about the ethics of different treatments is worth having.
- **Usefulness** – how useful are drugs for treating different types of impulse control disorder? Can a cognitive-behavioural treatment combat the pleasurable sensations caused by neurotransmitters?
- **Competing explanations** – there are different models here, as there are for all sections in this option, all of which have different assumptions. Comparing and contrasting is a high-level skill and is worth doing.

Cross check

Biological, cognitive and behavioural perspectives/models, page 92

Nature/nurture, page 103

Determinism, page 101

Reductionism, page 104

Expert tip

If you do the same issues for every topic area for this option, it does not matter. You only do one Section B exam question.

Anxiety disorders (phobias)

Revised

Definitions, types/examples (case studies) of phobias

Some people have **generalised anxiety disorder** meaning they might have a 'panic attack' but do not know its cause. On the other hand some people know the actual cause and this is called a phobia. The symptoms of generalised anxiety disorder are:

- excessive, uncontrollable and often irrational worry, which interferes with daily functioning
- physical symptoms of headaches, nausea, numbness in hands and feet, muscle tension, difficulty swallowing and/or breathing, trembling, twitching and sweating

In everyday life people say 'I have a phobia of...' when they don't like something. To be diagnosed formally as phobic there must be anxiety 'attacks' and the person must have 'difficulty in social and occupational functioning' because of it. For example, a person with agoraphobia may not have left their home for 6 months or more, they will have closed curtains and never go to a door because of their fear of the outside world.

There are many different phobias, some very common and some quite rare. Acoraphobia (heights) and agoraphobia (the 'outside') are common, while koumpounophobia (buttons) is rare. Blood-injury-injection phobia (a blood phobia is hemophobia) often results in the person fainting (see page 166). Cynophobia is a fear of dogs (see page 165).

There are two classic case studies about phobias in psychological literature: the case of Little Albert (based on classical conditioning – see page 31) and

Anxiety is a general feeling of dread or apprehensiveness accompanied by various physiological reactions such as increased heart rate, sweating, muscle tension, and rapid and shallow breathing.

A **phobia** is a persistent fear of an object or situation in which the sufferer does anything possible to avoid the feared object or situation.

the case of Little Hans (based on the psychodynamic approach of Freud – see page 34).

McGrath et al. (1990) report a case study about Lucy, a 9-year-old girl with a phobia of specific loud bangs such as fireworks and popping balloons. She was treated successfully with systematic desensitisation (see below). Saavedra and Silverman (2002) report on a 9-year-old with a fear of buttons. A large bowl of buttons fell on him while at school and from then on he would not wear clothes with buttons. Small, plastic buttons caused him most distress. Slow exposure with associated positive reinforcement led to improvements, but it was then discovered that he found buttons disgusting when they touched his body.

Expert tip

Although you might know a lot about Little Hans and Little Albert, remember that you are *not* writing an AS answer in detail on them. You are using them as brief examples of phobias.

Cross check

Case studies, page 76

Explanations of phobias

There are a number of different explanations for phobias.

Classical conditioning assumes that fears are acquired by a process of associating a conditioned stimulus (CS) – something unpleasant, such as pain – with an unconditioned stimulus (UCS) – such as a dog, a white rat or any other stimulus – via a traumatic experience. Watson and Raynor (1920) **classically conditioned** Little Albert (page 31). This demonstrated that phobias can be learned.

The **Freudian psychoanalytic** theory suggests that phobias are a defence mechanism against the anxiety created by the unresolved conflicts between the id and the superego. The ego attempts to resolve these conflicts by using the coping mechanisms of repression and displacement. In repression, the ego attempts to 'forget' that the conflict exists. In displacement the ego re-channels the anxiety, which is displaced from the feared impulse (such as hatred towards one's father) and moved towards an object or situation that is symbolically connected to it (such as Little Hans's father resembling a horse).

Genes may predispose some people to anxiety (and phobic) disorders. Kendler et al. (1992) argue that the genetic factor common to all phobias strongly predisposes a person to specific phobias such as blood phobia. Ost (1992) found that those with a specific phobia for blood injuries had 60% of first-degree relatives who also had the same phobia.

Expert tip

For any genetic explanation of a disorder such as schizophrenia, depression or a phobia, people don't inherit a specific gene for it. Rather, they inherit the vulnerability to it.

DiNardo et al. (1988) suggest a **cognitive** explanation for phobias. They found that only half of people who had a traumatic experience with a dog, even when pain was inflicted, developed a phobia of dogs. Why? DiNardo et al. believe that people who have *any* traumatic experience (e.g. with dogs) but do not develop a phobia must *interpret* the event differently from those who do develop a phobia. This means that it is the way people think about their experience that makes the difference. It is an exaggerated expectation of harm in some people that leads to the development of a phobia.

Cross check

Cognitive approach, page 87
Psychodymanic perspective, page 93
Behaviourist perspective, page 92
Biomedical approach, page 156

Treating phobias

Systematic desensitisation, based on classical conditioning, was developed by Wolpe in 1958, specifically for the counter-conditioning of fears, phobias and anxieties. The aim is to replace the conditioned fear, which is maladaptive, with relaxation, which is adaptive and desirable. It involves three phases:

- An **anxiety hierarchy** is constructed – a range of situations or events with which the fear is associated. These are arranged in order from the least fearful (e.g. *imagining* exposure) to the most fearful (e.g. in vivo).
- The person is trained in deep **muscle relaxation and deep breathing techniques**. This counteracts the effects of anxiety-related hormones such as adrenaline.
- The person then thinks about, or is brought into contact with, the least fearful item and applies relaxation techniques. When relaxed the next item

Now test yourself

45 Describe **one** study supporting the cognitive explanation for phobias.

Answer on p.202

Tested

in the hierarchy is presented. This continues systematically until all the items in the hierarchy have been removed and the person is desensitised.

Flooding (Stampfl, 1967) uses 'in vivo' exposure – actual exposure to the feared stimulus. A person is confronted with the feared stimulus and cannot withdraw. This causes a major anxiety attack, but after a while the stress hormones dissipate and eventually the person calms down. At this point they realise the feared stimulus has not 'killed them' and that their phobia is unjustified. Wolpe (1973) successfully used this technique with a girl with a car phobia. Many therapists do not use this because of its unethical nature.

Applied tension (Ost et al., 1989) is specifically for people with blood and injection phobias. At the sight of blood, blood pressure drops sharply (called vasovagal response), often leading the person to fainting (passing out). Applied tension involves tensing the muscles in the arms, legs and body for about 10–15 seconds, relaxing for 20–30 seconds and then repeating both these five times to raise blood pressure. Ost et al. found that 73% of patients were improved (i.e. no fainting) at the end of the treatment and 77% were improved at follow-up.

Ost and Westling (1995) compared **cognitive-behavioural therapy** (CBT) with applied relaxation in the treatment of panic disorder. Over 12 weekly sessions those in the applied relaxation group received training in deep muscle relaxation only. The CBT group also received training in restructuring the thoughts associated with the panic attacks. Results: the CBT group had a significant reduction in the number of panic attacks in the patients after treatment (74%), and 89% at follow-up.

Expert tip

There are three evaluation issues to consider:

- **Ethics** – flooding and systematic desensitisation are at the two extremes of the ethics spectrum, and therefore worth comparing.
- **Usefulness** – how useful is flooding? Can applied tension be used for anything else? Can systematic desensitisation be used to treat everything?
- **Competing explanations** – there are different models here, all of which have different assumptions. Comparing and contrasting is a high-level skill and is worth doing.

Cross check

Physiology of stress, page 139
Ethics, page 79

Now test yourself

46 Describe the applied tension technique for treating blood and injection phobias.

Answer on p.202

Tested

Expert tip

When you compare and contrast, don't describe one thing and then describe the other thing. Make a point and look at that point from one view and then from the opposing view.

Anxiety disorders (obsessions and compulsions)

Revised

Definitions, measures and examples of obsessions and compulsions

People can have obsessions, compulsions or both, with OCD being one of the most common anxiety disorders. Some estimate 69% of those diagnosed have obsessions *and* compulsions (with 25% just obsessions and 6% just compulsions). Generally there is some trigger event, followed by obsessive thoughts, which cause discomfort if not resolved (e.g. something might not have been done, or something might happen or cause a problem). There might then be the ritual of checking (e.g. to confirm something has been done) or washing (e.g. to remove a contamination). The compulsion involves repeating the action continually.

Examples of obsessions include:

- fearing contamination from dirt, bacteria, etc. when touching surfaces
- imagining a fire breaking out in every building entered

Compulsions include:

- *washing* hands many times until they are thoroughly clean
- *checking* fire exits or exit routes in every building entered
- *doubting* and so reading an email many times before sending it to ensure it is correct
- *touching* repeatedly, such as a door, to see if it is closed

An **obsession** is a recurring and persistent thought that interferes with normal behaviour.

A **compulsion** is a recurring action a person is forced to enact.

Obsessive-compulsive disorder is where irresistible thoughts and actions must be acted on.

Expert tip

This information is general and introductory. Try to quote psychological research, such as the case study and psychometric test below, which can be evaluated.

A **case study** of OCD is that of 'Charles' by Rapoport (1989). When aged 12 Charles started to wash compulsively. He followed the same ritual each day in the shower, which would take him up to 3 hours. Getting dressed would take another 2 hours. Charles was treated by Rapoport who prescribed the drug Anafranil and linked this with a behavioural management programme, such as washing in the evening. For a while the symptoms disappeared. Over time Charles went on to cope with his disorder.

Cross check

Case studies, page 76

The **Maudsley Obsessive-Compulsive Inventory** (MOCI) is a **psychometric test** originally designed by Hodgson and Rachman (1977) to assess OCD. It is a self-report questionnaire using a forced-choice 'yes' or 'no' format. It has 30 questions/items with four sub-scales:

- **Checking** (9 items), for example I frequently have to check things (gas or water taps, doors etc.) several times.
- **Cleaning/washing** (11 items), for example I am not unduly concerned about germs and diseases (reverse scored).
- **Slowness** (7 items), for example I am often late because I cannot seem to get through everything on time
- **Doubting** (7 items), for example I have a very strict conscience.

Expert tip

The MOCI is confusing! There are 30 questions and four appear in two sub-scales of checking and washing.

A person can have a total score between 0 (no symptoms) and 30 (maximum presence of symptoms). This determines the nature, extent and severity of the OCD.

Alternative measures include the **Yale-Brown Obsessive-Compulsive Scale** (Y-BOCS), which also has ratings, and cognitive measures such as the **Intrusive Thoughts Questionnaire**. **Physiological measures** can be taken to determine the levels of anxiety associated with a particular behaviour, and behavioural diaries used to determine the time taken for particular activities.

Now test yourself

47 Describe **one** way in which obsessive-compulsive disorder has been measured using a questionnaire

Answer on p.203

Tested

Explanations of obsessive-compulsive disorder

Biological explanations have been proposed. Altemus et al. (1993) suggest that OCD is caused by low serotonin levels, but so are many other disorders, so there must be some additional factor. Studies have also shown that people with OCD show abnormal functioning in the orbital region of the frontal cortex and/or the caudate nuclei. These regions are responsible for converting sensory input into thoughts and behaviours, and if these regions do not regulate activity (e.g. they become over-stimulated) this could account for the recurring thoughts and behaviour. Evidence for this is gained from brain scans and studies of people with brain injury in these regions (e.g. Paradis et al., 1992).

Cross check

Psychometric tests, page 98

Self-report questionnaires and rating scales, page 72

Physiological approach, page 89

The **behavioural** explanation suggests that people associate a particular 'thing' with fear and so they learn to avoid that 'thing' and perform ritualistic behaviour (the compulsion) to help reduce the anxiety and fear. The **cognitive** side looks at why people misinterpret their thoughts associated with the 'thing' and how these become obsessive.

The **psychodynamic** explanation of OCD follows the same principles as with other mental disorders: there is a conflict between the id and the ego, which creates anxiety. The impulsive nature of the id may be responsible for the creation of obsessive thoughts, while the ego, in an attempt to control the id, may create compulsive behaviour to try to counteract the obsessive thoughts and resolve the conflict.

Treatments for obsessive-compulsive disorder

Medical treatments assume that if OCD is caused by low serotonin levels, then drugs can be used to increase the activity of serotonin in the brain. This is exactly what clomipramine does. About 60% of patients with OCD improve with medication but a high dose of the drug needs to be taken for at least

12 weeks. Of those patients that do respond, at least 75% will relapse in the months after stopping the drug.

Traditional **psychoanalytic** and **psychodynamic psychotherapy** was, for many years, the only psychological approach used. This is a 'talking treatment' that aims to resolve the conflict arising from the id and ego. To access the unconscious, Freud used free association, which involves the client saying whatever comes into his or her mind. He also used dream analysis. Very few practitioners now use these techniques because they take too long and are ineffective, and much more effective treatments are available.

Given the **behavioural** view above, the way to resolve the problem is to confront the fear, rather than avoid it, so the performing of the ritual is unnecessary. This can best be done using **exposure and response prevention**. The exposure component involves the person being exposed to the feared 'thing', either directly or by imagining exposure to it, and gradually through anxiety management becoming less anxious about confronting it. If there is no anxiety then there is no need to perform the ritualistic behaviour, and so the response prevention is the removal of the compulsion. Linked to this is **cognitive therapy**, where the thoughts causing the anxiety need to be re-interpreted and re-evaluated, to show that what is believed to be true is not actually true. In theory this is simple to say, but quite difficult to achieve.

Expert tip

Don't just describe a specific treatment; also know the background or assumptions on which it is based. For example, exposure and response therapy is based on which model?

Cross check

Models, page 156
Approaches, page 87

Now test yourself Tested

48 Describe the assumptions of cognitive-behavioural therapy regarding obsessions and compulsions.

Answer on p.203

Expert tip

Any evaluation should include at least three issues and one of these must always be the named issue presented in the question.

Expert tip

There are three evaluation issues to consider:

- **Comparing and contrasting** – there are competing explanations here: medical, behaviourist and psychodynamic. Be able to compare and contrast them.
- **Usefulness** – treatments are suggested, but how useful are they?
- **Methodology** – there are strengths and weaknesses of case studies and there are strengths and weaknesses of self-report questionnaires.

4.5 Psychology and organisations

The selection of people for work

Revised

Selection of people for work

Selection procedures mainly involve:

- **personnel recruitment** – the means by which companies attract job applicants
- **personnel screening** – the process of reviewing information about job applicants to select workers
- **personnel selection** via interviewing

Human resource management (HRM) is the general name for a strategic and coherent approach to the management of the people working in an organisation.

The process of personnel recruitment might include: the production of a **job analysis** and **job description**; advertising the job via appropriate media; and production of an **application form**. The application form might be standard, weighted or a biographical information blank. A curriculum vitae (CV) and letter of application may also be required.

Psychometric, **screening** or **'employment' tests** can include assessment of:

- cognitive ability (e.g. aptitude and achievement tests)
- physical or mechanical ability
- motor/sensory ability
- job skills/knowledge
- personality (e.g. use of the 'big five' factors – openness to experience, conscientiousness, extraversion, agreeableness and neuroticism)
- a work sample or involve a test specific to the job/organisation

Any test used in the selection process should be both valid and reliable.

The selection process involves a **selection interview**. An interview needs questions and it needs at least one interviewer. To be valid, any question must relate to the **job description** (what the job actually is) and a **job specification** (information about the human characteristics needed for the job). The questions can be presented in three main ways:

- **Structured interview** – each participant is asked exactly the same questions in the same order.
- **Unstructured interview** – the researcher asks different questions, depending upon where the conversation/discussion takes them.
- **Semi-structured interview** – the researcher has a certain number of set questions, but can also ask other questions depending upon where the responses takes them. This way the researcher can find out about things in more depth and prompt a more detailed response.

With a single interviewer, drifting from the structure is more likely, as are bias and the incorrect appointment of an applicant. A team of interviewers, who are trained (or at least experienced), is highly desirable. They can compare notes at the end of all the interviews and hopefully they will agree on the best applicant for the job. This can then be part of a statistical decision-making process (as outlined below).

Now test yourself Tested

50 Describe structured and unstructured selection interviews.

Answer on p.203

Personnel selection decisions and job analysis

Selection decision strategies can be 'clinical', whereby a manager subjectively selects the person they *feel* will be best. This may be correct or it may be wrong and involve biases. A statistical strategy has more objectivity:

- **Multiple regression model** – this combines scores of each job factor statistically and the applicant with the highest number of points is appointed.
- **Multiple cut-off model** – this requires an applicant to obtain a minimum score or level of proficiency on each factor to be successful; otherwise the applicant is rejected.
- **Multiple hurdle model** – this requires an applicant to have achieved a sufficiently high score (e.g. on a series of tests or 'hurdles') at various stages (e.g. end of day 1), otherwise the applicant is rejected.

In many countries **equal opportunity** law requires the selection and decision-making process to be transparent: each decision needs clear and unambiguous evidence to show equality. Fairness is more likely if selection uses:

- structured (formal) interviews and a team of trained interviewers rather than just one, so decisions are based on consensus

Cross check

Reliability, page 82
Validity, page 86
Psychometric tests, page 98

Now test yourself

49 Describe **two** problems with psychometric tests used in personnel screening.

Answer on p.203

Tested

Personnel selection involves the choosing from a sample of job applicants the individual(s) best suited to the job(s) available.

A **selection interview** is the choosing from a sample of job applicants the individuals best suited to the jobs available through a 'conversation with a purpose'.

Cross check

Interviews, page 73
Inter-rater reliability, page 82

Expert tip

In this section both interviews and inter-rater reliability have been mentioned. You should know all about these from the AS course. Go back and check if you cannot remember.

- screening/psychometric tests, and interview questions that are valid
- a decision-making model with a statistical rating or scoring system rather than the 'clinical' subjective approach

A **job analysis** is a study of every aspect involved in the completion of a work task. It involves a **job description** (what the job actually is) and a **job specification** (information about the human characteristics that are needed for the job). Modern techniques focus on either the task (e.g. FJA) or worker (e.g. PAQ):

- FJA (**functional job analysis**), developed by Fine and Cronshaw (1944), has seven categories to describe tasks workers do in jobs. The categories are: things (with seven descriptor words), data (seven descriptors) and people (nine descriptors). The most recent version also includes worker instructions, reasoning, maths and language.
- PAQ (**positional analysis questionnaire**) uses a structured questionnaire to analyse jobs. It is completed by a trained job analyst. 195 statements are divided into the six categories of: information input, mental process, work output, relationships with others, job context, and 'other job characteristics'. Scoring is on a 6-point scale from N 'not apply' to 5 'very substantial use'.

Job analysis is the systematic study of the task, procedure, tools, duties and responsibilities involved in a job.

Both these techniques use rating scales. Other methods include the following:

- **Questionnaires** (open and closed) could be given to workers, and workers could be **observed**.
- **Work sampling** could be used – a statistical technique for determining the time spent by workers in various work activities (such as a teacher who prepares, teaches and marks work).
- The **critical incident technique** analyses events that are particularly positive or negative and usually involve a report by the worker concerned.

Cross check

Questionnaires, page 72
Sampling, page 83
Generalisations, page 97

Performance appraisal

Performance is appraised:

- for the organisation:
  - to assess productivity levels and decide on promotions, demotions, bonuses and firing
  - to provide information about training needs; to improve performance and quality
  - to validate employee selection (have the right people been chosen?) and to evaluate the effectiveness of any organisational change
- for the individual:
  - to provide feedback on how to improve performance; to remove weaknesses and to encourage the worker to work smarter rather than harder
  - as a basis for career advancement and continuing professional development
  - to determine whether they deserve more reward (e.g. pay), responsibility, promotion, etc.

Performance appraisal is the process of assessing or evaluating workers.

Ways to appraise include the following:

- **Rankings**: the rater ranks a worker on some aspect of performance, usually in relation to other workers. Sometimes, for example, workers are ranked in the top 10% or bottom 10% – a **forced distribution**.
- A **checklist** can be used and when rating an employee the supervisor checks all those statements that most closely describe the behaviour of the individual under assessment. Statements can be weighted and a total score can then be given to the worker.
- More formal techniques are BARS (**behaviourally anchored rating scales** and MBO (**management by objectives**). BARS combine rating scales and critical incidents of worker performance.

A number of **biases** can occur in the appraisal process:

- **Primacy effects** (or first impression). Appraisers should not make an overall judgement on the basis of just a few first (negative or positive) impressions. The **recency effect** can also apply and is where the most recent behaviour is used.
- **Halo effect**. An appraiser should not make an overall judgment on the basis of an assumption that if the worker is very good at one aspect then he/she will be good at all aspects of a job.
- **Averageness**. An appraiser may have a tendency not to use the extremes, putting most people in the middle or giving an average score.
- **Personal bias**. An appraiser may like some people more than others. This personal preference should never be part of any appraisal.
- **'Spill-over' effect**. This is the assumption that if a person has one poor appraisal they will be poor in every appraisal (and, of course, vice-versa).

Expert tip

Five biases are listed here. You don't need all five for a Section A question. Choose any two you can remember.

Biases can be **overcome** by using more than one appraiser and using inter-rater reliability checks. An appraiser trained in both appraising and giving feedback is always better than one who has not been trained. An **effective feedback interview** is crucial because, if done correctly, it can motivate, enthuse and reward a worker, suggesting ways in which performance can be improved and identifying professional development. Done poorly it can frustrate, demotivate and damage manager–worker relationships.

Expert tip

There are three evaluation issues to consider:

- **Methodology** – this is always worth considering and in this section interviews, questionnaires and observations apply (as well as inter-rater reliability).
- **Generalisations** – what may work in one organisation may not work or be applicable to another.
- **Subjective vs objective** – consider which procedures are personal and subjective and prone to bias and which are objective, scientific and fair to all.

Motivation to work

Revised

Need theories of motivation

All people have needs (e.g. to eat and drink) and we are motivated to satisfy them. We also have needs as people in a society and the need for achievement.

A **theory of motivation** is an analytic structure designed to explain the force that energises, directs and sustains behaviour.

Maslow's (1954) **needs hierarchy** proposed a five-tier hierarchy:

1 Physiological: food, drink, warmth, etc.
2 Safety: protection from harm, need for law and order.
3 Social: need for affection, relationships and family.
4 Esteem: need for achievement, mastery of skills, status.
5(7) Self-actualisation: realising potential; fulfilment.

Maslow believed that lower-level or basic needs had to be satisfied before the progressing to higher levels. In 1970 Maslow added two additional needs and added an eighth later on:

(5) Cognitive: having knowledge and understanding.
(6) Aesthetic: the appreciation and search for beauty.
(8) Transcendent: helping others to achieve self-actualisation.

Expert tip

Every student knows Maslow's five needs. But there is much more than this. Go beyond the basics. Maslow has eight needs not just five, and there are other needs theories in addition to Maslow's.

Aldefer (1972) re-categorised Maslow's hierarchy into three 'simpler' categories (ERG):

- **E**xistence needs (physiological and safety needs) – the need for the basic material necessities of life.

- **R**elatedness needs (social and self-esteem needs) – the need to have and maintain interpersonal relationships both at work and home.
- **G**rowth needs (self-actualisation) – the need for self-development and advancement.

McClelland's **achievement-motivation theory** (1961) suggests that we have three work-related needs:

- **Need for achievement** – the need to get a job done, to master a task, to be successful. People want to achieve on the basis of their hard work and effort rather than on the basis of luck.
- **Need for affiliation** – the need to be liked and accepted by other people; effort is applied to creating and maintaining social relationships and friendships.
- **Need for power** – this concerns being influential in the lives of others and also in the control of others; the need for discipline is important.

McClelland believes that a good manager should have the need for power, not necessarily need for achievement and certainly not the need for affiliation. McClelland used **thematic apperception tests** (TAT), involving looking at pictures followed by a description of the story each suggests. Is a projective test so does not have the reliability of a psychometric test.

Now test yourself

51 What are the three work-related needs outlined by McClelland?

Answer on p.203

Tested

Cross check

Reductionism and holism, page 104

Psychometric and projective tests, pages 98 and 58

Motivation and goal-setting

A person can be motivated by setting a goal and when it is achieved a sense of achievement and success follows. This is the basic principle underlying the application of **management by objectives**. One of the best ways of **setting effective goals** is to make them '**SMART**': goals should be Specific, Measurable, Attainable/agreed, Realistic/relevant and Time-based.

In the 1960s Locke suggested that working toward a goal provides a major source of motivation to reach the goal and, with appropriate feedback, improved performance. Latham proposed similar ideas and the combined **goal-setting theory** by Latham and Locke became popular. They believe goal-setting has five principles:

- **Clarity** – when a goal is clear and specific it is unambiguous and measurable.
- **Challenge** – goals that are relevant and linked to rewards are good motivators.
- **Commitment** – goals must be understood and agreed to be effective.
- **Effectiveness** – goal-setting must involve feedback on progress and achievement.
- **Task complexity** – tasks must be achievable and in a particular time period.

A **theory** can be defined as an analytic structure designed to explain a set of empirical observations.

Cognitive/rational theories of motivation view workers as rational, decision-making beings who cognitively assess (think about) the costs and benefits before acting. **Equity theory** assumes that workers expect to achieve pay, status and recognition according to what they bring to a job. This they do in comparison with others and if there is perceived inequality the worker will become de-motivated.

Expert tip

If a question asks you to explain 'a theory of..., ensure you refer to what a theory is in your answer.

The **VIE** (or **expectancy**) **theory** (Vroom, 1964) believes that workers are rational and decision making is guided by potential costs (negative outcomes) and rewards (positive outcomes). The theory is summarised by the equation: $M = E \times I \times V$ or motivation = expectancy × instrumentality × valence. M (motivation) is the amount a person will be motivated by the situation in which they find themselves, which is determined by: E (expectancy), which is the person's perception of the *extent* to which the amount of effort correlates with performance. I (instrumentality) is the person's perception of how performance will be rewarded. It is the extent to which the amount of reward matches the *amount of effort* required. V (valence) is the perceived *strength of the reward* or punishment. If the reward is small then so will be the motivation, even if *I* and *E* are high.

Motivators at work

Intrinsic motivation is an internal desire to perform a particular task because it gives pleasure or develops a particular skill. Motivation comes from the actual performance of the job or task and gives a sense of achievement and satisfaction. Praise, respect, recognition, empowerment and a sense of belonging are said to be far more powerful motivators than money.

Extrinsic motivation is the desire to do something because of an external reward such as money. Extrinsic rewards include: pay, promotion and fringe benefits such as commission and bonuses. Promotions and competitions/incentive schemes can be used against sales objectives such as volume, profitability and new account development. Extrinsic motivation can also include merchandise incentives such as a company car.

A **reward system** consists of intrinsic and extrinsic rewards used by an organisation to motivate employees.

Expert tip

There are three evaluation issues to consider:

- **Generalisations/individual differences** – what might motivate one person might not motivate another.
- **Reductionism vs holism** – theories want to reduce needs (for example) to a short list. Is this possible? Is it desirable?
- **Competing theories** – know some differences between each theory so you can evaluate them.

Now test yourself

52 Using examples, what is the difference between intrinsic and extrinsic motivation?

Answer on p.203

Tested

Leadership and management

Revised

Theories of leadership

Leadership can be said to be a form of social influence, where a person gains the aid or support of others to achieve a goal or task. This can apply to many different things in addition to an organisation. A **manager** works in an organisation and is concerned with the day-to-day planning, organising, controlling and coordinating of those for whom he or she is responsible. A manager may not be the leader, instead implementing the ideas and instructions of a leader. A leader can be a 'great person' or be charismatic, but a manager need not be.

A **theory of leadership** is an analytic structure designed to explain the ability to guide a group to achieve a goal.

Management style is the way in which people are directed toward the attainment of goals.

Universalist theories look at the major characteristics that are common among effective leaders. The **great man-woman theory** (e.g. Wood, 1913) argues that 'great leaders are born, not made' because they possess the personal qualities and abilities to make them great. **Charismatic** (or transformational) leaders are said to have the determination, energy, confidence and ability to inspire followers.

Expert tip

Make sure you know the difference between leadership and management.

McGregor (1960) outlines two types of leader belief: **theory X** is where workers are seen as unmotivated and will avoid work; **theory Y** is where workers are perceived as being self-motivated, will work hard and have organisational commitment.

Cross check

Nature/nurture, page 103
Individual vs situational, page 102

Now test yourself

Tested

53 What is the difference between a leader and a manager?

Answer on p.203

A **universalist theory of leadership** is an analytic structure designed to explain the major characteristics that are common among all effective leaders.

Behavioural theories look at the actual behaviour shown by leaders to determine which behaviours are successful and which are not. Researchers at Ohio State University (e.g. Halpin and Winer, 1957) developed the **Leader Behaviour Description Questionnaire** (LBDQ) with 1800 statements. Analysis suggested two types of leader:

- Leaders with **initiating structure** – the degree to which they define and structure their role. They initiate, organise, clarify and gather information.
- Leaders with **consideration** – the degree to which they act in a friendly and supportive manner to workers. They encourage, observe and listen, as coaches and mentors.

These two dimensions determine four styles, dependent on whether structure is high or low and whether consideration is high or low.

Researchers at the University of Michigan identified **task-oriented behaviours** (similar to 'initiating structure'), where the main concern is production rather than workers, and **relationship-oriented behaviour** (similar to 'consideration'), where the concern is for people. This extended into Blake and Moulton's (1985) **managerial grid** where the two styles resulted in five types of leader: country-club, team, impoverished, authority-compliant and middle-of-the-road.

A **behavioural theory of leadership** is an analytic structure designed to explain the behaviour shown by leaders to determine which behaviours are successful and which are not.

Leadership style and effectiveness

Fiedler (1976) assumed that a leader's ability to lead is **contingent** upon various situational factors, including, for example, the leader's preferred style, and the capabilities and behaviours of followers (workers). This means that the same person can behave differently in different situations.

Fielder used the **least-preferred co-worker** (LPC) scale, a questionnaire with 16 items, where leaders are asked about the person with whom they least prefer to work. This determines whether the leader is relationship-oriented (high LPC score) or task-oriented (low LPC score). Situational factors are dependent on:

- **leader–member relations** – the extent to which the leader is trusted and liked by workers, and the workers' willingness to follow the leader's guidance
- **task structure** – the extent to which the group's task has been defined and the extent to which it can be carried out
- **position power** – the power of the leader and the degree to which the leader can exercise authority over workers

Cross check

Questionnaires, page 72

The effectiveness of a leader is determined by the interaction of the leader's style of behaviour and the favourableness of the situational characteristics.

Now test yourself Tested

54 What is meant by a situational theory of leadership?

Answer on p.203

The **situational leadership** approach argues that no single leadership style best fits all situations. Instead successful leaders are those who can adapt their leadership style (e.g. as below) to the group they are attempting to lead. In the 1980s the theories by Hersey and Blanchard were merged and their combined theory has three main components:

- **Styles of leadership** (S) – Telling, Selling, Participating and Delegating (labelled S1 to S4)
- **Maturity levels** (M) – High, Moderate (2 levels) and Low (labelled M4 to M1)
- **Development levels** (D) – combinations of low and high competence with low and high commitment (D1 to D4)

Situational leadership is the view that there is no one 'best style'. Instead the best style is that which is appropriate to the task and the group being led; the specific situation.

House (1971) proposed that a leader affects the performance, satisfaction and motivation of a group of workers in different ways: offering rewards for achieving performance goals; clarifying routes towards these goals; removing obstacles to performance. The function of the leader is to ease the way to the group's goals by meeting the needs of the workers. The revised version (1996) suggests that a leader compensates for and complements deficiencies in those being led.

Muczyk and Reimann (1987) argue for four 'pure' patterns or **styles of leader behaviour**. They believe that:

- leaders can differ in the extent to which they involve others in decision making (extensive employee participation or no employee participation)
- the extent to which they are involved in the execution of the decision

Combinations of these two dimensions produce four styles of leader behaviour: directive democrat, directive autocrat, permissive democrat and permissive autocrat.

Expert tip

A question could ask you how you would find out which style a leader in an organisation has. Think about the method you might use and why you would choose this particular method.

Leaders and followers

In any organisation there are managers (or leaders) and there are workers. Often the satisfaction (or dissatisfaction) experienced by workers is determined by the relationship with management. A number of models, mostly based on leader–member exchange or LMX, have been proposed to explain the manager–worker relationship.

Dansereau et al. (1975) proposed the **vertical dyad linkage** (VDL) theory. The model suggested that leaders treat followers differently with respect to mutual trust, respect and obligation, creating an in-group (a small number of trusted followers) and an out-group (a larger number where the relationship remains a formal one). Since then research has gone in two directions. VDL theory became the **leader–member exchange model** and an alternative **individualised leadership model** by Danserau et al. (1995) was proposed where each follower is considered to be independent from others and each leader is viewed as unique.

Cross check

The core study by Tajfel on in-groups and out-groups, page 28

The Vroom and Yetton (1973) **normative decision model** proposes that the best leadership style depends on the situation and the followers (or group) to be included in the decision-making process, and that no one leadership style or decision-making process fits all situations. The model was updated in 1988 to be the **Vroom-Yetton-Jago decision-making model**. Depending on the group leader and situation one of five styles can apply:

- **Autocratic** (A1): the leader makes a decision without consultation.
- **Autocratic** (A2): the leader consults followers for information and then makes a decision.
- **Consultative** (C1): the leader shares the problem, consults individual followers for information and then makes a decision.
- **Consultative** (C2): the leader shares the problem, followers meet as a group and discuss it, but the leader makes a decision.
- **Group** (G): the leader shares the problem, consults the group and accepts the group decision.

Expert tip

There are three evaluation issues to consider:

- **Reductionism vs holism** – models want to reduce styles to a short list. Is this possible? Is it desirable?
- **Nature vs nurture** – are leaders born or made?
- **Individual vs situational** – does a leader apply their individual style or do they apply a style according to the situation they are in?

Group behaviour in organisations

Revised

Group dynamics, cohesiveness and teamwork

Two explanations of group (or team) development are those of Tuckman (1965) and Woodcock (1979). Tuckman outlines four stages of group development:

- **Forming** – where individuals begin to come together, get to know each other and agree on tasks and goals.
- **Storming** – where individuals will present ideas and sometimes these will be accepted and sometimes they will cause conflict.
- **Norming** – when members of the group agree a strategy, some members realising that for the good of the group their ideas are not accepted.
- **Performing** – when the group functions as a coherent unit, working effectively and efficiently without conflict.

A fifth stage (**adjourning**), where the group has completed a task and breaks up, was added in 1977.

Woodcock suggests four stages of team development:

- The **under-developed team** – feelings are avoided; objectives are uncertain and the leader makes decisions.
- The **experimenting team** – individuals listen to each other; they test each other out.
- The **consolidating team** – tasks are clarified, objectives are agreed and procedures are proposed.
- The **mature team** – feelings are shared, individuals are flexible and working methods are comfortable.

According to Belbin (1981) 'What is needed is not well-balanced individuals, but individuals who balance well with each other'. A **successful team** with **group cohesiveness** will be promoted by the extent to which members correctly recognise and adjust themselves to the relative strengths of the team, both in expertise and in ability to engage in specific team roles. Belbin believes that an ideal team would include: one coordinator (or shaper); one innovator; one monitor-evaluator; and one or more implementer, team worker, resource investigator and finisher-completer.

McGregor (1960) outlined 11 characteristics of effective and ineffective groups. Likert (1961) identified 18 and Zander (1982) 14.

Decision making

Decision making is said to be one of the most important and frequent tasks among managers and employees in an organisation. The entire process is dependent upon the right information being available to the right people at the right time.

Wedley and Field (1984) suggest that **pre-planning** for decision making leads to solutions of high quality, acceptability and originality. Pre-planning involves choosing a style of leadership, whether to involve others, how to gather information, who to contact, and how to generate alternative solutions.

There are different views (going back as far as Lewin et al., 1939) about which decision-making style the leader (or manager) will use. The main ones are as follows:

- **Autocratic** (directive or authoritarian) – the leader gives clear expectations of what needs to be done, when and how. There is little or no input from the group.
- **Consultative** – the leader consults, gathers information and then makes the decision.
- **Participative** (democratic or collaborative) – the problem is explained, with everyone being encouraged to participate, including the leader.

A **group** in an organisation refers to individuals who combine skills and resources to achieve a common goal.

Team building (or development) is the process of enhancing the effectiveness of teams.

Now test yourself

55 Identify the four stages of team development proposed by Woodcock.

56 Describe the four stages of group development according to Tuckman.

Answers on p.203

Tested

Expert tip

Look at questions 55 and 56. Make sure you know the difference between 'identify' and 'describe'.

Group cohesiveness is the team spirit developed by people working in unity.

Group decision making is a mental process of considering alternatives, resulting in a choice.

- **Delegative** (or laissez-faire) – the leader gives the responsibility for the decision to the group/team, with no structure or guidance.

A more recent decision-making model is the **Vroom-Yetton-Jago** (1988 – see page 175).

Groupthink is when the adoption of group norms unintentionally erodes the ability of an individual to evaluate independently. Janis (1972) suggests that it has eight features, including: an illusion of invulnerability – the belief that nothing can go wrong; and an illusion of unanimity – the belief that group members who respect each other will automatically agree. Groupthink means that discussion is limited, and that there is an absence of alternatives, support for confirming information, and a failure to plan for when things might go wrong.

Strategies to avoid groupthink include: encouraging individual evaluation; promoting open enquiry; breaking a full group into sub-groups; admitting shortcomings; holding second-chance meetings; and not rushing to a quick solution.

Group polarisation is the tendency for groups to make decisions that are 'more risky' (after Stoner, 1961) than an individual would make. If an individual makes a decision then he or she can be held solely responsible. However, if a group makes a decision then the responsibility (if it goes wrong) is diffused among the entire group.

Groupthink is a syndrome characterised by a concurrence-seeking tendency that overrides the ability of a cohesive group to make critical decisions (Janis, 1965).

Group polarisation involves groups making decisions that are more extreme than those made by individuals.

Bottger and Yetton (1987) suggest that individuals within a group can be trained to avoid poor decisions. For example, the levels of experience, expertise, competence and diversity of team members are important in group decision making and productivity. Having a trained 'facilitator', for example, resulted in many more ideas being generated than in groups that did not have one.

Group conflict

Conflict can occur on four levels, ranging from **interpersonal** to **organisational**:

- Intra-individual – conflict occurs when an individual is faced with a choice and must make a decision.
- Inter-individual – conflict between two people.
- Intra-group – conflict between a person and a group.
- Inter-group – conflict between two groups.

Group conflict is when individuals or groups express different or incompatible ideas.

There are different **causes of conflict**:

- **Distrust** – lack of trust among individuals; lack of trust of another company/organisation.
- **Helplessness** – because views and decisions are never accepted; the organisation is too powerful.
- **Injustice** – mistreatment by another individual or mistreatment by an organisation.
- **Superiority** – one person thinks that he or she is better than others; one organisation thinks it is better than another.
- **Vulnerability** – a position or job is under threat and needs defending; there is uncertainty and fear about the future.

To these can be added:

- **Task conflict** – when group members disagree over shared tasks.
- **Process conflict** – when members disagree over the way in which something should be done.
- **Personal conflict** – this can happen when two people simply do not like each other.

Expert tip

Go beyond the 1939 Lewin autocratic and democratic styles. Include others that are more up to date.

Conflict can be **negative**: it can harm group cohesiveness; it can inhibit effective communication and even lead to rumour and distrust; and it can lead to more 'fighting' and less productivity and goal achievement.

Conflict can be **positive**: it might energise the group, reducing complacency; it might stimulate creativity and innovation; it can increase the quality of decision making as each member contributes more.

Thomas (1976) suggests five strategies to resolve conflict:

- **competition** (one wins the other loses)
- **accommodation** (one side 'gives-in')
- **compromise** (both give up something)
- **collaboration** (cooperation to reach an agreed solution)
- **avoidance** (withdrawing or backing down from the conflict)

Cross check

Reductionism, page 104
Generalisations, page 97
Individual differences, page 91

Expert tip

There are three evaluation issues to consider:

- **Reductionism vs holism** – there are many lists here. Why do psychologists want to *reduce* everything to a list?
- **Generalisations** – what applies in one organisation might not apply in another. There are many different types of organisation and conflict can occur in different situations.
- **Individual differences** – some people accept the decisions of others, some people argue for the sake of it. There are individual differences in the way people behave in groups.

Expert tip

When planning an essay, don't just re-write what appears here. This is just information. Show that you understand what it means; explain and impress the examiner.

Organisational work conditions

Revised

Physical and psychological work conditions

The conditions of the physical and psychological working environment should make people feel safe, comfortable and they should not experience any negative effects, whether physical or mental. By the nature of the work, many environments are very aversive.

Physical conditions include the following:

- **Illumination** – lighting levels need to be appropriate to the task; not too dim or too bright. The type of light and glare, even from computer screens, can cause eyesight problems. Some workers must wear protective glasses. Grandjean (1988) makes recommendations for reducing glare.
- **Temperature** – some jobs require workers to experience very high or very low temperatures, but in an office, for example, temperature should neither be too high nor too low. Fanger (1970) found that raising the humidity of a room significantly decreases worker performance.
- Loud **noise** might be unavoidable for some, and ear protectors have to be worn. For most people, loud noise is aversive and noise should be within acceptable levels.
- Some workers experience extreme **motion**. For example, those working with heavy, vibrating machinery can experience long-term effects on their ability to hold things.
- **Posture** – office workers are provided with seats, but often these are poor quality and over time posture and back problems can result.

Psychological conditions include feelings of a **lack of privacy** or **crowding**, which can be experienced if too many people work in a small space (where social density is high). The opposite occurs is where a worker may have an **absence of social interaction**, being unable to talk to another person for large parts of their working day. For some workers a **sense of status** is important to them (and so they wear badges identifying their role, e.g. 'Supervisor'), while for others being anonymous is important.

Temporal conditions of work environments

The number of hours people work varies significantly and how those hours are organised is important:

- Many people work for 8 hours per day for 5 days per week (a 40-hour week).
- Those who are self-employed often work more hours than people who are employed. Some businesses (e.g. a shop) might open for 12 hours per day, for 7 days per week.
- A **compressed working week** might mean working 12 hours per day, for 3 days per week.
- People such as doctors work an **on-call system**, were they work as needed or all the time over a 36-hour period, for example.
- A **flexi-time system** means people work the same hours per week but can work whenever they choose (e.g. 7 a.m. to 3 p.m. or 11 a.m. to 7 p.m.).
- Many workers work shifts and usually there are three 8-hour shifts in a 24-hour period.

Temporal conditions of work environments refer to the time workers spend at work.

Typical mistake

Temporal has nothing whatsoever to do with temperature. *Tempus* is Latin for 'time'.

Shift-work causes sleep disturbances, and physical and mental fatigue. Pheasant (1991) suggests it causes primary chronic fatigue. More extreme is the view that shift-workers die younger compared with non-shift workers.

Shift patterns can be organised to minimise negative health effects:

- **Slow rotation theory** suggests shift change as infrequently as possible (the same shift for a least a month). This minimises health effects but is not popular for social reasons (workers want time with their families).
- **Rapid rotation theory** involves frequent shift change (e.g. once per week) so is preferred by workers doing the same shift for a short time. There are two types (and the rota continues, giving an equal balance of working all 7 days per week over time):
  - Metropolitan rota: work two early (6 a.m. to 2 p.m.), two late (2 p.m. to 10 p.m.), two night (10 p.m. to 6 a.m.), two rest.
  - Continental rota: work two early, two late, three night, two rest, then two early, three late, two night, three rest.

Expert tip

A question could ask you to suggest how *you* would organise a shift-work pattern if you were manager. You could also be asked to explain why you have chosen the theory you have.

Now test yourself Tested

57 **(a)** What is meant by the 'rapid rotation theory' of shiftwork.
(b) Describe **two** examples of rapid rotation theory.

Answers on p.203

Ergonomics

Should we fit the person to the job, or fit the job to the person? We do not want a person to experience stress or make an error. Instead, a happy, efficient, healthy and productive worker is highly desirable.

Ergonomics (or human factors in work design) is the scientific study of matching the design of tools, machines, work systems and work places to fit the skills and abilities of workers.

Chapanis (1976) outlines the **operator-machine system**, comprising: the **operator** (his or her senses, information-processing/decision-making ability and ability to control); the **machine** system (its controls, the way it is operated and its displays – feeding back to the senses).

Regarding the machine:

- **Controls** (such as knobs, switches, buttons, pedals and levers) should match the operator's body, be clearly marked and mirror the machine actions they produce.
- **Displays** can be visual (e.g. clock, speedometer) and need to be appropriate and legible, with optimal luminance, and not cause eye strain. Auditory displays (e.g. bell, buzzer, alarm) must have an appropriate tone and volume.

Studies of visual displays focus on: legibility, positioning, accuracy and speed (of reading).

Human decision making when operating a machine is just as important as the machine. Riggio (1990) suggests that when operating machines there can be errors of:

- omission – failing to do something, such as forgetting to turn something off
- commission – performing an act incorrectly, i.e. doing something wrong
- sequence – doing something out of order
- timing – doing something too quickly, or too slowly

Errors can be due to **tiredness/fatigue**, the use of **alcohol** and/or drugs (including medications for illnesses), or because of **accident proneness**. When something does go wrong it is often because people apply what are known as **motion stereotypes**: a behaviour that is familiar, and done without thinking about it.

Reason (2000) made the distinction between two causes of accident:

- **Theory A** – accidents are caused by the unsafe behaviour of **people**.
- **Theory B** – accidents are caused by unsafe (poorly designed) **systems** of work.

Errors such as these can be rectified either by:

- changing the design of the machine – fitting the job to the person
- selecting people who can operate the machine system that is being used – fitting the person to the job

Expert tip

There are three evaluation issues to consider:

- **Usefulness** – there are many recommendations, but how useful are they? Can organisations implement what is recommended?
- **Generalisations/individual differences** – organisations are very different and what might be a good procedure in one organisation might not be good in another. People are different: some can cope with physical and mental tasks, others cannot.
- **Individual vs situational** – are causes of accidents individual or situational, or is it inappropriate to make this distinction? Can causes be *reduced* to one or the other?

Expert tip

Do some research of your own here. Look for published examples of these four types of error. Do the same for the examples that follow.

Cross check

Reductionism, page 104
Generalisations, page 97
Individual differences, page 91
Individual vs situational, page 102

Now test yourself

58 Describe **two** types of error in operator–machine systems.

Answer on p.203

Tested

Expert tip

A topic area like this suggests that anecdotes (personal stories and examples) are acceptable. They are not. Always quote names (dates), psychological evidence and studies wherever possible.

Satisfaction at work

Revised

Job design

The Hackman and Oldham (1976) **job characteristics model** looks at the outcomes associated with the characteristics of a job or the psychological states of workers:

- **Core job characteristics**: (a) skills variety, task identity and task significance; (b) responsibility (autonomy); and (c) knowledge of outcome (feedback) from the job. These job characteristics lead to the calculation of a **motivating potential score** (MPS).
- **Psychological states**: (a) experiencing the work as meaningful; (b) experiencing personal responsibility; and (c) having knowledge of the actual result or outcome of the work.

Job satisfaction is how content or happy a person is with his or her job of work.

Outcomes can be internal motivation, growth satisfaction and general satisfaction. However, if any of the psychological states is absent then both motivation and job satisfaction are weakened.

The job characteristics model is tested with the **Job Diagnostics Survey** (JDS), a self-report questionnaire. The MPS, for example, is obtained by answering

23 questions (e.g. Q11: 'The job is quite simple and repetitive') on a 5-point scale ranging from 5 'very descriptive' to 1 'very non-descriptive'.

Job satisfaction can also be influenced by **job design**:

- **Job rotation** is where workers are moved from one task to another. This might be done on a daily, weekly or monthly basis, depending on the task. Job rotation can prevent boredom and monotony. It can enable a worker to widen his or her range of skills, giving an understanding of the overall work process.
- **Job enlargement** widens jobs and allows workers to take on additional tasks. This isn't working harder or repetitively, instead a number of workers may work together as a team to complete the product. It is working more holistically rather than in a reductionist way. There is no increase in responsibility but there can be an increased feeling of job satisfaction.
- **Job enrichment** is where workers are given more responsibility in the task they do. This might include redesigning a task (as they are the user, the expert) or it might involve being responsible for a team of workers completing a task. Job enlargement is a 'horizontal' extension of a person's job; job enrichment is a 'vertical' extension.

Job design involves matching the aims of producing a successful product and having happy, contented and satisfied workers.

Cross check

Self-report questionnaires, page 72
Reductionism vs holism, page 104
Generalisations, page 97

Measuring job satisfaction

Job satisfaction (and dissatisfaction) can be measured using self-report questionnaires and scales.

The **Job Descriptive Index** (JDI) devised by Smith et al. (1969) uses a scale ('yes', 'no', and 'don't know') in response to whether given statements about five major work aspects (pay, promotions and promotion opportunities, coworkers, supervision and the work itself) accurately describe their job.

Some argue that the **Minnesota Satisfaction Questionnaire** (MSQ) devised by Weiss et al. (1967) is better because it measures 20 aspects using 100 questions, so covering a wider range of job-related aspects. It uses a 5-point scale from 'very satisfied' through to 'very dissatisfied', giving the opportunity to express feelings a little more fully that the JDI. However, 100 questions takes longer to complete than the smaller number on the JDI.

Expert tip

A question could ask you to suggest how *you* would measure job satisfaction. Think about it now rather than in your examination.

The **critical incident technique** analyses events that are particularly positive or negative and usually involves a report by the worker concerned. The reason *why* the critical event happened is the focus because this could indicate the level of satisfaction or the level of dissatisfaction felt by the worker. This measure is usually done by an interview.

Thompson and Phua's (2012) **brief index of affective job satisfaction** (BIAJS) focuses on affective rather than cognitive aspects of job satisfaction. Affective satisfaction concerns the emotional feelings workers have about their job.

Cross check

Quantitative data and qualitative data, page 80

Attitudes to work

Herzberg proposed a **two-factor theory** (1959), believing that the factors causing job satisfaction and factors causing job dissatisfaction are separate. Herzberg distinguished between:

- **hygiene factors** (dissatisfiers) – company policy, supervision, work conditions, salary, relationships with peers and job security
- **motivational factors** (satisfiers) – achievement, recognition, responsibility, advancement and growth

Now test yourself

59 Describe **one** theory of job satisfaction/dissatisfaction.

Answer on p.203

Tested

Lack of job satisfaction can cause job withdrawal, absenteeism and sabotage. Withdrawal behaviours are when a person becomes physically and/or psychologically disengaged from the work or organisation. Physical withdrawal includes lateness, absenteeism and poor turnover. While sometimes **lateness** is unavoidable, chronic lateness is a sign of job dissatisfaction. **Absenteeism** might be involuntary (due to illness) but it can also be voluntary (another indicator of job dissatisfaction). Psychologically, disengagement can include minimal effort and passive compliance, and it can result in poor quality work and mistakes. Whether these behaviours are genuine or not can be judged according to the pattern, frequency and duration (Blau, 1994).

Industrial sabotage is 'rule-breaking which takes the form of conscious action or inaction directed towards the mutilation or destruction of the work environment' (Taylor and Walton, 1971).

Sabotage can be motivated by:

- frustration – spontaneous actions that indicate the powerlessness workers feel
- attempts to ease the work process – likely in industries where workers are paid by the hour and wages are dependent on output
- attempts to assert control, that is, to challenge authority

Some workers might not be happy and leave the organisation. **High turnover** can be a sign of job dissatisfaction. However, some workers might be happy and show **organisational commitment**, remaining with the organisation for a long time, showing loyalty and support. Organisational commitment can be measured using an **Organisational Commitment Questionnaire** (OCQ), where self-report questions are answered using a 7-point scale from 'strongly agree' through to 'strongly disagree'.

Now test yourself

60 Give **three** reasons why workers might commit industrial sabotage.

Answer on p.203

Tested

Expert tip

There are three evaluation issues to consider:

- **Individual differences** – there is an attempt to *reduce* behaviours to categories and types, but there are many individual differences that might make this difficult to do.
- **Quantitative vs qualitative data** – many questionnaires put workers on a scale and give them a number. How many interview the workers and ask about their feelings?
- **Methodology** – many questionnaires and rating scales are used here. This is an issue worth investigating in detail.

5 A Level Examination Guidance/ Questions and Answers

5.1 A level examination guidance

Specialist Choices

The A level examination consists of *one* paper, Specialist Choices. Although all five options appear on the same examination paper, you answer questions only from the two options you have studied.

Typical mistake

Do not choose to answer questions from options that you have not studied simply because you think you have had sufficient life experience in, say, healthcare or education. You need to be able to apply the appropriate psychological theory and evidence.

The format of the examination paper is exactly the same for all five options.

Section A

This section consists of one short-answer question, with two parts.

Part (a) will ask you to describe or explain in your own words a topic area of the syllabus. Part (b) will expand on the topic area of part (a) by asking you to describe a study, theory, therapy/treatment, measure, type, technique, application or example relating to that topic area.

Exam-style question

(a) Explain what is meant by the simulation method of measuring personal space. [2]
(b) Describe *one* study that has used the simulation method of measuring personal space. [4]

Exam-style question

(a) Describe what is meant by the term 'phobia'. [2]
(b) Describe *two* ways in which phobias can be treated. [4]

Expert tip

Do not learn a textbook definition for every possible term that needs explaining in part (a). There are only 2 marks allocated, so you do not need much detail, and it is much better to write your own answer, showing that you understand, rather than writing a definition that you might not understand.

Typical mistake

This is not an essay question. Although the question might be easy to answer, and you could write a lot, don't! You can only score a total of 6 marks.

Section B

This section consists of one essay question with two parts.

Part (a) assesses **descriptive** skills, concerned with what you know about psychology and whether you understand it. Examination questions testing what is known as AO1 ask you to **identify**, **outline** or **describe**. A more formal definition of this assessment objective is: *knowledge and understanding of psychological theories, terminology, concepts, studies and methods, and to express this knowledge and understanding in a clear and effective manner.*

Part (b) assesses **analytical and evaluative** skills, concerned with considering the quality of a study or theory, pointing out strengths and weaknesses such as methodological errors, and making valid generalisations. Examination questions testing AO2 would ask you to **evaluate** or **discuss**. A more formal definition of this assessment objective is: *ability to analyse and evaluate psychological theories, terminology, concepts, studies and methods and to apply psychological theories, concepts and studies to practical situations, everyday life and experience.*

Exam-style question

(a) Describe what psychologists have discovered about intelligence. [8]
(b) Evaluate what psychologists have discovered about intelligence and include a discussion of psychometric testing. [12]

Exam-style question

(a) Describe what psychologists have found out about stress. [8]

(b) Evaluate what psychologists have found out about stress and include a discussion of physiological measures. [12]

Part (a): Describing

For A level this term has not changed, so you can carry over what you learned for AS into A level. To 'describe' means that you reproduce knowledge that you have learned. It does not matter what option you have chosen or which of the five topic areas you choose. What you do is exactly the same each time. Consider the 'intelligence' question above. It begins with the injunction (command word) 'Describe', so this is what you do. But what do you describe? The Education part of the syllabus is worded as follows (but the same principle applies for all options):

f) Intelligence:

- *concept, types and tests of intelligence*

Concept of intelligence and IQ. Types of intelligence tests: Stanford-Binet; Wechsler (WAIS and WISC; BAS). Reliability, validity and predictive validity. Intelligence and educational performance.

- *theories of intelligence*

Factor-analytic approach (Cattell, 1971); multiple intelligences (Gardner, 1983); triarchic theory (Sternberg, 1988).

- *alternatives to intelligence*

Emotional intelligence (e.g. Goleman, 1995); creativity and unusual uses test (e.g. Guilford, 1950); problem-solving: means-end analysis, planning strategies and backwards searching.

You need to describe a range of evidence, so it is worth mentioning something from each bullet point – in this example, something about what intelligence is and types of test; something about theories; and something about alternatives to intelligence. In other words, cover a little from all three bullet points. How much detail to include? As you only have 20 minutes (the recommended time you give to this question part) you cannot mention everything in detail so mention some things briefly. For example, you could write 'there are a number of different theories of intelligence such as those by Cattell (1971), Gardner (1983) and Sternberg (1988)'. This would show an examiner that you know there are three theories. You might then describe one, perhaps two, in a little detail and simply have a sentence on the third. You have shown the examiner that you know something about each, but made the point that you do not have time to go into detail.

The mark scheme is flexible and there is no one correct answer that everyone writes. *You* are writing *your* essay and if you choose to mention the Cattell theory in detail that is acceptable. If someone else describes the Gardner theory in more detail and the Cattell in less detail then that is also perfectly acceptable. A third choice, because it is *your* choice, is to describe Sternberg in detail and briefly mention the other two. This format applies to the two other bullet points. You can write about one bullet point in detail (again of your choice) and briefly mention the other two. The aim is to show range (breadth) and detail (depth). This applies to every topic area from every option. Consider the mark scheme:

7–8 marks: Definition of terms is accurate and use of psychological terminology is comprehensive. Description is accurate, coherent and detailed. Understanding is very good. The answer is competently structured and organised.

This mark band is for 7–8 marks. There is no value in considering the other mark bands because a maximum mark is what you should aim to achieve. As you will note, there is nothing specific included with regard to exactly what you have to do. This is because answers that are very different can achieve just as much credit as each other provided they follow what is on the syllabus.

Typical mistake

Some try to describe everything that is listed on the syllabus, and in detail. This is impossible! Either they get half way through an answer, and find they don't have time to complete it, or they happily carry on describing and have no time at all to evaluate in part (b).

Part (b): Evaluating

'Evaluation issues' in the wide sense (see chapter 2 for full details) include:

- **methodology** – experiments, observations, questionnaires, case studies
- **methodological issues** – ethics, ecological validity, generalisations, validity, reliability, snapshot vs longitudinal, quantitative data vs qualitative data, controls, sampling
- **issues** – usefulness of research, psychometrics, use of children, use of animals, ethnocentrism
- **debates** – determinism vs free will, reductionism vs holism, nature vs nurture, individual vs situational
- **approaches and perspectives** – cognitive, physiological, social, developmental, individual differences, behaviourist, psychodynamic and humanistic

Any of these issues can be chosen to be included in the answer to part (b). For Paper 1 you evaluated using one issue in detail. For Paper 2 you wrote whole essay questions based on these issues. All you have to do now is to write about the same issues as they apply to your chosen option subject knowledge, but in less detail.

Expert tip

Think about what you are going to include in your part (a) answer. Think about the evaluation issues that clearly relate to that part (a) answer. Use those issues for part (b).

Typical mistake

Don't write about issues in part (b) and then begin to *describe* new information to support the issue. *Description* in part (b) scores *no marks*.

How to construct a discussion

The best way to evaluate is through a number of 'mini debates' or 'mini discussions'. A debate in its simplest form looks like this (a year 1 example has been chosen as this is familiar to everyone whatever A level options have been chosen):

- **Claim** – The samples used by Schachter and Singer in their study of emotion cannot be *generalised.*
- **Reason** – This is because Schachter and Singer only used male psychology students who were paid to carry out the research.
- **Conclusion** – We should be cautious when applying the findings from male psychology students who are paid to actual emotion in the 'real' world.

An answer like this would receive some marks because it is evaluation. But it could be taken to a higher level. Consider how much stronger your debate would be if you used *evidence* as well as *reason* to support your claim. So, in our example:

- **Claim** – The samples used by Schachter and Singer in their study of emotion cannot be generalised.
- **Reason** – This is because Schachter and Singer only used male psychology students who were paid to carry out the research.
- **Evidence** – Schachter and Singer used participants who were all male college students taking classes in introductory psychology at the University of Minnesota. Some 90% of students in these classes volunteered and received two extra points on their final exam for every hour they served as participants.
- **Conclusion** – We should be cautious when applying the findings from male psychology students who are paid to actual emotion in the 'real' world.

Now go one step further. Add *evaluative comment* to the evidence quoted:

- **Claim** (as previously)
- **Reason** (as previously)
- **Evidence** (as previously)
- **Evaluative comment** – The problem with this is that *male psychology students* who are getting *credit* for their degrees by taking part are likely to show uncharacteristic behaviour (different from females or non-students or people not being paid) by perhaps being more willing to give the researchers the findings they want. This is because they will be familiar with what is being tested from their own reading and may be tuned in to any cues the researcher may unconsciously give and also more likely to guess the researcher's aim. This is called showing demand characteristics.
- **Conclusion** (as previously)

Using this format you are well on the way to a really impressive evaluative answer. To be very thorough in demonstrating your understanding, you could add a *counter-comment* or *argument*. This would look like this:

- **Claim** (as previously)
- **Reason** (as previously)
- **Evidence** (as previously)
- **Evaluative comment** (as previously)
- **Counter-comment/argument** – On the other hand, Schachter and Singer needed to start to research somewhere. They needed the convenience of an opportunity sample who happened to be their own students to be able to complete their research in a reasonable time and against a limited budget. Also, from this initial research other studies could be done using different participants and a different topic area.
- **Conclusion** (as previously)

If you repeated this formula three (or more) times, then you would have a complete answer. Crucially, you do not have to follow this format exactly to achieve the full 12 marks. This format is simply the best way to show a range of high-level evaluative skills.

To summarise, you need to:

- present a number of evaluation issues (three or more)
- include the one named evaluation issue stated in the exam question as one of those three (or more) issues
- identify and describe the issue
- present advantages and disadvantages of that evaluation issue
- use examples from your description in part (a) to support your answer

Section C

This section consists of two 'applications' questions. You choose one question to answer. **Application** means that you have to use your psychological knowledge in an alternative situation; to consider how it can transfer from one situation to another; to think how it could be applied in different situations.

Expert tip

Read both questions carefully. Choose the one where you can answer *both* parts well to maximise marks.

One part of this question will ask you to *suggest* and one question part will ask you to *describe* knowledge relevant to the suggestion. Sometimes the suggestion part will be part (a) and sometimes it will be part (b). Whatever way round the question parts appear, the suggest part is worth 8 marks and the describe part 6 marks.

Exam-style question

(a) Describe *two* ways to measure non-adherence that do not involve self-report measures. [6]
(b) Suggest how *you* would measure non-adherence to medical requests using self-reports. [8]

Exam-style question

(a) Describe *two* types of shiftwork. [6]
(b) Suggest how *you* would measure the effects of shiftwork using physiological measures. [8]

Typical mistake

Don't describe in the 'suggest' part of the question. This part will always require you to suggest or apply something. You have to think what *you* would do. The emphasis is on the word 'you' and not what someone else did.

The 'describe' part

To be successful in this question part you need to *describe* a good range of evidence, or whatever evidence is appropriate to the question that is asked. In many ways this is half-way between a Section A (b) question worth 4 marks and the Section B (a) essay question worth 8 marks. All you are doing is describing relevant knowledge. Look at the mark scheme:

5–6 marks: Appropriate description of a good range of appropriate evidence with clear understanding.

The 'suggest' part

To be successful in this question part, consider the mark scheme:

7–8 marks: Suggestion is appropriate to the question and based explicitly on psychological knowledge. Description of explanation is accurate, coherent and detailed. Understanding is very good.

The idea of Section C questions is to get you to think. Your suggestion shows how much you can think, how much you know about psychological methods and how much you can apply psychological knowledge to your suggestion. It is *your* suggestion, so feel free to suggest whatever you think.

Typical mistake

If you feel your ideas have weaknesses, don't just sit there thinking and write nothing. Writing ideas (i.e. making suggestions) shows your ability to think, and that is what gets credit.

5.2 A level questions and answers

This section contains exam-style questions followed by example answers. The answers are followed by expert comments (shown by the icon ⓔ) that indicate where credit is due. In the weaker answers, they also point out areas for improvement, specific problems and common errors such as lack of clarity, weak or non-existent development, irrelevance, misinterpretation of the question and mistaken meanings of terms.

Specialist Choices

Section A

Question 1

(a) Explain, in your own words, what is meant by 'improving adherence to medical advice'. [2]

Answer A

(a) Improving adherence to medical advice means that when a patient visits a doctor they should improve their non-adherence to the doctor's request.

ⓔ *This answer is worth no marks at all. The answer merely rewords the question and adds nothing such as a definition or example to show understanding. There isn't even an indication of understanding of the term adherence.*

Question 2

(a) Explain, in your own words, what is meant by 'measuring stress'. [2]

Answer B

(a) Stress can be measured by conducting interviews with the particular patient, and asking them to describe what they are feeling and why they are stressed.

The answer does not tell us what stress is and, except for the idea of conducting an interview, there isn't very much knowledge expressed about the ways in which stress is actually measured. However, an interview could be conducted and this is what a medical practitioner would do (rather than a psychologist, who may give a questionnaire), so this answer scores 1 mark out of 2.

Question 3

(a) Explain, in your own words, what is meant by the term 'selection interview'. [2]

There is nothing complicated in this, or any other part (a) question. Simply explain what is meant by whatever term is presented.

Answer C

A selection interview is a meeting between the job applicant and the interviewer(s), in which the applicant is asked questions that the interviewer(s) believe will be helpful or essential in their selection of the candidate.

This answer tells us exactly why a selection interview is conducted and scores the full 2 marks.

Question 4

(b) Describe *two* behaviourist applications to learning. [4]

This question has two parts and so, for 2 marks each, relatively brief answers can be given, compared with one longer answer for 4 marks. The question wants a description of how the behaviourist perspective has been applied to learning.

Typical mistake

When two things are required, don't write about the first and then move on to the next question, forgetting to answer the second part.

Answer D

(b) One behaviourist application to learning is classical conditioning. An example is Pavlov's dogs. Ivan P. Pavlov wanted to see if, when he gave dogs food, they would salivate automatically. He wanted to see if he rang the bell at the same time whether he could condition the dogs. He found using a UCS, UCR, CS and CR that this was possible. Another behavioural application is Skinner...

There is no point in including the rest of this answer because it scores no marks at all. The basics of learning theory – the original experiments by Pavlov and Skinner – are not applications to education. So this does not answer the question.

Typical mistake

Classical and operant conditioning are not applications to education. They are theories of learning. An application concerns how these theories can be used in a classroom.

Answer E

(b) One behaviourist application is the use of positive reinforcement in a classroom. For example, if a child learns well and is given a reward by the teacher then the child is likely to want to learn well again and so they can get another reward. Another application is negative punishment. This is where a child misbehaves and as a punishment something the child enjoys (such as playing with a toy, or leaving the class early) is taken away. This means the child is unlikely to misbehave again and this is another way in which behaviourist applications apply to learning.

This is an excellent answer. It shows understanding of how the principles of operant conditioning apply in a classroom and explains the applications through examples. The terms positive reinforcement and negative punishment are used correctly, showing good understanding. This answer would receive full marks – 2 marks for the first application and 2 marks for the second application.

Expert tip

Write an amount appropriate to the marks allocated. If the answer is worth just 4 marks then write enough to get 4 marks, but do not waste time by writing more than is needed. These two examples are a suitable length.

Question 5

(b) Describe a structured and an unstructured selection interview. [4]

This is a 2 + 2 mark question. 2 marks are given for description of a structured interview and 2 marks for description of an unstructured interview.

Answer F

(b) A structured selection interview is when a selection of people are chosen throughout the company to do the interview with a set of questions that are structured, and is more formal. An unstructured selection interview is again when a selection of people have been chosen to do the interview but without a list of specific questions to ask, allowing the interview to go in its own direction.

This suggests, wrongly, that a selection interview is conducted by anyone in a company who happens to be chosen to do so, rather than a personnel manager and human resources team. No marks are given for this comment. However, '...set of questions that are structured, and is more formal' shows an understanding of a structured interview, and so this is given 1 mark. In the second sentence, 1 mark is awarded for 'without a list of specific questions', which shows an understanding of an unstructured interview and again 1 mark can be awarded. 2 out of 4 marks are awarded.

Answer G

(b) A structured interview is when an interviewer has a set of questions that they will ask the interviewee. This allows them to stay on topic, find out all the relevant information, and be equal and fair to all interviewees. The advantage is that there is no time wasted off topic, but the disadvantage is that the interviewer may not be able to see the many interesting things in an interviewee.

An unstructured interview is when the interviewer and interviewee have more of a conversation – the interviewer does not have a set list of questions and the conversation just flows. The advantage is that the interviewer can find out a lot about the person, but the conversation may go off topic and become irrelevant, which isn't fair to all interviewees.

Remember that answer F scored 2 marks for basic information about structured and unstructured interviews. This answer has more detail added to each component and shows quite good understanding. There is an awareness of equal opportunities and the fairness shown to all interviewees in a structured interview. This is a competent answer that is worth 4 marks out of 4.

Expert tip

If there are two components in a question give each one equal treatment, for example by writing the same amount for each. If there are two components and the question is for 4 marks, then the marks will be allocated as 2 + 2.

Section B

Question 6

(a) Describe what psychologists have discovered about learning and teaching styles. [8]

This question part is looking for a description of a range of information from the three bullet points in the syllabus. According to the mark scheme the answer should be accurate, use psychological terms, be coherent, have detail, show understanding and be logically structured.

Answer H

(a) Learning style is the reasonably consistent use of stimuli or a set pattern/behaviour adopted by the students in an educational context. Teaching style is the method/style with which a teacher teaches. There are two theories which explain learning style: Curry's onion model and Grasha's six learning styles. The right kind of learning and teaching style together is very important in the growth of both the teachers and the students. Teaching styles also vary from informal to formal and from student centric to teacher centric. A fair mix of these styles is highly beneficial while learning and teaching. These different styles can be used in varied proportions while teaching different types of students to match with the learning styles.

This answer mentions both teaching and learning styles and some relevant names (Curry and Grasha) and concepts (formal and informal; teacher and student centric). However, after mentioning the basics, there is no expansion of them at all. The description is accurate, generally coherent but lacks detail. Understanding is reasonable. *These are terms from the mark scheme to describe an answer worth 3–4 marks. This answer would score 3 marks, but no more, because of the lack of detail.*

(b) Evaluate what psychologists have discovered about learning and teaching styles and include a discussion about 'X'. [12]

This question part is looking for an evaluation of what has been written in part (a) – in this case teaching and learning styles. Crucially, one of the issues to be discussed must be the named issue. The named issue could be any issue relevant to this topic area such as individual differences, methodology, perspectives or reductionism. The other issues included are up to you.

(b) Learning styles are explained in two main theories, namely, Curry's onion model and Grasha's six learning styles. Curry's onion model states that a student learning style comprises three layers. The first and outermost layer is 'Institutional Preference' which is extremely volatile and changes with the kind of task at hand. The second and middle layer is 'Information Processing Style' which is only slightly volatile and although it changes with tasks sometimes, it is mostly the same. The third and innermost layer is 'Cognitive Personality Style' and is different from person to person and is the most stable of all. Learning styles can be classed using either the Myers-Briggs Learning Style Inventory, which classes learners as either: extroverts or introverts, sensors or intuitors, thinkers or feelers, judgers or perceivers. Students can have any kind of combination out of the 16. Grasha's six styles of learning are: Independent, Collaborative, Avoidant, Dependent, Competitive and Participant.

Teaching styles can be classed as formal or informal and student centric or teacher centric. These styles can be measured using several methods such as observation, self-reports, questionnaires, interviews and problem-solving activities. The factors of demand characteristics and social desirability may come into play when self-reports, questionnaires and interviews are used. Teachers and students can also be told to rate each other on a scale but this method may not always be effective. Observations may be an invasion of privacy, therefore consent must be sought. Debriefing must also be done before the problem-solving activities. During the use of all these methods, ecological validity must be the ultimate concern.

There is a major problem with this answer. Except for a few isolated sentences there is no evaluation, and instead this simply adds detail or elaboration to part (a). There are no marks for description in this question part – it is evaluation only. If this was added to part (a) then it would be worth 6–7 marks. But the examiner cannot do this – the answer is labelled as part (b) and that is how it will be marked. The instances of evaluation (the comment about rating not being effective or the reference to ethics) score just 1 mark out of 12. There is no attempt to address any issue, whether it is the named one or not.

Typical mistake

Not knowing the difference between the terms 'describe' and 'evaluate'.

Expert tip

Choose at least two evaluation issues of your own and with the named evaluation issue, done thoroughly, you should score high marks.

Question 7

(a) Describe what psychologists have found out about pain. **[8]**

This question part is looking for a description of a range of information from the three bullet points from the syllabus. According to the mark scheme the answer should be accurate, use psychological terms, be coherent, have detail, show understanding and be logically structured.

Answer I

(a) According to Mershey and Bogduch (1974), pain is defined as unpleasant sensory and emotional feelings along with potential tissue damage, or described in terms of such damage.

Psychologists have discovered many different types of pain. These include injury without pain, which includes episodic analgesia and congenital analgesia.

Pain without injury is another type of pain, where usually pain occurs after a nerve-damaging disease has ended, e.g. herpes. Pain without injury includes neuralgia and causalgia, where pain starts even with the slightest touch. Other types of pain include chronic pain, which can be permanent, acute pain, which is short-term and sometimes mild, organic pain, which includes pain where the only cause is tissue damage, and psychogenic pain, where there's no psychological explanation but the person can still feel it.

The main purpose of pain is to defend yourself when you know you are hurt, for example removing your hand once you touch something hot. Secondly, pain also helps us take remedial actions, once we experience the feeling. Psychologists have discovered many theories of pain, which include the 'specificity' and the 'gate-control' theories. Specificity theory was discovered by Von Frey (1895) who explained that tissue damage was the only explanation of pain, whereas the 'gate-control' theory by Melzack and Wall (1988) explained pain in terms of biological as well as psychological and social factors. It is called the 'bio-psychological' approach to pain. It explains that there's a gate in the body which either stops the pain messages or lets them travel to the brain.

Since everyone has the right to 'no pain', psychologists first discovered the techniques for measuring pain, to ensure the remedies for it. One of the best ways to measure pain is through self-reported methods, especially clinical interviews, as self-reports can tell us about the six elements that were defined by Karoly (1965), which must be present in self-reports – for example, neurophysiological factors, social factors etc. Although self-reports provide us with in-depth data, they may not always be reliable as patients might respond to demand characteristics through attention-seeking behaviour etc. Pain can be measured through psychometrics and rating scales such as one devised by Melzack, known as the 'McGill Pain Questionnaire', which includes many words that the patient must chose to describe his pain. It is one of the most widely used methods for measuring pain. The behavioural method is also another way for measuring pain and it uses tools such as the UAB pain behaviour scale, devised by Richards et al. (1987). Furthermore, psychologists have also discovered pain-measuring methods for children. One such tool was made by Varni et al, named the 'Varni-Thompson Paediatric Pain Questionnaire', which has visual analogue scales, on which the children point out their indication or severity of the pain. However, children who are too young to talk cannot use this technique, so the best method for them is an observational method performed by parents or physicians.

Remedial actions have also been taken and psychologists have discovered techniques for measuring pain. These include chemical treatments such as different painkillers, for example analgesics acting at the site of pain. Surgical attempts are also made but only as a last resort. Behavioural and cognitive therapies are also used, such as non-pain imagery attention diversion, but these may not be helpful for everyone and every type of pain. Alternative therapies such as microwave diathermy and acupuncture are also used. Techniques using electrical stimulation are also used, which include PENS and TENS, and must be used as a last resort.

This is a substantial answer! It covers all three bullet points from the syllabus. There is a definition, as well as types and theories of pain. There are various measures and there are ways in which pain can be managed. Each aspect is dealt with accurately and appropriate terminology is used throughout. There is ample detail, perhaps too much in terms of the time spent, and evidence of understanding. A maximum of 8 marks would be awarded.

Typical mistake

Don't write too much for part (a) and run out of time.

(b) Evaluate what psychologists have found out about pain and include a discussion about 'X'. **[12]**

This question part is looking for an evaluation of what has been written in part (a) – an evaluation of pain. Crucially, one of the issues to be discussed must be the named issue. The named issue could be any issue relevant to this topic area such as self-reports, methodology, reliability or physiological vs psychological explanations. The issue chosen for the following answer is competing theories.

(b) The discovery of the different types of pain has been very useful for doctors and psychologists as well. This is because the different types of pain can help us determine the cause of the pain, as well as the specific managing technique for it. For example, the phantom limb pain, where a person can feel pain even though that body part not there. This is defined as psychogenic pain, where the only cause is psychological.

Furthermore, the different theories devised by psychologists give us an explanation of why a specific pain is occurring. The specificity theory, although it gives us a cause of pain, is a reductionist approach because it only gives us tissue damage as the sole cause of pain. Moreover, the technique of neurography tells us that all nerves have sensory receptors, which respond to the sensation of pain. The 'gate-control' theory criticises the specificity theory and provides us with another explanation. It combines the 'bio-psychosocial' approach, but it can also be considered reductionist to some extent, because it overlooks the long-term causes and the external factors for pain.

Although the self-report methods are some of the most widely used methods for measuring pain they may not always be reliable because the patient may respond to demand characteristics. Clinical interviews are one of the best ways to measure pain as they give large, detailed and in-depth data, but they can be time consuming and expensive. Psychometrics are also the most widely used methods and even the most reliable because they give consistent scores, but some of the words used in the MPQ are difficult to understand and therefore the scale can be vulnerable to falsification. The tests results are reliable and are consistent for both UAB and MPQ so they can be considered a valid way for measuring pain. When measuring pain through behavioural methods one must be careful, because of the social reinforcement the person is getting. Furthermore, one must be cautious when measuring pain in children because some children may be stoical and calm, even when they are suffering from a lot of pain.

Chemical treatments provide quick and instant relief, but they may have side-effects, if a person becomes dependent on them. Surgical techniques on the other hand can be performed in every society and set up. The behavioural and cognitive therapies can only be used by people who are willing to talk about their pain behaviours, and imagery can only be performed by people who are good at imagining peaceful techniques. Lastly, the electrical stimulation techniques cannot be performed in every set up as they are expensive. Therefore, it can be said that psychologists' discoveries about pain have helped in measuring pain, as well as suggesting remedies.

This is a very good attempt at evaluation, but there are some weaknesses. The answer begins by contrasting different theories and makes some appropriate evaluative comments. It then mentions reductionism but does not say what reductionism is, or what is good or less good about being reductionist. The examples that are used for this issue are appropriate. The answer then considers methods for measuring pain and contrasts self-reports, clinical interviews and psychometric measures. The answer here is good, but has weaknesses: clinical interviews are not really time consuming (compared with an MPQ, for example) and they are certainly not expensive; there is no explanation of any term and there are no advantages and disadvantages of methods, just examples. In the final paragraph the answer contrasts different ways in which pain can be managed but no issues are raised here. In terms of marks, this is still a good answer. There is a range of issues and the named issue has been included. There is excellent use of examples, although the issues themselves are not developed and the advantages and disadvantages of these are not mentioned. Despite the weaknesses this answer would still score 10 marks out of 12.

Typical mistake

If you don't address the named issue you will limit yourself to a maximum of 6 marks. Alternatively, if you only address the named issue and no other issues, you will also limit yourself to a maximum of 6 marks.

Section C

Question 8

(a) Describe what psychologists have found that makes noise annoying. [6]

This question part is looking for a description of factors that make noise annoying, and the work of Kryter and Borsky (as mentioned on the syllabus) is the most likely source of examples.

Answer J

(a) According to Glass and Singer (1972), there are three main factors that make noise annoying: the volume (objective in decibels), the predictability of the noise, and person's perceived control (can they affect the noise in any way, such as switching off the source). They found that noise was most annoying when it was high volume, unpredictable, and there was low perceived control. Miedema and Vox (1999) said that there were other factors, such as if the person believed the noise was a hazard to their health or if it was associated with fear. Finally, some people may simply be more sensitive to noise than others – this was said by Taylor (1984).

Expert tip

To receive credit research does not have to be listed in the syllabus or included in this revision guide. Any *appropriate* research is credit-worthy. For example, the study by Miedema and Vos (not Vox) is not on the syllabus, but it is appropriate to this question.

This is a good answer that has all the appropriate features required by the question. It mentions the three crucial factors of loudness, unpredictability and uncontrollability, but attributes these to Glass and Singer (when they are factors derived from many studies). It also mentions fear and the work of Miedema and Vos (not Vox, but no credit is lost for incorrect spelling). The main weakness with this answer is the lack of detail for a question carrying 6 marks. It scores 5 out of 6 marks.

(b) Suggest how you would investigate how annoying the noise made by neighbours is. [8]

This question part is looking for a suggestion of how levels of annoyance, caused by 'noisy neighbours' can be investigated. This could be done using a questionnaire, or perhaps by taking some physiological recording, for example of blood pressure. Psychological and methodological knowledge should be evident in the answer.

(b) One way in which to measure how annoying noise is would be to operationalise aggression and see if it affected people to the point of anger. Donnerstein and Wilson (1976) did this in one lab experiment where they either played no noise (around 50 db) or 95 db of unpredictable, 1-second noise bursts. Half of the participants were angered, and the researchers measured shock intensity to see if participants became aggressive. They found that in the angered condition, noise led to more intense shocks than without noise. This suggests that anger – compounded by the annoying noise – made people more aggressive. Because it had a larger effect on the participants who were not angered, this can be an indicator that the noise was annoying.

Another way may be to test performance. If performance decreases in the presence of noise, then it may be an indicator of annoyance. Bronzhatt and McCarthy (1975) examined a school where one side was quiet and one side was noisy because it was next to elevated railway tracks. They found that the performance of children on the noisy side was worse and the reading scores of children on the quiet side were superior.

If noise does lead to elevated stress levels, then a physiological approach may be implemented. The levels of cortisol or adrenaline may be measured – higher levels mean higher stress, implying that noise is more annoying. Also, Matthews and Canon (1975) found that helping behaviour dropped from 80% to 15% when there was noise. A decrease in pro-social behaviour like helping may mean that noise is more annoying.

A further way to measure how annoying noise is is to simply ask. While participants are doing a task, experiments can test different variables and participants can tell the experimenter when it is becoming too annoying. Furnham, Dobbs and McClleland (2011) did something similar, although they examined how noise affected the performance on the task itself – similar to Bronzhatt and McCarthy.

This good answer makes a number of appropriate suggestions. However, there are two weaknesses. Firstly, none of the suggestions is developed in terms of how it could be investigated. For example, one suggestion is 'to simply ask'. The answer could suggest that this could be done with a questionnaire, which could be open-ended or closed, and then details of questions asked could be given. The second weakness is in describing the work of others rather than suggesting alternative methods. This answer is good and it does show understanding, scoring 3 marks out of 6.

Question 9

(a) Describe features of addiction, such as those outlined by Griffiths (1995). [6]

This question part is looking for a description of the features of addiction. The most likely answer will include the features outlined by Griffiths (1995), who produced a list that applies to any addiction.

Answer K

(a) The characteristics of addiction are generally the same in each case; however, some may differ from case to case. The most important symptom of addiction is the over-doing of something as your mind sends out a feeling of need. Addiction can be chemical or psychological. In both cases, withdrawal symptoms are present. If an addict cannot pursue their need to do something, they get nervous, agitated or angry. On the other hand, while doing the thing they are addicted to, they calm down and a feeling of elation and relaxation is experienced.

A person addicted to either an action or a substance, will eventually form an immunity to it and will need higher and higher doses to be kept happy. An addiction can also affect the person's safety and in that case it has become out of control.

This shows understanding of some of the basics of addiction. However, rather than identifying what the features are, the answer gives examples. The answer is vague in its use of terminology. For example, the last paragraph refers to 'immunity', but the correct term is tolerance. There is a mention of withdrawal symptoms, but rather than writing about physical or psychological dependence, the answer refers to 'chemical or psychological'. The answer is also quite brief and lacks detail. Overall it would score 3 marks out of 6.

(b) Suggest how the features of addiction apply to the behaviour of a person who may be gambling. [8]

This question is looking for suggestions for how the features of addiction described in part (a) apply to the specific behaviour of gambling.

(b) My son has been spending more money than he has on gambling. He loses money but still feels the need to gamble. Whenever I refuse to give him any more money, he finds a way to make money in order to gamble more. If I tell him about my concern, he denies the fact that he is addicted. However, when he doesn't go gambling for a while, he becomes easily angry and agitated. At first, he went a few times with his friends and as the time passed, he went more often. Now he goes a couple of times a week. This is concerning as he feels the need to go more and more often. Unfortunately, gambling is now a very big part of my son's life. He is either gambling, or thinking about it. Sometimes it is the only thing he talks about. Whenever he is angry or stressed he goes gambling because he says it helps, but every time he comes back, he is angry about losing more money.

e *This tells an interesting story, but the answer does not pick up on the features of addiction except for a brief mention of 'denial' and 'thinking about it' without implying that these are features of an addiction. For example, one feature is salience, where the addict is thinking about the addiction even when the addictive behaviour is not being performed. The answer doesn't pick up on any of the features mentioned in part (a). This vague answer scores no more than 1 mark out of the 8 available.*

Now test yourself answers

Core Studies

1 Liars are said to avoid eye contact and show signs of fidgeting such as touching their face, playing with objects, and putting their hand over their eyes and mouth.

2 The clips were sensitive and the fewer people who saw them the better. The agreement between the two observers was so high (0.95 or better for most things) that there was no need to code any more clips.

3 Mann et al. conclude that the most reliable indicators of telling a lie are pausing for longer and blinking less.

4 A false memory happens when post-event information changes the original memory, so a person believes that the false information really was part of the original event even though it never existed.

5 DV1: Percentage of participants recalling true and false events at all three stages. DV2: Ratings of clarity of memory scored from 1 (not clear at all) to 10 (extremely clear). DV3: Ratings of confidence in ability to recall more detail scored from 1 (not confident) to 5 (extremely confident).

6
- Participants are sent a booklet and fill in any memories they have about each of four events listed.
- Interview 1 conducted at university (or by telephone) 1–2 weeks after completion of booklet, recalling each event in as much detail as possible.
- Interview 2 conducted at university (or by telephone) 1–2 weeks after Interview 1, again recalling each event in as much detail as possible.

7 The first test of theory of mind was the 'Sally-Anne' test devised by Baron-Cohen, which looked at whether children could 'think what Sally was thinking'.

8 There are eight different problems. Most people start with the first two, which are:
- The original involved a forced choice between two alternatives meaning that there was a 50/50 guess.
- The results of the original test did not sufficiently discriminate between those with AS disorders and those without (such as a parent).

9 *Any two from:*
- The AS/HFA (autistics) will score lower on the eyes test than other groups.
- The AS/HFA (autistics) will score higher on the AQ test than other groups.
- Females will score higher than males on the eyes test.
- Males in the normal group will score higher than females on the AQ.
- Scores on the AQ and eyes test will be inversely correlated.

10 One difference was that Group X was reared in darkness from birth until member A attained the minimal size and coordinational capacity to move itself and its partner in the apparatus. This age varied between 8 and 12 weeks. Group Y received 3-hour daily exposure, beginning at 2 and ending at 10 weeks of age, to the patterned interior of the laboratory while restrained in holders that allowed some head movement but prevented locomotion.

Each of the eight pairs of both group X and group Y then began exposure in the apparatus for 3 hours daily.

11 Visually guided paw placement; avoidance of a visual cliff; blink to an approaching object

12 This is where a kitten has developed paw–eye coordination. A kitten will look and place its paw in a place where it has looked. A flippant example is that if a kitten with visually guided paw placement is dropped it will turn and successfully land on its feet. A kitten that does not have visually guided paw placement will hit the floor without turning and may not land on its feet.

13 (a) An advert was placed in a newspaper advertising a study on 'learning and memory' and stating that $4 would be paid (plus $.50 for travel). 40 males aged 20–50 with various occupations were chosen to participate. As people volunteered the sample is self-selecting.

(b) People who volunteer might have personality characteristics different from those who do not volunteer. Certain types of people may not read that newspaper or certain types of people may choose not to respond to such things.

14 (a) *Any two from:* the experimenter said that he was in charge and so was responsible; the 'stern' manner of the experimenter; his wearing of a grey lab-coat.

(b) *Any two from:* the study was conducted at the prestigious Yale University; it was a scientific experiment; it was conducted in a psychology laboratory; the shock generator and the electrodes and paste all added authenticity.

15 (a) *Any one from:* informed consent; deception; right to withdraw; physical and psychological harm

(b) *Any one from:* confidentiality; debriefing

16 (a) *Any two from:* khaki uniform, 'billy-club' (police stick), reflecting sunglasses and a whistle

(b) *Any two from:* muslin smock, no underwear, sandals, a prisoner number and a nylon stocking to cover their hair

17
- They were arrested at home, spread-eagled against the police car, searched and handcuffed.
- They were put into a police car and taken to the police station.
- They were formally booked and read their rights, finger-printed and put into a cell.

18 (a) The dispositional hypothesis was that the 'badness' in prisons (in the USA) was due to some feature of an individual person; their personality, their disposition.

(b) There was no support for the dispositional hypothesis. Instead Zimbardo believed it was the *situation* of being in a prison and playing roles that led to the guards behaving badly.

19 In 1964 Catherine 'Kitty' Genovese was attacked and murdered by Winston Moseley in the Queens borough of New York. Although it was claimed that 38 different witnesses saw or heard the event, not one of them reported it to the police.

20 If there is one person witnessing an event he or she is 100% responsible for helping. If there are more people then responsibility is diffused among them. If there are 10 people then they are each only 10% responsible. This means that they are less likely to help.

21 *Any two from:*

- An individual who appears to be ill is more likely to receive aid than is one who appears to be drunk, even when the immediate help needed is of the same kind.
- Given mixed groups of men and women, and a male victim, men are more likely to help than are women.
- Given mixed racial groups, there is some tendency for same-race helping to be more frequent. This tendency is increased when the victim is drunk as compared with apparently ill.
- There is no strong relationship between number of bystanders and speed of helping.
- The longer the emergency continues without help being offered:
  - the less impact a model has on the helping behaviour of observers
  - the more likely it is that individuals will leave the immediate area; that is, they appear to move purposively to another area in order to avoid the situation
  - the more likely it is that observers will discuss the incident and its implications for their behaviour

22 Three new groups of 16 boys in each group from the same school as for study 1.

23 (a) The study was a snapshot study because it probably took no more than 30 minutes to complete for each boy.

(b) A disadvantage of any snapshot study is that it only gives us an impression of behaviour at that moment and in that place. This might not be how a person usually behaves and it does not tell us that a person will continue to behave in the same way over a period of time.

24
- They were deceived because they thought it was an experiment on 'visual judgements' or 'artistic preference'.
- The boys thought they were categorised according to 'judgement' or 'preference' but they were deceived as allocation to groups was done randomly.

25 (a) Bandura et al. used time sampling. In this study a record was made every 5 seconds and as the test lasted for 20 minutes, 240 instances of behaviour were recorded.

(b) This meant that the observer had time to see the behaviour, look down at the sheet of response categories, find the correct box, tick it and be looking up and ready for the next.

26 *Any two from:* Imitative physical aggression; imitative verbal aggression. *Partial imitation*: mallet aggression; sits on bobo doll. *Non-imitative aggression*: punches bobo; aggressive gun play. *(Imitative aggression, for example, is not a category. Be precise!)*

27 (a) The children were matched by the experimenter and nursery teacher by rating each child on four aspects (e.g. physical aggression and verbal aggression) using a five-point scale.

(b) They were matched to achieve a balanced sample in each group to help prevent the result from being confounded (where it is not known whether the result is due to the IV or due to come confounding variable).

28
- Freud believes that 'Hans was not a normal child' and therefore no generalisations could be made from him to other children.
- Freud states: 'an analysis of a child conducted by his father, who went to work instilled by my theoretical views and infected with my prejudices, must be entirely devoid of any objective worth'.

29 One piece of evidence is the 'giraffe episode' in which Hans describes a story involving two giraffes. Freud's interpretation is that the tall giraffe is the father and the crumpled giraffe is the mother.

30 (a) One advantage is that behaviour can be studied in detail and over a period of time, so developmental changes can be recorded.

(b) Case studies like this one done by Freud rarely produce enough quantitative data for statistical testing; this means that some people regard case studies as little more than anecdotal evidence.

31 Forty one infants were excluded from study 1, three from study 2 and 11 from study 3.

Fussing means being bad-tempered, irritable, moody, temperamental and fractious. In other words, the baby would not settle to the task or concentrate on it without crying or being distracted from it.

32
- Preferences for attractiveness appear very early in life.
- They are consistent across various types of face.
- They generalise beyond visual behaviours to social and play behaviours.

33 Langlois et al. state: 'Exposure to cultural media does not seem to account for these preferences; rather, preferences for attractiveness are either innate or acquired with only minimal experience with faces in the environment'. Given that the infants were very young it is illogical to conclude that they are learned, but Langlois et al. are reluctant to commit themselves totally.

34 A motive (or intention) is the reason why a behaviour is done. In this study the intention could be good (play a game) or bad (hurt the other child). The consequences were the same as the ball hit the child on the head.

35 IV1: age – children are 3–4 years or 6–8 years. IV2: mode of presentation – verbal only; picture motive implicit; picture motive explicit. IV3: motive good or bad and outcome good or bad.

36 The participants, the children, do not know what the study is about. As Nelson is the interviewer, experimenter and designer of the study, she knows exactly what condition each child is in. This is a single-blind study.

37 Physiological arousal and psychological (or cognitive) interpretation

38 (a) The physiological component was manipulated by placing the participants into one of four groups: EPI MIS, EPI INF, EPI IGN and the placebo/control group.

(b) The psychological component was manipulated by placing the participants into either a euphoric or an anger-suggesting situation.

39 (a) The experiment could not work without the stooge suggesting to the participant a behaviour (euphoria or anger) to explain the physiological arousal. Without a stooge the participants would probably have just stood and chatted to each other.

(b) One problem is that the use of *any* stooge in any research is deception and is therefore unethical.

40 This would increase the ecological validity of the study. It might have no effect on the results because people nearly always have REM and NREM sleep. But there might be more REM and dreaming with more detail.

41 Scientific equipment is reliable, which means that it gives consistent recordings. It is also objective. For example if a person is entering REM sleep then the EEG records it without input from the participant.

42 (a) Self-reports were used when participants were woken up and asked to record any dream into the tape recorder next to the bed.

(b) Observations were used by the experimenters. They observed the EEG print-out to determine when REM and NREM sleep began and ended and to determine the direction of eye movements.

43 Topographical knowledge is thought to comprise information about both landmarks and spatial relations between landmarks.

44 Before they arrived for scanning, the participants completed and returned questionnaires about:

- areas of London with which they were most familiar
- films they would rate as very familiar
- individual landmarks from a list of 20 world-famous ones they had visited in person and could visualise in their mind's eye

45 The participants were 11 right-handed, qualified and licensed male London taxi drivers (mean age 45.7 years). None had a previous history of psychiatric or neurological illness. The average time spent working as a licensed London taxi driver was 14.55 years.

46 This is because females:

- are said to be more sensitive to olfactory cues than males
- might rely more on olfactory cues in mating behaviour than males

47 Controls could include:

- Presentations of each face-odour were counterbalanced.
- Presentations of pleasant–unpleasant odours were counterbalanced.
- Presentation time was standardised at 500 ms.
- Time for tone presentation and odour release was standardised.
- Odour 'strength' was standardised for each participant.

48
- The highest mean rating of male attractiveness was for male fragrance at 5.73 (scale 1–9), slightly better than clean air, second highest at 5.70.
- The lowest mean rating of male attractiveness was for body odour at 3.64.
- When the two pleasant odours were combined (mean of 4.42) and the two unpleasant odours combined (mean of 4.85) and compared with fresh air (mean of 4.9) participants evaluated male faces as being significantly less attractive with an unpleasant odour than with a pleasant or neutral odour.

49 The pseudo-patients were the stooges; the people recruited by Rosenhan to do the study as he did. The participants were the doctors and nurses who worked in the various mental institutions.

50 (a) Psychiatric diagnosis was reliable because all the pseudo-patients were admitted.

(b) Psychiatric diagnosis was not valid because the pseudo-patients were faking illness and it was not detected by the psychiatrists.

51 One explanation concerns the symptoms: sane people do not telephone a mental institution and ask for an appointment; sane people do not claim to hear voices; hearing voices is a legitimate symptom of schizophrenia. This creates doubt for a psychiatrist. It is better to admit someone who might be sick. A second explanation is that psychiatrists really cannot distinguish the sane from the insane.

52 We all have different personalities, we all play different roles and we behave differently with different people in different situations. But in everything we do we have a memory for it. A true 'multiple personality' would not recall what another personality does or thinks.

53 (a) *Any two from:*

- The shopping trip for which Eve White claimed to have no memory.
- The letter Thigpen received apparently started by Eve White and finished off by Eve Black.
- Eve White disappearing into the woods when she was a child, said to be a prank played by Eve Black.

(b) The problem with this type of evidence is that it can be true, partially true or made-up. We have no way of checking its validity at all.

54 (a) Wechsler-Bellevue intelligence scale or the Wechsler memory scale.

(b) Drawings of human figures or the Rorschach (ink blot) test.

(c) The EEG record, which tested the electrical activity of the brain.

55 Whether a person is an empathiser or a systemiser is naturally occurring. A person is one or the other (to differing degrees). It is not possible for an experimenter to manipulate this and tell a person to be an empathiser (or systemiser) when they are not.

56 The reliability of any questionnaire is usually tested by giving the test, obtaining a result and then giving the same test 3 weeks later and seeing if the result is the same (or very similar) to that obtained previously.

57 Aim 1 was: do males take science subjects and females humanities subjects? The findings were that 59.1% of males chose science subjects and 70.1% of females chose humanities subjects. The difference was significant ($p = 0.001$) so the aim was fully supported.

58 • Camouflaging (reported in 91% of cases)
- Comparing with others (88%)
- Checking appearance in mirrors or 'mirror-gazing' (87%).

59 • Avoidance of looking at a specific defect
- Using only 'good' mirrors and not 'bad' mirrors
- Using private mirrors rather than public mirrors
- Using only mirrors that were obscured (e.g. cracked), so that a full reflection could not be seen

60 *Any three from:*
- Use mirrors so they show most of the body, or the whole of the face rather than a specific part.
- Focus attention on the reflection rather than internal impression of feelings and not make an automatic 'ugly' judgment.
- Use a mirror for a function, such as shaving or to do make-up.
- Use different mirrors rather than the 'trusted' one and not use magnifying mirrors or mirrors that give ambiguous reflections.
- Not to use a mirror when they have the urge, but to delay and do other things instead.

Themes in Psychology

1 One similarity is that both are experiments, having an IV, a DV and control of variables in common. One difference is that one is conducted in a laboratory – a potentially artificial situation but where conditions can be very tightly controlled – and the other is conducted in a relatively natural environment where control of variables is more difficult.

2 One disadvantage of conducting a study in a laboratory is that it is low in ecological validity. The setting is artificial as the participants are travelling there and the task they are required to do may also be something they would never normally do in real life.

3 One advantage of conducting a field experiment is that it may be higher in ecological validity than a laboratory experiment but as it is an experiment there is an IV and a DV and there will also be a number of controls applied.

4 A repeated measures design is where each participant takes part in both conditions of the independent variable.

5 One way in which order effects can be overcome is to counterbalance. Participant 1 does condition A then B, participant 2 does condition B then condition A and the format is repeated for all participants.

6 Random allocation is done by giving each participant a 50/50 chance of being in either condition. This can be done by tossing a coin. It can only be done for an independent groups design.

7 Psychologists try to control for extraneous variables to try to ensure that the DV is the result of the IV and not some extraneous variable.

8 Situational variables, experimenter variables and participant variables

9 The victim always wore the same clothes such as an Eisenhower jacket; the victim fell over 70 seconds after leaving the station; the same subway line was used for each trial; the victim was always male.

10 This is where the questionnaire forces the respondent to commit themselves either to a positive response or to a negative response. There is no neutral or 'opt-out' choice. The advantage is that is prevents a respondent from giving a neutral answer to everything, resulting in data that surround a mid-point.

11 Open-ended questions are simply questions that ask the participant to give a response in his or her own words with no pre-determined way to answer. Closed questions on the other hand require the participant to choose from a range of pre-determined answers.

12 In a structured interview each participant is asked exactly the same questions in the same order. In an unstructured interview the researcher asks different questions, depending on where the discussion takes him or her. A semi-structured interview has some structured questions *and* some unstructured/open-ended questions.

13 • Participants may provide socially desirable responses; they may not give truthful answers; they may respond to demand characteristics.
- Researchers have to be careful about using leading questions, which can affect the validity of the data collected.
- Answers to open-ended questions may be time-consuming to categorise and difficult to analyse.

14 With a positive correlation, as one variable increases the other variable also increases (or both decrease). With a negative correlation, as one variable increases the other variable decreases (or one decreases while the other increases).

15 However strong a relationship might be, all we can conclude is that the two variables are related. We can *never* say that one variable *causes* another.

16 Controlled observation – Bandura et al.; naturalistic observation – Piliavin et al.; participant observation – Rosenhan

17 One advantage of an observation is that the observed behaviour is natural and can be measured objectively. In the study by Piliavin et al. participants did not know they were in a study and so responded as they would have done normally. A disadvantage of an observation is that participants cannot explain why they behaved in particular way. In the study by Piliavin et al. participants could not say why they behaved as they did. If they had been asked they might have been upset when realising they had been deceived.

18 Watson and Raynor classically conditioned Little Albert. Initially, Albert was not afraid of animals, and his favourite was a white rat. But then, every time the rat was presented to Albert, a loud noise, made by banging two mental bars together, made him jump and frightened him. Albert associated the fear with the rat, and this fear of the rat generalised to other animals too. This demonstrated that fears and phobias can be learned.

19 The advantage of a case study is that an individual can be studied in depth and a range of different data can be gathered. The study by Thigpen and Cleckley on Eve allowed them to gather lots of different data. They carried out IQ tests, memory tests, the Rorschach ink blot as well as interviewing her many times.

20 *Any two from:*

- It may be impossible, on a practical level, to create a real-life situation or make something happen naturally.
- There may be a lack of control over confounding variables. Experimenters cannot control all variables; they may not be able to isolate one variable from many others.
- If a study is conducted in a natural environment, the experimenter may not have obtained the participants' consent, so the study would be unethical.
- The data may be less reliable, i.e. if the study is repeated, entirely different data might be produced.

21 High ecological validity means that the study is close to real life (rather than being conducted in a laboratory). High levels of control mean that confounding variables are reduced and the DV is more likely to be due to the IV. In most experiments high control is preferred over high ecological validity. One way to achieve high levels of both these is to break ethical guidelines.

22 (a) Deception is when an experimenter (or stooge) acts or speaks in a way that induces a false belief in a participant.

(b) At the end of a study participants are told what was happening, asked if they have any concerns, and given any explanations they require. Anything that may have caused stress is smoothed over so that the participants can leave the study in the same state in which they arrived.

23 Studies should be ethical because no-one should be harmed or deceived in the pursuit of knowledge. Something may go wrong with a procedure and the participants may be harmed for life even though they may claim they are fine at the time of the study. However, it could be said that unethical studies are good because deceiving participants keeps them naive and they respond as they normally would. The ends might justify the means.

24 One weakness of quantitative data is that they do not give us a reason why participants behaved as they did. In his study Milgram knew that 63% went to 450 volts but he did not ask them why they did so; instead he assumed he knew the reason for their continuation with the study or their early withdrawal.

25

- The study by Dement and Kleitman on sleep and dreaming gathered qualitative data by asking participants to report the content of a dream. One participant reported that they had a dream about two people throwing tomatoes at each other.
- The study by Freud gathered qualitative data because Little Hans's father recorded conversations, 'episodes' and other events in the life of Little Hans.

26 Qualitative data are in the form of words. Examples include descriptions of events, quotes from participants, or descriptions of participants' responses to a task. Qualitative data can help us understand *why* people behave in a particular way.

27 Reliability is how consistent something is. For example the reliability of a questionnaire could be tested using test–retest and if the results are the same then the test is said to be reliable.

28 The reliability of a questionnaire involves administering the same test to the same person on two different occasions, such as intervals 3 weeks apart, and comparing the results. The results can then be correlated. The split-half method can also be used, which involves splitting the test into two and administering each half of the test to the same person.

29 The reliability of an observation can be checked using inter-rater reliability. This is where two or more observers watch the same behaviour and score it independently. The study by Bandura et al. had two observers and their agreement, measured by using a correlation test, was over 0.9.

30 Thigpen and Cleckley (multiple-personality disorder); Billington et al. (empathising and systemising); Baron-Cohen et al. (eyes test); Dement and Kleitman (sleep and dreaming)

31 A random sample is a sample that has been selected in a way that means everyone in the target population has an equal opportunity of being chosen. One way to try to eliminate participant variables is to randomly allocate participants to conditions. Random allocation is part of an independent groups design and is done by (for example) tossing a coin for each participant, giving them a 50/50 chance of doing condition 1 or condition 2 first.

32 A snapshot study is where, in the context of an entire lifetime, a few minutes in a study provides merely a snapshot of a person's behaviour and experience.

33

- It is not possible to study how behaviour may change over time (development), and one cannot see the long-term effectiveness or harm of exposure to certain stimuli.
- The behaviour recorded is limited to that time, in that place and in that culture.

34

- The study by Thigpen and Cleckley on Eve is longitudinal because it went on for at least 14 months and they could track the development of her disorder over time.
- The study by Freud is also longitudinal because the development of the phallic stage and Oedipus complex in Little Hans could be studied over several years.

35 (a) A longitudinal study takes place over a period of time, usually following one or more participants throughout the period (or visiting them at regular intervals) to monitor changes.

(b) One problem is that it can be difficult to track participants over a long period of time – for example, they may move house or may not want to continue participating. Thus, longitudinal studies tend to lose participants as they go along. This is called 'participant attrition'.

(c) One example is the study by Freud on Little Hans and a second is the study by Thigpen and Cleckley on Eve. Neither participant withdrew, with Eve being studied over at least 14 months and Little Hans for a number of years.

36 Validity is whether an experiment or procedure for collecting data actually measures or tests what it claims to measure or test. Concurrent validity could be checked by comparing the result of a test with an alternative that is known to measure what it claims to measure.

37 Construct validity shows how the measure matches up with theoretical ideas about what it is supposed to be measuring. Predictive validity shows how well the test correlates with some other measure, which is assessed after the test has been taken.

38 Cognitive psychology is about mental processes such as remembering, perceiving, understanding and producing language, solving problems, thinking and reasoning. The main assumption of the cognitive approach is that how we think is central in explaining how we behave and how we respond to different people and different situations.

39 Some psychologists say that this approach is less scientific because we cannot observe the subject matter directly – we are just inferring or guessing how people think or process information.

40 Freud and Held and Hein look at development over time. Bandura et al., Langlois et al. and Nelson are developmental approach studies.

41 This approach emphasises growth and change and how an experience at one point in life can have various consequences at later stages. It helps us to understand how children behave at various stages in their early life. For example, Little Hans progressed through a number of developmental stages, and at the time of the study was said to be in the phallic stage, having progressed through the oral and anal stages.

42 In the study by Dement and Kleitman an EEG was used to determine what stage of sleep (REM or NREM) the participants were in by recording the electrical activity of the brain.

43 The study by Maguire et al. used an MRI brain scanner. MRI stands for magnetic resonance imaging. This technique is non-invasive, in that no injection of a radioactive substance is needed. This is preferable to other types of scanning such as PET, where a radioactive injection is needed.

44 An assumption is that we can only understand people in the context of how they operate in their interactions and perceptions of others. Why does someone behave in a particular way in a particular situation? We only know by looking at the context of the people around them.

45 A script allows us to understand how most people will behave in social situations. Whatever we do in social life we can only interact if we can predict what people are likely to do and say.

46 One assumption is that in any group of people, there are differences between those people in terms of their personal qualities, the ways in which they respond to situations, etc. Any study can generalise but it will not apply to all people all of the time because there are always individual differences.

47 The studies by Billington and by Veale and Riley show both generalisations and individual differences. Billington shows that each person can be divided into two main cognitive types yet within these there are individual differences. Veale and Riley show common mirror-gazing behaviour in BBD patients yet also show that there are differences in the way various individuals behave.

48 One of the main assumptions of the behaviourist perspective is that all behaviour is learned through experience and nothing is inherited. This includes classical conditioning (Pavlov), operant conditioning (Skinner) and social learning theory/observational learning (Bandura). Bandura had children observe an aggressive model, which they later imitated.

49 Because behaviourism refuses to acknowledge how we think, how we make sense of the world, some explanations it provides are incomplete. Consider, for example, two people who are bitten by a dog. One develops a dog phobia and one does not. Why? It is probably because of the differing ways in which they make sense of the situation; the cognitions they have about the dog and other dogs. Behaviourism fails to account for this.

50 The conscious mind is where we are aware of our motivations for behaviour and can verbalise them explicitly. The weakness is that Freud believes we also have an 'unconscious' mind where the motivation for behaviour is related in some way to sex, and largely hidden from our conscious mind. The problem is that the 'unconscious' mind might not exist.

51 Freud proposed a theory of psychosexual development, describing a number of stages through which every child progresses. According to Freud, each stage has a particular (predetermined) focus of 'sexual gratification' and it is important that the conflict is resolved so that the child can continue into adulthood without any dysfunctional behaviour. The stages begin with the oral stage (age 0–1), with the focus on sucking and later biting, moving on to the anal stage (age 1–3), with the focus on expelling and retaining faeces. The phallic stage (3–6 years) focuses on the genitals and includes the Oedipus complex. After that (6–puberty) is a 'latency' stage where any conflicts from the previous stages should be resolved. Puberty brings normal adult sexual activity, remaining throughout life.

52
- If research is useful, it can be of benefit to society. It can improve the world in which we live, for example in understanding crime, mental illness and how students can learn more effectively.
- It helps us to understand social behaviour, our interactions with others, obedience, etc.
- If research is useful, it enhances the value and status of psychology as a subject.

53 *Any two from:*
- Useful studies should be ethical – participants should give informed consent and not be deceived. However, a study may need to be unethical to be really useful.
- Studies conducted in a laboratory may not be useful as they are low in ecological validity.
- Studies should use a representative sample and be generalisable. Useful research should apply worldwide so there is no ethnocentrism.

54 The term comes from the word *ethnos*, meaning 'nation' in modern Greek, and *kentro* meaning 'centre'.

55 According to Tajfel it is the mere categorisation of people into two (or more) groups that creates in-group favouritism and out-group discrimination.

56 A generalisation is when something applies to most people most of the time.

57 Schachter and Singer claim that emotion results from physiological arousal and cognitive (or psychological) interpretation. Perhaps this does apply to everyone rather than being just a generalisation.

58 • 'Metrics' refers to measurement and 'psycho' refers to psychological abilities, so psychometrics is the measurement of the mind.
- Psychometrics is the science of psychological assessment.

59 Thigpen and Cleckley used the Wechsler-Bellevue intelligence scale and the Wechsler memory scale to test Eve White and Eve Black. The results of the IQ tests were 110 for Eve White and 104 for Eve Black. Eve Black's memory function was on the same level as her IQ, while Mrs White's was on a much higher level than her IQ.

60 • It is important to study children because they represent the most important and formative period of human development. What happens in early life can determine many things in adult life.
- By understanding children's thoughts and behaviour, it might help us to understand adult thought and behaviour.
- In some ways, children are better participants than adults as they are naive and can be more open and truthful.

61 The study by Freud tracked the case of Little Hans over a period of time, for at least 3 years. This meant that Freud could get feedback and information on the psychosexual development of Hans as he progressed through the phallic stage and Oedipus complex.

62 There is no right or wrong answer to this one; it is asking you what you think. In a laboratory the experimenter has more control, but on the other hand such control is low in ecological validity and does not enable us to observe the behaviour of an animal in its natural environment. Which method is best?

63 Yet another one to ponder. What do you think? Again the answer is a matter of opinion and it is just a matter of weighting up the advantages and disadvantages and making a judgment.

64 (a) One study that shows environmental determinism is that by Bandura, in which children copied the aggression they had observed. Children who did not observe the aggression did not copy it.

(b) One study of biological determinism is that of Schachter and Singer, which involved causing physiological arousal in the participants, who were motivated so seek an explanation for it.

65 Yet another one to ponder. Some people believe we exercise free will all the time. Others think that we just think we do, whereas really it is an illusion and that *all* our choices are determined by other things. As usual with these questions there is no definitive answer and it is for you to think about, to discuss with your friends or in class and see what you can conclude.

66 An individual or dispositional explanation for behaviour will look to some feature or characteristic within the person rather than situational causes.

67 The study by Rosenhan showed that mental illness was perceived because of the situation and context. The study by Milgram showed that some participants obeyed the authority in the laboratory situation. The study by Haney et al. showed that both the guards and prisoners took on the roles associated with the situation.

68 The nature view believes that all behaviour is genetically (biologically) determined. The nurture view believes that behaviour is mainly, or entirely, acquired through experience and the influence of the environment is crucial. This is environmental determinism.

69 The nature view believes that all behaviour is genetically (biologically) determined and so this is reductionist. The nurture view believes that behaviour is learned, determined by the environment, and so this too is reductionist.

70 Reductionism is the process of explaining complex psychological phenomena by reducing them to their component parts. This is the opposite of holism, where the total is more than the sum of the parts.

71 • It helps us to understand the world because a fundamental way of understanding is to analyse, break things down into component parts, test them and then build them back up again. This is important in studying the natural world and humans in a scientific way.
- In theory it is easier to study one component rather than several interacting components. If one component is isolated and others are controlled then the study is more objective and scientifically acceptable.

Specialist Choices

1 The main features of humanistic cooperative learning are: each child is responsible and accountable for his or her role; a task can only be solved when all pupils make a contribution and only when each child has contributed equally and all can share the same success. Cooperative learning techniques include: the jigsaw technique, jigsaw II and reverse jigsaw; the reciprocal teaching technique; the Williams; and think pair share.

2 The zone of proximal development is the distance between what children can do by themselves and the next learning that they can be helped to achieve with competent assistance. Scaffolding is a 'framework' by a parent, teacher or other to help the child learn, and can include, for example, vertical scaffolding (extending the child's language) and instructional scaffolding (using more advanced language to help a child explain things).

3 Dyscalculia affects mathematical performance and processes such as addition, subtraction and dealing with money. Dyspraxia involves problems with fine and/or gross motor coordination. Dysgraphia is a disorder of writing, which can involve the physical aspects of writing, e.g. pencil grip and angle. *(Dyslexia could have been included as an alternative to one of these three.)*

4 One way in which a child can be educated is to use Hornsby and Shear's (1976) alpha-to-omega scheme. This is a highly structured multisensory approach (using sight and hearing) to write and read. The pupil is taught step by step, beginning with single letter sounds linked to letter names and letter shapes. Progress leads to learning single-syllable words, followed by complex multisyllabic words.

5
- An independent learner works and researches independently, seeking minimal guidance.
- A dependent learner relies on others, preferring to be told information and given work. Often learning rather than thinking.
- A competitive learner is motivated to do better than others.
- A collaborative learner likes small-group discussions and project work.
- An avoidant learner avoids working, lacks enthusiasm and does not enjoy study. May have learned helplessness.
- A participant learner enjoys class activities and is eager to please a teacher.

6 Learning effectiveness can be improved by using the PQRST technique. P is for preview, Q is for question, R is for read, S is for self-recitation and T is for test. This method is intended to improve the ability to study and remember material in a textbook. A second way is the SPELT method, which stands for Strategies Program for Effective Learning and Thinking. This approach makes the assumption that if a student knows how to learn then they can go about it more effectively.

7 One advantage of praise is that it provides information about the individual student's competencies in recognition of noteworthy effort or success at a difficult task. One disadvantage of praise is if it is given without regard to the effort needed to complete the task, or attributes success to ability alone or to external factors such as luck or the ease of the task.

8 Self-efficacy is the extent to which an individual believes that he or she is competent and can succeed at a particular task. Bandura (1977) believes that past achievements in the activity encourage a feeling of self-efficacy. Success raises it; failure lowers it. Seeing someone else, whom you believe to be of the same or lower standard to yourself, complete a task provides confidence to do the same. Encouragement and positive words from those close to you (e.g. a teacher) can instil confidence. Control over arousal and anxiety levels provides greater self-efficacy.

9 To prevent disruptive behaviour a school could have:
- high behavioural expectations by all staff, with commitment to enforcing rules promptly and consistently
- clear rules, sanctions and procedures (all pupils know what is and what is not acceptable)
- a warm school climate and friendly staff, with a visible and supportive head teacher

10 Preventive strategies involve anticipating disruptive behaviour and proactively working to stop a disruptive behaviour from starting. Corrective behaviour is responding retroactively to a disruptive behaviour and working to stop it happening again.

11 The Wechsler Adult Intelligence Scale test gives an overall IQ made up of a verbal IQ score and a performance IQ score. The verbal test includes: verbal comprehension – similarities, vocabulary; and working memory – digit span, arithmetic, letter–number sequencing.

The performance test includes: perceptual organisation/reasoning – block design, matrix reasoning, picture completion; and processing speed – symbol search, digit symbol coding.

12 Guilford devised several tests to measure creativity/divergent thinking: quick responses – a word association test; remote consequences – the suggestion of radical answers to unexpected events, such as loss of gravity; unusual uses test, which asks people to suggest unusual uses for everyday objects, such as a brick.

13 Safer (1979) suggests:
- Appraisal delay – Have I got any symptoms? Do I feel ill?
- Illness delay – Do I need medical help?
- Utilisation delay – Will the treatment work? Can I afford it?

14 Munchausen syndrome includes pathologic lying, peregrination (traveling or wandering), and recurrent, feigned or simulated illness. Aleem and Ajarim (1995) studied a 22-year-old female who had a painful swelling above her right breast. After many tests it was discovered that the girl had been injecting fecal material into herself and Munchausen syndrome was diagnosed. One weakness is that this is the case of just one person and so it is not possible to generalise to other people.

15 Validity refers to whether a measure actually measures what it intends. Pill counts should measure adherence. However: the fact that the pill has left the bottle does not mean it has been taken; a patient may simply throw away unconsumed medication and supplies are divided up; pills may be transferred to other containers.

16 Ley (for example) suggests *(any three from)*:
- Emphasise key information by stating why it is important and stating it early in the interaction.
- Simplify instructions and use clear and straightforward language.
- Use specific statements ('you should...') and have the patient repeat the instructions in their own words.
- Use written instructions, breaking down complex instructions into simpler ones.
- Use a combination of oral and visual information (such as diagrams).

17 There is no difference in the intensity of acute and chronic pain. Both can hurt just as much as each other. The difference is that acute pain is short-lived and does not last for very long, whereas chronic pain goes on for a longer period of time.

18 Turk suggests that people will show *(any three from)*:
- facial and/or audible expressions of distress, such as groaning and pulling a face
- distorted ambulation or posture, meaning that they might limp or hold the painful area
- irritability/bad mood
- avoidance activity, such as staying at home or resting

19 *Any two from:*

- Holmes and Rahe (1967) used the SRRS to measure life events, giving each a rank and a mean value. At the top of the list is 'death of spouse'; at the bottom is 'minor violations of the law'. Points are added to give a total score.
- Lazarus et al. (1981) devised the hassles and uplifts scale to record daily hassles, such as 'too many things to do'.
- Friedman and Rosenman (1974) devised the Type-A Personality Questionnaire to measure the behaviour of people who are said to be aggressive, assertive, competitive and time conscious.

20 *Any two from:*

- Blood pressure tests: Goldstein et al. (1992) found that paramedics' blood pressure (measured using a sphygmomanometer) was higher during ambulance runs or when at the hospital, compared with other work situations or when at home.
- Geer and Meisel (1972) used the Galvanic skin response (GSR), which calculates the electrical resistance of the skin (to indicate level of arousal in the autonomic nervous system) when participants viewed aversive photographs of dead bodies.
- Sample tests of blood or urine: Lundberg (1976) collected urine samples to measure the levels of stress caused by commuting to work; Johansson et al. (1978) found that the 'finishers' in a Swedish sawmill excreted more stress hormones than cleaners.

21 Fear arousal involves a message being presented to a target audience with the aim of scaring or creating fear in them in order to change their perceptions and motivate them to act.

22
- In the UK Tapper et al. (2000) used 'The Food Dudes' campaign aimed at promoting the eating of fruit and vegetables in schools. Extensive resources were provided: a Food Dude video; Food Dude rewards; a set of letters (for praise and encouragement); a home-pack; and a teacher handbook and support materials. Levels of fruit and vegetable consumption were measured and it was found that lunchtime and home consumption was higher than in the control group.
- Walter (1985) conducted a 5-year programme on nutrition, physical fitness and cigarette smoking prevention in children in schools in the Bronx, New York. After 1 year the programme group (compared with the control group) showed improved cholesterol levels, lower blood pressure and improved post-exercise pulse recovery rate.

23 Theory A is the person (or individual) approach, where accidents are attributed to the unsafe behaviour of people. Theory B is the systems approach, where accidents are said to be caused by unsafe systems at work.

24 The most likely are:

- The illusion of invulnerability – the belief that 'it will not happen to me', for example the sinking of the *Titanic* (1912), where the captain could be said to be to blame.
- Cognitive overload – when a person cannot cope with all the competing mental demands placed on them. An example of this is the air traffic controller who was blamed for an airplane crash in Zagreb.

25 Kryter (1970) suggests that noise is annoying if it is loud, uncontrollable and unpredictable. Borsky (1969) adds: if it is perceived as unnecessary; if those making the noise are unconcerned; and if the noise is yet another environmental stressor.

26 Chafin (2004) found that listening to classical music could reduce blood pressure. He took a baseline measure of blood pressure (sitting in silence) and then gave a stressful (mental arithmetic) task to participants, which increased blood pressure. He then played different types of music (classical, jazz, pop and no music) and he found that those given classical music recovered (blood pressure back to normal) more quickly than with any other type of music.

27 Density refers to physical conditions, whereas crowding is a psychological state. Spatial density is where the number of people remains the same and the size of space varies. Social density is where the size of space remains the same and the number of people varies. Crowding can vary between people because it depends on whether they perceive themselves to be crowded or not.

28
- Christian et al. report on a real-life event. Deer were released on James Island in 1916. The deer bred successfully, but in 1955 half of them died quite suddenly. Autopsies revealed enlarged adrenal glands, so it was concluded that the deer died from stress due to crowding.
- In 1965 Dubos wrote that lemmings jumped of the edge of cliffs because of biological pre-programming in order to regulate numbers due to high social density. However, other studies have shown that lemmings do not jump off cliffs.

29
- To plan escape strategies, so events do not happen or are not repeated.
- To determine how people behave during an event.
- To understand how survivors feel and respond so that appropriate therapies can be applied.

30 In the experiment by Mintz (1951) each participant pulled on a string attached to a cone in a bottle. Only one cone could be removed at a time and cones had to be removed before water filled the bottle. Mintz found that each participant pulled hard on their cone and all the cones jammed at the neck of the bottle, meaning that no-one escaped. This provides support for Le Bon's contagion explanation that people think about themselves only, and stampede in their rush to escape first.

31 Four ways are: simulation, stop–distance, natural observation and the comfortable interpersonal distance scale. The simulation method uses dolls or drawings rather than real people. One example is Little (1968), who investigated cultural differences in personal space. He created different social situations and participants had to place dolls at distances that reflected where they would stand in real social situations. Little found that Scottish females were placed furthest apart while Greek females were placed the closest.

32 *Any two from:*

- Participants cannot give informed consent because they would know that the invasion was about to take place and so it would not be an actual invasion.
- Participants may be psychologically harmed (at least temporarily so).

- Participants can experience embarrassment, and as they are likely to escape the situation as quickly as possible, this shows that harm is being caused.

33 The Pruitt-Igoe Project was a 57-acre urban housing project that relocated people into 43 high-rise buildings, each 11 stories high, with 2 762 apartments. There was a very high crime rate and the whole estate was demolished after a relatively short period of time.

34 Finlay et al. 2006 identify two main types of casino design:

- The Kranes playground model has features designed to induce pleasure, legibility and restoration. The design has an open space, high ceilings, vegetation and an entertaining, fantasy environment that is comfortable and pleasant.
- The Friedman design has low ceilings so the focus is on the slot or fruit machines. There is a maze-like design, so it is hard to find the exit, which encourages continuous playing of the machines.

35 *There are many different errors, but two of them are:*

- Euclidean bias is where people assume roads are grid-like, with right-angles, such as the design of Manhattan Island, New York, when in reality roads have angles and bends and rarely go in straight lines.
- Segmentation bias is when we estimate distances incorrectly when we break a journey into segments compared with when we estimate a journey as a whole.

36 Levine suggests that we should have:

- structure mapping – the map should reflect the layout and appearance of the setting it represents. This means that:
  - the map should be placed near an asymmetrical feature so more than one building is visible (the map should not be placed against a wall)
  - the map should include a landmark that is visible in reality (then the person can match the two and plan a route)
- orientation – the map should be aligned to match the setting and it should have forward equivalence (the top of the map should be straight ahead)

37 Deviation from statistical norms is simply deviating from the norm or average, as in a normal distribution curve. Anyone at either end of the curve is abnormal or atypical. A person who is very tall is abnormal, as is a person who is very short.

38 *Any three from:*

- Sensky et al. (2000) used CBT to treat schizophrenia.
- Covert sensitisation was used by Kohn and Antonuccio (2002) for kleptomania.
- Blaszcznski and Nower (2003) found that imaginal desensitisation was particularly effective with gamblers.
- Ost and Westling (1995) found that CBT led to a significant reduction in the number of panic attacks.
- Exposure and response prevention is used to treat obsessive-compulsive disorder.

39 *Any three from:*

- Disorganised (hebephrenic) involves incoherence, disorganised behaviour, disorganised delusions and vivid hallucinations.
- Simple involves a gradual withdrawal from reality.
- Catatonic involves impairment of motor activity, where the person often holds the same position for hours or days.
- Paranoid is where the person has well-organised, delusional thoughts (and hallucinations), but a high level of awareness.
- Undifferentiated/untypical is a category for sufferers who do not fit into any of the above categories.

40 Frith (1992) argues that schizophrenics have faulty information processing, particularly with 'mentalising', which is impairment in attributing mental states (thoughts, beliefs and intentions) to other people. They apparently have an impaired 'theory of mind'.

41 *Be careful here. The question refers to 'drug' and not 'medical' treatments, so ECT cannot be included.*

There are three types of drug used: MAOIs, SSRIs and SNRIs. Anti-depressants work by affecting neurotransmitters. Those most involved in depression are thought to be serotonin and noradrenaline. SRRIs inhibit serotonin and SNRIs inhibit both serotonin and noradrenaline. MAOIs inhibit a wider range of neurotransmitters, such as adrenaline and melatonin, in addition to serotonin and noradrenaline.

42 REBT focuses on how illogical beliefs are maintained such as musterbating (I must be perfect at all times) and I-can't-stand-it-itis (the belief that when something goes wrong it is a major disaster). The A, B, C, D and E are: A for the activating event, B for the belief held about A and C the consequences – thoughts, feelings or behaviours – resulting from A. To change to rational beliefs, Ellis suggests we must: D, dispute the irrational beliefs and E, experience the effects of successful disruption of the irrational beliefs.

43 Physical dependence is when the body has adjusted to the presence of a substance and incorporated it into the 'normal' functioning of the body's tissues. Psychological dependence is a state in which people feel a compulsion to use a substance for the pleasant effect it produces (which can happen without being physically dependent).

44 Before committing the act there is a growing tension. During the act the person feels pleasure from acting, and often feels relief from the urge. Afterwards the person may or may not feel guilt, regret or blame.

45 DiNardo et al. (1988) found that only half of all people who had a traumatic experience with a dog, even when pain was inflicted, went on to develop a phobia of dogs. They believe that people who have any traumatic experience (e.g. with dogs) but do not develop a phobia must interpret the event differently from those who do develop a phobia. This means that it is the way people think about their experience that makes the difference. They suggest it is an exaggerated expectation of harm in some people that leads to the development of a phobia.

46 When people see blood or a needle, their blood pressure drops sharply, often leading the person to faint or pass out. The way to counter the drop in blood pressure is to raise blood pressure. Ost et al. (1989) propose using applied tension. This involves tensing the muscles in the arms, legs and body for about 10–15 seconds, relaxing for 20–30 seconds and then repeating both these five times.

47 The Maudsley Obsessive-Compulsive Inventory (MOCI) is a psychometric test to assess obsessive-compulsive behaviour. It is a self-report questionnaire using a forced-choice 'yes' or 'no' format. It has 30 questions/items with four sub-scales: checking, cleaning/washing, slowness and doubting. When all the items are totalled, a person can have a score between 0 (no symptoms) and 30 (maximum presence of symptoms). The extent and severity of the OCD is determined by the score out of 30. *The Yale-Brown Obsessive-Compulsive Scale (Y-BOCS) is an acceptable alternative.*

48 Cognitive-behavioural therapy changes the way a person thinks (the cognitive part) and the way a person behaves (the behavioural part). It may focus on how a person responds to a particular situation. This is done not by going back to the cause of the problem, but by focusing on the present symptoms. It works by looking at how a person thinks about how an event has affected how he/she felt and what he/she did. If negative thoughts can be reinterpreted or changed for more positive or realistic thoughts, then the person will feel better and their behaviour will change.

49 Any psychometric test used in the selection process should be both reliable and valid. Does the test give consistent data over time? This means the results from one person should be comparable with results from another person. Does the test accurately measure a person's attributes, i.e. the aspect of the job that it is supposed to assess? If the measure does not, then it is not valid for that particular job.

50 A structured interview is where each participant is asked exactly the same questions, in the same order. An unstructured interview is where the researcher asks different questions, depending upon where the conversation/discussion takes them.

51 The *need for achievement* is the need to get a job done, to master a task, to be successful. The *need for affiliation* is the need to be liked and accepted by other people. The *need for power* concerns being influential in the lives of others and also in control of others.

52 Intrinsic motivation is an internal desire to perform a particular task. It gives pleasure, achievement and satisfaction or develops a particular skill. For example, praise, respect, recognition, empowerment and a sense of belonging are said to be far more powerful motivators than money. Extrinsic motivation is the desire to do something because of an external reward such as money, which can include pay, promotion and fringe benefits such as commission and bonuses.

53 A leader may have some charismatic characteristics (be a 'great' man or woman) exerting social influence to gain the aid or support of others in achieving a goal or task. A manager is concerned with the day-to-day planning, organising, controlling and coordinating of those in an organisation for whom he or she is responsible. A manager might not be the leader, but instead implements the ideas and instructions of a leader.

54 The situational leadership approach argues that there is no one leadership style that is best and fits all situations. Instead the most successful leaders are those who can adapt their leadership style to the individual or group they are attempting to lead.

55 The under-developed team, the experimenting team, the consolidating team and the mature team.

56
- Forming: where individuals begin to come together, get to know each other and agree on tasks and goals.
- Storming: where individuals will present ideas and sometimes these will be accepted and sometimes they will cause conflict.
- Norming: when members of the group agree a strategy, some members realising that for the good of the group their ideas are not accepted.
- Performing: when the group functions as a coherent unit, working effectively and efficiently without conflict.

57 (a) The rapid rotation theory is based on frequent shift change (e.g. once per week) and so it is preferred by workers who only do the same shift for a short time.

(b) There are two ways to organise a rapid rotation (and the rota continues, giving an equal balance of working all 7 days per week over time):

- Metropolitan rota: work two early (6 a.m. to 2 p.m.), two late (2 p.m. to 10 p.m.), two night (10 p.m. to 6 a.m.), two rest.
- Continental rota: work two early, two late, three night, two rest, then two early, three late, two night, three rest.

58 *Any two from:*
- Omission – failing to do something, such as forgetting to turn something off.
- Commission – performing an act incorrectly (i.e. doing something wrong).
- Sequence errors – doing something out of order.
- Timing errors – doing something too quickly, or too slowly.

59 Herzberg (1959) proposed a two-factor theory, believing that the factors that cause job satisfaction and the factors that cause job dissatisfaction are two separate things. Herzberg distinguished between: hygiene factors (causing dissatisfaction) – company policy, supervision, work conditions, salary, relationships with peers and job security; and motivational factors (causing satisfaction) – achievement, recognition, responsibility, advancement and growth.

60 Sabotage can be motivated by:
- frustration – spontaneous actions that indicate the powerlessness workers feel
- attempts to ease the work process – typical of industries where workers are paid by the hour and wages are dependent on output
- attempts to assert control, that is, to challenge authority